JFK
FIRST DAY
EVIDENCE

Stored away for 30 years in an old briefcase,
new evidence is now revealed
by former Dallas Police Crime Lab Detective
R. W. (Rusty) Livingston

GARY SAVAGE

THE SHOPPE PRESS
MONROE, LOUISIANA

Published, 1993, in the United States of America by
The Shoppe Press
P. O. Box 2741, Monroe, Louisiana 71207-2741
Published in 1993, this edition is unabridged and unaltered.
No parts of this book may be used or reproduced in any manner
without written permission of The Shoppe Press,
except in the case of brief quotations in critical articles or reviews.

Library of Congress Catalog Card Number: 93-85438

International Standard Book Number: 0-9638116-5-7

Manufactured in the United States of America
Copyright 1993 by The Shoppe Press
Monroe, LA

10 9 8 7 6 5 4 3 2 1

JFK
First Day Evidence

This work is dedicated to all Americans who honestly desire to seek the truth.

Contents

	PREFACE	7
	ACKNOWLEDGEMENTS	9
	PROLOGUE	13
	INTRODUCTION	21
CHAPTER I	The Assassination Weekend	29
CHAPTER II	The Crime Lab	69
CHAPTER III	The Old Briefcase	89
CHAPTER IV	The Prints	99
CHAPTER V	The Backyard Photographs	121
CHAPTER VI	The Map	143
CHAPTER VII	The Memorandum	185
CHAPTER VIII	The Spy Camera	205
CHAPTER IX	Jack Ruby	217
CHAPTER X	More Documents	237
CHAPTER XI	The Acoustics Evidence Disproved	265
CHAPTER XII	"Lone Nut" or "Lone Patsy?"	281
	EPILOGUE	299
	APPENDIX	313
	WORKS CITED	413
	BIBLIOGRAPHY	415

P R E F A C E

ONCE IN A LIFETIME AN OPPORTUNITY PRESENTS ITSELF THROUGH sheer coincidence, which from the outset can only be called amazing. One such occurence happened to me about four years ago after I read a book on the assassination of President John F. Kennedy.

I recalled, after studying many of the photographs in the book, that my Uncle Rusty had some assassination-related materials which he had held on to since his days with the Dallas Police Department. He had long since retired, and my interest in reviewing the old documents and photographs was gladly received by Rusty.

This book is a result of that chance encounter which set off a chain of events leading to this effort. The original Crime Lab photographs had been stored away by Rusty in an old briefcase for nearly three decades, almost forgotten along with the recollections of the men who made them. Some have passed on, but many of the old Dallas detectives are still alive. I asked Rusty if we might interview the men who had worked with him in the Crime Lab back in 1963, and he agreed.

Organizing the photographs and memories of those men who worked the evidence in the assassination of JFK was a tremendous undertaking requiring countless hours of organization and research. Having no grand budget, Rusty and I took it upon ourselves to learn the many accusations made through the years of a possible conspiracy and to try to develop only the facts according to the men who were there first. What we found on a regular basis continually surprised us and in most instances belied the existence of a second gunman, although through no grand design or pre-drawn conclusions on our part. Rusty and I always had and continue to maintain an open mind in regard to the true evidence in the case.

This book is a documentary showing much of the ORIGINAL evidence collected by the Dallas Police Crime Lab before the intrusion of the federal government as well as reflections and background of some of the Dallas officers working the case. All of the evidence presented, therefore, remains unfiltered through the 1964 Warren Commission (WC) or the 1979 House Select Committee on Assassinations (HSCA). It was our desire from the outset to reveal ALL of the information possessed by Rusty. If conspiracy charges are to be leveled, let the accusers be aware of all the evidence uncovered by the first men who were there.

Gary Savage, Monroe, Louisiana, 1993

ACKNOWLEDGEMENTS

IN THE COURSE OF RESEARCHING THE MATERIAL PRESENTED IN THIS book, many retired Dallas police officer witnesses were interviewed. Not one refused to speak to Rusty or me when asked. It was obvious after many interviews that the recalled knowledge of the assassination investigation was emblazoned on each man's mind as his own personal and individualized brush with history which was not easily forgotten. All were eager to share what they witnessed.

JOHN CARL DAY, the lieutenant in charge of the Dallas Crime Lab in 1963 and Rusty's immediate superior, was extremely gracious in detailing his memories of the investigation to Rusty and me. The long list of questions I presented to him were answered in meticulous detail. This one man, in essence, developed most of the crucial evidence which would later be examined in minute detail for generations to follow. He is, according to Rusty, "one heck of a good man." I thank him sincerely.

W. E. (PETE) BARNES was another Crime Lab man involved in the investigation. His brazen wit was a constant source of delight in composing some of the background stories developed for the book. Pete readily shared with Rusty and me his recollections of all of the evidence he personally developed in the case, which was extensive. Pete originally was the man who trained Rusty in the work of the Crime Lab, and through the stories told to me previously by Rusty, I felt as though I already knew him long before I actually met him. It was indeed a pleasure to get to know Pete.

BOBBY BROWN is another down-to-earth Crime Lab man interviewed by Rusty and me. His manner of "telling it like it is" was appreciated and greatly helped in providing an understanding of the events in much greater detail than was known before.

R. L. STUDEBAKER and H. R. WILLIAMS were also very gracious to take the time to share with Rusty and me their memories of the assassination investigation. Their recollections served to clarify many of the controversial issues arising years later and help set the record straight.

GUS ROSE, a former Dallas Police Homicide Officer, was the first man to formerly interview Lee Oswald after his arrest. Gus was always courteous and patient over the phone in answering my questions about his role in the investigation. It was a pleasure to later finally meet and talk with him in person.

JIM BOWLES, now the Sheriff of Dallas County, was a supervisor in the Communications Office of the Dallas Police in 1963. His study and later important documentation of the so-called "acoustics evidence" of the investigation has until now been largely overlooked. It is presented in this book by his graciously allowing Rusty and me to do so, and we wholeheartedly thank him.

Many researchers have been spoken to during the course of writing the book, including JIM MARRS, J. GARY SHAW, JACK WHITE, and others. Their questions about Rusty and his role in the Crime Lab eventually steered us in the direction of writing this book and interviewing the other men still living who were his co-workers in the Department. Their gentle nudges of us to pursue our course in developing the original Dallas police evidence was needed and appreciated.

JIM EWELL, one time a reporter for the *Dallas News*, was also kind enough to share his memories of November 22nd, 1963. During the course of our interview, Jim told Rusty and me, "The more I got into that situation that day, the less I became a reporter. My head started swirling to where I was living an out-of-body existence. The more that you heard what had happened to Kennedy, you felt like your feet were off the ground." The accurateness of his recollections helped me understand more fully the feelings experienced by those present, and I thank him.

CAPTAIN JERRY POWDRILL of the West Monroe Police Department provided unceasing expertise in a careful re-study of the fingerprints developed in the case. His conclusions, based on an examination of Rusty's photographs and fingerprint card of Oswald, were a tremendous help to Rusty and me. Thanks go out to you, my friend!

Thanks also go to the government publications staff at the Northeast Louisiana University Library in Monroe, Louisiana, for allowing me ready access to the volumes of the Warren Commission and HSCA as well as to their many other books on the assassination.

A special thanks is due to MONA OLIVER, Assistant Professor of English at Northeast Louisiana University. Her many careful hours of editing a sometimes roughly worded manuscript led to a coherence that even I can understand.

Finally, thanks to my wife, JENNY, and to my three children-- SARAH, REBEKAH, and THOMAS--for putting up with my obsession for over four years. Thanks also to my AUNT DAISIE for allowing me to practically steal her husband, my UNCLE RUSTY, away for so long.

GARY SAVAGE

P R O L O G U E

A R E L A T I V E   B A C K G R O U N D

It seemed I had a thousand questions to ask Rusty. Did you really see Oswald? Did you actually talk to him? Do you think that he pulled the trigger? A thousand questions.

He began to tell me, "Yes, I did see Oswald. No, I didn't actually talk directly to him while he was in custody. That was the job of the folks doing the actual interrogatin'. And yep, I think he really did it."

Suddenly he paused. I didn't know whether I had stirred an old memory or reached a point that he may not have wanted to pursue. But then in his quiet Texas drawl he simply told me, "Hang on a minute, Gary. You're gonna' have to slow down! You know, that's not the only case I ever worked on."

I knew my uncle was right. His even-toned directness reminded me of my sometimes annoying habit of rushing conversation. I knew Rusty had worked for the Dallas Police Department during the Kennedy investigation, and suddenly 28 years later my interest had been awakened with a vengeance.

Maturity hopefully brings with it an ability to recognize and be sensitive to the feelings of others. That aspect of my own maturity was certainly tested with Rusty's steady repetition: "That's not the only case I ever worked on." His response told me he was willing to talk, but not just about the Kennedy assassination. It was time to stop asking and start listening. I was selling a whole police career short and needed to slow down.

But Rusty had already sensed my excitement about his involvement with the Kennedy matter, and quickly began to tell me things I couldn't wait to hear. I was titillated by his brief answers, some directly contradicting what I'd just read in a current bestseller about the JFK assassination!

The sensationalism of the Kennedy assassination material possessed by my uncle was clearly exciting. Some I was to discover had not been seen by the public for nearly three decades.

Undaunted about my single-mindedness on the assassination, Rusty continued to expound about his time with the Dallas police. "I always did want to write a book one day about my time with the Department. You know, I do have a bunch of good stories that I'd bet people would be interested in."

Yeah, sure, I thought. Let's just get to the good stuff. I was eaten up with the JFK conspiracy thing, and my enthusiasm kept clouding my sensitivity. But Rusty wanted to tell me HIS story, not just about his involvement in the Kennedy investigation. I realized a need to appease my uncle out of respect as well as to get to what I really wanted to hear. It seemed a minor inconvenience. "OK," I said with affected interest. "So, let's hear some of your stories."

He started by telling me, "When I began full-time with the Dallas Police Department, I was working what they called 'fill-in.' One night we pulled up on a service station and an ol' boy had a crowbar under the window trying to pry it open. We caught him, searched him, then put on the handcuffs and put him in the back seat of the squad car. I piled in the back with the prisoner while my partner began driving us down to the station to begin the booking process."

Rusty leaned back in his kitchen table chair with a casual smirk and went on. "Suddenly I began to smell something quite out of the ordinary and looked over at our prisoner, who was still kind of shaken up by his predicament. I blurted out the obvious and asked him, 'Did you shit on yourself boy?' He turned my way with his head bowed down and told me, 'A little bit.'" The laughter between Rusty and myself had barely died down when I realized that he really had a story to tell.

A new world was beginning to come alive between my uncle

and me. My perturbed impatience had given way to an enjoyment of stories the tender years of my youth were not privileged to hear. My weathered uncle relaxed forward in his chair as I found my search leading to a new-found respect and friendship between us.

As a kid, I remember long family drives to visit my Uncle Rusty and Aunt Daisie in Dallas. Daisie is my mother's sister. Like the sisters, Rusty and my daddy had grown close as brothers-in-law. We'd leave from our home in Louisiana on Friday afternoons and drive old Highway 80 all the way to Dallas. When we arrived at Rusty's house, he'd sometimes just be leaving for work. He usually worked at night, and I can still recall him putting on his revolver and leaving by the front door. During our visits, I wouldn't see him until the following afternoon since he slept days while working nights.

My daddy would occasionally go with Rusty on those Friday or Saturday night shifts. Daddy seemed to enjoy being Rusty's temporary "partner" since it was quite a change from his construction work and the slower pace we enjoyed back in Monroe. The streets of "Big D" were filled with all kinds of people, different races and nationalities, a world away from the one in which my father was reared.

Rusty worked in the Crime Scene Search Section of the Identification Bureau of the Dallas Police Department during the 1960's. He had access to many graphic photographs showing all sorts of really "gross stuff." On cases that particularly interested him, or cases that he thought he might be called on later to testify, Rusty would usually make a reference or file copy for himself of the pictorial evidence of a crime scene. Fortunately for us today, that is exactly what he did with much of the Kennedy assassination-related material which is presented in this book.

During those weekend visits, I can remember more than once finding Rusty's photographs when the grownups were not around. The gory scenes were sometimes accidentally left scattered across the table, and I'd climb up and take a look. I still vividly recall the horrible shots of some unfortunate's leg lying in the grass on the side of a railroad track, another of a man with no top to his head sitting in a porch swing with a rifle lying precariously across his lap, and another with a naked woman lying in a pool of her own blood. Those indelible visions have remained with me today. When I recently viewed the same forbidden photographs, now 28 years later, I remembered that first shock when I was young.

It's been said that most can remember where they were when President Kennedy was assassinated, and I'm no exception. Ironically, President Kennedy himself made a similar statement shortly before he was killed by stating that most people could recall where they were when Franklin Roosevelt died.

Rusty's photographs of the JFK assassination flooded me with memories of November 22nd, 1963. I was in my fourth grade classroom when a teacher came to the door and announced the news in a low, reverent voice. Even though the peculiar sadness of her tone was uncomfortable, my reaction was at first nonchalant. That feeling quickly faded though, as my teacher began to tell us what a tragedy this was to our country. I remember beginning to understand and identify with the sadness of the adults. When I got home later that afternoon, I turned on the television to view the unexpected scenes in Dallas being broadcast instead of my usual *Quick Draw McGraw* cartoon show.

While certainly not aware of the politics of President Kennedy, my frustration at 8 years old over pre-empted afternoon cartoons gave way to the realization that what I was seeing was important. I stayed glued to the television all weekend watching Air Force One arrive back in Washington; the new President, Lyndon Johnson, attempting to speak words of comfort to a shocked nation; the funeral procession leading to Arlington Cemetery; and finally, the slaying of Lee Harvey Oswald in the basement of the Dallas Police Department. This was major stuff, even for an 8-year-old kid!

After the tragedy had occurred in Dallas, my family once again made the semi-annual pilgrimage to visit Rusty and Daisie. I vaguely recall my uncle showing us the photographs that he had of the Texas School Book Depository Building and Oswald in custody. The importance of what I was seeing at such a young age was not realized.

Rusty does tell today of the $50,000 offer that he received immediately after the assassination from a national magazine for the photographs he had in his possession. He declined it. I guess it had to do with something called ethics. It seems other people's standards weren't quite so high, however, since some of the same photographs were published soon afterwards anyway.[1]

The desire to write a book certainly has not been high on any priority lists that I ever made. The circumstances leading to the effort began to take shape during a recent visit to Dallas with my Uncle Rusty and my brother Steve. I had wanted to see for myself the assassination site at Houston and Elm Streets and check out the path that Oswald had taken during that fateful Friday afternoon. Rusty's knowledge of the city helped us trace Oswald's movements, and the comment was made of the proximity of Jack Ruby's apartment to Oswald's rooming house.

We roamed over the grassy knoll area at the assassination site, just as thousands have done over the years. We were typical rubber-necks, training our eyes upon the now permanently opened, glass-covered window on the sixth floor of the former Texas School Book Depository Building.

We visited The Sixth Floor, a new museum which is now located on the same floor from which shots were fired. My brother Steve and I stood at the window next to the so-called sniper's nest, which is now enclosed in glass (preventing a true view as seen by the sniper), and gazed down towards Elm Street. Being an avid hunter, my brother simply stood there and shook his head saying, "There's no way he could have made that last shot from here. It's just too far!"

As we left the museum, I became excited about our next stop. Prior to our arrival in Dallas, I had seen a segment on CNN about the new JFK Assassination Information Center which had been set up in Dallas' West End Marketplace as a nationwide clearinghouse for information relating to the assassination of President Kennedy. After viewing a new film on the assassination, we went through an adjoining exhibit area which showcased many different theories about the shooting.

One exhibit which caught Rusty's eye was a photograph of a man now deceased named Roscoe White. His son had recently claimed that his late father had been a gunman who had fired on the Kennedy motorcade from the grassy knoll area on the north side of Elm Street.[2] Although the claim to date has not been satisfactorily proven, Rusty did remember White as having been on the Dallas police force for a short time as a patrolman. When Rusty and I had completed viewing the exhibits, we began talking to one of the Center's founders, J. Gary Shaw.

Rusty introduced himself to Shaw as a retired detective from the Dallas Police Department. He wanted to know when the film we had just seen had been made because of L. C. Graves' appearance. Rusty had broken Graves in as a detective years before and had mistakenly thought that he had passed away. Shaw assured Rusty that Graves was alive and well.

L. C. Graves and Jim Leavelle were the two Dallas police officers who escorted Oswald at the time of his murder. Shaw asked Rusty if he knew Jim Leavelle and, of course, Rusty said, "Sure." Shaw then got Jim on the phone and passed it to Rusty who sat down and chatted for a few minutes to an old friend he'd not seen in years.

When Rusty rejoined us, Shaw asked him if he'd recognized Roscoe White's picture in the exhibit area. Rusty told him yes, that he did remember White's face as being someone on the force at one time. Rusty then began telling Shaw about his own work in the Crime Lab processing some of Oswald's fingerprints some 28 years ago, without going into much detail.

After mulling over a few other assassination-related points, the idea began to roll around in my head about Rusty's firsthand involvement in all of this. I began remembering the photographs that he had, which I had never seriously studied. I realized that here was an eyewitness to many of the events surrounding President Kennedy's assassination that had never before been approached to tell his story. I really wondered if he could begin to shed some new light on the whole affair.

"Maybe we ought to write a book, Rusty," I said kind of half-heartedly with a smile on my face. Gary Shaw looked at me and seriously said, "Maybe you should!"

With that, we headed back to Louisiana. The trip to Dallas had been inspiring to me, to say the least. I was overwhelmed and thoroughly impressed as Rusty's memory was triggered by our expedition. Rusty had viewed the museum exhibits as if browsing through an old family album. He knew many of the principles personally and provided amusing anecdotes and trivia that gave a depth of character not encountered in most JFK assassination-related books.

During our 5-hour trip home, the flippant suggestion of writing a book became a serious commitment. Rusty and I had taken a mutual plunge almost as nerve-wracking as a marriage proposal! The drive to Dallas became the first small step in a long journey back in time to gather fresh information on one of the most compelling mysteries of the twentieth century.

1. Jim Marrs, *Crossfire* (N.Y.: Carroll & Graf Publishers, Inc., 1989), 451.
2. "I Was Mandarin," *Texas Monthly*, December 1990, 133.

INTRODUCTION

RICHARD WARD LIVINGSTON HAS BEEN MORE OF A WITNESS TO recent American history than most. As a child standing on a street corner in Ardmore, Oklahoma in the late 1930's, Rusty unexpectedly witnessed a car crash and then the arrest of a notorious kidnaper named Harvey Bailey. As a young sailor in the World War II Pacific arena, he witnessed General Douglas MacArthur wade onto a Phillipine island after a triumphant return. Then, as fate would have it, as a detective in the Dallas Police Department, Rusty witnessed the arraignment of Lee Harvey Oswald for the assassination of President John F. Kennedy. Rusty has always seemed to end up in the right place at the right time.

The circumstances surrounding his association with the Dallas police began to take shape in the late 1940's. World War II had just ended, and the United States was beginning to enter into the postwar baby boom era. Rusty had served aboard the *USS Maryland* as a Navy frogman and after being discharged began kicking around a few odd jobs around north Texas. He worked on a construction job pushing concrete in a wheelbarrow. "That was a little too rough for me, so I had to quit," he told me with a laugh. Later, after a brief stint as a lineman with the telephone company, Rusty got a job as a security guard with an aircraft plant in Grand Prairie, Texas.

While Rusty was off fighting in the Pacific, his father, Jack, had gotten a job with the Grand Prairie Police Department, and the family had relocated from his boyhood home in Ardmore. Upon his return home, Rusty began to ride with his father on patrol around Grand Prairie occasionally. He witnessed firsthand how his father dealt with people, attempting to understand the reasons why they would do the things that they did. Rusty told me about his father, "I've seen him walk up to men that would want to fight any officer that tried to arrest them, and my father would calmly tell them to come on along with him, and they'd follow him to jail as meek as a kid. They had respect for him because they knew that he would treat them fairly. He would sit them down and talk to them like a father and point out their wrongs, and a lot of times leave them crying. I remember one of them told me, 'I wish Mr. Jack would just beat the crap out of me instead of talking to me. He makes me feel like a heel, and I guess I am.'"

Rusty's interest in police work began to take shape as he hung around the station in Grand Prairie where his father eventually became Chief of Police. "I used to hang around and look at all of his mug shots of criminals and such, and that sparked an interest in me. I never did particularly want to be a patrolman; I wanted to be a detective. I applied to the Dallas Police Department and passed both the physical and written examinations. I got called in to be interviewed and was accepted and then started to school at the Academy."

IT WAS 1951 WHEN RUSTY BEGAN HIS TRAINING AT THE DALLAS Police Academy. He started the six week course a week late along with another rookie named R. L. Bobo. The two of them were held over for an additional week following the graduation of the other class members since they had begun their training late. Both Rusty and R. L. stayed with the Dallas police until retirement.

The police chief at the time of the Kennedy assassination was Jesse Curry. Rusty told me, "Curry taught at the Police Academy for years. He was always a fair chief and did a good job and got along well with the men. He was what you would call a 'Policeman's Chief.' If a chief didn't get along with the men, he didn't last too long."

The first month in uniform for Rusty was, to say the least, enlightening. He told me, "I'll never forget the first night after I got into uniform after I graduated out of the Academy. We worked what they called 'fill-in' with the patrol squad. We would fill-in for an officer who worked a particular beat. When one of them was sick or on their day off, we'd fill-in for their regular partner. We were working the three to eleven shift that first day that I was in uniform."

"We got in the car and I was unsure, and wondering how much I had learned in the Academy was going to help me out on the street as a policeman. The first man that I went to work with that night was a nice ol' boy that stayed there until he retired."

"Anyway, the first thing that we did after we checked into service was to go down to the beat, which was the old 44 beat in south Dallas. After we got down on the beat, we pulled into a cafe and checked out for coffee. We sat and had a cup of coffee, and my partner was telling me about the beat and what went on. He told me not to be nervous and that everything was going to be all right and that he would take care of me. I told him that I felt so green and I didn't know whether I could handle the job or not."

"So after drinking our coffee, we checked back into service. Shortly after that the first call we got was a disturbance with a gun. Going through my mind at that time was the thought that it looks like I'm going to get shot the first day on the job. Most of the calls we got like that, we'd arrive and there wouldn't be a gun in sight, nothing at all going on. Sometimes there would just be an ol' boy waving a gun around threatening people, and he'd usually be gone from the scene."

Rusty was soon to experience some immediate misgivings about the police department that he had so longed to be a part of. He continued, "Later on, I hadn't been there too long, maybe into the next month, I was working the late night shift from eleven to seven in the morning. I was working in the south section of downtown, the old 41 beat. Incidentally, in that beat at that time, Jack Ruby had a night club down on South Ervay. The first thing that I remember on that particular beat, we got a call on a silent burglar alarm at a clothing manufacturing building on the edge of downtown Dallas where they made men's slacks."

"When we arrived, another uniform squad was already there along with a detective squad with a night lieutenant who was in charge of the detectives on the late night shift. They were carrying out handfuls of men's slacks and putting them in the trunk of the squad cars. I'm standing there with my mouth open, thinking about how I'm supposed to be out catching thieves and not being one. It shocked me, and I didn't know what to do. Even though I had been there only a short time, I knew how things were and that you didn't rat on another police officer. If you did, your career would end right there. I didn't say anything to anybody about it, but that was my thought at the time."

"Later on, they caught this night lieutenant and some of the other detectives that were there and some other patrolmen. They found out that they had been stealing on several occasions, and they filed on them for it. They tried the Lieutenant, and he eventually went to the penitentiary for his part in the stealing."

"They never called me to testify about what I saw that night, and I was glad of it. I don't know what I would have told them. I felt like telling the truth about everything, but like I've said at that time you had to kind of watch yourself. I wanted to be a detective, and I wanted to stay there on the job, so I didn't say anything. I was never questioned, and since I was just a rookie at the time anyway working fill-in, I was never suspected as being in on it. Thinking back now, I can see that there was a lot of graft going on in the Department at that time. Later on, it got pretty well cleaned up. It did get better as the years went on. We had a cleaner police department than when I went to work there in the beginning."

Rusty worked fill-in for about a year before getting a regular beat. His first partner was a brand new rookie named Warren Thurston. Thurston was voted "Rookie of the Year" while being teamed up with Rusty. During that year, Rusty held the record for the most burglars caught in one month.

He told me, "We caught four boys one night after they had burglarized a service station. We stopped them on the street and searched the car and found a lot of stolen articles in the car: cigarettes, candy, that type of thing. They took us back and showed us where they had broken into a service station."

"Later I caught two boys in a grocery store. We would drive by with our lights out, checking buildings for burglars, and we caught two in one grocery store there and two more at a cleaners. That was a pretty good month we had working late nights."

I asked Rusty what a typical day would be like for a Dallas patrolman back when he began in the early fifties.

He said, "Until you got broken in and got a regular beat of your own, you worked one of two shifts. You could work either the evening shift or the late night shift. You switched back and forth with each one. The evening shift was from three o'clock in the evening until eleven at night, and the late night shift went from eleven at night until seven in the morning. When I first went to work, one week we'd get two days off and the next week we'd get one day off, always in the middle of the week. We never got any weekends off. I enjoyed it so much that I hated to see quitting time come when I first started. I didn't like to be off. Sometimes we'd be off Friday and Saturday, and those were two of the busiest nights. I didn't like that much because I wanted to be in on where all the action was."

"We'd usually get to work at about 10:30 for the eleven o'clock shift so that we could change into our uniform and have assembly. We'd go down to the locker room and change clothes and put our uniforms on and then go on up to the assembly room. The Captain would give us a little pep talk and then the Sergeant would read out all of the offenses that had happened, the main ones that had happened in each district."

"We'd change shifts in the basement. The car would pull down the ramp into the parking garage. They'd leave half of them on the street, and the other half came on in and changed shifts. It would take about fifteen minutes. One shift would come in about thirty minutes before quitting time, and the other would come in about fifteen minutes before shift change, and they'd gas the car up for the new shift coming on. We'd walk out of the assembly room and take off."

Rusty said that when he began as a rookie, there was a three-month probation period. After that period was over, you were under civil service regulations. During the probationary period, you could be fired for practically no reason at all. After the three-month period, however, there had to be a cause to be laid off or fired. He said it depended on an officer's job performance as to when he got picked up for a regular beat.

I asked Rusty about the structure of the Department at that time. He told me, "Under the Chief of Police was the Assistant Chief. There were Deputy Chiefs over each Division such as Patrol, Traffic, Records, Dispatch, and the Jail. At that time there were three different Shift Captains. Each one was in charge of one shift and had his own men. They would change shifts every month. There was also a Captain over each detective office of Burglary and Theft, Homicide, Auto Theft, Forgery, and the Vice-Squad."

"We had a Sergeant over each beat or section of town. He'd stay out on patrol all the time. Anytime we'd have anything that we felt like we needed his advice on, we'd call and he'd come and meet us. Usually any major call like a burglar caught in a building, or a shooting, or a hijacking [armed robbery], or rape, the Sergeant was always there."

"Over the Sergeant was the Lieutenant. He would drive around town, but wouldn't stay out all the time. Over the Lieutenant was the Captain, who generally stayed in the office most of the time handling all the paperwork."

THIS WAS THE SAME BASIC STRUCTURE OF THE DALLAS POLICE Identification Bureau in 1963 when Kennedy was assassinated. Rusty had become a detective and was working in the Crime Lab, a rank basically equivalent to Sergeant. His boss was Lieutenant Day, whose desk was located in the same office. In a large outer connecting room was the desk of the man who ran the Identification Bureau, Captain George M. Doughty.

After his years as patrolman working beats all over Dallas, Rusty had made detective in 1956. He was assigned first to Burglary and Theft. During that period he developed personal friendships with many of the local merchants which later served him well in developing leads for various crimes that he would be investigating. Rusty enjoyed working out the leads in solving different crimes since he was mainly on his own.

A typical call in Burglary and Theft would be a reported burglary of a safe. Dallas seemed to have its share of "safe burglars." Rusty told me the story once about one particular safe burglar who had been brought into custody for questioning by the detectives.

He began, "This one ol' boy told the detectives that he had some nitro-glycerin in his house. Everybody got pretty excited about that, and they let the Department news-hounds know about it. Some of the police reporters and photographers went out there along with one of the men from the Crime Lab."

"Anyway, this was the type of story the reporters thought was newsworthy, so they stood around outside this house while the Burglary and Theft detectives and our Crime Lab man went through looking for this nitro. They searched the house high and low and didn't find anything, so one of the officers found a small medicine bottle and filled it about half full of water."

Rusty started smiling as he got to the end of his story, and somehow I already knew the punch-line. "So here was this officer carrying this bottle out of the front door, and all these news photographers were out there taking his picture. He got all the way down to the bottom of the steps there and caused himself to trip and threw that medicine bottle right into the middle of those reporters. They all just scattered! One of the police reporters told me later that he felt stupid since it wouldn't have done much good to run. He said he just couldn't stand still though when the officer fell down."

AFTER ABOUT THREE YEARS IN BURGLARY AND THEFT, RUSTY transferred to the Juvenile Division. He told me, "I got transferred to the Juvenile Bureau, which I hated thoroughly. It just never seemed to me like it was police work, handling juveniles all the time. It was a baby-sitting job, more or less. We'd handle missing kids or anything that had to do with anyone under seventeen years of age."

Finally Rusty got his chance to escape to an area of the Department that interested him. "An opening came up. They wanted somebody to work in the Crime Lab. They had picked one of the older detectives in Juvenile that liked his job there, and he didn't want to leave. I think that he didn't have to work very hard and liked the slow pace. Anyway, he had enough influence with the Captains to get me picked to go instead of him. But I was glad to get out of there. I enjoyed working in the Crime Lab."

And so began the job which, as fate would have it, would end up placing Rusty in the midst of the investigation of the shooting of President Kennedy. The Crime Lab Office located on the fourth floor of the Dallas Police Department would become Rusty's "home away from home" for the duration of the 1960's.

CHAPTER

I

The Assassination Weekend

FRIDAY, NOVEMBER 22ND, 1963, BEGAN FOR PRESIDENT JOHN F. Kennedy on an upbeat note. After spending the night in Fort Worth's Texas Hotel, the President awakened to sounds of people gathering outside across the street in a parking lot. A light rain continued to fall as the largely blue-collar crowd continued to swell to almost 5,000 to hear the President who was scheduled to speak.

Despite the rain, Kennedy did not wear a raincoat or hat as he made his way across the street. He climbed aboard a flat-bed trailer which was backed into place as a speaker's platform. As the crowd began to chant, "Where's Jackie?", the President looked back across to his hotel room and told them, "Mrs. Kennedy is organizing herself. It takes her a little longer, but of course, she looks better than us when she does it."

After a short address, Kennedy went back into the hotel and made his way into the ballroom where a Chamber of Commerce breakfast had just begun. Once again as Kennedy stood up to address the crowd, he commented on Jackie who had just arrived in the ballroom to join him twenty minutes late. "Two years ago I introduced myself in Paris by saying that I was the man who had accompanied Mrs. Kennedy to Paris." The crowd loved it and stood cheering the President and First Lady.

After the breakfast, the Kennedys went back up to their room, feeling wonderful about the warm reception they had just received. During the rare one hour rest period spent in the room, the President was shown an anti-Kennedy ad in the local morning paper. He handed it to Jackie and told her, "We're heading into nut country today. If anybody wants to shoot me from a window with a rifle, nobody can stop it."

Presidential Aide Ken O'Donnell placed a call to Secret Service Agent Roy Kellerman. A discussion was held concerning whether the clear bubble-top roof cover should be removed from the limousine for the Dallas motorcade. A decision was made to leave it off with the hope that there would be no rain.[1]

The President's entourage then left the hotel for Carswell Air Force Base and boarded Air Force One for the short flight to Dallas. The sun abruptly broke through the clouds as the President and Jackie arrived at Love Field in Dallas. A huge crowd composed largely of women and children had gathered on the tarmac behind a cyclone fence.

As the President and Jackie descended the stairs from Air Force One, the smiles and casual waves of America's first couple were eagerly sought by the excited spectators. The President broke away from his party to shake as many hands as he could. Jackie and he were separated temporarily, but reemerged together and were directed to their seats in the presidential limousine by the Secret Service.

1. Citizen photograph given to Dallas police showing the presidential limousine in the Dallas motorcade.

The motorcycle escort which typically rode alongside the presidential limousine was instructed beforehand by the Secret Service to ride in the procession directly behind the President.[2]

2. Citizen photograph given to Dallas police, taken from the rear of the Secret Service car following the President.

The clear plastic convertible top had been removed, and the motorcade began its trek toward downtown Dallas. The route had been planned by the Secret Service days before and been printed in the local Dallas newspaper. Washington-based Secret Service Agent Winston G. Lawson along with local Dallas Secret Service Agent Forrest Sorrels consulted with various members of the Dallas police in planning the placement of officers along the parade route as early as November 13th, 1963.[3] The destination of the motorcade was the Dallas Trade Mart, located just off the Stemmons Freeway. The President was scheduled to speak at a Trade Mart luncheon at 12:30 p.m.

People lining the parade route were extremely enthusiastic. The President and Jackie were overwhelmed by the excitement generated by the crowds. Kennedy had been warned by some of his friends back in Washington not to make the trip to Dallas in fear of his safety. Adlai Stevenson had been attacked only a month earlier by radicals in Dallas, and many believed that the President might also be at risk there. All of that had been temporarily forgotten as the motorcade made its way slowly through the roaring downtown crowds.

3. Citizen Photograph given to Dallas police showing the presidential limousine in the Dallas motorcade.

Few words were spoken by the occupants in the presidential limousine as they smiled and waved in awe of the overwhelming reception. The motorcade had been slightly delayed due to the massive surge of people into the streets and had fallen about 10 minutes behind its scheduled arrival time at the Trade Mart. At approximately 12:30, the motorcade broke through the shadows of the tall buildings of Dallas and entered Dealey Plaza, a two block wide open area on the west end of downtown.

In the northeast corner of the Plaza stood the seven story Texas School Book Depository Building, an old brick structure filled with stacked boxes of school textbooks. One of the shipping clerks who worked on the sixth floor had been temporarily hired

4. Citizen photograph given to Dallas police showing the Texas School Book Depository Building.

only a few weeks before. His name was Lee Harvey Oswald.

As the motorcade completed its predetermined journey past the Main Street crowds, a right turn was made onto Houston Street. Scores of people were on hand to catch a brief sought-after view of the current President of the United States.

The bright sunlight suddenly enveloped the occupants of the open limousine, and a sharp breeze brushed their faces as they headed one block north on Houston Street. Directly above and in front of the unsuspecting President stared Oswald from the towering sixth-floor Depository window. The easiest shot of the day was his for the taking, but he waited patiently.

5. Citizen photograph of the presidential limousine. Notice Jackie looking to her left, as she was told to do by aides.

The limousine then made an elongated 120 degree turn left onto Elm Street, practically struck the north curb, and slowed to approximately 11 miles per hour. The crowds had thinned, and the motorcade was free to pick up speed as it headed down the slight hill on Elm towards a triple railroad underpass.

6. Another citizen photograph showing the President leaning his right arm on the side of the limousine.

7. Citizen photograph given to Dallas police. Notice Kennedy's jump seat positioned him higher than Connally.

AS THE CROWD HAD ASSEMBLED THAT MORNING TO VIEW THE motorcade, surprisingly few had gathered in the middle grassy area of Dealey Plaza on the south side of Elm Street. The large vacancy appears in numerous photographs and films taken at the time of the shooting.

Earlier in the morning of the assassination, Abraham Zapruder, a ladies' dress manufacturer, had been urged by one of his employees to go home and retrieve his new 8 mm movie camera to film the President. Fortunately for the sake of history he did, and his home movie became the most important documentation that exists today of the assassination. Zapruder stood on a concrete pillar next to the grassy knoll on the north side of Elm Street, looking south. He continued filming during the entire shooting and realized the horror of what was happening before him as his camera rolled.

Each frame of the Elm Street footage of the assassination has since been assigned a number and meticulously studied. Robert Groden, a researcher who served as a photographic consultant to

8. Another citizen photograph given to police showing the closeness of the Secret Service follow up car.

the House Select Committee in the late seventies, has worked with the film to enhance each individual frame.[4]

It seems, after an objective reading of testimony from many of the eyewitnesses, that those standing near the upper end of Elm Street and those in the motorcade itself near the Depository Building felt as though most or all of the shots were fired from the Depository Building. Others on the lower end of Elm felt as though the shots possibly came from the fenced area over the grassy knoll. Some witnesses (including Secret Service personnel) felt as though the shots were fired from more than one location, with multiple shots occurring at the same moment.

Herein lies the controversy. A second gunman automatically entails a conspiracy of two or more people. Opinions drawn from those who have studied the assassination for years vary widely today. The conclusion drawn in 1964 by the Warren Commission, appointed by President Johnson to investigate the shooting, was that Lee Harvey Oswald was a lone gunman who fired on the motorcade.[5] Any other sounds of gunfire heard that day by eyewitnesses were dismissed as echoes or mistaken recollection.

Despite the various opinions of well-meaning (and some not-so-well-meaning) researchers, the events recorded through photographic and physical evidence and testimony of eyewitnesses can now be our only road to truth. Conclusions drawn about the events which occurred on Elm Street are destined to remain controversial. Only an open mind and study of the facts developed over years by governmental and private researchers can help us understand today what occurred on November 22nd, 1963, in Dallas.

As THE PRESIDENTIAL LIMOUSINE ROUNDED THE CORNER OF Houston onto Elm Street, Kennedy seemed relaxed and casually looked to his left as he waved his right hand at the bystanders. He then lowered his arm to rest it on the side of the open car. At that moment, the first shot rang out.

9. Dallas Police Crime Lab photograph looking north on Houston Street.

10. A second Dallas Police Crime Lab photograph looking north on Houston Street, slightly closer to the Depository.

Many of the witnesses who stood at the corner of Houston and Elm Street thought they had heard a backfire from a vehicle. Some thought a firecracker had been thrown and temporarily surmised a bad joke was being played. Two witnesses, Royce Skelton and Virgie Baker, later reported that the first shot had missed the limousine entirely and hit the sidewalk on the north side of Elm Street near the Stemmons Freeway sign.[6] The sniper's view was obscured by a Texas live oak tree below the sixth-floor Depository window. The bullet's impact on the sidewalk burst the concrete into a cloud of dust in a trajectory away from the Depository Building.

Stavis Ellis, one of the motorcycle escorts riding about 100 feet in front of the President, was looking rearward directly at the President as the first shot was fired. Ellis stated that the first shot hit the curb, not the President. He said that the President turned and looked over his shoulder after the first shot was fired.[7] This immediate reaction by the President as well as Governor Connally to the loud report can be seen on the Zapruder film as an abrupt turn by both men to the right. Key frames are omitted from the Zapruder film at the moment the shot hit the sidewalk. A casual viewing of the film indicates a very evident skip in the smooth flow of the action.

11. Dallas Police Crime Lab photograph looking east on Elm Street. Note the shadow of the photographer, as well as the box containing his photograph and fingerprint supplies. This is basically the same view seen by James Tague.

One bystander located on the south side of Elm Street next to the triple underpass was struck on the side of his face by a ricocheting piece of debris during the assassination. James Tague had pulled over to view the motorcade and was standing beside his car as the presidential motorcade approached. As the first shot rang out, Tague felt a sting on his cheek which probably triggered an instantaneous flight reaction. As he quickly ducked behind a

41

12. Dallas Police Crime Lab photograph showing a closeup view of the front of the Depository Building.

concrete pillar of the railroad underpass, Tague heard two more shots.[8] It seems probable that James Tague was struck by the ricocheting fragments of the first shot.

Governor Connally has steadfastly maintained that he was not hit by the first shot. He told the Warren Commission that he heard the first shot and immediately recognized it as a rifle and had the feeling that it was an assassination attempt. Connally instinctively turned to look over his right shoulder towards the direction from which he felt the shot had come.[9] Oswald probably fired his first shot from the southeast corner window of the sixth

13. Citizen photograph given to Dallas police showing Vice-President Johnson in right rear seat and Senator Ralph Yarborough in left rear seat waving. Lady Bird Johnson is seated between the two.

floor of the Depository Building and completely missed the presidential limousine.

Following the initial distraction of the first unexpected bullet, the President evidently did not realize what had just occurred. He continued to look to his right and then forward as he once again began to casually wave his right hand. During the next few frames of the Zapruder film, the limousine's occupants disappear from view behind the Stemmons freeway sign. It was precisely at that moment that the wound to the President's neck occurred. As the President reemerged from behind the sign, his arms had risen with clenched fists as though to protect himself. A back brace worn by the President probably contributed to his remaining in an upright position after being struck.

The neck wound to the President is the key to the 1964 Warren Commission lone-gunman theory, which holds that Lee Harvey Oswald fired three shots from the sixth floor of the School Book Depository Building. It was the Commission's conclusion that a shot from behind entered the back of the President and exited forward through his neck below the Adam's apple (the wound occurring behind the freeway sign). Commission attorneys theorized that the same bullet had also traveled forward to enter Connally's back, inflicting all of his injuries. Researchers today refer to this as the "single bullet theory." The Commission then determined that a second bullet from Oswald from the rear resulted in the fatal head shot of the President. A third shot had at some point been fired, but had missed the limousine.[10]

After being shot in the neck, Kennedy reappeared from behind the sign with his arms thrust upwards in a protective stance. About one second later, Governor Connally reacted to a shot in his back which critically injured him. Connally fell over into his wife Nellie's lap, who was seated to his left, as he screamed, "My God, they're going to kill us all!" Fortunately for the Governor, the positioning of his fall onto his wife's lap helped to seal the sucking wound he had received in his lung.

A definite pause between shots now momentarily allowed the two Secret Service Agents in the front of the limousine to look around and witness the horror in the rear seats. William Greer, the agent driving the car, applied the brakes after he realized that shots had been fired. This in turn caused the back-up car of Secret Service Agents to hit their brakes to avoid rear-ending the presidential limousine. Roy Kellerman, the agent in the right front seat of the President's car began to speak into his microphone as he leaned forward.

Jackie, seated to the left of the President, leaned toward her husband during the few moments of stunned silence. Her right arm rested on the rear of the seat, touching the President's left shoulder. She had just realized that something terrible had occurred. As the limousine slowed almost to a halt, the unexpected fatal shot was fired, striking the right side of the President's head. The President rocked violently back into the seat, falling lifeless into his horrified wife's lap. Jackie was showered with bloody brain tissue and screamed, "Oh, my God, they've shot my husband. I love you Jack."

Bobby Hargis, a motorcycle officer riding to the left rear of the limousine, was sprayed with bloody matter and bone fragments.[11] His first thought was that he had been shot himself. The sickening impact on the President's head was heard by the Secret Service Agents in the follow-up car as well as by Connally as he lay injured.

Seeing a piece of her husband's skull lying on the rear trunk lid of the car, Jackie instinctively dashed out of her seat to retrieve it. Secret Service Agent Clint Hill had already bolted from the follow-up car and barely secured his footing on the rear running board of the presidential limousine as it suddenly accelerated following the fatal head shot. Hill reached forward toward Jackie, who in effect paid him no attention. Although not recalled in her own memory, Jackie's action was a vain attempt to gather the scattered portions of the President's fractured head. During the frantic drive to Parkland Hospital which followed, Jackie attempted to hold the jumbled pieces of her husband's head together.

HAVING FIRED THREE SHOTS, LEE HARVEY OSWALD LEANED slightly forward and quickly glanced at the disappearing motorcade. Three spent rifle hulls had been ejected from the rifle and now lay on the wooden plank floor to his right. Oswald stood, turned rearward, and at a controlled but excited pace probably made his way down the long open aisle along the east wall of the sixth floor, carrying his rifle. As he reached the end of the unobstructed 90 foot long aisle, he made a left turn and briskly walked along the north side of the huge room of boxes, past the large freight elevators on the right.[12]

During his escape from the sixth-floor sniper's nest, whether predetermined or not, Oswald approached an opening in the tall stacks of boxes on his left. He stopped and leaned over a two-high stack of boxes and placed his rifle on the floor behind, concealing it from immediate view. He then turned and quickly entered the small stairs in the northwest corner of the Depository. After descending to the second floor, he exited the stairs and entered the second-floor lunchroom.

Dallas Police Officer Marrion Baker, a motorcycle escort in the motorcade, noticed pigeons flying from the roof of the Depository during the shooting. He hurriedly parked his motorcycle and dashed up the front steps into the Depository Building. Roy Truly, the building superintendent, quickly directed Officer Baker up the stairs to the upper floors, when Baker noticed movement in his peripheral vision of someone entering the second-floor lunchroom door.[13]

The officer had his revolver drawn as he confronted Oswald, who remained calm during the encounter. Truly, who had raced ahead of Officer Baker, returned and told him that Oswald was an employee. Baker then left Oswald in the second-floor lunchroom and headed back up the stairs, not surmising that Oswald had anything to do with the shooting. Oswald proceeded to buy a coke and then walked calmly out the front door of the Depository.

Following the shooting, the motorcade continued on its predetermined drive as it entered Stemmons Freeway. The original destination, however, had now tragically been changed to Parkland Hospital. Coincidentally, the route to Parkland led directly in front of the Trade Mart, where several motorcycle officers were awaiting the arrival of the President.

Pedestrians had lined up on both sides of the 10-lane highway and had begun to cut across the oncoming traffic to view the motorcade, which was now speeding past. Traveling the opposite way on Stemmons freeway southbound was a reporter for the *Dallas News* named Jim Ewell.

Ewell had just covered the President's arrival at Love Field for the newspaper, and was headed back in his pickup truck to the Dallas Police Department where he worked as a police reporter on the third floor. His news assignment was now basically over, except for a rewrite of the notes jotted down back at the airport.

Ewell stated that as he looked across the center highway divider at the high rate of speed of the passing motorcade, his first thought was that one of the pedestrians cutting across the highway may have been run over accidentally. He first noticed Chief Curry's car go by, followed by the open limousine carrying the fatally wounded President. He then noticed Clint Hill sprawled across the rear of the presidential limousine. The motorcade was "really strung out," according to Ewell with the three press buses going by spaced far apart from one another.

Ewell himself struggled to avoid hitting people cutting in front of his own vehicle. As he exited at Main Street and headed towards Police Headquarters, Ewell drove under the triple underpass into Dealey Plaza (from the opposite direction the motorcade had entered) approximately two to three minutes following the shooting. He told Rusty and me, "As I came out on Commerce, which then was still two-way, I looked over at the School Book Depository, and it looked like a disturbed ant-hill. I mean, people were spilling out and crying everywhere."

The screaming sirens of the motorcade now bypassed the Trade Mart, where the waiting crowd had gathered to see the now fatally wounded President. A few of the motorcycle officers parked in front of the Trade Mart joined in behind the speeding cars racing to the hospital. One motorcycle officer's radio "send" button had been stuck open for a few minutes as he sat waiting in front of the Trade Mart. (This will be discussed in a later chapter.)

As the motorcade arrived at the emergency room entrance, Secret Service Agents and Dallas Police Officers quickly rushed to the President and gasped at the gruesome scene. The President lay face up in Jackie's lap with his eyes open in a gaunt stare. Governor Connally first had to be removed in order to lift the President from the car. Connally temporarily regained consciousness and attempted to bring himself up, realizing that he was blocking the President in the car. The effort proved fruitless, however, and he fell back helplessly. He was quickly lifted onto a stretcher by the agents and officers and hurriedly wheeled inside to Parkland Hospital's Trauma Room #2.

Jackie, still holding the President's head in her lap, would not let go of her husband. Clint Hill quickly realized that Jackie could not bear for anyone to see her husband's wounds and volunteered his coat to cover the President's head. Kennedy was lifted out of the limousine, placed on a stretcher and wheeled into Trauma Room #1. As the room quickly began to fill up with medical personnel, a slight pulse and shallow breathing were detected. Lifesaving measures were attempted, but the President's injuries were fatal, and he died shortly. Nothing could possibly have been done to save him. President John F. Kennedy was officially pronounced dead at 1:00 p.m. Governor Connally was immediately rushed to surgery and eventually fully recovered from his wounds.

UPON THE DEATH OF KENNEDY, THE NEW PRESIDENT LYNDON Johnson was driven back to Love Field by Dallas Police Chief Jesse Curry. Vice-President Johnson had arrived in Dallas earlier aboard Air Force Two and was in the line of dignitaries waiting to greet the President. President Kennedy had arrived in Dallas after Johnson aboard Air Force One.

Air Force One and Air Force Two were alike in all aspects, except in name. However, when Johnson returned to Love Field after the assassination, he boarded Air Force One, the President's plane. He proceeded to the President's bedroom, where he began placing long distance calls back to Washington.[14]

Back at Parkland following the death of the President, a heated confrontation occurred between the Secret Service Agents and Dr. Earl Rose, the county medical examiner. The agents had ordered a coffin to be delivered to the hospital. After the arrival of the coffin, the body was placed inside, wrapped in sheets. A plastic bed liner had been placed first on the inside to protect the coffin's lining from being stained by the President's blood.[15]

As the Secret Service prepared to leave the hospital, Dr. Rose informed the agents that, by Texas law, he had to perform an autopsy on the President in Dallas. He told the agents that the autopsy could be done quickly to accommodate their desired departure back to Washington. At this point, the agents were no longer protecting the President. They were protecting a body. They were not willing to let Dr. Rose do an autopsy, however. Jackie did not want to leave Dallas without her husband's body, and the agents wanted the new President Johnson as well as Jackie back in the air for an immediate flight to Washington. A shoving and shouting match ensued in the hallway of the hospital. Some of the Secret Service Agents placed their hands over weapons concealed in their jackets and pushed the body past Dr. Rose. An ambulance was commandeered into which the body was loaded, and the Secret Service drove it with Jackie back to Love Field. The agents were fearful during the drive that at any time they might be stopped by the Dallas police and made to return to the hospital.

The agents had ordered the best coffin in stock, which came complete with bed springs, from a Dallas funeral home. It showed as they struggled to load the heavy bronze casket onto Air Force One. Kennedy's aides were surprised to find Johnson aboard, mistakingly believing he was already on his way to Washington aboard Air Force Two. Johnson had already assumed authority over Air Force One and told Kennedy's aides that he was delaying takeoff in order to be sworn in as President. Dumbfounded by the actions of the new President, the aides were told by Johnson that Attorney General Robert Kennedy had suggested that he be sworn in immediately at Dallas. Bobby later denied that he had advised Johnson of any such need to be sworn in at that time.[16]

Johnson had called an old friend of his, U. S. Federal Judge Sarah Hughes, to swear him in as President. The supplemental power had been cut off aboard Air Force One, and the cabin quickly heated up, causing all aboard to be extremely uncomfortable. Johnson requested that everyone come forward to the plane's stateroom to witness the swearing in, including Jackie. After the somber swearing in ceremony was completed, Police Chief Curry and Judge Hughes departed, and Air Force One was immediately ordered airborne by President Johnson.[17]

AS THIS HISTORIC EVENT TRANSPIRED, ACROSS TOWN IN THE DALLAS suburb of Oak Cliff, Dallas Police Officer J. D. Tippit was gunned

14. Dallas Police Crime Lab photo taken by Pete Barnes showing Officer Tippit's squad car following the shooting.

down. Eye-witness testimony related that a man had been stopped by an officer and leaned over the passenger side of the squad car as the officer remained inside. After a few words were exchanged, the officer emerged from his car. The man by the window started around to meet the officer at the front of the car. Suddenly, the man pulled out a revolver and fired four shots which killed the officer instantly. The man who murdered Officer Tippit fled the scene, reloading his revolver as he briskly walked away.

Witnesses to the shooting contacted the Dallas Police Dispatcher's Office within a few minutes, using the Tippit police radio. Units were dispatched immediately as the call went out that an officer was shot. In an adjoining alleyway next to the Tippit squad car, a jacket was found thrown under an automobile, and was pointed out and later photographed by the police.

A few minutes later Johnny Brewer, a shoe salesman on

15. Dallas Police Crime Lab photo taken by Pete Barnes showing the front of the Tippit squad car.

Jefferson Boulevard in the Dallas suburb of Oak Cliff, was listening to the radio and heard that a Dallas officer had been shot. As the police sirens screamed outside his storefront, Brewer noticed a nervous man stop to look in his sales window. The man kept glancing over his shoulder as if he were trying to avoid being seen and looked to Brewer as if he had been running. When the police cars passed, the man continued walking a few doors down to the Texas Theater. Brewer had grown suspicious of the individual, due to his knowledge of the officer being shot, and walked out front to see where the man would go. He witnessed the man duck inside the Texas Theater without paying. The theater cashier had not paid attention as the man went by, and Brewer walked over and suggested that she call the police.

Reporter Ewell had ridden along with the Captain of Personnel, "Pinky" Westbrook of the Dallas police, to the alleyway

16. Dallas Police Crime Lab photo taken by Pete Barnes showing the driver's-side view of the Tippit squad car.

where the jacket had been found. As the men stood around the scene, the call came across the police radio that someone had been seen entering the Texas Theater. Ewell stated that "I barely got in that car, because here they are spinning out, and I'm kind of hanging onto the door swinging out with it! Now that's how fast they were going back then. We parked exactly in front of the Texas Theater, and everybody got out and ran in."

The police had already been searching the area for a suspect in the killing of Tippit and so arrived quickly and in force. From the stage area of the theater, Brewer pointed out to the police the man he had seen earlier in his store front.[18]

At the time, the upper balcony of the theater was practically filled with high school boys who had skipped school that Friday afternoon to watch the movie "War Is Hell." Reporter Ewell had entered the front of the theater and, for no reason he could recall,

17. Citizen photograph given to Dallas police showing the front of the Texas Theater, site of Oswald's arrest.

raced up the stairs to the balcony as the Dallas officers continued into the lower seat area. As he was going up the stairs, he heard people yelling to turn up the house lights. Reaching the balcony, Ewell observed the large crowd of high school boys as the house lights suddenly came on. The boys, fearing that they had been discovered skipping school, began to pour down the stairs and out the front of the theater (helping to create the crowd which was widely reported to have gathered). In the rush to leave, one fellow hit his head on the low clearance at the rear of the balcony, falling to the floor as his buddies rushed over him. He later emerged from

18. Dallas Police Crime Lab photo taken by Pete Barnes. Dallas officer is indicating the theater seat Oswald used.

the theater with footprints covering his white tee shirt.[19]

Officer Nick McDonald walked from the rear screen area toward the front of the theater to the man that Brewer had pointed out. McDonald approached from the aisle on the seated man's right, avoiding eye contact. As he reached the aisle where the suspect was seated, Officer McDonald quickly turned towards the man and ordered him to stand up. As the suspect did, he yelled, "This is it!" The man then struck Officer McDonald with one hand while he pulled out his revolver with the other. McDonald managed to get his hand on the revolver to slow the hammer action on the firing pin, which resulted in a misfire. More officers instantly dove onto the man across the seats and knocked him to the floor between the rows. One officer standing behind the huddle of policemen attempted to point a shotgun over and down through the center of the struggle. An almost comical scene was witnessed by reporter

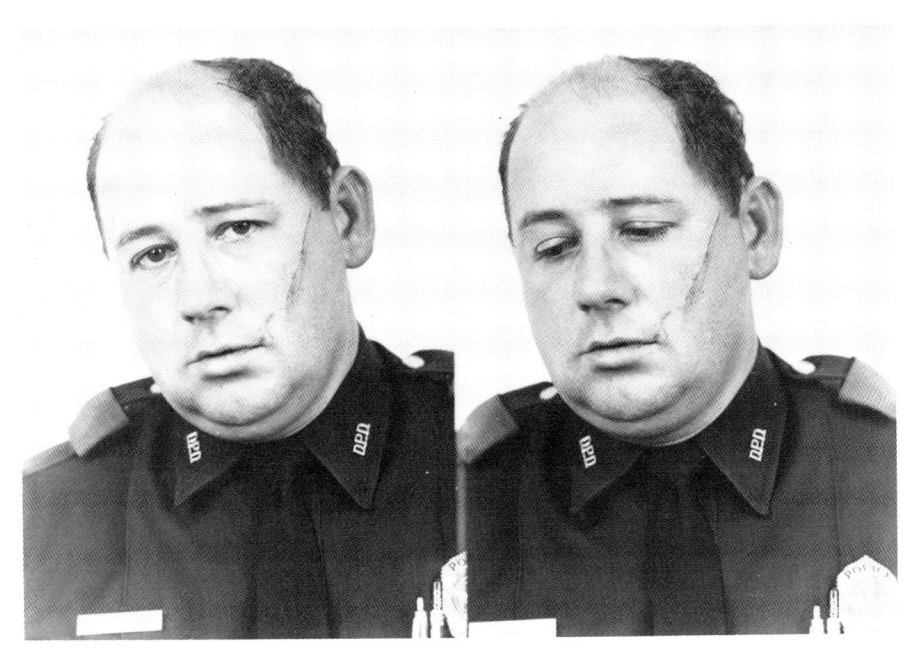

19. Dallas Police Crime Lab photo taken with the mug room camera showing Officer Nick McDonald. Photo was made to indicate facial injuries sustained by McDonald from a right-hand blow by Oswald at the Texas Theater.

Ewell as he looked down from the balcony above.

The man was subdued and handcuffed and taken to a police squad car parked in the front of the theater. The theater crowd had now spilled into the street, and other bystanders gathered to get a look at what was going on. The suspect was quickly placed in the car and driven to the Police Department.

The suspect was taken to the Homicide Offices on the third floor of the Dallas Police Building, where Homicide Detective Gus Rose first began talking to him in a front office. After a few moments, Detective Rose had the suspect brought into an interrogation room and began some initial questioning. Detective Rose attempted to determine who the suspect was but was told by the man, "You're the detective; you figure it out!" Rose then stood the man up and searched him and found two different pieces of identification on him, Alex Hidell and Lee Harvey Oswald.[20]

Homicide Captain Will Fritz had now assumed charge of the

20. Dallas Police Crime Lab photo taken by Pete Barnes showing the lobby of the Texas Theater.

21. Dallas police file copy of slain Officer J. D. Tippit.

investigation of the President's murder and had just returned to the Homicide Office from the Book Depository Building. Fritz had been informed of a missing Depository employee and wanted to send Detective Rose to locate the missing employee. Fritz tapped on Rose's door, interrupting the questioning of the Tippit shooting suspect. Detective Rose went to the door and was asked by Fritz to go immediately to try to locate the Depository employee. When the name Lee Oswald was given, Rose told Fritz that the man seated in his office might be Oswald. He was the same man just arrested in the Texas Theater as the suspect in the shooting of Police Officer Tippit.[21]

As Oswald was being arrested in Oak Cliff, police officers had descended en masse upon the Depository Building at the corner of Elm and Houston Streets, searching for the assassin and clues. After pushing through a stack of boxes at the southeast corner window on the sixth floor, three spent rifle hulls were found by a sheriff's deputy. Minutes later, following an intense search between stacks of boxes, a rifle was located. The rifle was carefully photographed and then lifted from its temporary hiding place. It was then taken to the Dallas Police Crime Lab Office for processing. The entire sixth floor was then photographed by Crime Scene Detectives during the afternoon and evening.

Dallas Homicide Detective Gus Rose along with two other Detectives made a second trip during the afternoon to Irving, this time to locate Wesley Frazier. Frazier had given Oswald a ride into work that morning. A polygraph test was administered to Frazier during the late evening. Rose stated that Frazier told him he was scheduled to pick up Oswald at the Paine residence that morning, but Oswald walked over to his house instead. He said Oswald was carrying a large object covered in brown wrapping paper with him to work that morning.

As AIR FORCE ONE WAS IN FLIGHT BACK TO WASHINGTON, arrangements were discussed with Jackie as to where the President's body would be taken. She agreed that Bethesda Naval Hospital

22. Dallas Police Crime Lab photo taken by Pete Barnes in Dealey Plaza on Monday, November 25th.

would be the logical place since her husband had been treated there previously. However, the radio communications between Air Force One and Washington do not reflect the decisiveness of a Bathesda decision. Walter Reed Army Hospital was also mentioned as a possible destination for the body.[22]

When the President's plane arrived back in Washington at Andrews Air Force Base, many dignitaries gathered to meet it. Robert Kennedy dashed up the front loading ramp and made his way to the rear compartment and joined Jackie by the President's coffin. The heavy bronze coffin was off-loaded into a waiting grey Navy ambulance by the Secret Service Agents accompanying the President in Dallas as the Kennedy aides and family watched. A ceremonial honor guard was ignored as the coffin was hastily delivered into the rear of the waiting ambulance.[23]

After the ambulance departed and the noise of a helicopter

23. Dallas Police Crime Lab photo taken by Pete Barnes on Monday, November 25th, showing the center area of Dealey Plaza between Elm and Main Streets. Numerous wreaths were quietly placed there by citizens.

rotor had faded into the background, Lyndon Johnson spoke live to the nation. He delivered a short text prepared on the flight back to Washington, which attempted to reassure the nation that, with their help and God's, the nation would go on. Johnson and Lady Bird then boarded a waiting presidential helicopter and flew to the White House.

The ambulance bearing the President's coffin made the 45 minute drive to Bethesda, where the body of the President underwent an autopsy and preparation for burial. The family waited above in the hospital while the Secret Service continued to protect access to the body of the President in the morgue below.

The autopsy was a fiasco. Many top military personnel were standing around barking orders as the autopsy commenced. The body had been delivered to the Bethesda morgue through a

24. Dallas Police Crime Lab photo taken by Pete Barnes on Monday, November 25th, overlooking Dealey Plaza. The view is basically the same seen by Abraham Zapruder as he made his 8 mm film of the assassination.

rear entrance. The President's body, wrapped in sheets, was lifted by the doctors and other hospital personnel from the heavy bronze casket onto a stainless steel autopsy table perforated with hundreds of holes.[24] The plastic bed liner from Parkland had partially stuck to the body due to a seepage of blood from the wounds. The naval officers quickly cut away the liner and completely unwrapped the sheets in preparation for the autopsy.

The Navy doctors who performed the procedure, inexperienced or not, did an extremely incomplete job of record keeping. The wounds were not sufficiently probed in order to show proper bullet entry and exit orientation. Even today, the x-rays and autopsy photographs remain controversial. It becomes evident that most of the actions of the Secret Service personnel who handled the body in Dallas and later in Washington showed a total lack of

25. Dallas Police Crime Lab photo taken by Pete Barnes on Monday, November 25th, showing Dealey Plaza.

respect for procedure. Much of the confusion which exists today could have been avoided if the autopsy had been done by Dr. Rose back in Dallas as Texas law at the time demanded.

AS THE LONG EVENING WORE ON IN DALLAS, OSWALD WAS interrogated by Homicide Captain Fritz while in the presence of FBI and Secret Service agents. The Dallas police did not typically record interrogation of a suspect, and no recordings were made of the Oswald interviews. Oswald was fingerprinted in Captain Fritz's third-floor office.[25] Oswald's wife, Marina, was brought down to the Homicide Bureau on the third floor of the Police Department. The rifle found in the Depository earlier in the day was brought down from the fourth-floor Crime Lab Office for Marina to identify as belonging to her husband.

The Dallas police brought in witnesses to the Tippit shooting and placed Oswald in several line-ups to be viewed. Due to the overwhelming physical evidence collected by the police during the day, Oswald was arraigned for the murder of Officer Tippit and later for the murder of "One, John F. Kennedy." Much of the evidence against Oswald had already been processed in the short time span of the first day by the Dallas police, but outside government forces were already at work to interrupt their progress.

J. Edgar Hoover's FBI wanted control of the assassination investigation. The ball had been dropped by the FBI in the failure to notify the Dallas police about Oswald. Hoover knew it, and began to exercise damage control. Local Dallas FBI Agent James Hosty had attempted to contact Oswald in the weeks prior to the shooting, but was not successful. Hosty had spoken to Marina Oswald at the residence of the lady who had befriended and taken her in, Ruth Paine. Lee Oswald was told by his wife of Agent Hosty's visit, and went to the local FBI office to register a complaint concerning it. He delivered a note which may have been some sort of threat to the Bureau, and the note was passed on to Agent Hosty.

Following the assassination, Hosty destroyed the note after being told by a superior to do so.[26] Hoover's FBI was beginning to manipulate evidence out of fear of losing face for not making the local authorities aware of Oswald as being a threat to the President. The FBI was aware of Oswald's previous actions in New Orleans with the Fair Play For Cuba Committee, and had attempted to keep an eye on him in Dallas. Police Chief Curry became aware of the FBI's knowledge immediately following the assassination and went public with the news, to the chagrin of J. Edgar Hoover.

At the time, the murder of the President was not a Federal crime, and the local authorities had jurisdiction in the investigation. However, the Dallas police were asked to release the rifle to the FBI on the night of the shooting. It was given by Dallas Police Crime Lab Lieutenant John Carl Day to FBI Agent Vincent Drain at approximately 11:30 p.m., witnessed by Rusty in the Crime Lab Office. The rifle was the only item requested to be released by the FBI at that time. A palm print identified as Oswald's had been located and lifted from the disassembled rifle barrel by Lieutenant Day before the FBI took possession of it. The lift of the palm print was not given to FBI Agent Drain at that time since the rifle had been the only item requested to be released.

THE EVENING OF THE ASSASSINATION DAY SLIPPED INTO THE morning of the next, almost unnoticed by the numb participants. As the nation began to absorb the tragedy of the loss of a president, Dallas police officers were working overtime to collect and process the evidence gathered. The Dallas Police Department was now dealing with two homicides which occurred on November 22nd, 1963 (along with other routine police business). The death of the President as well as the death of one of their own had become intertwined with a common suspect, Lee Oswald.

Back in Washington, following the autopsy and preparation for burial, the body of the late President was placed in another coffin which had been ordered locally. It was transported to the East Room of the White House early Saturday morning. Dignitaries from around the world began to send messages of condolence to Washington, D. C. The burial site, not yet determined, was first speculated by newsmen possibly to be Boston. Arlington Cemetery was later decided upon by the President's family as the final resting place. The funeral was scheduled for Monday, November 25th. This day was declared by President Johnson as a national day of mourning. It was decided that the coffin lid would remain closed during the public viewing.[27]

Throughout Saturday, Oswald was interrogated by Dallas Police Homicide Captain Will Fritz in the presence of various representatives of the Secret Service and FBI. Residents of Dallas began to cover Dealey Plaza with flowers in memory of the slain President. Television news coverage was continuous, and by Saturday evening, a complete profile of Oswald was broadcast nationwide.

The rifle found on the sixth floor of the Depository was eventually traced by the FBI to a Chicago mail order house.[28] The name on the order blank was A. Hidell, one of the names which appeared in the identification found in Oswald's wallet at the time of his arrest. Oswald was shown a photograph found in his belongings with him holding the rifle in a backyard pose. He denied that the photograph was legitimate, claiming that it had been doctored to show his face on someone else's body. Oswald repeatedly denied shooting anyone on the previous day and requested that a New York lawyer named John Abt be called to help in his defense. After being interrogated at various times throughout the day, Oswald was once again retired to his cell on the fifth floor of the Dallas Police Department for the night.

Sunday morning began early for workers at Arlington Cemetery in Washington. The burial site was still being prepared and was made complete with a gas-powered eternal flame. The President's body remained in the East Room of the White House in a flag-draped coffin, and was scheduled to be taken to the Capital Rotunda at around noon.

In Dallas, Oswald was awakened and escorted back to the office of Captain Fritz for a final interrogation before a scheduled transferral to the Dallas County Jail, a routine procedure for the Department. However, since this was not a routine prisoner, elaborate security precautions were taken. It was decided at the last moment to transport Oswald in an unmarked car. An armored truck was backed into position to act as a decoy.

After the brief interrogation of the prisoner had been completed without any confession of guilt admitted, Oswald was taken to the jail elevator and brought down to the basement parking garage in the Dallas Police Building. As the elevator door opened, television cameras broadcast the scene live to the nation. Oswald was flanked on both sides by Dallas Police Detectives. An all clear was given,[29] and the men made their way to a waiting car which, unfortunately, had not been backed up to its proper position.

Oswald was escorted through a line of police officials and passed a crowd of reporters on his left. The newsmen had surged forward over a railing, against the security wishes of the police, in anticipation of photographing and questioning Oswald as he passed. Unnoticed by the police, an unidentified man had gained entry into the supposedly secure parking basement. As Oswald began to make his way past the reporters, he made eye contact with the man and then looked away. Oswald was asked if he had anything to say in his defense. Immediately the man in the crowd rushed to face the suspect and quickly fired one shot into Oswald's abdomen. Oswald moaned and fell immediately to the floor. The detectives pounced on the man, preventing any more shots from being fired. As the man was brought under control and stood up, he was recognized by some of the officers. His name was Jack Ruby, a local night club operator. A live execution had just been broadcast on national television, and it seemed that pandemonium had broken loose in the nation.

Oswald was given improper first aid at the scene,[30] and eventually loaded into an ambulance. He was driven to Parkland Hospital, where at that very moment Nellie Connally, the wife of the wounded Governor, was making her first public statement.

The body of the President in Washington was being loaded and transported to the Capitol at the same hour. Just after the body of the President was placed into the Rotunda, the death of Oswald occurred at Parkland Hospital. Many citizens stated at that moment that Ruby should be given a medal for murdering the accused assassin.

As Ruby sat in his jail cell not knowing if his single bullet had accomplished his goal of murder, he perspired heavily and asked for a cigarette. His heart was palpitating heavily as he sat on the jail cell bunk after being strip-searched by the police. A Dallas officer then entered the cell and informed Ruby that it looked as though he would get the electric chair because Oswald had just died. According to the officer, Ruby relaxed. He was then asked if he wanted another cigarette and surprised the officer with his response. Ruby told him that he didn't smoke. It seemed obvious to the officer that Ruby was relieved Oswald had died.[31]

Crowds continued to file past the flag-draped coffin as

representatives of each branch of the armed forces stood at staunch attention as honor guards. President Johnson held meetings with Kennedy's Cabinet members and urged them to stay on. Viet Nam was discussed, and the continuation of American presence there was considered.

Meanwhile, a news conference was held by Henry Wade, the District Attorney of Dallas, making public the evidence gathered by police against Oswald. He announced that the investigation would not be closed with the death of Oswald. As the long, solemn weekend drew to an end, a line formed five abreast and three miles long to continuously view the President's coffin throughout Sunday night, and police began to discourage people from joining it.

AS MONDAY MORNING BEGAN, PREPARATIONS FOR THE PRESIDENT'S funeral had been largely completed. Jackie, retaining a gallant composure, returned from the White House to the Capitol Rotunda around 10:30 a.m. to accompany the President's body back to the White House. The coffin was carried down the Capital steps by an honor guard and placed on a horse-drawn caisson. The family returned with the body to the White House and emerged to begin a final walk to St. Matthew's Cathedral with foreign leaders following the caisson. The body was taken inside and placed in the center aisle of the church, and a funeral mass was held. As the service ended, the people emerged to continue their slow march to Arlington Cemetery.

The eternal flame was in place by the graveside and ready to be lit by the President's family. As the procession arrived, the huge crowd remained hauntingly silent. Jet planes whisked through the still air above, and the flag was removed from the coffin. A 21-gun salute broke the silence as the benediction was offered. The flag was presented to Jackie. The gas flame sputtered to life as Jackie placed the torch to the ground. She handed it to the President's brothers who in turn did the same.

As the throngs departed the graveside in Washington, two other funerals occurred almost simultaneously back in Texas.

Officer J. D. Tippit was buried with full police honors. The man accused but never tried of the murder of both the President and Tippit, Lee Oswald, was also buried.

1. William R. Manchester, *The Death of a President* (N.Y.: Harper & Row, 1967), 122.
2. Jesse Curry, *JFK Assassination File,* Limited Collectors Edition (Dallas, TX: American Poster & Publishing Co., 1969), 16.
3. Ibid., 9.
4. Robert J. Groden and Harrison Edward Livingstone, *High Treason* (N.Y.: Berkley Books, 1989), 340.
5. Warren Commission, *Report of President's Commission on the Assassination of President John F. Kennedy* (Washington, D.C.: U. S. Government Printing Office, 1964), 18.
6. Warren Commission, *Hearings Before the President's Commission on the Assassination of President Kennedy,* 26 vols.(Washington, D.C.: U. S. Government Printing Office, 1964), VI: 236. Also House Select Committee on Assassinations (HSCA), *Investigation of the Assassination of President John F. Kennedy,* 12 vols. (Washington, D.C.: U. S. Government Printing Office, 1979), XII: 20.
7. HSCA, XII: 23.
8. Jim Marrs, *Crossfire* (N.Y.: Carroll & Graf Publishers, Inc., 1989), 60-64.
9. Warren Commission, *Hearings,* IV: 132-133.
10. Warren Commission, *Report, 111.*
11. Warren Commission, *Hearings,* VI: 294.
12. Conclusions drawn by study of Dallas Police Crime Lab sixth-floor photos and map drawn by Crime Lab Detective R. L. Studebaker on November 22nd, 1963.
13. Warren Commission, *Hearings,* III: 250.
14. Manchester, 267.
15. David S. Lifton, *Best Evidence* (N.Y.: Carroll & Graf Publishers, Inc., 1988), 674.
16. Manchester, 271.
17. Ibid., 326.
18. Warren Commission, *Report,* 7-8.
19. Jim Ewell, taped personal interview, 8 January 1992.
20. Warren Commission, *Hearings,* VII: 228.
21. Former Dallas Homicide Detective Gus Rose, taped personal interview, 16 February 1993.
22. Lifton, 681.
23. Ibid., 682-683.
24. Manchester, 400.
25. Warren Commission, *Hearings,* VII: 285.
26. Marrs, 233.
27. Manchester, 452.
28. Ibid., 94.
29. Warren Commission, *Hearings,* XV: 151.
30. Jim Moore, *Conspiracy Of One* (Fort Worth, TX: The Summit Group, 1990), 178-179.
31. Interview of Dallas Policeman Don Archer in *The Men Who Killed Kennedy,* videotape, prod. Central Independent Television, P. L. C., 1988.

CHAPTER

II

The Crime Lab

THE CRIME LAB

IN 1963, THE DALLAS POLICE DEPARTMENT'S CRIME SCENE SEARCH Section of the Identification Bureau was located on the fourth floor of the newly remodeled building which had formerly been Dallas City Hall. A new city hall had been built adjacent to the old one, and the Police Department had inherited the entire old city hall for their offices.

At the time of President Kennedy's assassination, Rusty was working nights and was at home asleep. He first heard of the assassination when his wife, Daisie, had awakened him with the news she'd just heard on television. He told me, "I called in and talked to Captain Doughty to see if they needed me to come in and help out. He told me not to come in until my regular time, which was eleven in the evening."

When Rusty arrived that evening, he rode the elevator up from the basement as usual to the fourth floor of the Department to the Identification Bureau. Upon exiting the elevator, he turned right and made his usual walk through a large inner room which housed the Police Department files and file clerk areas. After passing a long counter on his right where history would be made within a few hours, he turned left, entering the Crime Lab Office, which was located off the large open area of identification files.

Rusty told me about that first night of the assassination: "When I came in, I talked to some boys that were on duty there. I don't recall exactly who it was or how many were there. But they told me that Oswald was back in the Mug Room where they did the fingerprinting and the photographing of people under arrest." The

26. Photograph showing Rusty alongside the fourth-floor Identification Bureau files. This open area was used to store numerous arrest records. The door on the left wall led into the Crime Lab Office.

Mug Room faced the same large inner room that Rusty's Lab Office did and was located only a few doors down. This took place around midnight after Oswald had been brought into the Identification Bureau following a five minute press conference which had just been carried live on television.

H. R. Williams was one of the Crime Lab Detectives working the 3 p.m. to 11 p.m. shift. He told Rusty and me, "I worked off and on in that darkroom printing pictures of the Kennedy assassination for weeks. It seemed like everybody wanted pictures, the Secret Service and the FBI." He told Rusty and me that the Dallas police did "a damn good job, and the FBI came in and screwed everything up." H. R. was not interviewed by the Warren Commission, or anyone else through the years.

H. R. was the man who took the mug shot of Oswald. He told us, "I saw him [Oswald] down in Homicide and, you know the

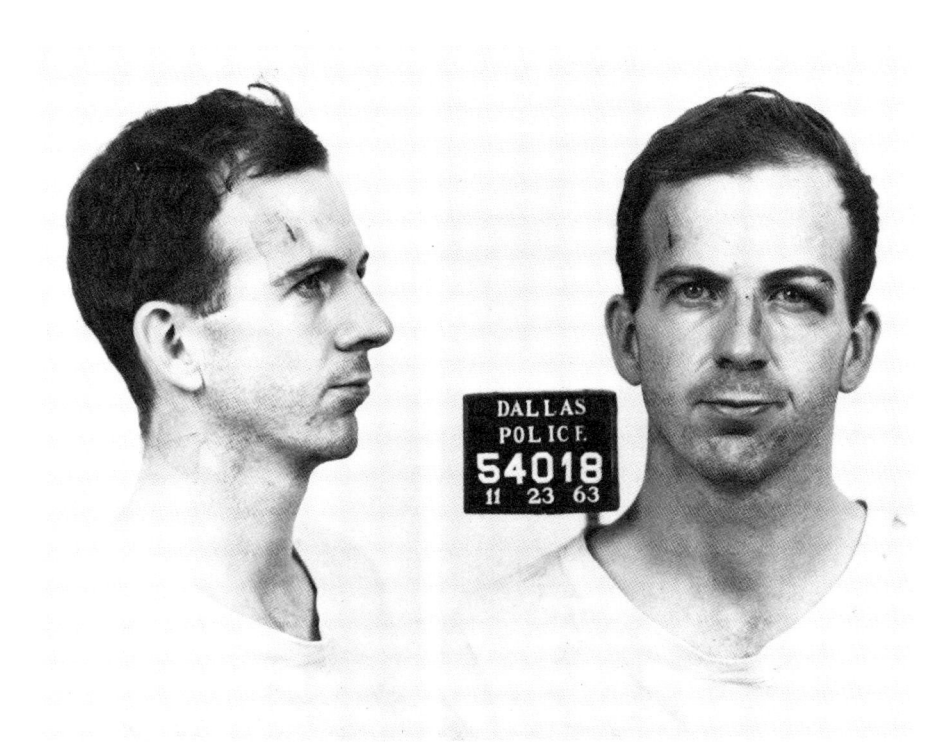

27. Dallas Police Crime Lab photo taken by H. R. Williams. This was a typical mug shot taken by the Identification Bureau of Oswald in the Mug Room. Oswald was fingerprinted after the photograph was made.

mug shot? In fact, I snapped the picture. K. P. [Knight] was standing right there. They knew they would just get one chance at it, and they were afraid of errors, and so I focused it and took a picture." He stated later that Lieutenant Day was also present when the mug shot was taken of Oswald, using the large mug camera. The full body shots were taken at a different time using a 4"x5" Graflex hand-held camera, according to H. R. He said that Oswald was taken into the mug room twice.

    H. R. told us that Oswald was talking a lot when the mug shots were being taken. From the things he was saying, H. R. felt as though Oswald was "a smart alec and real arrogant." He said that Oswald didn't talk about the assassination. H. R. also witnessed Oswald being fingerprinted in the Mug Room at the same time period. Lieutenant Day told Rusty and me that there were multiple

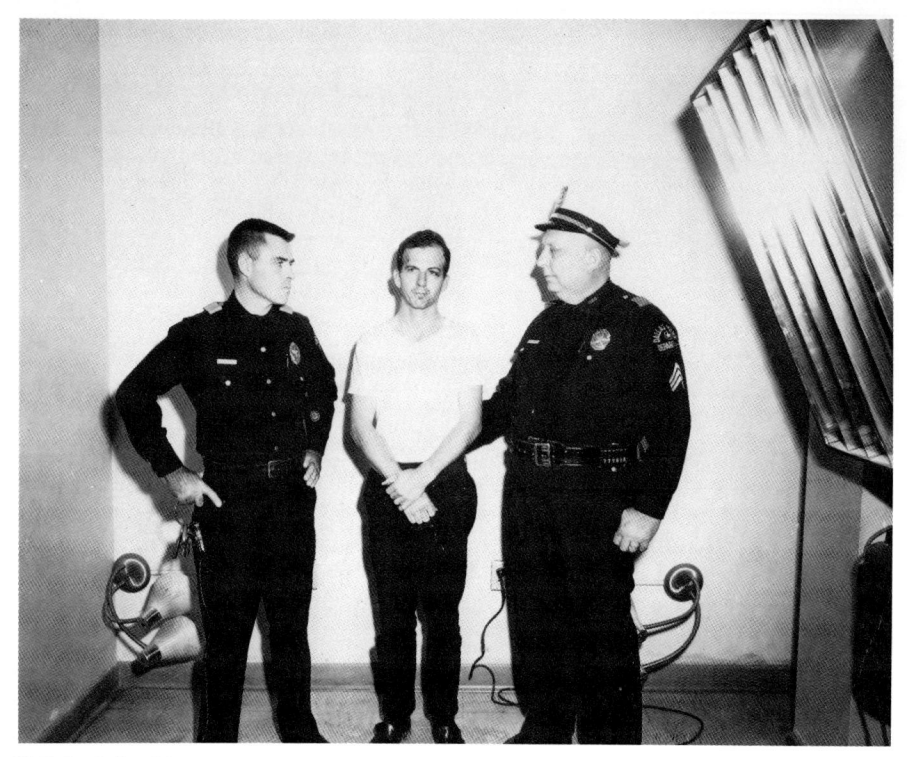

28. Dallas Police Crime Lab photo taken by the Identification Bureau. The photo shows Oswald in the center with Patrolman Todd on the left and Jail Sergeant Warren on the right.

requests for fingerprint cards of Oswald, and several were made in the Identification Bureau Mug Room.

H. R. said that he was eating lunch at home when he heard the news of the assassination on television. He called into the office and was told to come in at his regular time at 3 p.m., but came right on in anyway. When he arrived at the Crime Lab Office, everybody was still down at the Depository Building, so he went on down there. Lieutenant Day, R. L. Studebaker, and J. B. Hicks were still on the scene when he arrived, and were still working on gathering evidence. After seeing that he wasn't needed at the time, he headed back to the Crime Lab Office.

Rusty told me that he witnessed the men taking the stand up photographs of Oswald. He told me, "I walked back to the door and looked in, and they were just taking Oswald's photograph with the officers standing beside him. One was Sergeant 'Slick' Warren, we called him. The other boy was named Todd. He was a patrolman assigned to the Jail Office."

"When they got through taking his picture and fingerprinting him, Oswald was evidently taken up to the fifth-floor jail. Later on, they brought him from the jail to the long counter in the large open file room." This is the counter located just outside Rusty's office. "There was a Justice of the Peace in there and also I think some Secret Service and FBI men. The Justice of the Peace was named Johnston. He was standing behind the long counter, and I went and stood slightly behind and beside him. Some of the Secret Service and FBI men were back in there with us. Johnston arraigned Oswald for the murder of one, John F. Kennedy, right there in the Identification Bureau that night. After the arraignment, the jail officers took him down through the door that leads into the fourth-floor Jail Office."

This sequence of events helps those studying the assassination to understand the arraignment of Oswald for the Kennedy murder more fully. It was known that Oswald had been left in the custody of the fourth-floor Jail Office after being photographed in the Identification Bureau, but there was no record of his having been checked out by anyone at the time he was to have been arraigned. According to Rusty, however, Oswald was accompanied by the jail sergeant and patrolman who, in fact, were the same two that had taken him down to the midnight press conference and was photographed, fingerprinted, and later arraigned by Justice of the Peace David Johnston outside the Crime Lab Office in the Identification Bureau.[1] He was then led by the two officers into the fourth-floor Jail Office and back up to his fifth-floor cell for the night. Rusty told me that since the jail officers were accompanying Oswald themselves, it would not have been unusual for him not to have been "checked out" of his cell.

The arraignment of Oswald was witnessed by several Dallas officers, including Captain Fritz and Lieutenant Day. Day stated

29. Photograph taken on the fourth floor of the Dallas Police Department. In the right rear appears the long counter where Oswald was charged with the murder of "One, John F. Kennedy." Justice of the Peace Johnston stood on the side of the cabinet shown in the photo surrounded by Dallas officers including Rusty, the FBI, and the Secret Service. Oswald stood on the opposite side of the counter (out of view of the photo) flanked by Dallas officers.

that the arraignment of Oswald occurred soon after he had released the rifle to FBI Agent Drain. He told me that he went home shortly after this happened. Captain Fritz also stated to the Warren Commission that Oswald probably was not checked out of jail at the time since he was accompanied by two jail officers.

The fourth-floor Jail Office was located behind the Crime Lab Office where Rusty worked. On opposite sides of the Jail Office were a men's and women's jail which held minor offenders. There were stairs leading from the fourth-floor Jail Office to the fifth-floor jail which was used mostly for major offenders. The jail also had its own elevator for transporting those arrested between all of the Department's floors.

There were actually two Jail Offices, one in the basement by the parking area and one on the fourth floor between the men's and the women's jail. Rusty told me that "when we brought in an arrested person, we'd first take them to the basement Jail Office. Usually there was a jail lieutenant or sergeant at the desk who would tell us whether or not to take the person on up to the fourth-floor Jail Office. This depended on whether or not they wanted to go ahead and charge the arrested person and put him in jail. We'd then go to the jail elevator located behind the counter and take them up to the fourth-floor Jail Office."

Rusty's presence in the Identification Bureau at the time of the arraignment of Oswald was verified, though not specifically, by the testimony of David Johnston, the Justice of the Peace. Johnston told the Warren Commission interrogator, Mr. Hubert, while being questioned about Oswald's arraignment for Kennedy's murder, that "there was some seven or eight officer witnesses to that arraignment."

Rusty continued, "I remember Oswald was doing a lot of talking that night about how he was being mistreated. He claimed his rights were being violated and that he had not been allowed to speak to an attorney. Whether they actually had at that time or not, I don't know. This was on the night of the 22nd."

"After that was over with, I went into the Lab Office and talked to the officer who was on duty during the three to eleven shift. He was showing me some of the pictures that they had taken and printed and also pictures of everything that was taken from Oswald's house, or rooming house. He had all kinds of things that they had taken from there and photographed. They photographed the rifle there too. It was on the counter in the Crime Lab Office where I worked when they photographed it. This had happened sometime during the day. I am sure that Lieutenant Day, who was in charge of the Crime Lab, dusted the rifle that was found on the sixth floor of the School Book Depository, and lifted a partial palm print off the underside of the barrel after the rifle was taken apart.[2] They had the actual print there in the office that night. I compared it myself with Oswald's palm print, and it looked to me like there was enough there to say yes, it was Oswald's palm print. I think all the other people on the day shift had already looked at the palm print before I arrived that night, but I went ahead and looked at the palm print myself and was satisfied that it was Oswald's."

Rusty went on to tell me that many times, when a print had

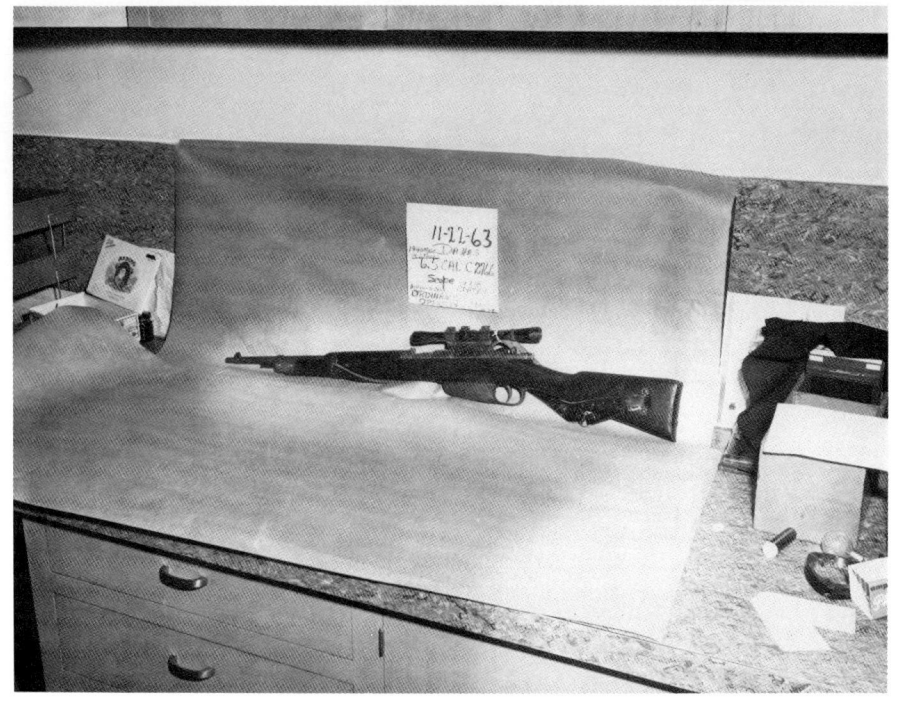

30. Dallas Police Crime Lab photo taken by Lt. Day in his Crime Lab Office showing the 6.5 mm Mannlicher Carcano found about an hour following the assassination on the sixth floor of the Texas School Book Depository Building.

been lifted at a crime scene and been brought back to the lab for analysis, it would be looked at by the other detectives. "That happened all the time," he told me. "After we had made a comparison and felt as though we had a match, if someone else was in the office, they'd usually take a look too and help to verify the match."

The controversy surrounding the palm print that Lieutenant Day had lifted from the rifle before releasing it to the FBI Friday night is an issue that some feel has never been thoroughly resolved. But here is an eyewitness on the night in question that actually saw the palm print before the FBI took possession of the rifle!

Over the years, charges have been leveled towards the Dallas police, particularly Lieutenant Day, concerning the palm print of Oswald found by him on the day of the assassination. During the

31. Photograph taken in the fourth-floor Crime Lab Office showing Rusty seated in front of the same counter shown in Photo 30 where the Oswald rifle was dusted and photographed by Lt. Day.

afternoon that Lieutenant Day possessed the rifle, a palm print was discovered when he had disassembled the rifle. Day compared it, after obtaining a card with Oswald's palm print, and the two matched. Lieutenant Day had "lifted" the print, leaving the FBI, who later in the evening took possession of the rifle, no obvious evidence of any pre-existing palm print.

Today some assassination researchers do not believe that Lieutenant Day actually did lift the palm print of Oswald from the rifle. He did, however, and most, if not all, other Crime Lab Officers saw and compared the palm print themselves, including Rusty, Pete Barnes, H. R. Williams, and Bobby Brown. Ample opportunity to compare the palm print lifted from the rifle existed since it remained in the Crime Lab Office for several days, and each officer recalled the lift and had no doubt that it was Oswald's.

Bobby Brown told Rusty and me that he remembered looking

at the palm print lifted by Lieutenant Day. He stated that there was no doubt that it was Oswald's palm print and said he looked at the palm print the day after the shooting. His scheduled hours for work on Saturday were from 7 a.m. to 3 p.m. Brown said that he didn't come in on the day of the assassination.

An explanation was given by Lieutenant Day concerning his not turning over the palm print to FBI Agent Vince Drain on the night of the assassination in Warren Commission Exhibit 3145.[3] Drain stated that Lieutenant Day told him that "he took the wooden part of the rifle off by loosening three or four screws and uncovered what he considered to be an old dry print with a loop formation underneath the barrel. He stated this appeared to him to be the right palm print of some individual. This print was found on the underside of the barrel which was completely covered by the wooden stock of the gun and not visible until he had removed the wooden portion of the gun. Lieutenant Day estimated this print was within three inches of the front end of the wooden stock. Lieutenant Day advised he dusted this print with black powder and made one lift."

Drain continued, "Lieutenant Day stated at this point he received instructions from Chief of Police Jesse E. Curry not to do anything else concerning the examination of evidence as it was to be immediately turned over to SA Vincent E. Drain of the Federal Bureau of Investigation for transmittal to the FBI Laboratory. Lieutenant Day stated he normally would have photographed this print, but since his instructions from the Chief of Police were not to do anything further, he literally took him at his word." As Rusty told me, "Lieutenant Day did everything by the book and followed orders to the letter."

One interesting event also occurred earlier in the afternoon, according to Detective Barnes. Lieutenant Day had brought the rifle back to the Crime Lab Office and then left to go back to the Depository. As Pete was continuing his work developing the photographs, a Secret Service Agent came into the office. Pete told us that he "wanted me to turn the gun over to him to make sure that we didn't mess up the prints on it. I told him, 'Partner, I'll bet I've dusted more fingerprint powder than you've ever seen in your lifetime.' He thought he was smart, but I told him I wasn't worried about it getting messed up because we had some good technicians in here."[4]

The palm print lifted by Lieutenant Day was not turned over with the other items taken by the FBI on the night of the assassination. He felt that enough of the palm print remained so that the FBI could also do a lift of their own. But the FBI was not able to lift the palm print after receiving the rifle. They later determined, however, that the palm print they received from Lieutenant Day was lifted from exactly where he stated that it was by comparing the irregularities found on the rifle barrel to the lifted palm print. Lee Harvey Oswald's palm print was found on the disassembled rifle discovered on the sixth floor of the Depository.

IN SUMMATION, THE PALM PRINT SPOKEN OF HERE WAS SEEN BY Rusty and others before the FBI took possession of the rifle. Vince Drain came into Rusty's office around midnight and took the rifle as evidence as Rusty looked on. The palm print developed and observed by the men in the Crime Lab Office that day was not released to the FBI at that time, but four days later. That delay instigated the controversy.

Critics have speculated over the years about the fact that the incriminating palm print was not released to the FBI on the night of the assassination and have emphatically, but incorrectly, claimed that it never existed. Many have actually charged that Lieutenant Day never found or lifted a palm print, yet as explained here, they did so without full knowledge of all the facts. They have continued even today to speculate that someone, possibly the FBI, sinisterly placed the palm print on the rifle and somehow later, in unison with Lieutenant Day, produced it as hard evidence. Further, an explanation was offered speculating that the FBI had visited the funeral home where Oswald lay in his open coffin and placed Oswald's dead hand directly on the disassembled rifle barrel on

Monday, November 24th.

As was previously explained, Rusty as well as at least four other officers saw and compared for themselves the palm print in question on the day of and immediately following the assassination. According to Miller Funeral Home Director Paul Groody, some men from an unspecified agency (he did not know which agency) came and fingerprinted Oswald after the body had been prepared and placed in the coffin. Groody stated that he had a difficult time removing the fingerprint ink from Oswald's hands when they left.

Rusty told me that he does not know for sure why any government agency, either the FBI or Secret Service, would need to fingerprint Oswald at that point in time. However, Rusty and J. B. Hicks had gone to the Parkland Hospital morgue and fingerprinted Oswald to verify that it was indeed the same individual in order to clear the Dallas police records. Possibly the FBI or Secret Service may have done the same thing, not reaching Oswald before his body had been prepared for burial. There is also the possibility that another set of prints were needed by some government agency for future comparison purposes.

A TYPICAL RESPONSE FOR THE CRIME LAB ON A MURDER CASE would involve dusting the area for fingerprints with fingerprint powder and a camel hair brush. The prints would be lifted, the scene would be photographed, and all other evidence would then be gathered. Rusty elaborated, "On a murder scene we'd usually make a scaled drawing of the scene. No matter what shift it was on, it had to be ready the next morning when the Chief arrived. We'd have to send it to him. That took up a lot of time."

Rusty made this point to me during one of our interviews, and at the time it didn't seem very important to me. However, later I would discover the relevance: making a scaled drawing of a murder crime scene and having it completed for the Chief to see the next morning helps support the validity of the date shown on the map which Detective R. L. Studebaker prepared of the sixth floor of the Depository. The map itself will be explored fully later.

32. Photograph taken in the fourth-floor Crime Lab Office showing Rusty seated in front of the door leading into the small corner evidence room.

Rusty continued telling me about the typical procedure the Crime Lab used in investigations. "We gathered the evidence and preserved it and put it in our evidence room and made our reports. If it came up for trial, we'd have to testify as to what we'd found. Our Crime Lab Office was about fourteen feet wide and about twenty feet deep. Over in one corner of the office was the evidence room. It was about six by seven feet with a solid locked door on it. The Lieutenant kept a key to it with him, and another was left in the office desk. Anybody who was working in the Lab Office could use the key. The only ones that had access to the evidence room would be the detectives working directly in the office. A lot of times on late nights when we left, there wouldn't be but one man on duty. When we left the office, we'd lock the key up in the desk drawer and lock the door to the Lab Office and also the outside door going into the Identification Bureau from the elevator."

He continued telling me about the inner-workings of the Crime Lab Office. "At the time that I went to work in the Crime Scene Search Bureau, we had Lieutenant Day, usually two or three men on the day shift, two or three men on the evening shift, and myself working the night shift. Later Lieutenant Day put in a shift from six in the evening until two in the morning with another man. So that man would overlap me with the night shift. So we had about eight or nine men assigned to the Crime Lab. Later on they hired a female to do the typing of our reports, and even later hired another girl to be a file clerk to keep their files up. Then they eventually added a civilian to do the darkroom work."

"We were usually pretty busy; I think busier on the day shift and the evening shift than on the late night shift. On the late night shift, we'd usually get more serious calls like murders and rapes, that type of thing. On the day shift you usually got business burglaries when people opened up and discovered that they had been broken into. On the evening shift, you'd usually get a lot of residential burglary calls from people who'd been at work all day."

"In working the Crime Lab, we were on call all the time and were pretty well restricted and stayed in the office. We'd spend our time there doing fingerprint comparison work, darkroom work and processing other types of evidence in between calls."

"When I was working late nights, sometimes I'd spend three or four days a week in court. I'd work all night and then have to go to court. A lot of times we were there all day long, particularly in murder cases and rape cases. In the witness room during the trial, you could pretty well judge when you were going on the stand and when you weren't, and we'd get a little nap sitting in the chair with our feet propped up. We'd usually be out of court by five o'clock, sometimes earlier. I'd get about four good hours of sleep before I'd have to go back in."

"On late nights, the door to the Identification Bureau was kept locked. Sometimes the jailors that had a key to the door going into the jail would come in there and shoot the breeze."

RECENTLY, RUSTY AND I DROVE INTO DALLAS AND WENT BY TO SEE the old Police Department offices. After entering through the front doors, we made our way to the basement area parking garage where Oswald was shot by Jack Ruby. After milling around the area, which I already felt strangely familiar with through my study of Rusty's photos, we made our way to an adjacent office where we spoke to the night sergeant who was with a patrolman. (Later Rusty told me that in 1963, this was the old property room where Oswald's belongings had been laid out and photographed.) Rusty told them who he was and asked if it would be alright if we went up to the fourth floor to have a look around at his old office. The sergeant said "OK," and sent the patrolman with us up to the place I'd already visited in my mind for months.

We rode the main elevator up to the fourth floor, which at the time was not occupied. The patrolman who accompanied us told us that he had never been up to the fourth or fifth floor either, and was curious to see the place for himself. As the elevator door opened, we stood facing a wall about five feet in front of us. Turning right, we immediately came upon a locked door with a glass insert.

"That's the big room where the files and clerk's desks were in the Identification Bureau," Rusty told me. Since that time though, partitions had been added, making the once open room into a series of smaller offices. Peering through the locked door, I could see the door that Rusty pointed out to me that once led into his Lab Office. Seeing the offices gave me a good perspective of a forgotten setting of events that had occurred more than twenty-eight years before.

The fourth floor was being remodeled for a new office area. The construction allowed us access between the old areas of the fourth-floor Identification Bureau and fourth and fifth-floor jails.

Rusty and I climbed the old marble steps to the fifth-floor jail area where Oswald was held. It was eerie peering down the shoulder-width aisles between the cramped cells. It made me recall the story Bobby Brown had told us concerning his trip up to the fifth-floor cell.

An FBI agent had approached Detective Brown in the Crime Lab Office and asked him to go get a hair sample from Oswald. Brown found a pair of scissors and climbed the stairs to the fifth-floor cell area. He said that after he told Oswald what he was there for, Oswald reached up and yanked out some hairs and gave them to him! The scissors weren't needed. Brown said that Oswald was just a real "asshole."[5]

Even before the current remodeling work, the fourth floor had already undergone some alterations since Rusty had worked there. The once large open file area had been divided into smaller offices. The walls around Rusty's office had been moved, although we did determine--using the still existing jail area--about where the old Crime Lab Office door once was.

After pointing out where the counter was and where he was standing when Oswald was charged with the murder of Kennedy, Rusty commented that "The place really is run down. It's a shame that they let it get like this."

The remodeling being done was a welcome sight to Rusty since the place looked like it had been deserted for years. The Crime Lab Offices were later relocated to the basement of the Police Department. Today the Crime Lab is located in a separate building across town from the original downtown location.

THE FIRST DAY EVIDENCE WHICH MY UNCLE POSSESSES OF THE Kennedy investigation gives a more complete picture of all of the previously known evidence collected by the Dallas Police Department. The purpose of this book is to present all of the evidence that Rusty possesses. I will explain what the evidence is and why it is important, and give the unique perspective of a man who witnessed Oswald in police custody and helped to process some of the evidence against him.

Rusty has just recently told me, "If the Dallas police had been left alone to investigate the assassination without the intervention of the Secret Service and the FBI, we could have possibly developed more crime scene evidence. But with the FBI taking over the investigation on the first day, which by the way was not in their jurisdiction, and the Secret Service taking away the presidential limousine, we didn't devote any more time to it [in the Crime Lab]. I remember the feeling around the Department at that time was that if that's the way the FBI wanted it to be, then let them have it."

"We always stayed busy in our office. It's not like many people think, that since it was the President of the United States, we would devote all of our time to investigating it. Since the Secret Service and the FBI took over the investigation, we basically dropped it and went on with our other cases the next day." However, the Homicide detectives continued to pursue the investigation for two to three months following the assassination, according to Gus Rose.[6]

THE ABUNDANCE OF EVIDENCE COLLECTED ON THE FIRST DAY OF the investigation and the processing of it will now be looked at closely. I will give an explanation as to what each piece of evidence is and how the Crime Lab handled its brief possession of this evidence. I will not speak of conspiracy, only of the first day evidence itself. Any conclusions that I draw from the evidence I hope will be obvious to the readers themselves after viewing the photographs. My main goal is to present some previously unseen and some previously seen, but clearer, photographs and documents in an uncensored or uncropped format. My hope is that future researchers will take this material and use it to get closer to the truth, keeping in mind that we, not a non-elected bureaucratic agency, are the government.

1. Warren Commission, *Hearings Before the President's Commission on the Assassination of President Kennedy,* 26 vols. (Washington, D.C.: U.S. Government Printing Office, 1964), XV: 508.
2. Warren Commission, *Hearings,* IV: 260.
3. Ibid., 261.
4. Former Crime Lab Detective W. E. Barnes, taped personal interview, 4 April 1992.
5. Former Crime Lab Detective Bobby Brown, taped personal interview, 25 April 1992.
6. Former Homicide Detective Gus Rose, taped personal interview, 16 February 1993.

CHAPTER

III

The Old Briefcase

THE WEEK FOLLOWING OUR TRIP TO DALLAS, I GAVE RUSTY A CALL to see when we might get together to start getting his story on tape. He said Saturday would be fine, and so the next weekend I headed into the northern Louisiana hills where my uncle now lives. Upon arrival, I proceeded with what eventually became a weekend ritual. I pulled out my videotape gear and climbed the steps to the front door of Rusty and Daisie's home.

Once the equipment was in place, Rusty set off to his bedroom to retrieve his old leather briefcase that contained crime scene photographs from his days with the Dallas police. He brought them into the dining room and pulled out about six manila envelopes from the briefcase which were crammed full of items representing a past lifetime of police work. The memories flooded back for me when I saw the photographs, some that could make even a hard-crusted person gag.

Of course my interest lay in the assassination photos, which he then produced. He first pulled out a map and said, "Here's the map that Studebaker made on the 22nd of the sixth floor of the Depository." I didn't know at that moment how important that map would later be to me in my research. He continued to pull out all of his photographs of the sixth-floor crime scene. Some contained a handwritten number on the back of them, while others did not. There were also some outside views of the Depository taken on the afternoon of and the day following the assassination as well as various views of the second-floor lunchroom area where Oswald claimed he was during the time of the shooting.

THE LIVE MURDER OF OSWALD ON NATIONAL TELEVISION TOOK place in the basement of the Dallas Police Department on the Sunday following Kennedy's Friday assassination. Rusty had numerous photographs of the area that Ruby had entered, which was used as a parking garage for Police Department personnel.

I was shown photographs of Oswald's effects found on his person when he was arrested in the Texas Theater as well as photographs of the inside of the theater. Rusty also had some photographs of the J. D. Tippit crime scene, showing the murdered Policeman's squad car.

Lying between some of the now 28 year-old black and white Police Department photographs was an old carbon copy of a document. It consisted of two pages with the original signature of J. C. Day, the Crime Scene Search Section's Lieutenant and Rusty's immediate supervisor at the time. It was an inter-office memorandum written to Chief Curry, explaining Day's work on the assassination and laying out the steps taken on November 22nd, 1963, point by point.

The next few items shown to me were five photographs of some latent prints developed on the trigger housing of the Mannlicher Carcano rifle that Lieutenant Day had taken the afternoon of the assassination in the Crime Lab Office. The photographs showed different lighting contrasts Lieutenant Day had done to highlight the faint fingerprint detail on the rifle. The fingerprints are visible to the naked eye in the photographs and are very noticeable on enlargements done by fingerprint comparison equipment.

Rusty then pulled out photographs of the rifle, taken in his office by Lieutenant Day the day of the assassination before it was released to the FBI that night. A faded copy of an old magazine ad fell from among the documents. It was a duplicate of the one from which Oswald ordered his rifle and revolver under the alias A.

Hidell. Rusty had also copied the facing page opposite the ad in the magazine.

Suddenly a small card appeared which measured about three by six inches. I asked Rusty what it was, and he told me, "Oh that's a fingerprint card that we rolled off Oswald."

"What?" I stood up in my surprise and bent over to take a closer look. Earlier Rusty had told me that he hadn't been in on the actual interrogation of Oswald. Therefore, I had wrongly assumed that he was not in on any part of the investigation.

"Yeah," Rusty responded in his characteristically modest tone. "J. B. Hicks and I rolled them off Oswald down in the Parkland morgue after they had done his autopsy."

"But why did you go down there?" I couldn't recall at this point having read anything about this before.

"Aw, it was just a routine thing. Normally when a person is killed in an accident or a homicide or sometimes even a natural death, if they had a record in our Identification Bureau, we'd go out and fingerprint them to verify that yes, that was the person in order to clear our files. J. B. Hicks and I went down to the morgue at Parkland Hospital and fingerprinted him."

So here I was in 1991, looking at an actual fingerprint card rolled off of one of the most famous suspected assassins of recent American history, and my uncle had rolled it himself! This, I thought to myself, had to be important. I figured a document of this importance would long ago have found its way into a museum. Finding a treasure like this in the hands of an old retired detective seemed to me like something you read about in a cheap crime novel.

At the same time that the fingerprints were taken by Rusty and J. B. Hicks, an autopsy photograph was taken which Rusty now showed to me. The photograph has appeared before in a book written by former Dallas Police Chief Jesse Curry called the *JFK Assassination File*.

Next Rusty showed me the now infamous pictures which came to be known as the "backyard photographs" of Oswald with a revolver strapped to his waist holding the Mannlicher Carcano rifle and some Communist newspapers in his hand. At that first viewing, I did not realize that one of the photographs was actually the third backyard photo (designated today as 133-C) which had not been published until the House Select Committee on Assassinations conducted its hearings in the late seventies.[1] A photo of retired Dallas Detective Bobby Brown recreating Oswald's backyard photo was also included in Rusty's collection.

Rusty then showed me various snapshots which had been taken by citizens viewing the motorcade through Dallas. He told me that a civilian employee that worked in the dark room had been given the snapshots and photographed them with the Crime Lab's copy camera following the assassination. The quality of the photographic copies seemed as good as the original snapshots themselves. They obviously appear to be taken by various camera types.

I asked Rusty about their copy camera. He said that it produced a negative which measured about 5"x7." The clarity of this camera could even fool experts, as will be discussed in depth later.

The Texas Theater was photographed by Crime Lab Detective Pete Barnes shortly after Oswald's arrest,[2] and Rusty has two views of the interior of the theater.

At the time of the assassination, Detective Barnes was at the dentist. He told Rusty and me that when he heard the news, he immediately drove back to the Crime Lab Office and was told by the Identification Bureau's Captain Doughty to remain there. After Officer Tippit was shot, he and Captain Doughty went to the crime scene at 10th and Patton in Oak Cliff to photograph the car and check for prints.

Detective Barnes related that he collected some spent revolver hulls from an officer named Joe Poe at the scene and marked them with a diamond-point pen.[3] Barnes was also called over to the spot in an adjacent alley where a jacket had been tossed under a parked car and photographed it. Rusty does not have a photograph of the jacket, but does have a copy of four of the Tippit car crime scene photographs.

After leaving the Tippit crime scene, Detective Barnes went to photograph a major accident. After leaving the accident, he proceeded to the Texas Theater to take the photographs showing where Oswald was arrested. Barnes worked until about 4 a.m. the following morning, putting in many hours of overtime, as did most of the Dallas Crime Scene officers in order to process much of the photographic and physical evidence gathered.

The next photograph I was shown was a collection of items taken on the day of the shooting. Some of Oswald's belongings are shown, which were seized by the Dallas police from the Paine residence where Marina Oswald was staying at the time of the assassination. After speaking to other researchers, I learned that one of these photographs had not been seen before by the public. The photo exposes some items belonging to Oswald that the FBI and possibly others may not have wanted the public to know about.

We then turned to some Dallas Police Department documents which included the Lee Harvey Oswald and Jack Ruby arrest reports and copies of the homicide report of John F. Kennedy and Lee Harvey Oswald. There were also mug shots of Ruby and Oswald. Rusty pointed out to me that Ruby's mug shot number of 36398 and Oswald's mug shot number of 54018 show that Ruby "had a police record going way back."

Each person placed under arrest is assigned a number by the Dallas Police Department, which is then displayed alongside the individual when the mug shot is made. If Ruby had not had a previous record in the Department, his number would have been slightly higher than Oswald's since Ruby was arrested for Oswald's murder only two days after Oswald was arrested.

OVER THE YEARS, RUSTY HAS NOT BEEN PHOTOGRAPHED OFTEN. Fortunately, however, a few pictures were taken showing him in the

Crime Lab Office and Identification Bureau file room during his years of service with the Dallas police. A perspective of the offices on the fourth floor of the Department can still be gained by a viewing of the old shots. (See Chapter II.)

A copy of the case report of Oswald was also included in the documents Rusty possesses. It lists the officer witnesses who saw or investigated the assassination. The typed list also includes names of individuals who witnessed events that occurred during the assassination.

FROM THE FIRST VIEWING OF THE EVIDENCE WHICH RUSTY HAS IN his possession, even a novice to the Kennedy assassination would be impressed. I then made it my goal to become my own researcher, so that I could fully understand what I was seeing. I felt Rusty did not even know the importance of the evidence which has remained in his old briefcase in a closet since November of 1963.

Later on, as I became more knowledgeable concerning the events of that day and the many conspiracy theories that have been tossed about, I began to realize the tremendous importance of what Rusty possessed. Even he eventually told me, "If only I had known what I had."

1. House Select Committee on Assassinations (HSCA), *Investigation of the Assassination of President John F. Kennedy,* 12 vols. (Washington, D.C.: U.S. Government Printing Office, 1979), VI: 171.
2. Warren Commission, *Hearings Before the President's Commission on the Assassination of President Kennedy,* 26 vols. (Washington D.C.: U.S. Government Printing Office, 1964), VII: 276.
3. Ibid., 275.

CHAPTER

IV

The Prints

CONTROVERSY HAS FOLLOWED THE KENNEDY ASSASSINATION investigation since day one. Many events seemed to work in concert to produce such a situation. However, when one examines the first day evidence as found by the Dallas police and notes when and by whom it was found or developed, a clear sequence of events will unfold. The evidence contained in Rusty's briefcase provides a tremendous amount of previously unpublished information. Many of the conspiratorial charges leveled toward the Dallas police over the last 28 years may now be laid to rest in a new viewing of the evidence collected first by the Dallas Crime Lab.

Rusty has copies of five photographs taken by Lieutenant Day made directly from the original Dallas police negatives which show latent fingerprints found on the trigger housing of the Mannlicher Carcano rifle from the sixth floor of the Depository. The fingerprints are visible to the naked eye even before enhancement. Each of the fingerprint photographs was taken with a light shining on the trigger housing from different directions in order to produce various contrasts of the fingerprints. This was an attempt by Lieutenant Day to bring out as much of the ridge detail as possible in order to do a comparison for identification of whoever had previously handled the rifle (the shooter). Fingerprint ridges are the lines running around each finger from one side of the nail to the other. The raised ridges are unique to every person.

The rifle was completely covered with black fingerprint powder by Lieutenant Day in order to check for prints after he had

33. Dallas Police Crime Lab photo taken by Lieutenant Day showing the latent fingerprints found on the left side of the 6.5 Mannlicher Carcano. This particular exposure proved to be the best in highlighting the ridge detail. It was the primary photo used for comparison by Captain Powdrill. (2 of the 5 trigger-housing photos appear in the Warren Commission as Exhibits 720 and 721.)

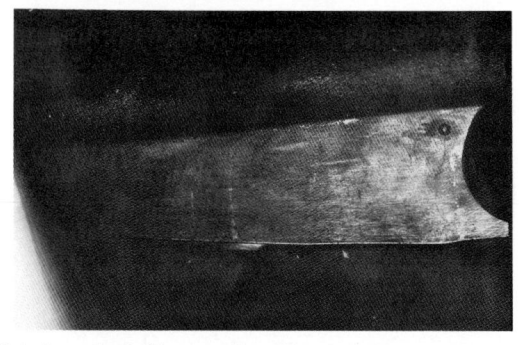

34. Dallas Police Crime Lab photo taken by Lieutenant Day with a second lighting contrast to highlight fingerprints.

THE PRINTS

35. Dallas Police Crime Lab photo taken by Lieutenant Day with a third lighting contrast to highlight fingerprints.

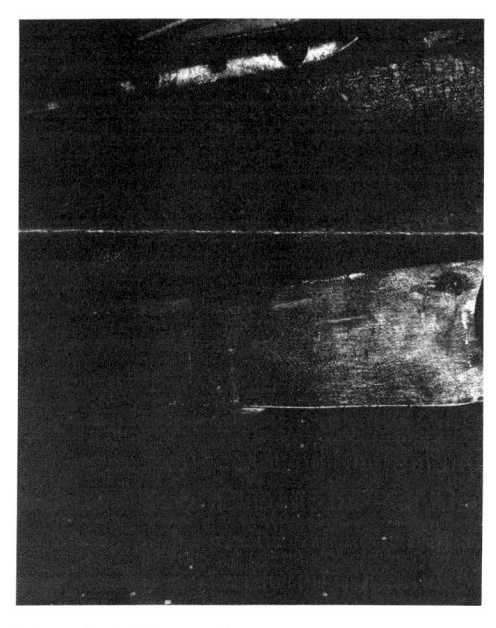

36. Dallas Police Crime Lab photo taken by Lieutenant Day with a fourth lighting contrast to highlight fingerprints.

103

37. Dallas Police Crime Lab photo taken by Lieutenant Day. This is the fifth and final photo showing the latent trigger-housing fingerprints. All of the original five trigger-housing photos were 5"x7"and were taken with the mug room copy camera. This particular print is the only full size photo possessed by Rusty. Unfortunately, the previous four prints were made on 4"x5" paper, omitting the peripheral detail of the gun barrel and scope.

returned to the Crime Lab around dusk on the evening of the assassination.[1]

The fingerprint photographs which Rusty retained copies of should not be confused with the palm print that Lieutenant Day found underneath the barrel of the disassembled rifle. This evidence is in addition to that. Many studying the assassination have confused the issue of what prints were found on the rifle as well as where and who actually found them.

Two different areas of prints were found on the rifle taken from the sixth floor of the Texas School Book Depository by Lieutenant Day. The first area of fingerprints was located on the left side of the trigger housing of the rifle as it was held in a

38. Dallas Police Crime Lab photo taken by Lieutenant Day of the 6.5 Mannlicher Carcano in his fourth-floor office.

forward position. A second area containing a palm print was found on the underside of the disassembled rifle barrel later in the evening of the assassination after further examination by Lieutenant Day.

The latent fingerprints appeared immediately while the rifle was being dusted on the sixth floor after it was located behind the stacks of boxes. This action was captured on film by a news photographer who had been allowed on the sixth floor by police. The fingerprints were then photographed by Lieutenant Day after bringing the rifle back to the Crime Lab Office and are the photographs which Rusty has copies of today.

Crime Lab Detective Barnes was in the office at the time Lieutenant Day photographed the trigger-housing fingerprints. He later compared the trigger-housing photographs himself to a print card of Oswald and told us that he found 3 points of identity. Pete told Rusty and me that there was not a doubt in his mind that it was

Oswald's fingerprint.²

Verification of ownership of the rifle was initially developed by Homicide Detective Gus Rose for Captain Fritz. On the afternoon of the assassination, Gus was the first officer to speak to Oswald's wife, Marina, about the rifle at the Paine home in Irving. He asked Marina if her husband owned a rifle, and through the translation of Ruth Paine into Russian, Marina responded, "Yes."

Gus said Marina then led them to a door in the kitchen which opened into the garage and pointed out a blanket and told them in Russian that "there is the rifle." Gus picked up the blanket, which was tied with a piece of cord, but the blanket was empty.

Michael Paine arrived at the Paine residence during the time Gus and other detectives were inside. Michael did not realize that the officers were inside when he exclaimed while coming to the front door, "I heard about the shooting, and I came to see if ya'll needed any help." After a brief search of the residence, Gus brought Marina, her two children, and Ruth Paine back to the Dallas Police Department and turned them over to Homicide Captain Fritz.³

THE TRIGGER-HOUSING FINGERPRINTS

THE FINGERPRINT TRACES FOUND ON THE SIDE OF THE TRIGGER housing of the rifle were first photographed and then covered with cellophane tape by Lieutenant Day to protect them for shipment to the FBI lab in Washington, D. C. Lieutenant Day had determined that the fingerprints were too light to do a lift first and then photograph, so he photographed the fingerprints before covering them with the tape.⁴ He also scratched his name on the stock of the rifle. When testifying later in Washington to the Warren Commission, Lieutenant Day told Rusty and me that he had some trouble finding his name because it was very faint.⁵

As Lieutenant Day worked on the rifle during the evening,

Chief Curry came into the Crime Lab Office. Lieutenant Day told him at the time that he had located a trace of a print on the trigger housing, but he had not yet had a chance to do a comparison check with Oswald's print card. He told Rusty and me that the Chief then went back down to the third floor and told the newsmen that we had a print. He said that he had not told Chief Curry that it was Oswald's print at that time.

LIEUTENANT DAY HAD FOREKNOWLEDGE OF THE FBI WANTING TO get the rifle from the Dallas Police before the order came to release it from his own superiors. Earlier in the evening Forrest Sorrels, the local Secret Service Agent, told Lieutenant Day, "The FBI is trying to get that gun. I told him that was fine with me if somebody wanted to work on it."

Lieutenant Day did not try to lift the fingerprints that he found on the trigger housing of the rifle on November 22nd, 1963. He photographed them only, and later did try to do a fingerprint comparison from a print card of Oswald to determine if he had held the rifle. Day stated to the Warren Commission that he could not exclude all possibility as to whose prints they were, but he did say that he thought that they were the right middle and right ring finger of Oswald.[6]

Lieutenant Day recalled that, as he was beginning to dust the rest of the rifle following the photographing of the trigger-housing prints, Captain Doughty came in and told him to stop working on the rifle. He said this was probably about 8:30 or 9:00 p.m. A few minutes later, Captain Fritz came into the Crime Lab Office and told him that Marina Oswald was in his office and he needed some information about the gun. He needed to know if Lee Oswald's prints were on the rifle. So Lieutenant Day began to once again dust the Mannlicher Carcano and soon located a palm print.

THE PALM PRINT

THE LIFT OF THE PALM PRINT FROM THE RIFLE BY LIEUTENANT DAY has sparked controversy over the years due to what has been labeled an "interrupted chain of evidence." This misunderstanding developed from the FBI's intrusion into the Dallas police investigation on the night of the assassination. The rifle was taken away from Lieutenant Day by the FBI before he had completed his analysis of it. At that time, the FBI did not receive the palm print just developed by Lieutenant Day. The print evidence stayed in the Crime Lab Office, and only the rifle was taken by FBI Agent Drain.

Lieutenant Day told us that, after he had photographed the trigger-housing prints and been stopped by Captain Doughty, he continued work on the rifle under the order of Captain Fritz. It was at that time that he noticed a print sticking out from the barrel. He said it was obvious that part of it was under the wooden stock, so he took the stock off and finished dusting the barrel. He said he could tell it was part of a palm print, and so he proceeded with a lift.

He told Rusty and me that he could tell it wasn't put on there recently by the way it took the fingerprint powder. He said what makes a print of this sort is a lack of moisture, and this print had dried out. He said he took a small camel hair brush and dipped it in fingerprint powder and lightly brushed it. He then placed a strip of 2" scotch tape over the developed print and rubbed it down before finally lifting the tape containing the print off and placed it on a card. He said he then compared the lift to Oswald's palm print card and was certain that it was Oswald's. He also said that after the lift, he could still see an impression of the palm print left on the barrel.

Next, Lieutenant Day had intended to photograph the area of the rifle barrel from which the palm print lift had been made, but was again interrupted by Captain Doughty at about 10:00 p.m. He was told once again to stop working on the gun and release it to FBI Agent Drain, who would arrive about 11:30 p.m. Lieutenant Day

THE PRINTS

did not have time to write any reports about what he had found, but did have time to reassemble the rifle before Drain arrived.

DRAIN TOOK THE RIFLE FROM THE DALLAS POLICE AT MIDNIGHT ON the day of the assassination and flew it to the FBI laboratory in Washington, D. C.[7] The palm print lift done earlier by Lieutenant Day had left too little powder residue on the rifle barrel to be readily identified a second time when the FBI received it in Washington. The FBI was not aware that the palm print had been lifted at the time of their initial examination of the rifle.

When the FBI received the rifle Saturday in Washington, a comparison of the faint latent fingerprints found by Lieutenant Day on the trigger housing of the rifle was attempted by Sabastian Latona, the Supervisor of the Latent Fingerprint Section of the FBI's Identification Division.[8] In Washington, Latona also photographed the fingerprints on the trigger housing which had already been photographed by Lieutenant Day in Dallas prior to his placing cellophane tape over them.

Latona could not make a positive identification since the fingerprints were extremely faint following the removal of the protective tape. Lieutenant Day's trigger-housing photographs (which Rusty has first generation copies of), made in the Dallas Crime Lab Office, were the best quality photographs made of the fingerprints found on the side of the trigger housing. The Dallas Crime Lab received the rifle back from the FBI in a pasteboard box. It remained unopened in the evidence room along with other physical evidence in the case. After a few days passed, orders came to release all of the physical evidence to the FBI. That is when the palm print was released for the first time to the FBI.

Lieutenant Day said that a few days after all of the evidence was turned over, an FBI Agent came to his house. He wanted to know when Lieutenant Day had lifted the palm print included in the evidence they had received because they had positively identified it themselves as Oswald's palm print. Lieutenant Day got the impression from the Agent that they thought they had missed it and

109

he could "envision J. Edgar Hoover going into orbit." He then informed the Agent that he had lifted the palm print before releasing the gun on the night of the assassination.

The FBI requested and received the remaining physical evidence from the Dallas police on the Tuesday following the assassination, not aware of the palm print's existence. To say the least, they were surprised upon discovering the palm print included with the evidence. By matching irregularities found on the rifle barrel to it, the FBI later verified that the palm print lift that was delivered was, in fact, genuine.

Lieutenant Day believed at the time that he had not completely obliterated the palm print on the barrel after his lift and later stated that he had pointed out the area of the palm print to FBI Agent Drain when turning the rifle over to him. Drain, on the other hand, did not recall being shown the palm print.

Rusty was standing by as Lieutenant Day gave the rifle to Drain. Rusty told me that Drain was in a hurry to leave and was distracted by another FBI agent who was hurrying him to leave. According to Rusty, "Drain was half listening to Lieutenant Day and half to the other FBI man and evidently didn't get the word about the palm print at that time."

A NEW COMPARISON OF THE OSWALD FINGERPRINTS

As stated earlier, Rusty has an original fingerprint card that he and J. B. Hicks made of Oswald following his murder while his body lay in the morgue at Parkland Hospital Sunday night. At that time, the Dallas Police Department used a small fingerprint card which was manufactured by the Faurot Company of New York. To use the card, an invisible chemical was placed on the victim's fingers, and the card was then rolled over them. The paper that the card was made from then reacted to the chemical from the

THE PRINTS

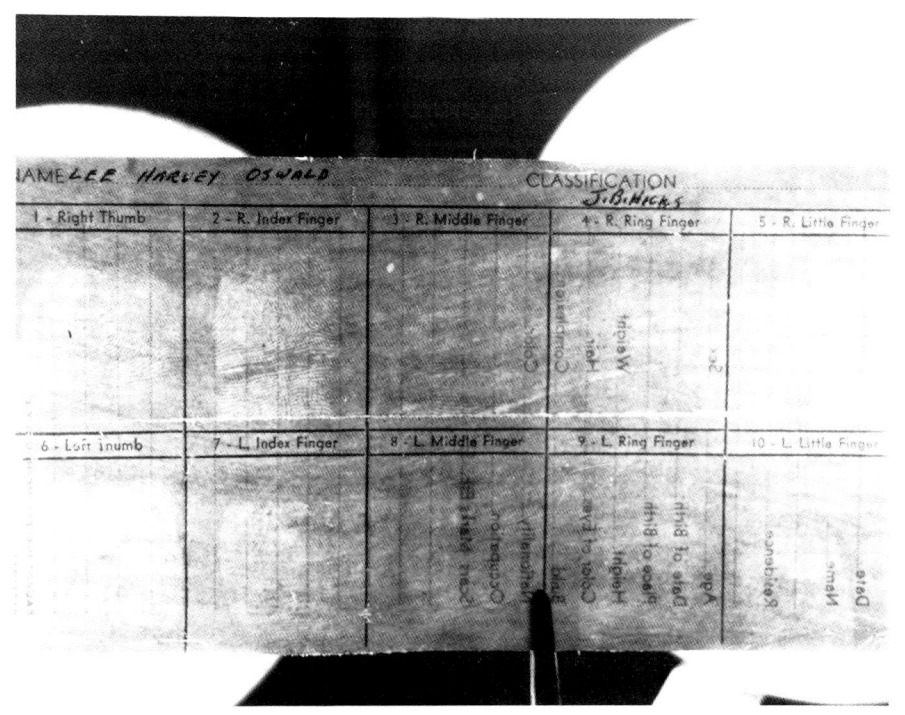

39. Photograph taken by Captain Jerry Powdrill of the West Monroe Police Department. This is the original fingerprint card made by Rusty and J. B. Hicks in the Parkland morgue of Lee Harvey Oswald. The card has faded severely through the years and was backlit to highlight the ridge detail.

finger, producing a print on the card. This type of card was typically used by detectives on deceased individuals in order to avoid leaving ink stains on a body already prepared for burial.

The reason Rusty and J. B. Hicks took a photograph and fingerprinted Oswald in the morgue was actually a routine assignment for the Crime Lab.

Rusty told me, "In fingerprinting, normally a lot of times we would have to go to a mortuary where a body had already been prepared for burial, and if we didn't get to it beforehand, we had to go to the mortuary and roll a set of prints. We did roll some prints while Oswald was in the morgue. He hadn't been prepared for burial."

Rusty and J. B. Hicks rolled at least three inkless cards and one inked card of Oswald that Sunday night in the Parkland

111

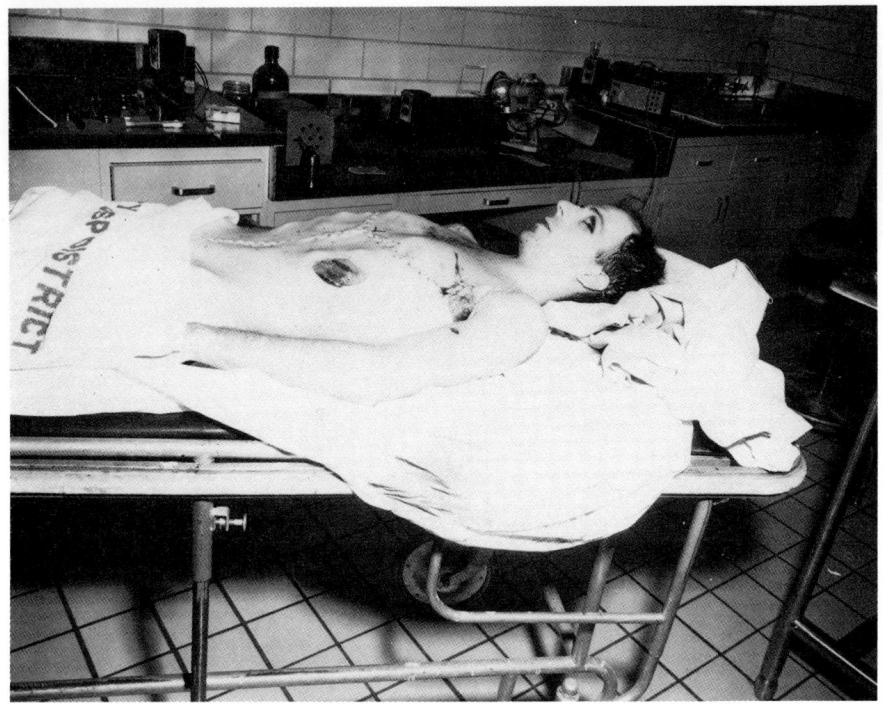

40. Dallas Police Crime Lab photo taken of Oswald's body by Rusty and J. B. Hicks in the Parkland morgue on Sunday night following the assassination. Numerous inkless fingerprint cards and one inked card were rolled off Oswald immediately after this photo was taken. The entry area of Ruby's bullet appears on Oswald's left side. The "Y" incision from the autopsy is also visible.

morgue. Rusty retained one inkless card for his reference. The inked card was taken back to the Identification Bureau and was checked the following day against Oswald's prints taken the previous Friday. Rusty told me it was typical that, when a detective back at the office verified that the prints were indeed from the same person, the fingerprint card was usually initialed by him, showing it had been done.

A firsthand witness with a fingerprint card in his possession helps to verify the fact that the Oswald killed by Jack Ruby, buried in Fort Worth, and later exhumed was the same Oswald who was in police custody charged with the murder of two people. Along with all the other first day evidence in Rusty's possession, this card establishes a chain of evidence to conclude that simple truth. Also, the card could be used to establish one more major fact, again for the sake of history: Do the fingerprints found on the trigger housing of the rifle match the fingerprints on the card possessed today by Rusty?

It was suggested at a second meeting with researcher Gary Shaw that Rusty and I try to find someone locally who was trained in fingerprint analysis to work with the evidence that we possessed. After doing some checking, it didn't take long to locate our local expert. Getting to know a dedicated professional who showed an unwavering and businesslike approach in getting to the truth of the evidence, be it condemning or not, was an exciting time for us.

CAPTAIN JERRY POWDRILL IS TODAY A MEMBER OF THE WEST Monroe Police Department and is a qualified fingerprint expert. He is often called to testify in court over photographic and fingerprint analysis work that he develops in his Crime Lab in West Monroe, Louisiana. He agreed to help Rusty and me in trying to determine two basic points with our evidence.

Before beginning, however, the first and main problem that Captain Powdrill encountered was to deal with the fading over the years of the fingerprint image on Rusty's card. The inkless card was not designed to be a permanent storage method for fingerprints. The inked cards were used for that. So here we were in 1992, left to deal with the faded card from 1963.

I placed a call to the Faurot Company in New York and was told that fading was indeed a problem with their cards over an extended period of time. They told me that they did not know of a chemical or any other process to enhance the card, and in fact asked me if I discovered a way to enhance the card to let them know! I laughingly told them, "Thanks a lot!" And so we were left to deal with the card on our own.

In fluorescent light, the ridges of the individual prints on the card are still visible to the naked eye; however, it quickly became apparent that it was painstakingly difficult on the eyes to make a point-by-point comparison between the prints. It was decided early on to make a series of photographs of the card to try to enhance the fingerprint images. Captain Powdrill was successful in bringing out the images better by simply shining a light through the back of the card, which was then photographed from the front. He then proceeded with the comparison.

THE FIRST MAJOR POINT WE ASKED CAPTAIN POWDRILL TO VERIFY was that Rusty's card matched the other known prints taken of Oswald at various points in his life, such as his military ID, cards taken while he was in police custody in New Orleans, Dallas, and so on. These prints have been widely published in various books through the years, and it was a simple matter for Captain Powdrill to verify the fact that Rusty's card did indeed match the known fingerprint cards taken previously of Oswald. Captain Powdrill stated that he is one hundred percent certain that Rusty's card matches those known prints of Oswald. The claim cannot be made that Oswald's prints have never been sufficiently verified by a failure to maintain a sufficient chain of evidence, or that the Dallas police somehow substituted someone else's prints on Oswald's fingerprint card in an elaborate conspiracy.

The chain of evidence that Rusty possesses is firsthand. It starts and stops with him. He owns the fingerprint card which he and J. B. Hicks rolled themselves. How many other researchers have a fingerprint card of Lee Harvey Oswald that they rolled themselves?

At some point in time all the nay-sayers can no longer sway opinion when faced with firsthand evidence and firsthand witnesses to an event. For all assassination devotees, check Warren Commission Volume XIX, Batchelor Exhibit No. 5002, page 18 under the CRIME SCENE SEARCH SECTION list of employees for employee number seven, Richard W. Livingston. Rusty was there. He worked in the Dallas Police Crime Lab. He took the prints of Oswald himself in the Parkland morgue. He helped develop stacks of photographs of the Kennedy investigation. He's held on to a fingerprint card for twenty-eight years in a briefcase in his closet.

My family and I have known him our entire lives and know him to be an extremely trustworthy and conscientious person.

Rusty has no reason to lie about what he did at the time of the assassination. In fact, if it were not for my curiosity, all of this evidence would still be sitting in his closet, probably destined never to be seen. Rusty didn't realize that what he possessed mattered anymore. If he did, I'm sure he would have shown it to the world sooner. What he's doing now will hopefully be a contribution to those striving for years to make sense of the awful events that happened so long ago.

The second area pursued by Captain Powdrill was a comparison of Rusty's fingerprint card to the five trigger-housing photographs taken by Lieutenant Day. Keep in mind that Lieutenant Day found what he thought to be the right middle and right ring fingerprints of Oswald, and Captain Powdrill proceeded with this information as an assumption.

After taking and developing an 8"x10" black and white photograph of Rusty's fingerprint card, Captain Powdrill determined that the card, although viewable, was painstakingly slow to use as a comparison print source. I took it upon myself to order JFK Exhibit F-400 from the HSCA files, which is an excellent photograph of Oswald's fingerprint card taken in New Orleans on August 9th, 1963. Captain Powdrill then compared Rusty's card to the JFK Exhibit print card photograph and determined a one hundred percent match. This proved the man arrested by the Dallas police was the same man arrested in New Orleans handing out Fair Play for Cuba literature. Captain Powdrill then used the JFK print card as a source for comparison with the old trigger-housing photographs (still in almost perfect condition).

As stated in his conclusions, many similarities do exist. His comparison focused on the right middle fingerprint of Oswald since it was one of the clearest of the trigger-housing fingerprints. He concluded,

"Examination revealed that the right middle finger (#3

finger) of Lee Harvey Oswald and partial latents seen in one of the black and white photographs have the following similarities:
1) Both were ulnar loops (type of fingerprint pattern).
2) Both have a ridge count of 15 to 16 (friction ridge count from delta to core).
3) Three (3) points of identity in the photographs matched three (3) points in the known inked cards.
4) Three (3) other points of identity in the photographed latent had very similar characteristics as in the known inked cards, but positive points of identity could not be made."

Three points matched and three other points possibly matched. Most states require seven to ten points of comparison for a conviction. Captain Powdrill further stated,

"To make positive identification through fingerprint comparison, a certain number of 'points of identity' must be made. The number of points of identity used for positive identification vary in the law enforcement community, wherein some agencies may require a minimum amount of six points and others may require as many as twelve.

Upon looking at the above-mentioned photographs and inked cards for countless hours, I can say that sufficient evidence does not exist to conclude that the latent print (in the photograph) is in fact that of Lee Harvey Oswald; however, there are enough similarities to suggest that it is possible they are one in the same."

BEFORE TAKING RUSTY'S FINGERPRINT CARD AND TRIGGER-HOUSING photographs to Captain Powdrill, in the back of my mind was the slight fear of what it would mean if the prints did not match.

City of West Monroe

Larry M. LaBorde
CHIEF OF POLICE

POLICE DEPARTMENT
2301 NORTH SEVENTH
WEST MONROE, LOUISIANA 71291

February 9, 1993

Mr. Gary Savage
Monroe, Louisiana

RE: Fingerprint Comparison

Dear Mr. Savage:

In October, 1991, you approached me with a request to compare latent fingerprints to known inked prints. At that time, I received from you the following items:

1) One inkless method type fingerprint card containing fingerprints, believed to be that of Lee Harvey Oswald and obtained by Officer J. B. Hicks, Dallas Police Department. (The above-mentioned inkless fingerprints were later compared to known inked prints of Lee Harvey Oswald, dated 8/9/63, taken by Arthur M. James with "JFK Exhibit F-400." The fingerprints on the inkless card and the fingerprints on the "JFK Exhibit F-400" were one in the same.)

2) Four black and white photographs depicting the trigger guard of the rifle found on the sixth floor of the former Texas School Book Depository building in Dallas, Texas. On each of the four photographs a partial latent fingerprint can be seen.

Upon examination of the above-listed items, the inkless card and the known inked impressions on "JFK Exhibit F-400" were compared to the unknown partial latents shown in the four (4) black and white photographs.

Examination revealed that the right middle finger (#3 finger) of Lee Harvey Oswald and partial latents seen in one of the black and white photographs have the following similarities:

1) Both were ulnar loops (type of fingerprint pattern).

2) Both have a ridge count of 15 to 16 (friction ridge count from delta to core).

41. Page 1 of a letter from Captain Powdrill to the author indicating his findings regarding the trigger-housing photos.

> Mr. Gary Savage
> Page 2
> February 9, 1993
>
> 3) Three (3) points of identity in the photographs matched three (3) points in the known inked cards.
>
> 4) Three (3) other points of identity in the photographed latent had very similar characteristics as in the known inked cards, but positive points of identity could not be made.
>
> To make positive identification through fingerprint comparison, a certain number of "points of identity" must be made. The number of points of identity used for positive identification vary in the law enforcement community, wherein some agencies may require a minimum amount of six points and others may require as many as twelve.
>
> Upon looking at the above-mentioned photographs and inked cards for countless hours, I can say that sufficient evidence does not exist to conclude that the latent print (in the photograph) is in fact that of Lee Harvey Oswald; however, there are enough similarities to suggest that it is possible they are one in the same.
>
> Respectfully,
>
> *Jerry L. Powdrill*
> Jerry L. Powdrill, Captain
> Expert Fingerprint Examiner
>
> JLP:rh

42. Page 2 of the letter from Captain Powdrill to the author.

Captain Powdrill told me at the outset of his comparison that if he found any contradiction, he would immediately stop his work. He found no contradictions. As he stated in his conclusions concerning the right middle fingerprint comparison, "Both were ulnar loops," and "Both had a ridge count of 15 to 16."

A total of six points of comparison in the fingerprint had been examined closely by Captain Powdrill as being similar. Counting the number of ridges between the ridge intersections or loops enables examiners to make a positive identification of an individual. Due to the lightness of the fingerprints on the trigger housing, a good ridge count was difficult to see.

During the course of his examination, Captain Powdrill told me, if someone in his department had brought the fingerprints to him that we had and he had made a comparison check as he did for Rusty and me, that he would tell his man to try his best to pursue the individual. He had a "gut feeling" that the fingerprints were a match and would pursue the suspect, trying to locate more evidence in order to get a conviction.

Remember that Lieutenant Day had also examined these same fingerprints and stated to the Warren Commission that "They appeared to be the right middle and right ring finger of . . . Lee Harvey Oswald." The examination by Captain Powdrill has concluded almost exactly what was stated by Lieutenant Day 28 years ago. Also Captain Powdrill's additional evidence he hypothetically would look for, as stated above, could directly apply here. The palm print of Oswald was also found by Lieutenant Day on the rifle!

The more research I did during the months after first interviewing Rusty, the more I realized the importance of what he knew and possessed for the sake of history. The determination to write about it and help all of those who have struggled over the years to set the record straight became a conviction with me. I began to devour the endless Warren Commission volumes and the House Select Committee volumes dealing with the Kennedy assassination to try to understand if what Rusty possessed was important. I came to the conclusion that it was extremely important in order to help clarify much of the controversy that has developed over the years.

Having the fingerprints on the rifle found at a murder scene where an employee worked would convict an accused person in most courts. Besides that fact, Oswald left the Depository Building after the shooting. He made a stop at his rooming house and picked up his revolver. This revolver was in his possession when he later was arrested at the Texas Theater, making him the prime suspect in the shooting of Officer J. D. Tippit[9] and eventually President Kennedy. And finally, at least three backyard photographs were taken of Oswald, probably by his wife Marina, holding the rifle found in the Depository . . . extremely incriminating photographs.

119

Author's Note

As the book was headed to press, an independent examination of Rusty's trigger-housing photos was done for the television program *FRONTLINE* by Vincent J. Scalice, a Certified Latent Print Examiner. Scalice was the fingerprint expert used by the HSCA in 1978. He stated in a letter of conclusions to the author that "Based upon the results of this examination and comparison, it is logical to assume that all of these photographs, which exhibit varying degrees of contrast, were not available for detailed comparison purposes in 1963 or 1978." Scalice had not seen all of the photos possessed by Rusty before.

Instead of focusing on only the clearest photograph (detailed in this chapter as performed by Captain Powdrill), Scalice used different enhancement techniques with all of the photographs. He stated, "It was necessary to utilize all of the photographs in order to carry out this procedure as the photographs were taken at different exposures ranging from light to medium and dark. As a result of the varying degrees of contrast from photo to photo, it became possible to locate and identify a sufficient amount of identifying characteristics on which to base a positive identification. As a result of an exacting and detailed examination and comparison under varying degrees of magnification and illumination, I have reached the conclusion that the developed latent prints are the fingerprints of Lee Harvey Oswald's right middle finger (#3) and right ring finger (#4) as they appear on the inked fingerprint card [JFK Exhibit F-400 of the HSCA]."

A comparison was also done by Scalice of Rusty's fingerprint card to JFK Exhibit F-400. He determined that "the inkless prints taken by Rusty [and J. B. Hicks] were indeed those of Lee Harvey Oswald, as they compared favorably with the inked impressions taken on 8-9-63."

Although the trigger-housing fingerprints were "extremely faint and barely distinguishable" and "partially distorted," a positive identification of Lee Harvey Oswald was made by Scalice. This is perhaps the most important finding made since the time of the assassination. It may now be stated as fact that the fingerprints of Lee Harvey Oswald were left behind on the trigger housing of the rifle found on the sixth floor of the Book Depository.

---

1. Former Crime Lab Lt. John Carl Day, taped personal interview, 18 December 1991.
2. Former Crime Lab Detective W. E. Barnes, taped personal interview, 4 April 1992.
3. Former Homicide Detective Gus Rose, taped personal interview, 16 February 1993.
4. Warren Commission, *Hearings Before the President's Commission on the Assassination of President Kennedy,* 26 vols. (Washington, D.C.: U.S. Government Printing Office, 1964), IV: 260-261.
5. John Carl Day interview.
6. Warren Commission, *Hearings,* IV: 261.
7. Ibid.
8. Ibid., 48.
9. Warren Commission, *Hearings,* III: 301.

CHAPTER

V

The Backyard Photographs

THE BACKYARD PHOTOGRAPHS

EXPERTS HAVE WRITTEN VOLUMES CONCERNING THREE photographs and one negative found among the belongings of Marina and Lee Oswald in the garage of Ruth Paine, a lady who befriended and helped the struggling young couple in Dallas. At the time of the assassination, Lee was staying in a small room he had rented in Oak Cliff near downtown Dallas, and Marina was staying with Mrs. Paine in Irving, a suburb of Dallas. Many of their meager possessions were stored in the Paine garage, and the Dallas police collected them as evidence on that Friday and Saturday following the assassination.

Note the date found in photo 81 (page 208). The sign shows that the Dallas police collected many items on the day of the assassination from Ruth Paine and Mrs. Oswald at the Paine residence, although they had no search warrant. Upon their arrival on that Friday afternoon, Mrs. Paine voluntarily gave the police whatever was deemed necessary for seizure as evidence.[1] Some of the officers involved in the search testified Mrs. Paine had stated that she had been expecting them after hearing the news of shots being fired from the Book Depository where Lee was working at the time. The police also returned the following day with a search warrant[2] to collect other items, and the backyard photos were included among the items collected on one of the two searches of the residence. (All of the officers testified that the photographs were found on the second search on Saturday.)

Those unfamiliar with the assassination might wonder about

123

the significance of the three backyard photographs. As evidence, they place the accused shooter, Oswald, with the rifle which was later to be found on the sixth floor of the Depository after the assassination, in his hands. They also show a revolver strapped to his waist similiar to the one the Dallas officers reported he was carrying with him at the time of his arrest in the Texas Theater for the murder of Dallas Police Officer J. D. Tippit.

The only thing that could make the rifle and revolver disappear from Oswald's hands would be to prove the photographs taken were faked, thus supporting his claim while in police custody that he did not at that time own a rifle. He did not deny owning the revolver, but claimed that he had bought it in Fort Worth a few months prior.[3] It should be noted here that Oswald lied to the Dallas police in practically every response dealing with himself personally after his arrest.

THE TESTIMONY OF THE DALLAS OFFICERS WHO FOUND THE backyard photographs was not fully developed by the Commission questioners (on the record, anyway). Detective Rose, one of the Dallas officers who initiated the search warrant on the second search of the Paine home on Saturday, told the Warren Commission that he found "two sea bags, three suitcases, and two cardboard boxes" which contained "numerous items of property of Oswald."[4]

Rose further stated that he found two negatives and one print while observing Irving Police Officer John McCabe locating another print almost simultaneously in one of the off-white seabags. Another Dallas officer present was Richard Stovall. He told the Commission that Rose found the snapshots, and "when he looked at them, he said, 'Look at this.' At the time he said that, he showed us the snapshots and the negatives to me."[5] Stovall did not specify how many different photographs were found. Another officer named Adamcik spoke only of "one picture of Oswald," though in the context of his testimony he was not asked how many photographs or negatives were found, but "Did you find the picture of Oswald with the rifle?"[6]

I recently spoke to Gus Rose. Although the assassination happened twenty-eight years ago, he spoke of it as if the event had just occurred. Rusty had already told me that Gus was an extremely good officer. Rusty had called Gus, spoken to him briefly, and asked if it would be all right for me to speak to him about Oswald. Gus told Rusty, "Sure," and added that he'd tell me, "anything I wanted to know and some things I probably didn't even want to know."

Gus told me that he had found the photographs of Oswald with the rifle in a seabag in the Paine's garage. I asked him if they had been on the top of one of the bags and by themselves. He told me that they were down in the seabag along with other pictures.

Gus also told me that he had been in on some interrogations of Oswald and said that he was really an "absolute nut." He was very adamant to me and said that he sincerely believed that Oswald was crazy and compared him to John Hinckley, the man who attempted to murder President Reagan. He said if I had been there as he was and listened for only thirty minutes, that I would have been convinced that he (Oswald) was "nuts." He believes today (as do many of the retired officers spoken to by Rusty and me) that Oswald committed the assassination entirely on his own.

Most of the officers Rusty and I have interviewed have read little on the assassination through the years or even the Report issued by the Warren Commission. In fact, one retired officer asked if I would send him a copy of his 1964 interview, which I gladly did later.

Many have capitalized upon the seemingly disorganized search conducted in the Paine garage by the officers, since in hindsight today the importance of the backyard photographs seems immediately evident in placing the guilt upon Oswald as the shooter. The evidence presented here, which Rusty possesses, does not contradict the officers' testimony.

The officers were conducting a search which turned up many items belonging to Oswald in the garage and collected multiple pieces of evidence at the time, which included the backyard photographs. Detective Rose told Rusty and me that he recalled at least one negative was found to go with one of the backyard photographs. An effort was made to locate the negatives of each of the backyard photograph prints, but apparently only one was found.

ONE OF THE MORE INTERESTING POINTS ABOUT THE BACKYARD photographs concerns the Imperial Reflex camera which was later proven by the HSCA to have been used to take the snapshots.[7] The Dallas police did not find the camera after two extensive searches of the Paine home. The FBI later claimed that the camera was found two weeks after the assassination by Robert Oswald, Lee's brother, who turned it over to the Bureau. Marina Oswald, however, said that she didn't remember the camera. The camera needed repair to the shutter lever before it could be used by the FBI to make comparison photographs.[8]

Much information which attempts to question the authenticity of the photographs has been developed by researchers through the years. The Warren Commission and HSCA determined that the photographs found in the Paine garage were genuine. It is a prudent exercise, however, to explore the arguments put forth by both sides in order to come to a better understanding and finally a judgement as to whether the photographs are genuine or fake.

One factor that most would not dispute is that if someone desired to frame Oswald for the assassination and fake a photograph showing him with the murder weapons in his hands, why go to the trouble of faking more than one photograph when one would do the job? Since there are three different backyard photograph poses existing today, the odds of discovering a fake have gone up dramatically since one can be compared to the next for continuity.

Although Rusty has had a copy of the third backyard photograph (133-C) since the time of the assassination, that particular pose was not revealed until the HSCA hearings were held in the late seventies. Rusty was not aware at that time that the photographs he had were important any longer. (He retired in

1974.) Rusty incorrectly assumed that all of what he possessed had already been published.

Marina Oswald first denied using the Imperial Reflex camera, but later stated after examination that she may have taken one of the photographs. Later she changed her story and said she may have taken two.[9] Due to the eventual changes made in her recollection of the photo-taking session, a case could be made against believing any version at all.

Oswald told Homicide Captain Fritz that the pictures were faked, and if he had time, he could show how they were done. Of course, Oswald never had the chance, since he was murdered on the following Sunday.

During an interrogation on Saturday, the day after the assassination, Oswald did make one comment which is worth noting. According to the Warren Commission testimony of Captain Fritz, Oswald was shown an 8"x10" enlargement made by the Crime Lab (possibly by Rusty) of one of the small backyard snapshots found by the officers. Having had previous experience in photography, Oswald was making a case to Fritz about the enlarged backyard photograph being a fake and said that someone "has taken my picture and that is my face and put a different body on it." Oswald was attempting to convince the police of his knowledge of photography techniques.

After being shown the enlarged photograph made by the Crime Lab, Fritz showed Oswald the small original snapshot found in the Paine garage. This print would have been instantly recognized by Oswald if indeed it were his. Instead of reinforcing his knowledge of photography to the police by saying that the enlarged photograph was made from the original small photograph, Fritz stated that Oswald told him, "That is a picture that has been reduced from the big one."[10] In stating the reverse of what had occurred, Oswald may have been attempting to further confuse the interrogators with another quick-thinking fabrication.

RUSTY HAS TWO BACKYARD PHOTOGRAPH PRINTS MADE FROM THE

43. Dallas Police Crime Lab photo taken by Rusty of the original Oswald snapshot with the mug room copy camera. This particular backyard pose was designated 133-A by the Warren Commission.

THE BACKYARD PHOTOGRAPHS

44. Dallas Police Crime Lab photo taken by Rusty of another original Oswald snapshot with the mug room copy camera. Copies of the Dallas police prints were retained by various officers in the Dapartment. The HSCA designated this particular backyard pose as 133-C.

Crime Lab copy camera. The copy camera, which was located in the Identification Bureau's Mug Room, was routinely used to make copies of various photographs, as well as photographs of crime scene evidence. The 5"x7" negatives it created made excellent black and white photographs which were sometimes difficult to tell from the original item copied. The photographs it made of evidence were typically stored in the permanent record files of the Dallas Police Department. A great deal of weight was placed upon a pictorial record of any crime scene, as was the case with the backyard photograph copies made by Rusty.

Confusion was obvious in the HSCA investigation concerning the origin of the photograph copies placed into evidence during the second governmental investigation of the JFK assassination. The original 1964 Warren Commission designated exhibit numbers for two of the three poses, 133-A and 133-B. The Commission was not aware at the time of the existence of a third pose. The HSCA later designated the newly surfaced pose as 133-C.

Back in November 1963, Rusty worked with only two of the three backyard snapshots found in the Paine garage and produced copies of 133-A and 133-C. He used the Crime Lab copy camera to photograph two of the original snapshots, which produced a 5"x7" negative. Multiple 5"x7" photographic prints were then made of the two backyard poses by Rusty (and possibly other Crime Lab detectives) in the Crime Lab darkroom.

The only pose that Rusty does not have is 133-B, which is the only photograph found with an original negative (according to the Warren Commission). Rusty does not remember working with drugstore type negatives when making the copies of the backyard photographs. Therefore, 133-A and 133-C must have been found as snapshot prints. Rusty simply photographed the snapshots given to him by the Homicide detectives.

Rusty ended up with a copy camera print of 133-A and 133-C. Geneva White Galle, the wife of deceased Dallas Patrolman Roscoe White, ended up with a copy camera print of 133-C. Dallas

Officer Richard Stovall, who had helped in the execution of the search warrant of the Paine residence, also ended up with a copy camera print of 133-A and 133-C. All of the Dallas officers' print copies were made in the Dallas Crime Lab.

It is interesting to note that none of the officers had a copy of the second backyard photograph 133-B, the only photographic negative apparently found and later given to the Warren Commission. Also only two of the snapshots, 133-A and 133-B, were eventually delivered to the Warren Commission investigators. However, three drugstore snapshot prints were evidently found, with Rusty photographing two out of the three. What happened to the third original snapshot of 133-C is today unknown. The negatives for 133-A and 133-C may also have existed at the time of the search of the garage, but were not reported found. All of the physical evidence collected by the Dallas police was later turned over to the FBI.

It should be noted also that according to Oswald's mother, a fourth backyard photograph once existed showing Oswald holding his rifle with both hands over his head. She stated that Marina had found it immediately after the assassination and that they had burned and flushed it down the toilet since it was so incriminating.[11] No negative was ever reported found of this pose by investigators.

The book *The Death of a President*, by William Manchester, mentions that Marina sold a copy of one of the backyard photographs for $5000.00 (apparently to *Life* magazine, since 133-A appeared on the cover soon after the shooting).[12] It would be interesting to know how and where she obtained her copy. This seems contradictory since she originally denied taking the backyard photographs.

EXPERTS TESTIFIED TO THE HSCA THAT THE BACKYARD photographs, including the newly discovered officer prints, were all genuine first generation prints from the original Imperial Reflex camera negatives belonging to Oswald.[13] Clearly, the Committee's experts could not tell the difference between the work of the Dallas police copy camera prints and the original snapshots. They assumed that the Dallas police had at one time possessed all of the original Imperial Reflex negatives and worked only with them to produce the enlargements shown to Oswald and the print copies given to the various officers. This was not the case. The copy camera fooled the experts.

Rusty told me, "The copy camera had one of the best lenses that I've ever seen. It could make a copy of a photograph just about as clear as an original negative. I wish I had that lens now!" The camera was permanently mounted on a long table with casters in the Identification Bureau in a room used at the time to take mug shots. That same room was also the place where arrested suspects were fingerprinted.

The experts on the HSCA did not know of the existence of the Dallas police copy camera. (Or if they did, they did not make it known.) Oswald's interrogator, Captain Fritz, testified that Oswald was shown one of the backyard photographs which had been enlarged. He did not say how the photograph had been enlarged, however. Today, Rusty has in his possession an 8"x10" print of backyard photograph 133-A which may have been printed at the same time as the photograph shown to Oswald. It is possible that Rusty was the one who did the enlargement of the photograph, although he says he cannot be one hundred percent sure. However, he feels there is a high probability that he could have been the one who did since he does possess the 8"x10" enlargement.

According to Rusty's wife, Daisie, Rusty stayed at work about twenty-three hours straight the day of the assassination, beginning at around 10 p.m. Friday night until about 9 p.m. Saturday night. Daisie told me that Rusty had not been working on Friday and Saturday nights at that particular time, but was told to come in that Friday night, his scheduled night off, due to all of the darkroom work that had to be done. According to Rusty, much of his time was spent in the dark room making copies of the crime scene photographs. After going home Saturday night around 9 p.m., Rusty did not return to work until Sunday night, his next scheduled work night.

It's relatively easy to spot the copy camera's work. The photographs of the backyard poses of Oswald taken by the camera and entered into evidence of the HSCA are cut off at the sides, or cropped. In other words, the copy camera photographs are rectangular with the sides cut off. The original Oswald snapshots made by the Imperial Reflex camera are basically square.

Was there some sinister reason that the photographs that Rusty produced were cropped? Not really, as Rusty explained to me, "The original photograph that I worked with was square, and when it was photographed with the copy camera, it naturally would be square on the new 5"x7" negative. To get a negative that would make a good clear photograph, you tried to focus the camera to where your image would cover as much of the negative as possible."

"Since the photograph was square and the negative was oblong [rectangular], it was necessary that two of the edges had to be left off in order to fill up the other edges of the negative. It was not to try to cover up anything. It was done to get the clearest photograph possible of the main subject, which was Oswald holding the rifle."

Admittedly, their conclusion concerning the origin of the officer's prints was incorrect, but the HSCA experts determined there was not credible evidence to show the backyard photographs were fake. They determined that the background in each of the photographs examined was different and carefully measured areas such as fence posts to note differences in each. Note the movement of the branch over the stairs in the left of each of the two photographs shown on pages 128 and 129.

SOME INDEPENDENT RESEARCHERS BELIEVE, HOWEVER, THAT THE background of all three backyard photographs is the same. A leader in the attempt to prove someone made a concerted effort to frame Oswald by the manufacture of fake photographs is Jack White of Fort Worth, Texas. Jack testified before the HSCA and attempted to prove with prepared overlays and transparencies that the photographs were composite fakes.

Recently Rusty and I made a trip to Texas to visit Jack and let him examine Rusty's photographs. We'd hoped to get feedback from him as to the importance of the copies that Rusty has. After getting acquainted, we settled down in Jack's office, where he then proceeded to show Rusty and me his own copies of all three of the backyard photographs.

After more than twenty-five years of study, Jack has arrived at some very convincing arguments that make most listeners take a strong second look at the three photographs. In order to understand how Jack has arrived at his conclusions, it is necessary to examine his version of the chronology of what he believes took place to develop them.

Jack began by showing us copies he had obtained from the National Archives of the first two backyard photographs originally published by the Warren Commission in 1964 (133-A and 133-B). He then turned to another print of 133-A which surfaced four years following the assassination. The photograph was obviously not studied by the Warren Commission, but was later examined by the HSCA. Known today as the DeMohrenschildt print (133-A DEM), the photograph is the clearest copy known to exist of the first pose. It contains more background than the original snapshots found in Oswald's two seabags.

The DeMohrenschildt print was discovered by George and Jeanne DeMohrenschildt among their personal possessions stored away after they returned to the United States in early 1967. They later claimed that they had never before seen the photo until its discovery. On the rear of the photograph was written in English, "To my friend George from Lee Oswald." Also written, but in Russian Cyrillic script, was the phrase, "Hunter of fascists Ha-ha-ha!" It was dated 5/IV/63.

The DeMohrenschildts had befriended Lee and Marina in Dallas prior to the assassination. The social status of the poor Oswald couple was in stark contrast to the well-off

DeMohrenschildt couple, a seemingly odd relationship. All were versed in the Russian language, however, and used occasional meetings to converse in it.

A close examination of the DeMohrenschildt print reveals more background than any of the other backyard prints existing. It is of such clarity that some of the newsprint is readable on the paper which Oswald is holding in his hand. Jack emphasized the point that he felt a cheap, mass produced plastic camera such as the Imperial Reflex would not capture such fine detail from the distance shown in each photograph, and noted such detail is not found on the snapshots from the Paine garage.

The DeMohrenschildt photograph is surrounded by a black border, indicating a full print made directly from the original negative. This is not the type of print obtained from a drugstore, which crops around the edges of the negative to produce a finished product with a white border. The Oswald snapshots contain the typical type of border which has omitted a small portion of the actual rough edges surrounding the negative to make a more pleasing finished product.

There is no denying, in a comparison between the DeMohrenschildt print and the snapshots of 133-A, that the DeMohrenschildt print is clearer as a full print directly from the original negative. The HSCA experts determined, however, that the DeMohrenschildt print was made by the Imperial Reflex camera given to the FBI. This was done by comparing certain imperfections found along the black border surrounding the print which matched the aperture of the camera. The border lines vary from camera to camera, and produce an identifiable "print" enabling experts to determine if a particular camera made a particular negative.

JACK BELIEVES THAT ALL OF THE BACKYARD PHOTOGRAPHS ARE composite fakes, meaning that someone put together various elements from multiple photographs in order to make one large, possibly 16"x16" sized photograph. Then, using a camera with an excellent lens, a photograph was made of the large composite photograph which may have then been retouched. Jack theorizes that the Imperial Reflex camera may then have been used to make the final copies which would leave a negative aperture traceable to the Oswald camera.

After viewing Jack's backyard photograph prints, we turned our attention to Rusty's copies. Rusty reached inside his old briefcase and pulled out two 5"x7" black and white prints buried deep among the stacks of old photographs. They were the copies he had made himself years before of the two backyard snapshots delivered to the Crime Lab by the Homicide detectives. He also pulled out the 8"x10" enlargement of 133-A (perhaps the one identical to the photograph shown to Oswald).

Jack studied the photographs with a careful eye. He commented that the 5"x7" photograph of 133-C was one of the clearest that he had ever seen. The 5"x7" of 133-A he felt was not as clear as his copy of the DeMohrenschildt print, which he believes is one generation nearer to the original.

I asked Jack about the leaves that appear to have moved over the steps in the left of Rusty's two photographs. He told me that, when the original photograph had been made, the leaves and shadows could have been painted on. Jack believes that the same background was used for all three poses, with the different perspectives achieved by cropping and tilting the background easel during development of the doctored photographs. I'll leave it to the reader to decide whether the backgrounds are alike or different. Other compelling anomalies exist, however, in the subject of the photograph, Oswald.

Jack believes that the body in the photograph is not Oswald, as was originally claimed by the suspect to Captain Fritz. Jack pointed out that the shirt worn in the photograph was not found among Oswald's personal effects. Knowing Oswald was frugal, Jack felt it unlikely that the shirt would have been thrown out. The pullover type shirt also was not the style that Oswald typically wore. A point was also made concerning the watch worn by

Oswald. There are no other known photographs in which Oswald is shown wearing a watch.

Another item recently pointed out by Jack in 133-C dealt with *The Militant,* a communist newspaper, held by Oswald. The actual width of the newspaper is eleven inches. Using the paper as a standard for measurement within the photograph, when projecting the full length of the body from head to heel, Oswald measures only four feet, eleven inches in height. The real Oswald was reported to be five feet, nine inches tall. Jack asserted that when the paper was placed into the photograph, the assembler failed to keep the different elements scaled properly.

Another argument put forth by Jack is that Oswald's head appears to be pasted onto the backyard photographs from the chin up. It was observed that his chin appears square, while in the police mug shot it appears more rounded. As successive generations of the backyard photographs are produced, a line appears to form between the chin and the lower lip.

RECENTLY, A NATIONALLY BROADCAST TELEVISION PROGRAM featured one of Rusty's former coworkers in the Crime Lab, Bobby Brown. The files at the Dallas Police Department are now open to the public, and a photograph of Brown in the Neely Street backyard had been found along with a duplicate photograph of Brown's body silhouette cut out of a duplicate photograph. The logical question was asked of Brown as to why he would do such a thing. The question is only relevant now in hindsight due to speculation of the genuineness of the backyard photographs. Though careful not to state specifically, the show attempted to fuel speculation that Brown may have been in on an attempt to help fake the original Oswald backyard photographs.

Rusty and I visited Bobby after seeing the program in order to find out all that he remembered about the investigation of the Crime Lab. Bobby told us that he arrived at work on Saturday morning, the day following the shooting. He helped in the development of the crime scene photographs, as did everyone else

45. Dallas Police Crime Lab photo taken by a Secret Service agent showing Detective Bobby Brown posing basically the same as Oswald had for reconstruction purposes. The reenactment was done for the Secret Service.

at the time.

Bobby told Rusty and me that a few days after the assassination, Forrest Sorrels of the Secret Service in Dallas called Captain Fritz and told him to get someone from the Crime Lab to go out and photograph the Neely Street backyard. Bobby was the only man from the Crime Lab to go, and was accompanied by Captain Fritz, a couple of Fritz's detectives (one he recalled was Elmer Boyd), and a couple of Secret Service Agents.

Bobby said that the Secret Service wanted a reenactment of the backyard photograph showing Oswald with the rifle to demonstrate where they were made. Bobby stated that he was the youngest one there and was elected to do the posing because no one else wanted to be in the photograph.

Bobby said that Captain Fritz got an old 35 caliber

46. Dallas Police Crime Lab photo taken probably by Bobby Brown of the front of the Neely Street apartment in Dallas, site of the backyard photos.

Remington from his car to use in the recreation. Bobby then had to show one of the other men how to use the 4"x5" Graflex camera and where to stand to keep the photograph in focus. He told us that they used possibly two of the backyard photographs as a reference to pose the reenactment, and several shots were then taken.

Bobby told us that the request to go to Neely Street was handled just like any other routine call. He made a call sheet on it, just as he typically did when the office was asked to do work, detailing who requested it and what the work performed was. He said that no one ever told him not to talk about what he did on the call and that copies were made later and given to the Secret Service as they had requested. Lieutenant Day was not around the office at the time Bobby received the call and did not recall who told him to

139

go to Neely Street.

I asked Bobby very specifically what would possess him to cut out his silhouette from the reenacted photographs. He was adamant to me that he only wanted to take himself out of the photograph since it was the background that was the subject, and not himself. He said that he did this entirely on his own, and that no one told him to do so. He said he cut his image out of a developed photograph and placed a white piece of paper behind it and rephotographed the reenactment.

It is obvious that the silhouette photograph made by Brown was done at the time he stated simply by comparing the growth of the bush in the background to the original Oswald backyard poses, probably taken in March or April of 1963. The reenactment photographs were made in late November or early December of 1963, in the days following the assassination, simply to document the location where the original Oswald photographs were taken.[14] From the beginning, Bobby Brown did not want to be in the reenacted photograph, but was told to do so by a superior. The photographs were made solely to show where the original backyard photographs were taken. Bobby was only doing his job as a Crime Scene Search Section Detective of the Dallas Police Department, and followed orders simply to document where the original backyard photographs were taken.

BY NOW UNDERSTANDING THE ORIGIN OF THE DALLAS POLICE photograph copies of the original backyard photographs, and with the knowledge that only one snapshot negative and probably three snapshot prints made by the Imperial Reflex camera were found in the Paine garage, along with additional facts developed through the years, some conclusions may possibly be drawn. Although it is not really the intention of this book to deal with speculation, but simply to present fact, in a close examination of the evidence, it seems that a pattern did develop.

Oswald ordered the rifle and the revolver from Klein's Sporting Goods Co., of Chicago, Illinois on March 20th, 1963.[15]

After receiving the items in late March or early April, Lee probably had Marina take the backyard poses (along with other family photos), using the Imperial Reflex camera. The snapshots were then developed by a local drugstore, producing the small square snapshot prints. After viewing the prints, Oswald possibly desired to print more copies of the infamous 133-A pose to pass around to his friends.

It was during this time period (October 12th, 1962[16] through April 6th, 1963[17]) that Oswald worked for Jaggers-Chiles-Stoval, a photography firm in Dallas. Keeping in mind that Marina produced a copy of 133-A for *Life* magazine following the assassination, and that George DeMohrenschildt later produced a copy of 133-A in 1967 (which was shown by the HSCA to be a full print from the original negative produced by the Imperial Reflex camera), a plausible explanation for the origin of 133-A emerges.

In the photography firm where he was employed, Oswald himself may have produced multiple copies of 133-A as full prints from the original Imperial Reflex negative. He may have then passed out copies to his friends (e.g. signing the rear of the Demohrenschildt print copy). Marina probably recalled where Lee had stored the copy(ies) and retained one of them, which she later sold. The snapshot negative of 133-A, you will recall, was NOT located in the seabag along with the snapshot print. Oswald may have left the negative in a separate location after making the print copies.

The arguments put forth by those who believe the backyard photographs are fake should be carefully studied and weighed against the conclusion of authenticity drawn by the Warren Commission and the HSCA. With the clarity presented here of 133-A and 133-C, the opportunity to compare exists for all to see and judge for themselves. Please examine for yourself the photographs marked 133-A and 133-C. These are from Rusty's photographs taken directly from the Police Department's 5"x7" copy camera negatives of the backyard photographs, and are quite possibly the clearest prints yet available to the general public.

1. Warren Commission, *Hearings Before the President's Commission on the Assassination of President Kennedy,* 26 vols. (Washington, D.C.: U.S. Government Printing Office, 1964), VII: 229.
2. Ibid., 231.
3. Warren Commission, *Hearings,* IV: 224.
4. Warren Commission, *Hearings,* VII: 231.
5. Ibid., 104.
6. Ibid., 209.
7. House Select Committee on Assassinations (HSCA), *Investigation of the Assassination of President John F. Kennedy,* 12 vols. (Washington, D.C.: U.S. Government Printing Office, 1979), VI: 140.
8. Jim Marrs, *Crossfire* (N.Y.: Carroll & Graf Publishers, Inc., 1989), 452.
9. HSCA, VI: 141.
10. Warren Commission, *Hearings,* IV: 226.
11. Marrs, 451.
12. William R. Manchester, *The Death of a President* (N.Y.: Harper & Row, 1967), 101.
13. HSCA, VI: 143.
14. Former Crime Lab Detective Bobby Brown, taped personal interview, 25 April 1992.
15. Warren Commission, *Report of President's Commission on the Assassination of President John F. Kennedy* (Washington, D.C.: U. S. Government Printing Office, 1964), 118.
16. Ibid., 403.
17. Janet M. Knight, *Three Assassinations* (N.Y.: Facts on File, Inc., 1971), 60.

CHAPTER

VI

The Map

INCLUDED AMONG THE KENNEDY ASSASSINATION EVIDENCE WHICH Rusty possesses is a copy of a map drawn by Dallas Police Crime Lab Detective R. L. Studebaker on Friday, November 22nd, 1963. The map shows the general layout of the sixth-floor crime scene of the Texas School Book Depository Building and notes a number and the direction of photographs taken by Detective Studebaker and Lieutenant Day during the day.

It was fleetingly referred to in Lieutenant Day's testimony before the Warren Commission when he was explaining what he did on that Friday afternoon.[1] After taking the rifle found on the sixth floor back to his Crime Lab Office, Lieutenant Day had returned to the Depository. He told the Commission, "It was around three that I got back, and I was in that building until about six, directing the other officers as to what we needed in the way of photographs and some drawing, and so forth."

The map was also referred to by Detective Studebaker himself in his testimony to the Warren Commission when he was asked by his interrogator, Mr. Ball, "Now, do you have some more pictures to show me?" Mr. Studebaker replied, "Well, I've got a bunch of them. I made this diagram of the whole sixth floor of that building. This isn't the original, and J. B. Hicks and I measured this thing, and I drew the diagram."[2]

The map is significant as an aide in organization of the photographs taken by the Dallas Crime Lab detectives on the sixth floor of the Depository. The Dallas police did an extremely capable

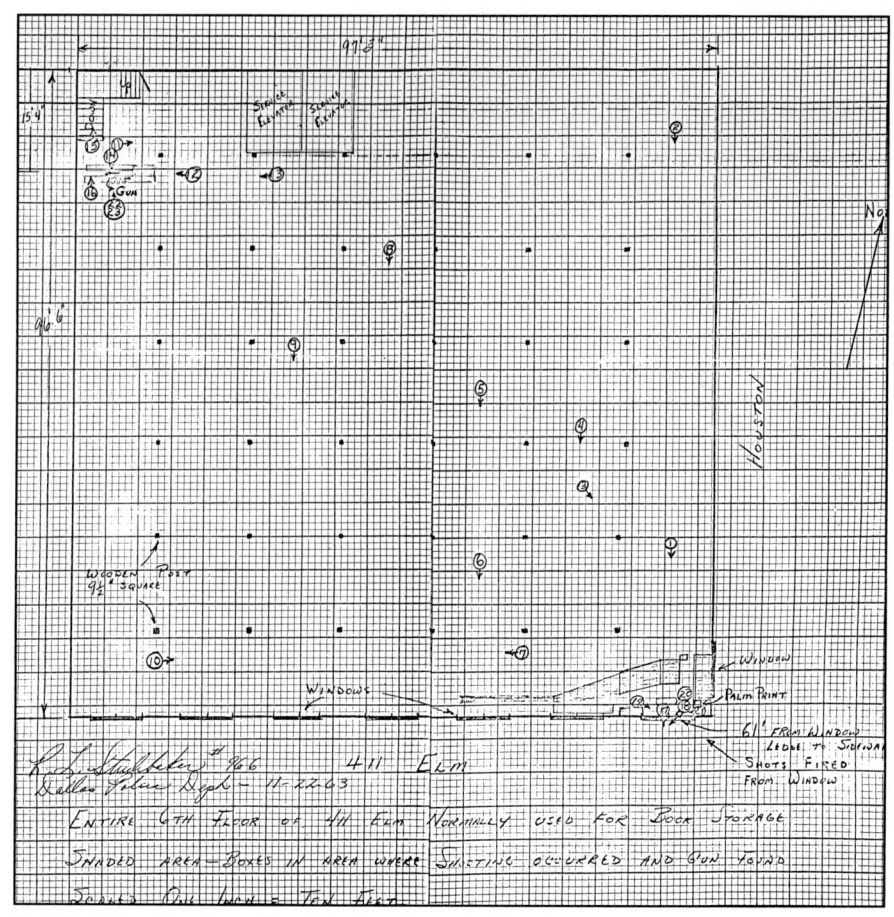

47. Dallas Police Crime Scene Map of the sixth floor of the Texas School Book Depository Building drawn by Detective R. L. Studebaker on November 22nd, 1963.

job of documenting with photographs the crime scene that had just been discovered. Lieutenant Day and Detective Studebaker quickly determined what evidence was relevant to the investigation and gathered an abundance of evidence which would have been used against Oswald if a trial had been held.

Lieutenant Day selected only certain photographs to take with him when he testified to the Warren Commission. Mr. Belin, a Warren Commission questioner, would occasionally refer to the photographs the Dallas police were entering into the Commission's evidence, using the numbers established by Detective Studebaker's map. For example, at one point Belin asks, "Your pictures which have been marked No. 22 and No. 23 [Photo 52 and 53] were both made, one was made by you, is that Commission Exhibit 718--" Lieutenant Day replied, "Yes sir."[3]

Rusty has told me that he and other officers were experienced in testifying in court and that he and others always gave direct and succinct answers to questions posed. They would not expand on the answers given unless asked to do so in order to avoid objections by counselors. It seems obvious in a reading of the officer testimony that expansion on some of the answers was not given. They did, however, tell the Commission all that was asked of them, but the map was not specifically addressed or placed into the exhibits of the Warren Commission.

The numbers represented on the map at first glance appear to represent the order of the photographs taken by Lieutenant Day and Detective Studebaker. This is not the case. Rusty and I asked both men to look at the map again in a recent interview and were told that the photographs were not taken in the numerical order shown on the map. The numbers simply represent a system of organization of the photographs assigned by Detective Studebaker. In fact, it appears that the numbers assigned to the photographs by Detective Studebaker fall into three basic groups which include the sniper's nest area, the area where the rifle was found, and the remaining entire area of the sixth floor.

A CONSIDERABLE AMOUNT OF SPECULATION AND CONSPIRACY charges have been leveled at all of the agencies involved in the investigation of President Kennedy's assassination, including the local Dallas Police Department. Only a partial knowledge of the evidence could tend to lead to such accusations. Hopefully, with a fuller knowledge gained through a viewing of the evidence gathered by the original men on the scene, a clearer judgement can be made.

Although many of the sixth-floor photographs have been

published, this presentation provides an organized format showing the clearest first generation photographs ever before seen. The images were made from the original Dallas police press camera negatives by Rusty at the same time multiple sets were being copied for federal and state agencies. The set copies given out to the various investigators were not typically numbered using the Studebaker map-numbering system. The map was an in-house type of reference system for the Crime Lab detectives. Fortunately for us today, Rusty took the time to number a set for himself of the sixth-floor photos, using Studebaker's map as a guide.

THE ORIGINAL 4" x 5" PRESS CAMERA NEGATIVES OF THE SIXTH-FLOOR photographs made by the detectives were retained by the Dallas Crime Lab. Rusty made a new set of negatives by using the department's copy camera to photograph the original photographs taken on the sixth floor. The second generation negatives were then given to the FBI by the Dallas police. The photograph copies that the FBI gave to the Warren Commission were probably second or third generation photographs produced from the second generation negatives made by the Dallas police copy camera or later generation negatives produced by the FBI themselves. However, at least one first generation set of photograph prints from the original Dallas police negatives probably was given to the FBI along with the new set of second generation negatives.

A casual reading of Lieutenant Day's testimony does not reveal that fact, although with the knowledge of it, a rereading of his testimony proves it. Lieutenant Day was shown Warren Commission Exhibit 514, which had been given to the Commission presumably by the FBI. It was the same photograph that Lieutenant Day had brought with him, which is shown here as DP #22 (Dallas Police Number 22), taken from the original 4"x5" press camera negatives. DP #22 was then entered into the Warren Commission as Exhibit 718.

The Warren Commission interrogator, Mr. Belin, asked Lieutenant Day, "Is Commission Exhibit 718 a print from the same negative as Commission Exhibit 514?"

Day responded, "No, I don't think so. This is a copy of this picture."

Mr. Belin then asks, "You are saying 514 was made, I assume, as a copy of 718. By that you mean a negative, a second negative, was made of 718 from which 514 was taken?"

"Yes, sir," Day tells him. Lieutenant Day had not let his original negatives leave his office and had ordered the new set of negatives made to give to the FBI.

Mr. Belin even stated that "718 appears to be a little clearer and sharper."

Lieutenant Day did not elaborate about the new set of negatives made for the FBI. Most who read the testimony would probably assume that the FBI did the copying, although now it has been shown that Rusty did it with the Department's copy camera. The photographs shown here are first generation photographs from the original Dallas police press camera negatives and are reproduced without any cropping to provide a complete viewing of the evidence.

BEFORE BEGINNING THE SEQUENCE OF CRIME LAB PHOTOGRAPHS, IT would help to examine the movements of the man who discovered the sniper's nest soon after it had been vacated by the shooter. At 12:30 on November 22nd, 1963, Deputy Sheriff Luke Mooney was standing near Dealey Plaza in front of the Sheriff's Office on Main Street as the presidential motorcade went by. After the President had passed, Mooney testified to the Warren Commission[4] that he had turned away and suddenly heard shots being fired. Instantly, he began running across the grass between Main and Elm Streets towards the location where Kennedy received the fatal head shot. He bolted across the street and up the embankment, jumping over the fence into the railroad yards. After milling around with other spectators and policemen for a few seconds, Mooney received orders through another officer that Sheriff Bill Decker had wanted his men to go inspect the Depository Building.

Mooney testified that he, along with two other deputy sheriffs, ran to the rear of the Depository Building and immediately closed two large iron gates, giving an order to a civilian present to keep them shut until another officer could take his place. He then entered the back door of the Depository and immediately took the west freight elevator to the second floor when he experienced a power loss to the elevator. Hurriedly locating the northwest stairs, Mooney began climbing and exited coincidentally at the sixth floor.

After a quick run through the sixth floor with nothing in particular attracting his attention, Mooney headed up to the seventh floor, again using the small northwest corner stairs. There he encountered other officers already searching the floor. He then headed back down the stairs to the sixth floor, meeting a photographer coming up, and began once again to do a search of the area. By chance, Mooney headed directly to the furthermost corner of the ninety foot room on the opposite end of the building.

48. Dallas Police Crime Lab reconstruction photo of the sniper's nest, taken by Day/Studebaker November 25th, 1963.

After squeezing through an area of stacked boxes encircling the southeastern window, he noticed three spent rifle hulls lying on the plank floor. Mooney claimed that he did not disturb the crime scene at all and leaned out of the window by the stacked boxes, calling below to other officers that he had found the location of the sniper.

THE THREE RIFLE HULLS

AT AROUND 1:00, HOMICIDE CAPTAIN WILL FRITZ OF THE DALLAS police arrived at the sixth floor of the Depository from Parkland Hospital under orders of Police Chief Curry.[5] Captain Fritz was accompanied by Homicide Detectives Richard Sims and Elmer Boyd. After participating in a floor by floor search along with a multitude of other officers, a voice called out that rifle hulls had been found on the sixth. Captain Fritz immediately entered the sixth floor and quickly ordered Officers L. D. Montgomery and Marvin Johnson to guard the area found by Mooney in the southeast window.

At approximately the same time, Lieutenant Day received a call from the Police Dispatcher while in the Crime Lab Office on the fourth floor of the Dallas Police Department. He was told to go to 411 Elm Street in Dallas, the Texas School Book Depository Building. He immediately left with Detective R. L. Studebaker and took the Crime Lab's station wagon which was loaded with photographic and fingerprinting equipment. They arrived at the Depository around 1:12 p.m. Police Inspector Sawyer was standing in the front door of the Depository and directed Lieutenant Day and Detective Studebaker to the sixth floor.

After a failed attempt to use the elevator, the two men climbed the stairs to the sixth floor. Upon reaching the head of the stairs, Lieutenant Day stated, "I believe it was the patrolman standing there, I am not sure, stated they had found some hulls over

49. (DP #19) Dallas Police Crime Lab photo taken by Day/Studebaker showing two of the three hulls on the floor.

in the . . . southeast corner of the building." Studebaker told Rusty and me that this was the area photographed first by himself and Lieutenant Day.

In his testimony before the Warren Commission concerning the photographing of the sniper's nest, Lieutenant Day stated, "They [the photographs] had been taken before anything was moved, to the best of my knowledge. I was advised when I got there nothing had been moved."

His questioner, Mr. Belin, then asked, "Who so advised you?"

Lieutenant Day responded, "I believe it was Detective Sims standing there, but I could be wrong about that." DP #19 may have been the first photograph made by the Crime Lab on the sixth floor. It was taken from the west side of the sniper's nest looking east. Only two of the hulls appear in this particular view since a box

50. (DP #20) Dallas Police Crime Lab photo taken by Day/Studebaker showing the three rifle hulls on the floor.

is in the way in the foreground. Both DP #20 and DP #21 were taken from the opposite side looking east to west. All three hulls appear in these two photographs. The three stacked boxes used as a rifle perch appear in the foreground of DP #20 and DP #21. After the hulls were photographed in place, Detective Sims, who had also been apparently guarding the area, picked them up.

Lieutenant Day testified that "I processed these three hulls for fingerprints, using a powder. Mr. Sims picked them up by the ends and handed them to me. I processed each of the three; did not find fingerprints. As I had finished that, Captain Fritz sent word for me to come to the northwest part of the building, the rifle had been found, and he wanted photographs."

Detective Studebaker testified about the same event occurring as the rifle hulls were being photographed. He explained, "Right after these were taken [the hull photographs], they said they

JFK FIRST DAY EVIDENCE

51. (DP #21) Dallas Police Crime Lab photo taken by Day/Studebaker. This is a second photo of the three rifle hulls.

had found a rifle and to bring the cameras over to the northwest corner of the building where the rifle was found, and I loaded everything up and carried it over there."

THE PAPER BAG USED TO CONCEAL THE RIFLE

OFFICERS JOHNSON AND MONTGOMERY HAD BEEN GUARDING THE area around the sniper's nest, keeping away anyone that might disturb the crime scene. As Lieutenant Day and Detective Studebaker began making photographs of the southeast window area, Johnson stated to the Warren Commission that he "stayed closer to that pop bottle while we were waiting for the crime lab to finish their work."[6] The area Johnson spoke of was on the third aisle over from the sniper's window and is shown in DP #7 (Photo 60, p. 170). Johnson testified that Montgomery stayed over "by the corner" at the first set of windows. He also said that nothing had been moved as Lieutenant Day and Detective Studebaker came and took photographs.

When the sniper's nest was first discovered by Mooney, a paper bag approximately 42" long by 8" wide lay folded in the extreme southeast corner of the sixth floor to the left of the window. It was constructed from the same type of wrapping paper and tape used in the shipping department of the Depository. It seemed evident to the investigators that it could have been used to carry in a concealed rifle. Latent prints later identified as Oswald's were found on the bag.[7]

It was later determined that on the morning of the assassination, Oswald had ridden into work with Wesley Frazier, a neighbor of the Paine's. Frazier told Detective Gus Rose in an interview conducted on the night of the assassination that he had met Oswald that morning coming into his yard carrying a long paper bag. The bag was also seen by Frazier's sister as Oswald strolled past her kitchen window.

Frazier stated to Detective Rose that he had asked Oswald what was inside the bag and that Oswald replied to him that it was curtain rods. He asked Oswald when they arrived at work if he wanted to lock the curtain rods in the trunk of the car for the day and that Oswald told him, "No, I'm going to need these today." Oswald then ran ahead of Frazier into the rear of the Depository, carrying the object in the paper bag. Incidentally, the rooming house that Oswald was staying in at the time already had curtains.

Unfortunately, no photograph was taken of the paper bag as it was found on the sixth floor before it was removed by the officers. As Lieutenant Day and Detective Studebaker began taking photographs of the hulls on the floor, the bag probably had not yet been specifically pointed out to them. As they picked up their photographic and fingerprint equipment and moved to the opposite end of the sixth floor to photograph the rifle, an error was made by

155

one of the men guarding the hulls and the paper bag.

Johnson and Montgomery incorrectly assumed that Lieutenant Day and Detective Studebaker had completed taking photographs of the hulls as well as the paper bag in the corner when, in fact, they had only photographed the hulls. Montgomery, probably believing the bag had been photographed, then picked the bag up and examined it. Johnson testified about the bag, stating that "the first I saw of it, L. D. Montgomery, my partner, picked it up off the floor, and it was folded up, and he unfolded it. I was standing there when he picked it up." He later stated that "it appeared to be about the same shape as a rifle case would be. In other words, we made the remark that that is what he probably brought it in. That is why, the reason we saved it."

Montgomery in his testimony to the Commission evidently was aware that he had disturbed evidence at the crime scene. Rusty told me that "we had a heck of a time with some officers picking up things at a crime scene before we had photographs." As Montgomery testified, he was asked if he had picked up the bag in which the rifle had been reportedly brought into the building. He responded with, "Yes."

The questioner responded, "You picked it up?"

Montgomery then said, "Wait just a minute--no. I didn't pick it up. I believe Mr. Studebaker did. We left it laying right there so they could check it for prints."[8]

Actually Montgomery was not entirely at fault. He had assumed that the bag had already been photographed, when in fact it had not. Later, however, the testimony of many officers placed the bag in the corner window when it was originally found. Rusty does not possess any photograph of the bag found in place by the detectives, and it is safe to assume that none was made.

THE 6.5 mm MANNLICHER CARCANO RIFLE

A RIFLE WAS FOUND ON THE SIXTH FLOOR OF THE DEPOSITORY NEAR the northwest corner stairs by Deputy Sheriff Eugene Boone and Deputy Constable Seymour Weitzman as the hulls were being photographed.[9] Deputy Boone called out to Captain Fritz that he found the rifle. He stated that he and Weitzman did not touch the rifle, but guarded it until Captain Fritz came over. Captain Fritz then called for Lieutenant Day to come and photograph it.

A manufactured controversy has evolved through the years concerning the rifle found on the sixth floor. Speculation has been fueled by a non-belief of the real evidence but a quick belief of conspiracy in all areas, mainly as a result of minor discrepancies. The testimony of the men who actually found and saw the rifle is taken out of context and exploited without a complete knowledge of all the facts.

The only rifle found or photographed on the sixth floor (not including the shotguns, rifles, or handguns carried by the multitudes of officers in and around the Depository) was a 6.5 mm Mannlicher Carcano rifle. A story widely circulated was that the rifle found was a Mauser. Once again, an examination of the true facts will explain how the story began as well as why it should be ended.

It has been speculated by believers in a multiple conspiracy that two rifles were on the sixth floor and that some type of switch occurred involving the officers who found the actual rifle which was photographed on the sixth floor. The switch was done, they believe, to substitute the rifle first found with yet another rifle which was then photographed by the Crime Lab in order to frame Oswald for the crime. Let us examine step by step the progress of the officers who found the rifle and what they actually stated about their experience on the sixth floor.

The first evidence to be examined will be a report filed by the Sheriff's Department officer who found the rifle. The report was filed by Officer Eugene Boone, dated Nov. 22, 1963, the day of the assassination. He states to his superior, Sheriff Bill Decker:

> Mr. Decker:
>
> I was assisting in the search of the 6th floor of the Dallas County Book Depository at Elm St. and Houston St. proceeding from the east side of the building. Officer Weitzman DPD and I were together as we approached the Northwest corner of the building. I saw the rifle partially hidden behind a row of books with two (2) other boxes of books against the rifle. The rifle appeared to be a 7.65mm Mauser with a telescope sight on the rifle. Capt. Fritz was called to the scene and also someone from the ID [Bureau.] pictures were taken and then Capt. Fritz picked up the rifle. I first saw the rifle at 1:22 pm date.
>
> E. L. Boone 240 DSO

A second report gave other details concerning Boone's discovery of the rifle:

> I got a battery powered light and went over to the Texas School Book Depository to help with the search of the building. I proceeded to the sixth floor of the building to search for the rifle. I started on the east end of the building and worked my way to the west end of the building. In the northwest corner of the building approximately three (3) feet from the east wall of the stairwell and behind a row of cases of books, I saw the rifle, what appeared to be a 7.65mm Mauser with a telescopic site. The rifle had what appeared to be a brownish, black stock and blue steel, metal parts. Capt. Fritz DPD was called to this location and along with an ID man DPD took charge of the rifle.[10]

Note that Officer Boone stated twice that the rifle

APPEARED to be a 7.65 Mauser, and was PARTIALLY HIDDEN between the boxes. He states that Captain Fritz picked up the rifle and photographs were taken by the ID man, who was Lieutenant Day. Boone did not handle the rifle. The rifle Boone discovered was then photographed on 16mm movie film as Captain Fritz handled it and Lieutenant Day dusted the trigger guard for prints. The tape shows the same 6.5 mm Mannlicher Carcano photographed later in the Identification Bureau by Lieutenant Day. There was only one gun found.

Later, Officer Boone was questioned by the Warren Commission about his statement filed in the Sheriff's Office naming the gun found as a Mauser. He clarifies what actually took place when asked by his interrogator:

> *Mr. Ball: There is one question. Did you hear anybody refer to this rifle as a Mauser that day?*
> *Mr. Boone: Yes I did. And at first, not knowing what it was, I thought it was a 7.65 Mauser.*
> *Mr. Ball: Who referred to it as a Mauser that day?*
> *Mr. Boone: I believe Captain Fritz. He had knelt down there to look at it, and before he removed it, not knowing what it was, he said that is what it looks like. This is when Lieutenant Day, I believe his name is, the ID man was getting ready to photograph it. We were just discussing it back and forth. And he said it looks like a 7.65 Mauser.*[11]

The Mauser episode began entirely as pure speculation by the officers standing around the just discovered rifle before it had been unwedged from between the stacked boxes. The speculation by the men standing around was incorrect, but the rumor was started and perpetuated by news reporters overhearing the officers.

Note that Officer Boone was not privy to the work done by Lieutenant Day in determining that the rifle was a 6.5 mm Mannlicher Carcano before he filed his report on the day of the assassination. But knowing the correct rifle type later in his testimony to the Warren Commission, he explained the Mauser story as purely speculation before the rifle was uncovered from between the boxes. Only later was he informed of the actual type of rifle from the work of the Dallas Police Crime Lab.

Another Officer, Seymour Weitzman, was beside Officer Boone and spotted the rifle almost simultaneously with him. Weitzman told the Warren Commission about the rifle:

> *Mr. Weitzman: It was covered with boxes. It was well protected as far as the naked eye because I would venture to say eight or nine of us stumbled over that gun a couple times before we thoroughly searched the building.*
> *Mr. Ball: Did you touch it?*
> *Mr. Weitzman: No, sir; we made a man-tight barricade until the crime lab came up and removed the gun itself.*
> *Mr. Ball: The crime lab from the Dallas Police Department?*
> *Mr. Weitzman: Yes, sir.*[12]

Once again it was stated by Officer Weitzman that the rifle found was the same one picked up by Captain Fritz and examined by Lieutenant Day of the Dallas Crime Lab.

One more officer witness to the discovery of the gun is included with hesitation. More exploitation has occurred through the years due to the outspoken inaccuracies of Roger Craig than any other. He was, however, present at the time of the discovery of the rifle, and his original testimony under oath to the Warren Commission is included here, with explanation given as to why he is "not to be believed," according to Rusty.

Roger Craig, a Dallas County Deputy Sheriff in 1963, was interviewed by the Warren Commission on April 1, 1963. He explained what he observed as the rifle was found:

Mr. Craig: And as I got nearly to the west end of the building, Officer Boone--Eugene Boone with the sheriff's office--hollered that here was the rifle.
Mr. Belin: How far were you from Officer Boone when he hollered?
Mr. Craig: About 8-foot.
Mr. Belin: What did you do then?
Mr. Craig: I went over to the cluster of boxes where he was standing and looked down between the boxes and saw the rifle lying on the floor.

Craig later stated that he did not handle the gun:

Mr. Craig: Officer Mooney and several of the city officers; Will Fritz came over, Capt. Will Fritz, with the city of Dallas; some of his investigators, I didn't know them; and a criminal identification man, I believe, from the city of Dallas, then came over there to take pictures of the weapon.
Mr. Belin: The weapon was moved by the time the pictures were taken?
Mr. Craig: No; no. The pictures were taken as the weapon was found lying there.

He later stated:

Everybody stayed there, you know, and sort of mingled around and uh, I then went back downstairs after the weapon was picked up. The identification man from the city of Dallas then, after he took his pictures, picked the weapon up and handed it to Will Fritz. And I then went back downstairs and over to the sheriff's office.[13]

Years later in a taped interview, Roger Craig embellished his story with additional remarks concerning the rifle, which he did not talk about under oath and which contradicts all of the other officers' testimony shown here. The story of the Mauser has been shown to be purely speculation by the officers standing around BEFORE the rifle had been removed from between the boxes. Rusty has severe doubts about the statements from Roger Craig that follow:

> Boone looked over into it and said "Here it is. Here's the rifle." So I immediately went over beside him and looked over and there was a rifle. We didn't touch it until Captain Fritz and Lieutenant Day of the Dallas Police Department got there. . . they got there and took some pictures of the rifle. I believe Day pulled the rifle out and handed it to Captain Fritz who held it up by the strap. . . and asked if anyone knew what kind of rifle it was.
> By that time, Deputy Constable Seymour Weitzman had joined us. Weitzman was a gun buff. He had a sporting goods store at one time and he was very good with weapons and he said it looks like a Mauser. And he walked over to Fritz and Captain Fritz was holding the rifle up in the air and I was standing next to Weitzman who was standing next to Fritz. And we were no more than 6 to 8 inches from the rifle and stamped right on the barrel of the rifle was 7.65 Mauser. And that's when Weitzman said, "It is a Mauser," and pointed to the 7.65 Mauser stamp on the barrel."[14]

THIS INTERVIEW WAS CONDUCTED IN 1976, ALMOST 13 YEARS following the assassination. The story related here has changed significantly in many respects from the one told by the other officers as well as the one told by Craig to the Warren Commission back in 1964.
Craig now states that the discussion concerning the rifle

52. (DP #22) Dallas Police Crime Lab photo taken by Day/Studebaker showing the rifle as it was found on the floor.

being a Mauser occurred AFTER the rifle was pulled out. Remember this action is on tape showing Lieutenant Day and Captain Fritz. The gun shown on the tape is the 6.5 mm Mannlicher Carcano. It was not stamped 7.65 Mauser, and Seymour Weitzman never claimed that he READ 7.65 Mauser off of the rifle, only that he speculated that it was a Mauser BEFORE the rifle was unwedged from between the boxes. The most important point Craig could make to the Warren Commission about the rifle found on the sixth floor being stamped 7.65 Mauser on the side seems to have slipped his mind while he was under oath.

One other fact debunking the Mauser myth was brought to light in a recent interview with Detective Studebaker. Rusty and I asked if he ever heard the term *Mauser* used to describe the rifle. Studebaker told us bluntly that he never heard the term *Mauser* used to describe the rifle found on the sixth floor, and he had

53. (DP #23) Dallas Police Crime Lab photo taken by Day/Studebaker showing the rifle. Studebaker's knee appears in the lower right of the photo as he braced himself on boxes above the rifle looking down.

remained on the sixth floor until 1 a.m. the following morning making the map and documenting the crime scene (except for a brief time during the evening when he went back down to the office to develop a few of his photographs and then returned to the Depository).

Detective Studebaker was photographing the hulls at the time the rifle was found. He had made his way across the large room to photograph the rifle in place. He then witnessed Lieutenant Day and Captain Fritz pick up and examine the rifle. Remembering that Studebaker did not hear mention of a Mauser during the entire day, note that this is the point at which Roger Craig stated that Weitzman saw 7.65 Mauser stamped on the rifle as Studebaker stood by. Craig had heard the term *Mauser* speculated only before the rifle was lifted from the boxes from Captain Fritz and Deputy

164

Weitzman, but later exaggerated and confused the issue. He is the principle reason for the perpetuation of a disproved rumor. All of the other men later admitted their error in speculation except for Roger Craig.

DP #22 AND DP #23 (PHOTO 52 AND 53) ARE PHOTOGRAPHS OF THE rifle taken as it was found in between layers of boxes on the northwest corner of the sixth floor near the stairs. The photographs were taken at about 1:25 p.m. according to an inter-office memorandum later written by Lieutenant Day. Detective Studebaker's knee appears in the lower right of photograph DP #23, which was entered into the Warren Commission as Studebaker Exhibit C.

54. (DP #1) Dallas Police Crime Lab photo taken by Day/Studebaker showing the rear of the sniper's nest.

165

JFK FIRST DAY EVIDENCE

THE SIXTH-FLOOR CRIME SCENE PHOTOGRAPHS

THE REMAINING PHOTOGRAPHS OF THE SIXTH FLOOR OF THE Depository present an overview of the roughly 98'x98' room of stacked boxes of school textbooks. A concerted effort was made by Detective Studebaker and Lieutenant Day to document with photographs the entire area. The series begins with DP #1 showing the rear of the sniper's nest, which Deputy Mooney had just discovered.

For the sake of clarity, no officers would appear in the photographs. Only the crime scene evidence, which was undisturbed, was photographed. DP #2 was taken from the same direction, with the photographer having simply backed up all the way across the building along the east wall.

55. (DP #2) Dallas Police Crime Lab photo taken by Day/Studebaker showing the rear of the sniper's nest along the east wall. Oswald may have run down this clear aisle when making his way to the northwest corner stairs.

The positioning of DP #3 on Studebaker's map is slightly off the mark. After careful study of DP #1 and DP #3, however, the viewer can well understand the precise position when the photograph was taken. A minor error on the part of Detective Studebaker seems to be the case here.

In order to achieve the view of the boxes in the window from behind, one stack of boxes has been moved back. Note in viewing DP #1 and DP #3 how only one stack of boxes has been pulled back out of the way to allow a clear view of the sniper's window.

DP #4 was taken on the second aisle over from the sniper's nest. It shows a continuation of the boxes which were stacked as a shield for Oswald in a semi-circular fashion. This would be the second set of arched windows on the south side of the Depository Building.

56. (DP #3) Dallas Police Crime Lab photo taken by Day/Studebaker showing a row of boxes removed to reveal the sniper's window beyond.

JFK FIRST DAY EVIDENCE

57. (DP #4) Dallas Police Crime Lab photo taken by Day/Studebaker showing the second aisle from the east wall.

58. (DP # 5) Dallas Police Crime Lab photo taken by Day/Studebaker showing the third aisle from the east wall.

59. (DP #6) Dallas Police Crime Lab photo taken by Day/Studebaker showing a Dr. Pepper bottle and a paper lunch sack. This is the third aisle over from the east wall. The sack is on the floor between the 2 stacked boxes in the center of the photo and the push cart.

DP #5 and DP #6 are photographs taken on the third aisle over from the sniper's nest. A Dr. Pepper bottle, along with a small lunch sack with leftover chicken bones and Fritos, was found in this area. Lieutenant Day checked the bottle for prints and found none. He also questioned a Depository employee on November 25th named Bonnie Ray Williams. Williams told Lieutenant Day that he had eaten lunch in that location on the previous Friday. Lieutenant Day, therefore, discounted this particular evidence as having been associated with Oswald.[15]

DP #7 is another view of the Dr. Pepper bottle taken from a different angle looking west. The arched windows running along the Elm Street side of the building are to the photographer's left.

DP #8 was taken of the fourth aisle over from the sniper's nest looking south towards the arched windows on Elm Street. DP #9 is looking down the fifth and sixth aisles of the Depository in the same direction as DP #8.

JFK FIRST DAY EVIDENCE

60. (DP #7) Dallas Police Crime Lab photo taken by Day/Studebaker showing another view of the cart and bottle.

61. (DP #8) Dallas Police Crime Lab photo taken by Day/Studebaker showing the fourth aisle over from the east wall.

THE MAP

62. (DP #9) Dallas Police Crime Lab photo taken by Day/Studebaker showing the fifth aisle over from the east wall.

DP #10 is a view looking eastward along the south wall of the Depository. It clearly shows the plywood which had just begun to be laid a few days before over the wood subfloor of the sixth floor. A point of controversy here has developed over the years concerning the laying of this new floor.

IT HAS BEEN PUT FORTH BY SOME THAT SINCE THIS WORK WAS BEING done on the sixth floor, other workers could have handled the boxes (including Oswald) and arbitrarily stacked boxes in the southeast corner which inadvertently formed the semi-circular pattern around the sniper's nest window. DP #10 clearly shows the work was just beginning on the westernmost side of the Depository. The sniper's nest was in the far corner on the opposite end of the building in this photograph. Taking into account the weight of just one box of books, it is doubtful that any worker would have carried stacks of boxes to the far end of the building and then carried them all the way back across the building in order to lay the new floor. The

171

63. (DP #10) Dallas Police Crime Lab photo taken by Day/Studebaker showing the north wall along Elm Street.

argument that other workers may have stacked the boxes to form the sniper's nest during the process of laying a new floor rings shallow when a practical approach to movement of the boxes as the work was being done is offered.

By examination of DP #10, an assumption can be made as to how the floor was laid on the sixth floor. Beginning on the west side of the building, the boxes could have been moved over one aisle, clearing a path upon which the first row of plywood was laid end to end. After completing a row or two of new plywood, the boxes were probably then stacked back onto the new plywood floor, creating an open area upon which the next row of plywood was to be laid. It was probably this point at which the workers broke for lunch to view the motorcade. It also seems highly improbable that anyone would want to carry book boxes 90 feet across a room and then bring them back 90 feet in order to lay the plywood flooring.

It is somewhat doubtful that anyone other than Oswald would have been working to stack boxes in the southeast corner window on that particular day. Workers would not likely have been on that end of the building stacking boxes when work had commenced on the opposite end.

Oswald did, however, work on the sixth floor regularly and would have left fingerprints on many boxes in the area over a period of time. But, according to Rusty, who actually processed some of the prints on the boxes which had been brought back to the Crime Lab Office, Oswald's were the FRESHEST prints on the boxes. According to Rusty, Oswald was the last person to touch them. Rusty explained that, "When you have a print on paper, the oils from your skin over time cause the ridges of the print on the paper to spread out. Oswald's prints that I found were fresh prints with good ridge detail. His were the freshest prints on the boxes."

Having Oswald as the last person to handle the boxes stacked to form a visual barricade is certainly a condemning fact. If someone else had stacked the boxes for the sniper's nest, their prints would have shown up as the freshest prints and would have been seen by Rusty and others who dusted the boxes for prints (unless of course they were wearing gloves). Additional prints were also found of various officers who handled the boxes in processing them as evidence. Rusty was himself fingerprinted by the FBI later to omit his fingerprints found on the boxes.

AFTER TAKING DP #10, LIEUTENANT DAY AND DETECTIVE Studebaker made their way back to the area of the staircase and elevator area at the north side of the sixth floor. Here a series of photographs were taken around the location where the rifle had been discovered. This includes DP #12, DP #14, and DP #16. A study of the map showing the photograph locations and direction helps the viewer to understand the proximity of the rifle location to the stairs used for Oswald's quick exit of the sixth floor.

DP #11 is a photograph looking east towards the freight

64. (DP #11) Dallas Police Crime Lab photo taken by Day/Studebaker showing one of the large freight elevators.

65. (DP #12) Dallas Police Crime Lab photo taken by Day/Studebaker showing an overview of the rifle location.

THE MAP

66. (DP #13) Dallas Police Crime Lab photo taken by Day/Studebaker showing the west wall of the sixth floor.

elevator used by the employees to transport book cartons between floors while filling orders. The photographer made DP #12 by turning to his rear and backing up a few steps looking westward. The photograph shows the sign for the stairway which Oswald used to make his way to the second-floor lunchroom where he was seen entering approximately 90 seconds after the shots occurred.

In DP # 13, notice that in the left of the photograph appears the cart upon which rests the plywood which was being laid. The workers had started work on the westernmost wall of the sixth floor. DP #14 was taken looking south and immediately behind the location of the rifle, which at this point had probably been found.

DP #15 is a photograph looking down the stairs which were located in the northwest corner of the Depository. This is where the detectives had entered the sixth floor and where Oswald had exited after firing his rifle. DP #16 shows the same general area of the stairs with the photographer once again simply backing up for a wider view of the area.

175

67. (DP #14) Dallas Police Crime Lab photo taken by Day/Studebaker showing the rear of the rifle location.

68. (DP #15) Dallas Police Crime Lab photo taken by Day/Studebaker showing the northwest corner stairs down.

69. (DP #16) Dallas Police Crime Lab photo taken by Day/Studebaker showing a wider view of the stairwell.

DP #17 was taken back in the window used by the sniper. It shows the view as seen by the sniper looking down Houston Street, which is where the President's motorcade approached before turning left onto Elm Street. No shots were reported fired before the President's vehicle made the turn onto Elm.

DP #18 is the exact view as seen by Oswald looking towards the motorcade at the moment shots were fired. It was obvious to the detectives that the boxes had been stacked in the window as a gun perch for the sniper. In fact, Detective Studebaker pointed out to the Warren Commission an area on the top of the stack of three boxes in the window marked by an indention which he strongly felt was made as the rifle rested on it. (See Photo 72.) The indentation is concave, and measures about one inch wide, about four inches long, and about one-eighth inch deep. Note that the trigger guard of the rifle shown on page 78 is rounded on the front, which would create such an impression as the shooter moved the rifle left to right along the box (which was still full of books), applying pressure.

177

JFK FIRST DAY EVIDENCE

70. (DP #17) Dallas Police Crime Lab photo taken by Day/Studebaker showing the sniper's view of Houston Street.

71. (DP #18) Dallas Police Crime Lab photo taken by Day/Studebaker showing the sniper's view down Elm Street.

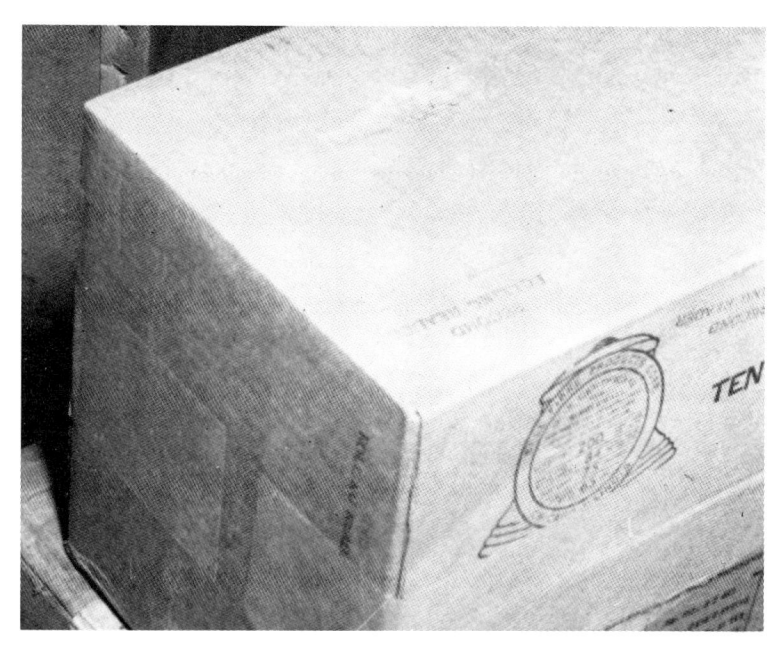

72. Closeup view of Dallas Police Crime Lab photo by Day/Studebaker on November 25th, 1963, showing an indentation made as the rifle was moved along the top of the box.

IT WAS THE INTENT OF LIEUTENANT DAY AND DETECTIVE Studebaker to photograph the entire sixth-floor area including the cramped sniper's nest window area. The hulls were first photographed on the floor, and later, the view as seen by the sniper was photographed. The three stacked boxes in the window were moved around in order to achieve the clearest view in each photograph.

On the afternoon of the assassination, Lieutenant Day and Detective Studebaker dusted the three stacked boxes in the sniper's nest window for prints at the scene. They also dusted a box lying to the left of the window and found a partial palm print where it was speculated that Oswald sat prior to the shooting. A 6"x6" portion of the box lid containing the palm print was at that time torn off and brought back to the Crime Lab Office, leaving the box in its original position on the sixth floor. The other three boxes were also left where they were found by the window.

JFK FIRST DAY EVIDENCE

73. Dallas Police Crime Lab photo taken by Day/Studebaker on November 25th, 1963 showing the box Oswald sat on. A palm print was developed on the left edge of the box.

According to statements found in Warren Commission Exhibit 3131, Captain Doughty (Lieutenant Day's superior in the Identification Bureau) "advised on August 31, 1964, that the four cardboard boxes, which were recovered from the sixth floor of the Texas School Book Depository by Lieutenant J. Carl Day and Detective R. L. Studebaker, were brought to the Dallas Police Crime Laboratory on the morning of November 25, 1963." Captain Doughty stated he had made a survey of his department, and the following individuals had handled these boxes: Captain Doughty, Lieutenant Day, Detective R. W. (Rusty) Livingston, and Detective Studebaker.

RUSTY TOLD ME THAT HE HELPED TO PROCESS THE BOXES IN THE Crime Lab Office after they had been brought down on the Monday

73A. Dallas Police Crime Lab photo taken by Day/Studebaker. This particular photo may have been taken immediately before the boxes were rearranged to reflect the reconstruction photos on Monday, November 25th, 1963. Lt. Day stated that the boxes had been positioned by newsmen during the weekend for photos and, in fact, this arrangement was published in news photos showing the sniper's nest.

following the assassination. This is confirmed in the Warren Commission Exhibit which was an interview conducted by FBI Agents James Bookhout and Vincent Drain. It states that Rusty "stated the only time he handled the four cardboard boxes found at the crime scene at the Texas School Book Depository Building, which were believed to have been used by Lee Harvey Oswald in his shooting of President Kennedy on November 22, 1963, was at the Dallas Police Department." Rusty told me that he did develop some prints on the boxes using silver nitrate and determined that they were Oswald's.

The boxes in the sniper's nest were photographed by newsmen on the day after the assassination according to statements from Detective Studebaker and Lieutenant Day. Detective

Studebaker stated in Exhibit 3131 that "on Saturday, November 23, 1963, newsmen were all over the building and particularly on the sixth floor photographing and generally looking for and examining anything that might have been related to the shooting of President Kennedy and Governor Connally." He also stated that on November 24th, 1963 (Sunday), he was again at the Texas School Book Depository and observed dozens of newsmen in the building. Lieutenant Day stated the same thing and added that he saw "many empty film pack cartons near where the boxes were located, and the boxes had been re-arranged, apparently for the purpose of taking photographs."

In a recent interview with Lieutenant Day, he told Rusty and me that, "We took a lot of pictures of the gun and the hulls and other stuff. That was all done on the Friday afternoon, because this stuff had been moved all around when we got back up there Sunday. I had a key to it [the Depository Building], and I didn't know they were going to let anybody in the building. But they had somebody in there shooting a bunch of pictures, and stuff had been moved around Sunday morning. But our purpose then was drawings more than anything else. It wasn't taking pictures."

According to the Warren Commission testimony of Lieutenant Day, Commission Exhibit 733 (Photo 78) and Commission Exhibit 734 (Photo 79) were taken on Monday, November 25th. The photographs depict the sniper's nest area as discovered first by the officers. The boxes are seen in the foreground of DP #19. The top box was resting with one edge on the window sill at a slightly downward angle. This matches perfectly with the widely seen photograph taken at the moment of the shooting in front of the Depository by a newsman riding in the motorcade.

THE SIXTH-FLOOR PHOTOGRAPHS ARE ONLY A SMALL PART OF THE evidence which Rusty possesses. The remainder of *JFK First Day Evidence* will deal with every piece of photographic and photocopied evidence collected by Rusty, no matter how insignificant. Much of it has been seen, though not with as much clarity, and some has not been seen. The explanations offered here will hopefully dispel many of the charges leveled by so many people over the years. The investigation by the Dallas Police Crime Lab detectives was intruded upon by the FBI before it was completed. What you have just read concerning the work of the men who were there first will hopefully give a clearer focus of the true evidence documented on the sixth floor of the Texas School Book Depository Building.

1. Warren Commission, *Hearings Before the President's Commission on the Assassination of President Kennedy,* 26 vols. (Washington, D.C.: U.S. Government Printing Office, 1964), IV: 264.
2. Warren Commission, *Hearings,* VII: 146.
3. Warren Commission, *Hearings,* IV: 257.
4. Warren Commission, *Hearings,* III: 281.
5. Warren Commission, *Hearings,* IV: 204.
6. Warren Commission, *Hearings,* VII: 102.
7. Jesse Curry, *JFK Assassination File,* Limited Collectors Edition (Dallas, TX: American Poster & Publishing Co., 1969), 94.
8. Warren Commission, *Hearings,* VII: 98.
9. Ibid., 105-109. Also Warren Commission, *Hearings,* XIX: Decker Exhibit 5323.
10. Warren Commission, *Hearings,* XIX: Decker Exhibit 5323.
11. Warren Commission, *Hearings,* III: 295.
12. Warren Commission, *Hearings,* VII: 107.
13. Warren Commission, *Hearings,* VI: 269.
14. *Two Men In Dallas,* videotape, prod. Tapeworm Distributors, 1987.
15. Warren Commission, *Hearings,* IV: 278.

CHAPTER

VII

The Memorandum

THE MEMORANDUM

74. Photograph of former Crime Lab Lieutenant John Carl Day.

LIEUTENANT JOHN CARL DAY, RUSTY'S CRIME LAB BOSS, WROTE A memorandum to Chief of Police Jesse Curry and Deputy of Police G. L. Lumpkin detailing his entire investigation of the shooting of President John F. Kennedy. He made seven or eight carbon copies of it and signed each one personally as shown here in Photo 75 and Photo 76. A copy of the document appears in the Warren Commission as Exhibit 3145. Most of the evidence presented in this book is mentioned in the memorandum, including the map drawn by Detective R. L. Studebaker on November 22nd, 1963. (See preceding chapter.)

187

January 8, 1964

Mr. J. E. Curry
Chief of Police

Subject: Crime Scene Search Investigation of
the Shooting of President John F.
Kennedy on Offense #F-89055

Sir:

At 1:12 p.m., November 22, 1963, Lieutenant J. C. Day, #591 and Detective R. L. Studebaker, #986 arrived at 411 Elm Street in response to a call from the Police Dispatcher. Detectives J. B. Hicks, #441 and H. R. Williams, #777 arrived about 3:00 p.m. to assist in the investigation of the shooting of President John F. Kennedy on Offense #F-89055.

Lieutenant Day and Detective Studebaker on arrival were directed to the sixth floor of the Texas School Book Depository Building. Three spent rifle shells had been found in the southeast corner of the building.

Photographs were taken of the three hulls as found. They were checked for prints, marked for identification and released to Detective R. M. Sims, #629 of the Homicide Bureau. The hulls were 6.5 caliber and no legible prints were found.

About 1:25 p.m., Captain J. W. Fritz, #9 directed Lieutenant Day to the northwest portion of the sixth floor where a rifle had been found between some cartons near the stairs. Photographs were taken of the rifle as found, then it was picked up by Lieutenant Day in such a way as to destroy no fingerprints that might be present. With Lieutenant Day holding the gun, Captain Fritz opened the bolt and a live shell fell from the barrel. This shell was in position to fire should the trigger be pulled. The live shell was checked for prints, marked for identification and released to Captain Fritz. No fingerprints were found.

The rifle, a 6.5 caliber, made in Italy in 1940, Serial #C2766, was taken by Lieutenant Day to the Identification Bureau about 2:00 p.m. and locked in an evidence box until further checking could be done. Agent Odum, Dallas office of the Federal Bureau of Investigation, drove Lieutenant Day to the City Hall. The rifle had no manufacturer's name and had a telescope sight mounted on it which was marked as follows: 4 x 18 coated Ordinance Optics, Inc., Hollywood, California. There was a small cloverleaf design with "OSC" stamped inside the cloverleaf.

Lieutenant Day returned to 411 Elm Street about 2:45 p.m. and continued the investigation with other Crime Scene Search officers.

75. Photograph of a carbon copy of page 1 of the original memorandum written by Lt. J. C. Day detailing his actions in the assassination investigation.

Crime Scene Search Investigation of
the Shooting of President John F.
Kennedy on Offense #F88056
Page 2
January 8, 1964

About fifty (50) photographs were made of the area involved in the shooting and a scale drawing was made of the sixth floor by Detectives J. B. Hicks and R. L. Studebaker.

The cartons in the area where the rifle was found, and also the cartons near the window where the spent hulls were found, were dusted for prints. A palm print was found on the top northwest corner of a carton that appeared to have been used by the assassin to sit on while aiming the rifle. This palm print was collected and preserved, along with the carton it came off, and three cartons stacked by the window apparently to rest the rifle on. The palm print lifted off the carton Oswald apparently sat on by the sixth floor window was positively identified before being released to the Federal Bureau of Investigation as the right palm of Lee Harvey Oswald.

Lieutenant Day returned to the Identification Bureau about 7:00 p.m. and started checking the rifle for prints. Two fingerprints were found on the side of the rifle near the trigger and magazine housing and a palm print was found on the underside of the gun barrel near the end of the stock. It appeared probable these prints were from the right palm and fingers of Lee Harvey Oswald, but the rifle was released to the Federal Bureau of Investigation to be sent to Washington, D. C. before the examination was completed and positive identification of the prints could be made. The prints were not very good for comparison purposes.

Paraffin casts were made of Oswald's hands and the right side of his face about 9:00 p.m., November 22, 1963, in the Homicide Bureau office by Sergeant W. E. Barnes, #756 and Detective J. B. Hicks. Those casts were sent to DCCCIL November 23, 1963 for nitrate tests.

All other evidence collected by the Crime Scene Search was released at 11:45 p.m., November 22, 1963 to Agent Vince Drain to be delivered to the Federal Bureau of Identification headquarters at Washington, D. C.

Respectfully submitted,

JCD:mol:fb

J. C. Day, #391
Lieutenant of Police
Identification Bureau

76. Photograph of a carbon copy of page 2 of the original memorandum written by Lt. J. C. Day.

The narrative is a total summation of the Crime Lab's activities concerning the Kennedy investigation, including conclusions drawn by Lieutenant Day and others. The date of the memo is January 8th, 1964, approximately one and a half months following the assassination.

Studebaker told us that, at the time of the assassination, he had only been a detective with the Crime Lab for a few months and still was "a little green." He said at the time he felt that he was just an old "hey-boy," meaning that everyone would tell him what to do by hollering "Hey-boy!" He also expressed to us that he had the feeling that he got elected to do a lot of the work on the sixth floor because he was the new kid on the block. He was in good hands, however, working directly under the supervision of the veteran Crime Lab man, Lieutenant Day.

Lieutenant Day and Detective R. L. Studebaker arrived at the Depository around 1:12 p.m. that Friday afternoon, about forty-two minutes following the shooting. At the beginning of the memorandum, Lieutenant Day mentions that three spent hulls had been found. He does not mention the time that the hulls were found, only that "three spent rifle shells had been found in the southeast corner of the building." He does, however, mention the time the rifle was found: "About 1:25 p.m., Captain J. W. Fritz, #9, directed Lieutenant Day to the northwest portion of the sixth floor where a rifle had been found between some cartons near the stairs."

Rusty told me that "Lieutenant Day always told us to take two pictures of crime scene evidence every time so that if one didn't come out, we'd have a backup." This seems to be the case during that day since Lieutenant Day states that "About fifty (50) photographs were made of the area involved in the shooting, and a scaled drawing was made of the sixth floor by Detectives J. B. Hicks and R. L. Studebaker."

Although about fifty photographs were taken, only twenty-three were noted on the map. The detectives probably picked the best of each two photographs to represent each number designated on the map. Also keep in mind that the press camera that was used would accept two slides at a time, helping to keep the photographs organized in sets of two.

Outlining the progress of events in the memo, Lieutenant Day first states that "Photographs were taken of the three hulls found. They were checked for prints, marked for identification and released to Detective R. M. Sims, #629 of the Homicide Bureau. The hulls were 6.5 caliber and no legible prints were found." This correlates with the progression of the photographs taken beginning with DP #19 through DP #21 on Studebaker's map.

Detective Studebaker stated in his testimony to the Warren Commission that "they said they had found a rifle and to bring the cameras over to the northwest corner of the building where the rifle was found, and I loaded everything up and carried it over there." This occurred as the hulls were being photographed. (See p. 153-154.)

Studebaker was then asked by his interrogator, Mr. Ball, "Did you take a picture of that," referring to the rifle.

Detective Studebaker responded, "Yes sir; on these, Lieutenant Day also took pictures of those, and he also took pictures of this gun. We took two shots apiece."[1]

The four photographs taken at this point appear on the map as DP #22 and DP #23. (See p. 163 and 164.) The best photograph of each set of two was entered into the map as one photograph. Knowing this fact helps in understanding Detective Studebaker as he continued his testimony when he was asked by Mr. Ball, "You have handed me a picture now that I will have marked as 'Exhibit C' and it is your No. 22. That is a picture taken by you of the location of the gun; that was before anyone moved it?" Detective Studebaker replied, "Yes."

Ball then asked, "Do you have another shot of that other picture?"

Detective Studebaker told him, "No, [but] we took two from the same location when we was up on top of the stack of boxes shooting down at it, before they picked it up. Actually, there was four negatives of them of the gun, but they are all in the same

191

location, shooting straight down and they were taken on different exposures." Detective Studebaker here tells us that four photographs were taken, yet only two are represented on the map that he drew.

Rusty told me that "We kept the file in a long cardboard box locked up in our evidence room in the Crime Lab Office. The Kennedy file had all our documents and photographs and so forth in it, which were kept locked up in the evidence room in our Crime Lab Office."

Lieutenant Day determined at the scene that no prints could be found on the stock of the rifle. He picked up the gun, and after looking over the knob at the end of the bolt-action mechanism, determined that no print was on the knob. Captain Fritz then ejected one remaining live round from the rifle, using only the small knob. When it was found, the rifle had been in a position to fire by simply pulling the trigger. Lieutenant Day told Captain Fritz that he needed to take the rifle down to his office in order to do a more thorough job of checking it for prints.

After taking the rifle back to his office and locking it in the Crime Lab evidence room, Lieutenant Day returned to the Depository Building around 2:45 p.m. At this time, the boxes in the sniper's nest were being dusted for prints. Day states that "the cartons in the area where the rifle was found, and also the cartons near the window where the spent hulls were found, were dusted for prints."

LIEUTENANT DAY STATED THAT AT NO TIME DID HE MAKE ANY statements to the press concerning the rifle. This would include the time on the night of the assassination that the well-publicized photographs and films were made of him carrying the gun over his head down the crowded third-floor hallway at the Police Department.

At that time, Lieutenant Day had been asked by Captain Fritz to bring the gun down from the fourth-floor Crime Lab Office to the third-floor Homicide Office. This was done to allow Oswald's wife, Marina, an opportunity to identify the rifle as having belonged to her husband. Lieutenant Day carried the rifle high overhead so that no one could touch it since he had just covered the entire weapon with fingerprint powder. He held the rifle high in the air, but not to parade the murder weapon for the press to see, as was widely reported. He was holding the rifle by the strap high overhead so that no one would touch the weapon and possibly destroy any fingerprints still undeveloped.[2]

The rifle is positively identified in the memorandum as being "a 6.5 caliber, made in Italy in 1940, Serial #C2766." Day states that "the rifle had no manufacturer's name and had a telescope sight mounted on it which was marked as follows: 4x18 coated Ordinance Optics, Inc., Hollywood, California. There was a small cloverleaf design with 'OSC' stamped inside the cloverleaf."

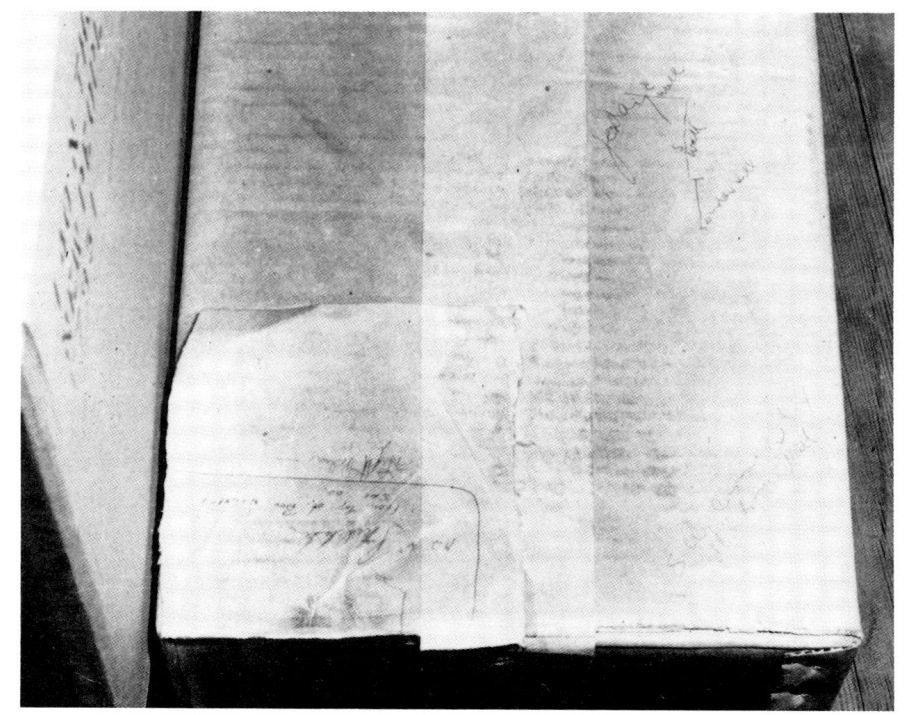

77. Closeup of Dallas Police Crime Lab reconstruction photo taken by Day/Studebaker on Monday, November 25th, 1963, showing the box used by Oswald to sit on while waiting for the motorcade. A palm print was developed on the top edge of the torn off portion of the box, which was replaced for the reconstruction.

Lieutenant Day stated that "A palm print was found on the top northwest corner of a carton that appeared to have been used by the assassin to sit on while aiming the rifle." Lieutenant Day told Rusty and me that the palm print on the box in the corner that Oswald sat on meant a lot to him at the time he was searching for prints. He said that he tore the portion off the box that contained the palm print and brought it back with him to the Crime Lab Office. They later returned to the scene on the following Monday, November 25th, and photographed the scene as a reenactment with the torn portion of the box replaced, which is evident in Photo 77. The three boxes upon which the shooter rested his weapon were placed back in the approximate position which had been photographed by the Crime Lab detectives.

LIEUTENANT DAY WAS ASKED ABOUT WARREN COMMISSION EXHIBIT 733 (Photo 78) and Exhibit 734 (Photo 79). The reenacted photographs show the boxes stacked as they were found at the crime scene. Day told the Commission, "This is the southeast corner of the sixth floor at the window where the shooting apparently occurred. The boxes in front of the window, to the best of our knowledge, [are] in the position they were in when we arrived there on November 22, 1963."

He is then asked by his questioner, Mr. Belin, "So 733 represents a reconstruction in that sense, is that correct?"

Lieutenant Day replied, "Yes sir. . . This, by the way, was taken on November 25, 1963."[3]

Lieutenant Day is then asked by Belin, "I want to turn for the moment to 729. I notice that the box on 729 appears to have a portion of it torn off and then replaced again. Is this correct or not?"

Lieutenant Day tells him, "Yes Sir," and later adds, "After I returned to the sixth floor of the Texas School Book Depository after delivering the gun to my office, we processed the boxes in that area, in the area of the window where the shooting apparently occurred, with powder. This particular box was processed and a palm print, a legible palm print, developed on the northwest corner

78. Dallas Police Crime Lab photo taken by Day/Studebaker on November 25th, 1963, showing a reconstruction of the sniper's nest (Warren Commission Exhibit 733).

79. Dallas Police Crime Lab photo taken by Day/Studebaker on November 25th, 1963, showing a wider view of the reconstructed sniper's nest (Warren Commission Exhibit 734).

of the box, on the top of the box as it was sitting on the floor. I placed a piece of transparent tape, ordinary Scotch tape, which we use for fingerprint work, over the developed palm print. I tore the cardboard from the box that contained the palm print."

Lieutenant Day continued, "Later that night [before the FBI had seized his evidence] when I had a chance to get palm prints from Lee Harvey Oswald, I made a comparison with the palm print off of the box, your 729, and determined that the palm print on the box was made by the right palm of Lee Harvey Oswald." Rusty remembers seeing the palm print on the piece of cardboard on the night of the assassination. In comparing it himself, he also determined that it was the palm print of Oswald.

Lieutenant Day, according to the memorandum, collected "three cartons stacked by the window apparently to rest the rifle on." This was done on Monday, November 25th, 1963, according to an FBI interview conducted later of Lieutenant Day. Rusty recalled processing the boxes and told me that he compared the prints that he found on the boxes with Oswald's and that they matched. Also on the night of the assassination, Rusty saw the palm print that Lieutenant Day had found on the underside of the barrel of the rifle found earlier in the day and concurred that the palm print was Oswald's. The latent fingerprints found on the trigger housing of the rifle which Lieutenant Day had photographed would require more study, since they were only faint, partial prints. (See Chapter IV.)

This sequence of events was also covered in the memorandum to Chief Curry by Lieutenant Day. He states that "two fingerprints were found on the side of the rifle near the trigger and magazine housing, and a palm print was found on the underside of the gun barrel near the end of the stock. It appeared probably these prints were from the right palm and fingers of Lee Harvey Oswald, but the rifle was released to the Federal Bureau of Investigation to be sent to Washington, D.C., before the examination was completed and positive identification of the prints could be made. The prints were not very good for comparison purposes" (the fingerprints on the trigger housing).

ALL THE EVIDENCE GATHERED BY THE DALLAS DETECTIVES HAS since been examined meticulously, with any minor discrepancy exploited by critics to the point of becoming sinister. The last item covered by Lieutenant Day's memorandum involves the paraffin casts made of Oswald in the office of Captain Fritz the night of the assassination.

Paraffin casts are made when a person has been suspected of firing a pistol or revolver and will detect nitrate residue left on the subject's hands. Lieutenant Day stated in the memorandum that "Paraffin casts were made of Oswald's hands and the right side of his face about 9:00 p.m., November 22, 1963, in the Homicide Bureau Office by Sergeant W. E. Barnes, #598, and Detective J. B. Hicks. These casts were sent to DCCIL [Dallas City County Criminal Investigation Laboratory] November 23, 1963 for nitrate tests." The casts were usually done in the Crime Lab, but an exception was made in order not to have Oswald shuttled back and forth in the hallways more than was necessary.

Detective R. L. Studebaker had come back to the fourth-floor Crime Lab Office to develop some of his negatives right before the men had gone down to the third floor to do the paraffin casts. He told Rusty and me that he also went down to the third-floor office and witnessed the procedure done to Oswald.

As Pete Barnes was administering the paraffin to Oswald, he told us that Oswald did make a few comments. He said Oswald told him after he had set up his equipment for the test, "I know why you are doing this."

Pete then asked him in his typical, right to the point style, "Why?"

Oswald replied, "You want to find out if I fired a gun."

Pete said he told him, "You're probably right."

The paraffin casts were made of Oswald's hands and right cheek before he was fingerprinted. Taking prints before administering the paraffin test would have affected the results of the paraffin test, according to Pete. Before leaving the Homicide

197

80. Photograph taken of Detective W. E. (Pete) Barnes in the third-floor hallway by the Homicide Bureau. Barnes is holding the palm print card he has just made of Lee Harvey Oswald.

Office, Detective Barnes made a palm print of Oswald on a large card which he then carried back with him to the fourth-floor Crime Lab Office.

On his way back to the Crime Lab, Pete once again passed through the crowd of reporters. His photograph was taken with him holding the inked palm print of Oswald. (See Photo 80.) As the reporters saw him pass, they shouted out questions. Pete told Rusty and me that he didn't answer them about what he was doing. He said, when he got back to the fourth-floor office, Lieutenant Day was still working on the rifle. The palm print card was then used for comparison with the palm print lifted from the rifle by Lieutenant Day, and the two were a match.

Pete Barnes told Rusty and me that he could make a better paraffin cast than most of his buddies and shared his secret with us.

He said that "the other detectives didn't get the paraffin hot enough" and that they were "afraid that they would burn him [the suspect]." Pete said with a grin that he, "didn't mind if it burned the bad guys a little in order to get a good cast."

The paraffin test on the hands of Oswald came back positive, but the test on the side of the face was negative. According to Lieutenant Day, the negative result of the test done on the side of Oswald's face did not necessarily mean that he had not fired a rifle. Lieutenant Day explained about the face test to the Warren Commission.

He stated that "had it not been for the particular type of case and this particular situation here--we would not have [done the paraffin test] at this time. It was just something that was done to actually keep from someone saying later on, 'Why didn't you do it?' Actually, in my experience shooting a rifle with a telescopic sight, there would be no chance for nitrates to get way back or on the side of the face from a rifle. I would not be surprised if there would be no nitrates from a man firing a rifle."[4] Lieutenant Day's precaution may have ultimately backfired since much was made of the negative result on the cheek later by critics.

The positive result of the paraffin test done on Oswald's hands was another matter. According to witnesses, the alleged shooting of Officer J. D. Tippit was done by Oswald with a hand gun. Oswald had a revolver with him when he was eventually arrested. The test confirmed nitrates on his hands, which would be consistent with having recently discharged a handgun. However, nitrate residue also is detectable from urine that could be on a subject's hands, which could also produce a positive result.

THE LAST ITEM MENTIONED IN THE MEMORANDUM TOLD OF AN event witnessed by Rusty and others in the Crime Lab Office on the night of the assassination. Day states, "All other evidence collected by the Crime Scene Search was released at 11:45 p.m., November 22, 1963 to Agent Vince Drain to be delivered to the Federal Bureau of Identification headquarters at Washington, D.C."

Rusty pointed out to me that this was a minor misstatement on Lieutenant Day's part. The only piece of evidence released to the FBI on November 22nd was the rifle. At the time the memorandum was written, however, all of the remaining evidence, including the palm print (which ultimately reached the FBI in Washington on November 29th), had been released to the FBI. Lieutenant Day's retention of the palm print that he had lifted from the rifle was done with the belief that traces of the palm print were still visible on the rifle. He felt at the time that the FBI would be able to get a lift as he had done already and, therefore, kept the palm print that he had lifted so that he could make a comparison for identification.

Lieutenant Day's job was largely over at that point in time. His gathering of evidence at the scene and brief possession of it developed a tremendously incriminating case against only one subject, Lee Harvey Oswald. When the FBI intervened and seized all of the developed evidence, the work of the Dallas Police Crime Scene Search Section basically was over.

As the chain of evidence is traced today, the photographic and documentary evidence possessed by Rusty gives a clear and firsthand look at the original evidence before it passed into the hands of others. After reading the testimony of many of the Dallas officers, I believe that *JFK First Day Evidence* will aide in organization of the bits and pieces of the heretofore known evidence with the new evidence shown here. The thorough job done by the Dallas police officers appears obvious in consideration of the impossibly short time they had to work on the assassination evidence.

IT IS MY PURPOSE HERE ONLY TO TRY TO PRESENT THE FIRST DAY evidence that Rusty possesses along with his firsthand testimony in order to help lay some speculation to rest. The conclusions that I draw are based strictly on the evidence which was presented to me by someone who was there at the time and quietly observed what was happening around him.

Rusty was well liked by the other officers on the force, and from personal experience of knowing him my entire life, I can testify to the fact that he is an extremely truthful individual. If he does not believe what he is saying is the whole truth, he qualifies his answer. All of the things that he has related to me after many taped hours of conversation eventually were proven true to me through other means of verification by research. I trust what he tells me to be absolutely true, at least to the best of his 28-year-old recollection.

Rusty related to me the work he did that Friday night after arriving for his late shift in the Crime Lab. "Instructions were left to me by Lieutenant Day to print several copies of the negatives of evidence photographs that were taken, which I did in the darkroom. I printed several copies of them because it seemed like the FBI, the Secret Service, the Governor's Office, the State Police, President Johnson, everybody wanted a copy of them. It seems like I made about forty-something sets of them. I spent the night mostly doing that in between other calls that were answered, routine calls."

Here was one of the men behind the scenes doing the copy work in the Crime Lab. He was never interviewed by the Warren Commission or the House Select Committee, though he was intimately involved in the processing of the evidence the first night following the assassination. Some of Rusty's co-workers likewise were never interviewed by the Warren Commission or the HSCA, including H. R. Williams and Bobby Brown.

Rusty made himself a reference copy of the photographs he developed and also took the time to number a set using Studebaker's map as a guide. (See Chapter VI.) He made a copy of the backyard photos 133-A and 133-C plus copies of a series of photographs of the sixth-floor crime scene. He made a copy of Oswald's possessions which were photographed in the Crime Lab Office. These he has retained since the time of the assassination.

Why did Rusty remain in the background? Remember that his boss, Lieutenant Day, was not happy with having been ordered by his superiors to turn over the evidence that he had collected to the FBI (which he did do the first night). Lieutenant Day did things by the book, and was very particular about what went on in his crime lab. While Rusty and others did the busy work, Lieutenant Day took the responsibility for his men. There was no reason to bring up Rusty's name to the Warren Commission (although he was mentioned by W. E. "Pete" Barnes in his testimony to the Warren Commission in Volume VII on page 277 as having worked in the Crime Lab that day).

TO HELP IN UNDERSTANDING THE DEDICATION AND DETERMINATION of Lieutenant Day, Rusty had once related to me, "When I first started working in the Crime Lab, I was working days. We'd got a call to go down near the city market, which was about five blocks south of city hall. There at the market across the street they had a bunch of old shotgun houses. They found a body in one of those old empty houses down there, and it had been there a couple of weeks, I guess, and it was really smelling. It had swollen up and burst in fact."

"Lieutenant Day was a real stickler for fingerprints. That's what most of his career had been, with the Identification Bureau in charge of the Crime Lab. He liked to keep the records straight. Anytime anybody was murdered or killed accidentally we had to fingerprint them so we could run them through the files and check to see if they had a record. If they did have a record, we would clear with the FBI that they were deceased, and we would take them out of the files."

"In this particular case, this ol' boy was really rotten. Lieutenant Day went out on the call with me, and he decided that we wanted that man fingerprinted. I tried to argue him out of it because he was stinking, and I said, 'Why don't you wait until they take him up to the morgue and put him in that cooler for a while and then he won't smell so bad?'"

"Naw," he said. "I'll fingerprint him."

"I walked in there with him, and he tried to roll a set of prints on him, and he got hold of one finger and tried to ink it, and the finger was so rotten that the bone came out of the end."

"It makes me kind of sick to think about it now. But you get used to that, so you can stand it to a certain extent. I always had a pretty strong stomach. I never really got sick."

He continued, "The Lieutenant always wanted us to fingerprint a victim at the scene. I always preferred waiting until they took him out to the morgue and did an autopsy on him. They'd have him in the cooler out there, and then he didn't smell so bad."

Again, Lieutenant Day was a man who did things by the book. His insistence that the victim be fingerprinted at the scene before being moved even with an atrocious odor to contend with, is an excellent example of his dedication to his job.

Lieutenant Day did not like his evidence being taken from him the night of November 22nd, 1963. He had collected it and was puzzled as to why the FBI would intervene as they did in a case where he had jurisdiction. He didn't have time to conduct a complete examination of the evidence. If he had been left alone to work with the evidence collected with no interference by the FBI to take it away the first day, many of the later charges of "cover-up" might have been thwarted. The reason for this intrusion was unknown to the guys in the Dallas Crime Lab. At the least, the decision of the FBI to take charge of the investigation being conducted by the Dallas police demonstrated a desire for their total control over all of the evidence gathered in the assassination.

1. Warren Commission, *Hearings Before the President's Commission on the Assassination of President Kennedy,* 26 vols. (Washington, D.C.: U. S. Government Printing Office, 1964), VII: 140.
2. Former Crime Lab Lt. John Carl Day, taped personal interview, 18 December 1991.
3. Warren Commission, *Hearings,* IV: 269.
4. Ibid., 276.

CHAPTER

VIII

The Spy Camera

THE SPY CAMERA

ONE CONTROVERSIAL PIECE OF NEW EVIDENCE THAT RUSTY possesses is a photograph of part of the items collected by the Dallas police from the Paine residence on November 22nd, 1963. (See Photo 81.) The photograph does not appear in the Warren Commission Volumes. The reason for the apparent omission is due to the Pandora's box which might have been opened if the public became aware that Lee Harvey Oswald possessed a small German-made Minox spy camera.

The FBI went to a concerted effort to hide the fact that Oswald possessed a spy camera. One of the officers that conducted two searches of the Paine home, Gus Rose, stated that he found the small Minox camera with film in it inside one of Oswald's seabags during one of the searches following the assassination. He told Rusty and me in an interview that "We probably got everything that belonged to Oswald."

All of the items recovered from the Paine residence were brought back to the Department, examined, and then marked by the detectives. A list was compiled of each item. After the accounting was complete, the inventory was locked in a closet in the Homicide Office.[1]

The FBI eventually took possession of all the evidence that the Dallas police had collected. Before the FBI did so, however, photographs were made by the Dallas police of the evidence. Fortunately, one of the photographs Rusty has of a portion of the evidence is the one which happens to show the Minox spy camera

JFK FIRST DAY EVIDENCE

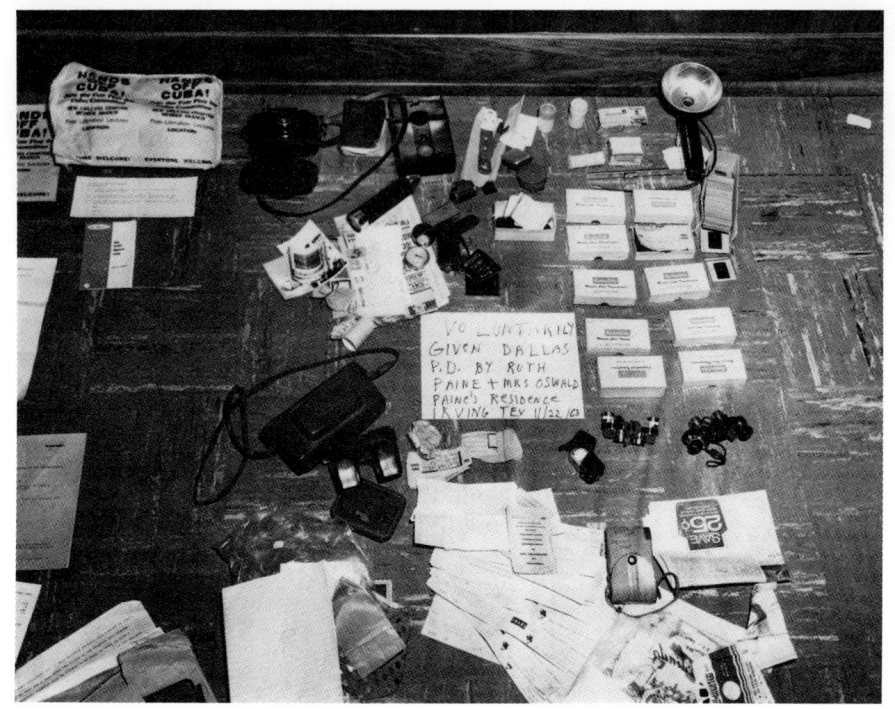

81. Dallas Police Crime Lab photo showing some of the belongings of Oswald. Several photos were taken of many items laid out on the basement property-room floor before they were released to the FBI. In the center of the photo is the small Minox camera located on top of the open camera case. The chain on the side was used to judge distance from the item to be photographed.

that the FBI almost successfully manipulated into oblivion.

According to Gus Rose, the photographs of the evidence were made in the property room of the Dallas police before being released to the FBI. Other photographs of the evidence were shown in Chief Curry's *JFK Assassination File,* which was released after the Warren Commission had completed its investigation. Rusty's photograph was not contained in the book. It is possible that the FBI seized all of the other copies and the negative of the print from the Dallas police, not being aware that Rusty had made one for himself while doing the Crime Lab's photographic work.

REPORTER EARL GOLZ DETAILED THE EVENTS SURROUNDING THE missing camera in *The Dallas Morning News* on August 7, 1978. At

208

THE SPY CAMERA

82. A blowup of the Minox camera shown in Photo 81. Although hard to detect, it seems that the word MINOX vaguely appears in the upper left on the camera case.

the time of the report, a photograph of the camera was not known to exist. The FBI stated that they did not believe that Oswald had possessed such a camera. The fact that Rusty has a photograph of the camera is more proof of at best incompetence in the handling of such an important piece of evidence that could aid researchers in attempting to reach further truth about this mysterious individual.

Many assassination researchers have speculated for years that Oswald may have been some type of low-level government agent. The fact that he possessed a spy camera with photographs of individuals behind wire fences might tend to lead some to the same conclusion. Oswald's wife, Marina, recently stated in an article appearing in *The Ladies Home Journal* in November, 1988, that "Now, looking back at his character, I can see that he had certain traits of professional training, like being secretive, and I believe he

83. Dallas Police Crime Lab photo showing more of the belongings of Oswald on the property-room floor.

worked for the American Government."

She continued, "He was taught the Russian language when he was in the military. Do you think that is usual, that an ordinary soldier is taught Russian? Also, he got in and out of Russia quite easily, and he got me out quite easily. How did this happen?" She believes that Lee kept secrets from her by saying that "Perhaps he told me so little because he was trying to protect me."

The evidence born out of Oswald's possession of the spy camera shown in Rusty's photograph might one day link Oswald to some governmental agency. With the FBI so intently and immediately concerned with the photograph of the spy camera being found and with such a past effort to cover up the fact, intense speculation will certainly continue by critics.

Of course, omitting the photograph from evidence was not the only simple act that the FBI did in order to make the camera go away. According to the Golz article, the FBI "tried unsuccessfully to pressure police into changing their inventory list to read a Minox light meter, not a camera." A light meter also appears in the photograph along with the spy camera.

THE FBI AGENT WHO HAD CUSTODY OF THE OSWALD PROPERTY WHEN the camera with film disappeared was Warren De Brueys. De Brueys was quoted as saying to Dallas reporter Golz that "I can state without any reservation that there was no collusion, no effort not to disclose anything. Nothing purposely, to my knowledge, was done to conceal anything. That would be the farthest thing from our minds at that time." But he added that there were "limitations as to what I can say. I've signed the secrecy agreement before leaving the bureau." De Brueys also stated that he could not remember whether a Minox camera was in Oswald's possessions.

The FBI agent continued, "There were quite a number of articles. I guess I spent all night cataloging those things and I at the moment can't remember that particular item, frankly."

Reporter Golz contacted the man that back in 1963 was in charge of distribution for the Minox Corporation in New York City, Kurt Lohn. Lohn told him the specifics of the spy camera produced by his company, beginning in the late 1930's. He said it was used extensively during World War II as a "spy camera." He explained that the camera was "about three inches long and an inch wide." Also, Lohn informed Golz that a camera of this type would contain a six-digit serial number. The FBI inadvertently listed a five-digit serial number for the "Paine's" camera.

Another article written by Golz appeared in *The Dallas Morning News* on June 15th, 1978, carrying the banner, "Oswald camera disappeared during FBI investigation." The article states that Dallas Police Detective Gus Rose told investigators with the House Select Committee on Assassinations that he did find the small camera.

THE FBI AT THE TIME TRIED TO PRESSURE ROSE INTO CHANGING HIS testimony from finding a Minox camera to a Minox light meter. Rose would not do so. In order to satisfy reporters' questions, who had gotten word about the FBI attempting to alter the police inventory list, the Bureau simply placed into their records two months later that the Minox camera found was not Oswald's. The FBI fabricated the story that the Bureau obtained a Minox III camera from Ruth Paine on January 31st, 1964. Ruth Paine did not recall that event ever happening. She said that she recalled no search of her home following the initial two-day search by the Dallas police.

I spoke to Gus Rose concerning the camera. He told me that he did find the small camera. He told me that "the FBI came back three times trying to convince me and Captain Fritz that what I had found was a light meter. Captain Fritz told them on the third visit not to come to him again about the camera." Fritz stood behind his man and today is vindicated through Rusty's photograph. Gus stood with the truth, Fritz stood by his man, and both were eventually proven correct!

After I told Gus about Rusty's photograph, he seemed pleasantly surprised. He told me that he had initialed the camera and asked if his initials were visible in the photograph. I told him I'd take a look. Although hard to see in a blowup of the photograph, an area does appear to have been marked by a dark pen. Later on, Rusty and I showed the photograph to Gus, and he stated that it appeared to be the camera that he found and initialed. He said that "There was film still in it, and we examined it and looked at it and noted that there was film still in it. But after that, I never saw it again after we put it in the property room."

DETECTIVE ROSE MADE ONE INTERESTING POINT TO ME ABOUT AN incident involving Oswald earlier in 1963. On the evening of April 10th, only four days after being fired from his photography job, Oswald attempted to kill Major General Edwin A. Walker, a right-wing conservative. Walker told the Dallas police that he was sitting at his desk filling out his income tax form. When he dropped a piece of paper and bent down to pick it up, a shot came through the window, hitting the wall right above his head. He said he immediately got on the floor.

Bobby Brown was the Crime Lab man investigating the incident.[2] He said that the police had Walker sit back in his chair to line up where the bullet was fired from. It appeared to come from behind a small picket fence in an alleyway. Bobby told Rusty and me that he collected the bullet and took it back to the station.

After the assassination, investigators found a note written by Oswald concerning the Walker shooting. Marina had mentioned that Lee had said something about it, and so the bullet from the Walker shooting was retrieved from the evidence room and tested for a match to the Oswald rifle found on the sixth floor. A definite match was not achieved, but a high possibility existed for the bullet to have been fired from the same gun. The slug was determined to be 6.5 mm, the same caliber as the Oswald rifle.[3]

DETECTIVE ROSE DOES NOT BELIEVE THAT OSWALD HAD ANY intelligence connections simply because he possessed the spy camera. He told us that "the political spectrum between General Walker and President Kennedy was vast. They were on complete opposite ends from one another. The guy that tries to kill Walker is not the same kind of guy that tries to kill the President." He felt that Oswald was a "radical, radical." He told us "he didn't smoke or drink and he didn't do drugs; he wasn't that kind." Rose read some of Oswald's writings and told us that they were outlandish.

Richard Stovall, the Dallas policeman who assisted in the search of the Paine residence, helped compile the inventory of the property taken. One of the items on that list is a "small German camera and black case on chain and film."[4] The description fits the small camera shown in Rusty's photograph exactly (although of course no film can be seen in the camera).

De Brueys was not the only FBI agent involved in the effort to make the camera disappear. According to Golz, Robert Gemberling, an FBI agent who wrote the first report submitted to the Warren Commission, was contacted in 1978 and asked about the FBI report concerning the camera obtained from the Paines. He stood by his fifteen-year-old report by commenting, "If that's what the report says, I feel sure that's true."

The agent-in-charge of the Dallas FBI office during the assassination investigation was J. Gordon Shanklin. He claimed that he could not recall the camera incident. However, an inventory list was made in his Dallas FBI office on November 26th, 1963, of the evidence obtained from the Dallas police. It listed "one Minox camera" under item number 375, which was witnessed by De Brueys himself as well as Dallas Police Captain J. M. English of the Property Bureau.[5]

However, upon arrival in Washington, a SECOND inventory list was made by De Brueys and another agent, Vince Drain. Item number 375 at that point became a "Minox light meter." Still included among the evidence were two rolls of "apparently exposed" and two rolls of undeveloped Minox film, supporting the fact that there must have been a camera to take the photographs. Remember, the FBI agents "could not recall" the camera at all.

Also shown in the photograph are two pair of small binoculars, a stereo camera, a stereo viewer, as well as numerous slides and photographs. Jack White, a researcher in Fort Worth, commented after seeing the photograph that it "seemed strange to him that Oswald would possess such an abundance of photographic equipment since he was portrayed as such a frugal individual." That is, of course, unless the items were stolen, or supplied to him by someone else.

RECENTLY, A COPY OF THE SPY CAMERA PHOTOGRAPH WAS SHOWN to Michael Paine by the PBS Television show *Frontline*. Paine was the man whose garage was used to store the meager possessions of Marina and Lee Oswald.

Paine stated to the interviewer that the Minox camera was actually his and that much of the other photographic equipment appearing in the Dallas police photograph also belonged to him, not

Oswald.

Paine stated that following the assassination, the FBI returned much of the photographic equipment to him, including the spy camera. He added that about five years after the assassination, most of the items were then stolen along with all his photographs from that era.

Under the Freedom of Information Act, investigators have obtained copies of the Minox photographs stated to have been in the camera at the time it was found in the Paine garage. The photographs tend to corroborate Paine's claim of ownership of the camera, since he was in the locations shown in the photographs.

However, the fact remains that the FBI attempted to conceal the existence of the camera, and then suddenly returned it to Michael Paine. (One wonders how they knew it was his. Was it not listed as Oswald's camera?) This seems to have escaped the knowledge of the FBI agents questioned in the 1970's, since they claimed ignorance even to the existence of the Minox camera.

As has been stated earlier, the evidence which Rusty possesses has remained with him from the day of the assassination. It has not been tampered with and has remained untouched by anyone other that Rusty and his immediate family. Rusty was not aware of the significance of what he possessed simply because he had never seriously studied all the aspects of the assassination. He was just working the night shift in the Crime Lab and kept a copy of the evidence in the case, not realizing that one day it would become one of the most direct links to the originally developed evidence.

Such a sensational find as the photograph of the Minox spy camera found in Lee Harvey Oswald's seabag makes one wonder, at the very least, why the FBI wanted to make it disappear. But the most compelling question to arise out of the evidence is--why did the FBI tell the Dallas police the camera did not exist, and then later KNOW the camera belonged to Michael Paine, and return it?

1. Former Homicide Detective Gus Rose, taped personal interview, 16 February 1993.
2. Former Crime Lab Detective Bobby Brown, taped personal interview, 25 April 1992.
3. Warren Commission, *Report of President's Commission on the Assassination of President John F. Kennedy* (Washington, D.C.: U.S. Government Printing Office, 1964), 18.
4. Warren Commission, *Hearings Before the President's Commission on the Assassination of President Kennedy,* 26 vols. (Washington D.C.: U.S. Government Printing Office, 1964), XXIV: 349.
5. Ibid., 340.

CHAPTER

IX

Jack Ruby

THE SECOND MAJOR TRAGEDY THRUSTING THE DALLAS POLICE Department into the national spotlight occurred on November 24th, 1963, two days following the assassination of President Kennedy. Lee Harvey Oswald was shot and killed by Jack Ruby, a small time night club owner in Dallas. The shooting occurred in the basement parking garage area of the Police Department during the transfer of Oswald from the City Jail to the County Jail, a standard procedure for someone charged with a felony. (See Photo 84 which shows an officer in the position of Oswald at the time he was shot.)

The crime scene in the basement was photographed by H. R. Williams at about 4 p.m. Sunday, November 24th.[1] He told Rusty and me that a man was placed on the ramp to keep traffic out while the photographs were taken.

Although the transfer was carried out as a highly visible public event, it was done with what was thought to have been thorough security precautions. Avoiding police detection, however, Ruby slipped unnoticed into a crowd of reporters and television cameramen gathered to witness the transfer. The observers were positioned by a railing directly across an access ramp separating the basement Jail Office from the parking garage (Photo 85). The ramp ran down from Main Street (Photo 86) through the basement (Photo 87) and back up to Commerce Street (Photo 88). Ruby knew his way around the Police Department Building, having been there before, dealing with eight previous arrests mainly concerning his night clubs.[2]

The activities of Ruby during the weekend of the

84. Dallas Police Crime Lab photo taken by H. R. Williams showing an officer in the place where Oswald was shot.

85. Dallas Police Crime Lab photo taken by H. R. Williams showing the railing in front of a parked car which reporters were supposed to stay behind.

86. Dallas Police Crime Lab photo taken by H. R. Williams looking down the Main Street ramp.

assassination have been extremely well documented. At 12:30 p.m. on Friday, November 22nd, Ruby was in the offices of a Dallas newspaper composing weekend advertisements for his Carousel and Vegas nightclubs.³ Immediately after the shooting occurred, calls began pouring in from advertisers about closing their businesses out of respect for the slain President. Ruby may have been thinking along the same lines as he left and quickly drove in his car to Parkland Hospital.

Ruby always seemed to enjoy being around where the action was. He was possibly seen at Parkland Hospital, according to Seth Kantor, a news reporter covering the President.⁴ Ruby had asked Kantor whether he thought he (Ruby) should shut his clubs down that weekend or not. Kantor advised him that it sounded like a good idea. At that point Ruby headed back to his car and went to the Carousel Club, where he gave orders to his errand boy, Andrew Armstrong, Jr., to begin notifying his employees that he intended to close down for the weekend.

87. Dallas Police Crime Lab photo taken by H. R. Williams showing the middle of the parking entrance/exit ramp.

Kantor, in his book *Who Was Jack Ruby?*, later speculated that he did not believe that Ruby had gone to Parkland Hospital in order to plant the "magic bullet" (the Warren Commission's prime exhibit supporting their conclusion of Oswald as the lone assassin). The nearly intact bullet was found by Darrell Tomlinson, the hospital's chief engineer, on an empty stretcher left in a hallway by hospital personnel.[5] Tomlinson stated that he did not know for certain if the stretcher which the bullet came from was the one used to transport Connally earlier.

Concerning a conspiracy involving Ruby planting a bullet at Parkland, Kantor reasoned, "in order for that to have happened, there would have had to be a sort of central assassination command post, where the impact of the shots fired into the President's car could be quickly analyzed, with orders relayed then for a messenger to head straight to Parkland with a slightly damaged bullet, which

88. Dallas Police Crime Lab photo taken by H. R. Williams looking up the Commerce Street exit ramp.

could be matched to the rifle that could be traced to Oswald."

Kantor continued his scenario by stating, "That kind of thing would have been questionable even on the TV series *Mission: Impossible*. But had there been such a push-button conspiracy, it would have been too smooth to have selected Jack Ruby--with his propensity for reckless driving, his craving for publicity and his mood swings--for the role of messenger on that job. No. He went to Parkland because of his own compulsions to go."

RUBY ATTENDED THE PRESS CONFERENCE OF OSWALD HELD BY police on the night of the assassination in the basement assembly room of the Police Department. At that time, Ruby was masquerading as a reporter and stood on a table at the back of the room. It has been speculated that Ruby may have known Oswald prior to the assassination, and the possibility existed for recognition of Ruby by Oswald.

Beverly Oliver, a night club dancer in the early sixties, today claims that she was introduced by Ruby to "my good friend Lee" in his club two weeks before the assassination. She said the man called Lee was recognized by her after the President's death as Lee Harvey Oswald. Oliver did not tell her story of the chance meeting until recently, saying that she didn't want to meet the same fate of others who she believed had been murdered to keep silent. Her story is the same as a dancer Ruby had imported from New Orleans named "Jada."

Jada claimed soon after the assassination that she had recognized Oswald as a man she had seen before in the club with Ruby. She died shortly thereafter.

One other interesting fact which may help support a Ruby-Oswald connection surfaced during the news conference. District Attorney Henry Wade was giving background on Oswald following Oswald's departure from the room. He told reporters that Oswald belonged to the Free Cuba Committee. Jack Ruby spoke up at this point, correcting Wade by stating, "Henry, that's the Fair Play for Cuba Committee."[6] Did Ruby have prior knowledge of Oswald's background?

It is interesting that Ruby did not move on Oswald at the time, which may have been the first encounter of the two following the death of the President (although there are some officers who saw Ruby around the Department earlier in the evening of the assassination).

H. R. WILLIAMS RECALLED SEEING RUBY TWICE ON THE WEEKEND OF the assassination at the Department. He told Rusty and me that he saw him on Friday night, the day of the assassination, visiting someone in jail. The visitor area was located two doors down from the Crime Lab Office. He stated that he also saw Ruby when he accompanied Lieutenant Day down to the third floor with the rifle. He said that he remembered Ruby coming to the fourth-floor jail to visit people he "assumed were his employees picked up on one thing or another." He said that he didn't see Ruby again after he shot Oswald.

Ruby's involvement in the assassination appears to many to have begun only after Oswald was captured by the Dallas police. Ruby may even have made a call to the police warning them of an impending attack on Oswald during the transfer.

On November 24th at around two o'clock in the morning, Billy Grammer was the Communications Officer on duty in the Dallas Police Building. He stated that he received an anonymous caller who detailed the transfer plans to him, down to the decoy vehicle. Grammer stated that the man knew him and called him by name and told him, "You're going to have to make some other plans or WE are going to kill him." Grammer thought he recognized the voice of the caller, but could not put a face to it. He made out the report to the Chief before leaving and went home to bed. The next day Grammer was awakened by his wife and told that Oswald had been murdered by Jack Ruby. It was at that time, in horror, that Grammer put the face of Jack Ruby with the familiar voice he'd heard the night before.[7]

RUSTY HAD KNOWN JACK RUBY AND HAD BEEN INSIDE RUBY'S CLUBS before. Earlier in his career as a patrolman, one of Ruby's clubs had been located on Rusty's beat. At that time he had thought of Ruby as "just a thug." Rusty said Ruby never did have a bouncer in his night clubs. Ruby took care of his own problem patrons with a set of brass knuckles. Rusty laughs off the notion of Ruby's reason for murdering Oswald as having been out of concern for Mrs. Kennedy.

Ruby in later years passed a note claiming that the Kennedy motivation had been a defense proposed to him by his first attorney, Tom Howard.[8] Coincidentally or not, Howard was standing near Ruby and witnessed the shooting of Oswald. Rusty told me that Tom Howard was known to "hit the bottle frequently."

ACCORDING TO RUBY HIMSELF, THE TIMING OF THE SHOOTING COULD

not have been better. At 11:17 a.m. he had just been to a Western Union Office located only 350 feet from the top of the Main Street ramp which leads down into the Police Department parking garage. This would have been only four minutes prior to the shooting, which occurred at 11:21 a.m. After leaving the Western Union Office, Ruby claimed to have entered the Main Street ramp passing Officer Roy Vaughn, who had stepped out to allow a car to exit. Vaughn vehemently denied through the years that Ruby passed by his location at the head of the ramp.

However, according to Seth Kantor in his book *The Ruby Cover-up,* Ruby may have taken another route down to the basement parking garage via an unguarded public stairway. The stairs had been used immediately before the shooting by reporters in a race down from the third floor to cover the basement transfer. This might well have been Ruby's entry point from Main Street into the first-floor public lobby adjacent to the parking garage. Since Ruby had wandered about the Police Department Building at will during the entire weekend posing as a reporter, it stands to reason that he might not have stood out and been noticed by police to have his presence challenged.

Most of the speculation concerning the actual route taken by Ruby today ultimately leads down an empty road. Ruby may have slipped by the officer on the ramp unnoticed. However, no one was ever able to show that anyone in the Dallas Police Department knowingly allowed Ruby entrance to the parking basement. If Ruby was allowed to enter the parking basement by a member of the Department, it may have simply been due to recognition by an officer of a known individual who was not seen as a threat. It is also unlikely that any officer would admit to an error in judgment which unintentionally led to Oswald's death.

TELEVISION CAMERAS HAD BEEN SET UP BEHIND THE RAILING SEEN in Photo 89, which shows one of the white bars of the railing across the center of the photograph. Photo 90 gives a wider perspective than Photo 89, and has a car parked in the area where the television

89. Dallas Police Crime Lab photo taken by H. R. Williams showing the view behind the railing as seen by reporters.

90. Dallas Police Crime Lab photo taken by H. R. Williams showing a wider view of the railing area.

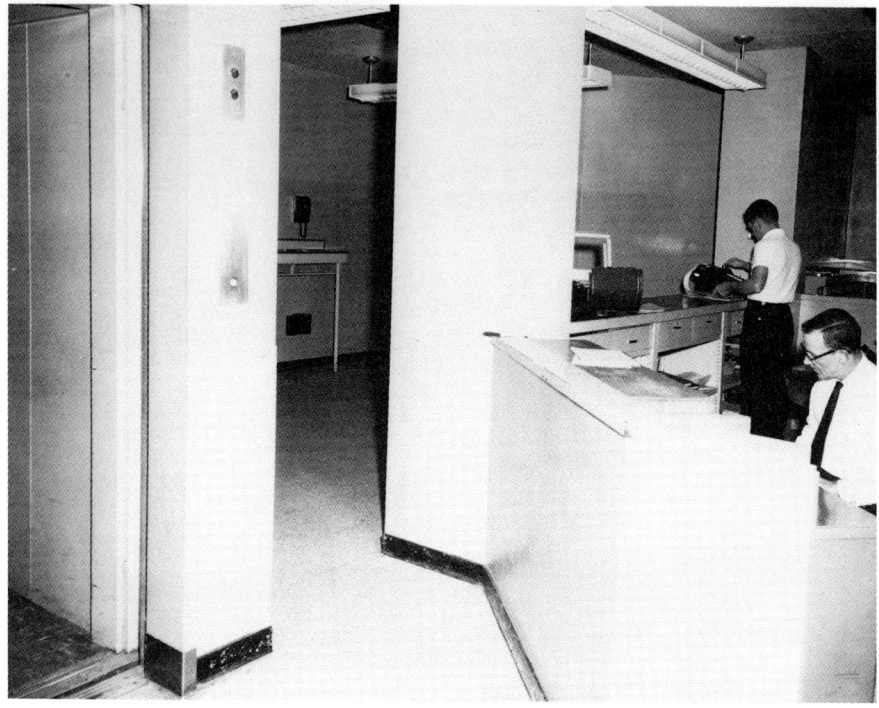

JFK FIRST DAY EVIDENCE

91. Dallas Police Crime Lab photo taken by H. R. Williams showing the open elevator used to transport Oswald.

cameras were set up. (The car area is where Photo 89 was taken from.) The reporters had managed to mingle with police in front of the railing in an effort to get closer to Oswald during the transfer to shout questions. Ruby was able to blend into this crowd in front of the railing.

The plan set out by police called for Oswald to be escorted directly to a waiting, unmarked car between a solid line of policemen on both sides. The officers had not, however, sealed off the reporters, allowing them to get an unobstructed view of the transfer. An armored car waiting at the top of the Commerce Street ramp was to be used as a decoy in a last-minute change in the transfer plan. Oswald was to be taken in an unmarked car which would then veer off from the armored car motorcade, taking an alternate route to the County Jail.

Photo 91 shows the open jail elevator taken by Oswald and

92. Dallas Police Crime Lab photo taken by H. R. Williams showing the view as seen by Oswald exiting the elevator.

his escorts down to the parking basement from Captain Fritz's third-floor office, where Oswald's final interrogation had just been completed. Photo 92 is the view which Jim Leavelle and L. C. Graves (the officers on each side of Oswald) had across the Jail Office after exiting the jail elevator.

A small discussion was held here as to whether all was in place for the transfer. After being told everything was set, although the unmarked car was not actually yet in position, they proceeded around the U-shaped jail office desk. Photo 93 is the next view detectives had as they escorted Oswald around the desk. They then proceeded through the door with the small glass insert seen in the center of the photograph.

As the escorted prisoner and the detectives walked through the Jail Office door into the basement, they would have had the same perspective as shown in Photo 94, filled with police and

JFK FIRST DAY EVIDENCE

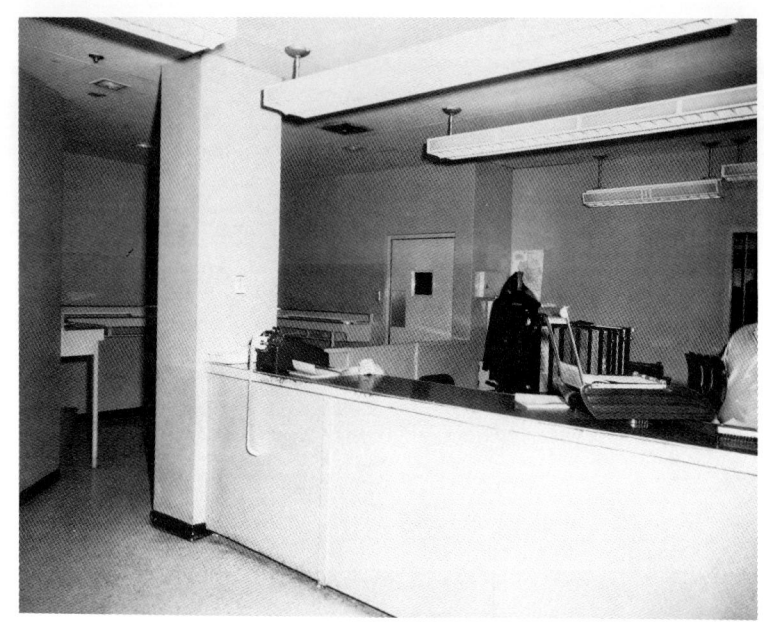

93. Dallas Police Crime Lab photo taken by H. R. Williams showing the U-shaped Jail Office desk.

94. Dallas Police Crime Lab photo taken by H. R. Williams showing the view as seen by detectives escorting Oswald at the moment he was shot by Ruby.

reporters. As soon as they entered through the door, however, television lights were turned on, practically blinding the view of Oswald and his escorts.

As the men with Oswald approached the waiting reporters, they realized all was not in place. The unmarked car had not been properly backed up to complete the simple transfer. As the car was backing up and the men continued towards it, reporter Ike Pappas reached forward with his microphone and asked Oswald if he had anything to say. Immediately Ruby dashed out by Pappas and fired the fatal shot into Oswald's abdomen. The blinding television lights and the transfer car not being in place ultimately contributed to the split second delay on the part of the nearby officers in responding to Ruby as he quickly leaped forward. Photo 85 shows an overview of the parking garage area used by the Dallas police that Ruby may have made his way across.

Immediately after Ruby fired his lone shot into Oswald, Detective L. C. Graves (who, incidentally, was broken-in as a detective by Rusty) grabbed the revolver and prevented Ruby from getting off any more shots. After scuffling with officers, Ruby was hustled out of the basement and escorted to the jail elevator which Oswald had just been brought down on. He was taken up to the fifth-floor jail and stripped to his underwear.

One humerous sidenote was recalled by Crime Lab Detective Bobby Brown who was in the fourth-floor Crime Lab Office at the time Oswald was shot. Shortly after the shooting, Brown got a call from a Homicide lieutenant. The officer requested that someone come down from the lab and do a parrafin cast on Ruby's hands. Bobby told us he asked the Lieutenant, "Don't you think that you have enough witnesses?" The man coyly told Bobby, "I'll get back to you." Of course, he never did.[9]

Dallas Officer Don Archer stated that at the time Ruby was placed in his cell, he noticed that Ruby was breathing heavily, with his heart racing. Later, Archer told that after he advised Ruby that Oswald had died, Ruby began to calm down. It seemed as if his life had depended on eliminating Oswald, having less fear of being

JFK FIRST DAY EVIDENCE

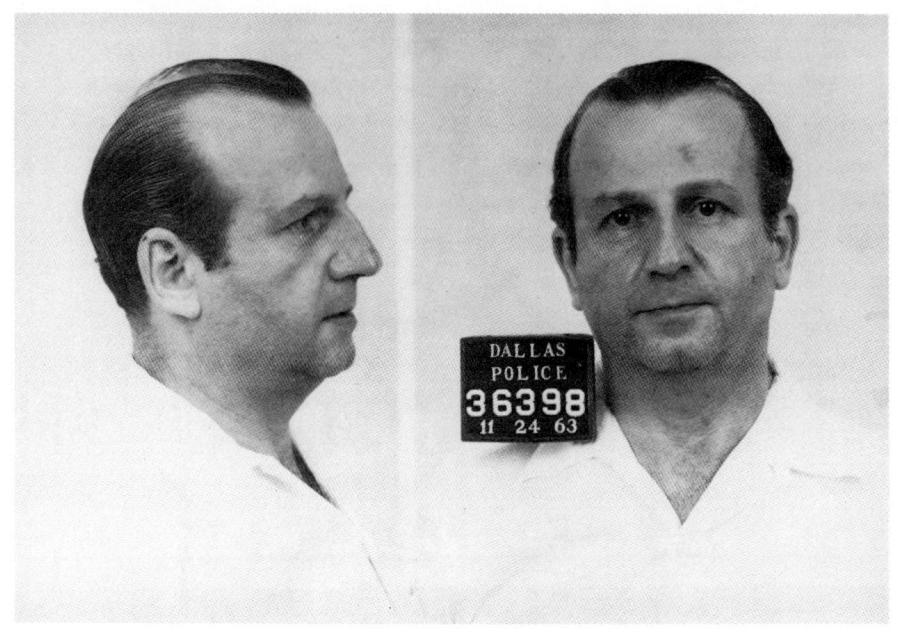

95. Dallas Police Crime Lab mug shot of Jack Ruby following his arrest for shooting Oswald.

in the custody of police charged with murder than possibly facing judgement of the underworld.

AFTER BEING CHARGED WITH THE MURDER OF OSWALD, RUBY WAS led into the Identification Bureau's fourth-floor Mug Room to be fingerprinted and photographed. His mug shot appears in Photo 95 and a full body shot is shown in Photo 96, taken following his arrest.

Investigation of Jack Ruby today should concentrate on his motive for slaying Oswald rather than on Dallas police complicity. Ruby's ties to the underworld have been documented extensively in the past few years, notably by author David E. Scheim in his book *Contract on America*. Ruby made several trips to Cuba to meet with various members of organized crime. Also Ruby had a twenty-fold increase in phone calls to numerous underworld figures in the months preceding the November assassination.

Ruby grew up in Chicago and in the 1930's was an errand

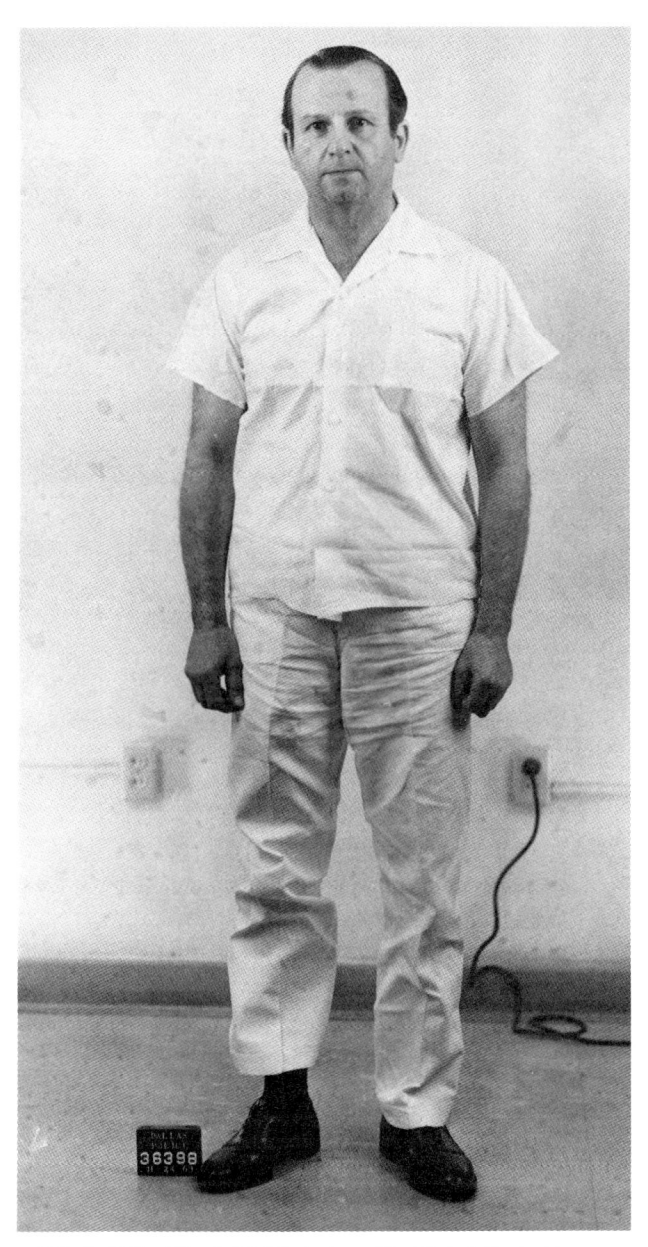

96. Dallas Police Crime Lab full-body photo of Jack Ruby following his arrest.

boy for Al Capone. He later worked in some legitimate and some illegitimate jobs, showing early that he could use his fists.

"Sparky," as he was known then, was out to prove that he was "a man as well as a Jew." He would take on anyone who cared to heckle his faith and would strike out at anyone quickly to prove his manhood. He was arrested in 1927 after having been caught scalping tickets, and in 1930 was sentenced for selling pirated music sheets. He worked many other odd jobs, including one as a bouncer in a nightclub.

In 1943, Ruby was drafted into World War II and served until he was discharged from the military in 1946. He briefly went into a business partnership with his two brothers, Earl and Sam, which ended the following year when the brothers realized they could not get along. In 1947, Jack left Chicago and moved to Dallas. According to Dallas Reporter Seth Kantor, a crime syndicate boss named Paul Rowland Jones had at that time wanted to export his criminal activities into Dallas, and Ruby was his new front man.

During his years in Dallas, none of the charges Ruby was arrested for amounted to much, however, except a traffic summons for which he paid a $35 fine. Rusty told me that he felt as though Ruby treated officers with drinks and prostitutes in his club in order to receive favors from the police when he got into trouble.

RUBY'S TRIAL FOR MURDERING OSWALD ENDED ON MARCH 14TH, 1964, with a jury ordering a predicted date with the electric chair. It was unexpected for Ruby, who had somehow believed that the jury would go easier on his taking vengeance into his own hands by killing a despised presidential assassin. The verdict was appealed. Ruby became severely depressed, eventually attempting to commit suicide in his jail cell. When Ruby was interviewed by the Warren Commission after his trial, he repeatedly asked to be removed from Dallas, stating that he could not speak freely there. Earl Warren stated that it was not possible for Ruby to leave Dallas, but Ruby persisted, claiming that his life was in danger if he were to speak the truth there. After Warren declined again to take Ruby away from Dallas, Ruby said, "Well, you won't ever see me again. I tell you that." He was right in his prediction.

Jack Ruby died on January 3rd, 1967, in Parkland Hospital from complications due to cancer. Dr. Earl Rose, the Dallas County medical examiner, determined that the immediate cause of death was due to a pulmonary embolism--a massive blood clot which had formed in Ruby's leg and passed through the heart into the lung. There were traces of cancerous tumors throughout his body, with the heaviest concentration found in the right lung.

The death of Jack Ruby closed another chapter in the events surrounding the assassination of John F. Kennedy. However, speculation will probably continue for years in an effort to reach an understanding of Jack Ruby's "true motives."

1. Former Crime Lab Detective H. R. Williams, taped personal interview, 25 April 1992.
2. Warren Commission, *Report of President's Commission on the Assassination of President John F. Kennedy,* (Washington, D.C.: U. S. Government Printing Office, 1964), 800.
3. Seth Kantor, *The Ruby Cover-up* (N.Y.: Zebra Books, 1978), 84.
4. Ibid., 8.
5. Warren Commission, *Report,* 81.
6. Ibid., 342.
7. Interview of Dallas Policeman Billy Grammer in *The Men Who Killed Kennedy,* videotape, prod. Central Independent Television, P. L. C., 1988.
8. Kantor, 130.
9. Former Crime Lab Detective Bobby Brown, taped personal interview, 25 April 1992.

CHAPTER

X

More Documents

MUCH OF THE REMAINING EVIDENCE THAT RUSTY HAS INCLUDES various Police documents, many having been seen before and thoroughly studied by others, as well as some of the identification cards and personal effects found on Oswald after his arrest. As has been stated previously, all of the evidence which Rusty possesses will be included in the presentation of the evidence, no matter how insignificant. Even though much of the evidence has been shown in former years in other books or publications, it will be shown here again as proof that it was originally collected by the Dallas police since it was in Rusty's possession as first day evidence.

Due to the lingering doubts raised over the years concerning the FBI's handling or alteration of documents, Rusty's evidence may now set to rest some of the questions of authenticity since it is direct from the Dallas police files. The evidence went through no one else, and appears today just as it did when it was first discovered and developed by the Dallas police in 1963.

PHOTO 97 IS A COPY OF THE HOMICIDE REPORT MADE BY THE DALLAS police on President John F. Kennedy. It is shown to have been filled out on November 23rd, the day following the assassination and notes near the bottom left that Lee Harvey Oswald was arrested for the crime. Rusty told me that most of the Dallas police officers felt in the years following the assassination that Oswald had committed the crime due to the overwhelming physical evidence gathered by the Department. No evidence gathered by the Dallas police led them to anyone other than Oswald as a suspect.

JFK FIRST DAY EVIEDNCE

97. Copy of Dallas Police Homicide Report of President John F. Kennedy.

    The details of the offense shown in the Police Homicide Report are stated as, "The expired was riding in motorcade with wife and Governor John Connally, and his wife. Witnesses heard

240

98. Copy of Dallas Police Homicide Report of Lee Harvey Oswald.

gun shot and saw the expired slump forward. More shots were heard and the expired fell into his wife's lap. Governor Connally was also shot at this time. Car in which they were riding was escorted to Parkland Hospital by Dallas police officers." The report states that "All witnesses affidavits are in Homicide Office." Rusty does not possess copies of any affidavits from witnesses.

Photo 98 is a copy of the Homicide Report of Lee Harvey Oswald. It was made out the same day the murder occurred as the nation watched the accused assassin being escorted to a waiting vehicle in the parking garage basement of the Dallas Police Department. The details of the offense reads, "Deceased was in custody being handcuffed to Detective J. R. Leavelle's left wrist with Detective L. C. Graves holding to deceased's left arm. Deceased was marched out of the Jail Office into the basement to be placed in a waiting automobile for transfer to the County Jail. Deceased had been charged with the Murder of Police Officer J. D. Tippit and President John F. Kennedy. As deceased and Detectives approached the car, a white male dashed from the throng of newspaper reporters and television cameramen and fired one time with a 38 caliber revolver striking the deceased in the left side. Deceased taken to Parkland Hospital where he was undergoing emergency operation at the time he expired. Judge McBride ordered Post Mortem. Suspect was arrested at the scene."

The person arrested for the crime was, of course, Jack Ruby. The weekend stalking of Oswald culminated in one quick shot from Ruby at 11:20 a.m. on the Sunday morning following the assassination. Ruby silenced Oswald forever from telling his reasons or motives in the shooting. The question still remains why Ruby would shoot Oswald. Was it for the sake of Mrs. Kennedy or simply to silence Oswald?

The final Homicide Report is of Dallas Police Officer J. D. Tippit (Photo 99). The report was written by Captain C. E. Talbert, Head of the Patrol Division in Oak Cliff. The report states, "Deceased driving Squad Car #10 east on Tenth stopped to interrogate a suspect who was walking west on Tenth. Suspect walked to officer's car on the right-hand side, [and] they talked through the closed window for a few seconds. Deceased got out of the car and started to walk around the front of the car to suspect; as

MORE DOCUMENTS

```
OLICE DEPARTMENT                    ...MICIDE REPORT                          CITY OF DALLAS
```

Name of Person Killed TIPPITT, J. D.	First Name	Middle Name	Race Sex Age w/m/34	Residence of Person Killed 238 Glencairn CA42294	Offense Serial No. F 85827
Reported By Bus: Police Officer #884 City of Dallas	Title or Relationship		Race Sex Age	Address of Person Reporting RI 89711	Phone of Person Reporting
Offense as Reported (Crime) MURDER				After Investigation Changed to	
Place of Occurrence — Street and Number or Intersection 400 blk E. Tenth			Division R	Platoon 2	Beat 108	Officers Making Report C. E. Talbert 463	I.D. No.	Status	I.D. No.
Day of Week Fri	Date of Occurrence 11-22-63	Time of Day 1:18pm		Date Reported 11-22-63	Time Reported 1:18pm	Report Received By Cave	Received—Time—Typed 5pm—same

DESCRIPTION OF DEAD PERSON

Age	Height	Weight	Eyes	Hair	Beard	Complexion	Identifying Marks, Scars, Etc.	Clothing

Coroner Notified: Judge Joe B Brown Jr.
Name of Coroner Attending—Time of Arrival   A.M. P.M.
Name of Prosecutor Attending—Time of Arrival   A.M. P.M.

Pronounced Dead by Physician: Dr. Liguori   Address: Methodist Hospital   DOA at 1:30pm
Person With Whom Accused Lived or Associated

DETAILS OF OFFENSE (Give Circumstances of Occurrence of Offense and its Investigation) Use Both Sides of This Sheet.
Deceased driving Squad Car #10 east on Tenth stopped to interrogate a suspect who was walking west on Tenth. Suspect walked to Officer's car on the right hand side, they talked through the closed window for a few seconds. Deceased got out of the car and started to walk around the front of the car to suspect, as he reached the hood of car suspect started shooting striking deceased once in the right temple, once in right side of chest and once in center of stomach. Suspect ran south on Patton from location toward Jefferson. Suspect was later arrested in the balcony of the Texas Theatre at 231 W. Jefferson. Suspect's gun a 38 Special was recovered and turned over to Homicide Bureau. Deceased taken to Methodist Hospital by Dudley-Hughes ambulance and pronounced DOA at 1:30pm by Dr. Liguori, Judge Joe B. Brown, Jr ordered autopsy. ... to Parkland Hospital. Next of Kin ... Personal effects placed in property room.

Known, Suspected or Possible Motives

DESCRIPTION OF SUSPECTS OR PERSONS WANTED

Name if Known	Alias	Address	Sex	Color	Age	Height	Weight	Eyes	Hair	Complexion
	Activity	Occupation	Dress and Other Marks					Cause for Suspicion		
Name if Known	Alias	Address	Sex	Color	Age	Height	Weight	Eyes	Hair	Complexion
	Activity	Occupation	Dress and Other Marks					Cause for Suspicion		
Name if Known	Alias	Address	Sex	Color	Age	Height	Weight	Eyes	Hair	Complexion
	Activity	Occupation	Dress and Other Marks					Cause for Suspicion		

Persons Arrested—Name—Address Lee Oswald			Race Sex Age w/m/24	Arresting Officers	I.D. No.	Charge

99. Copy of Dallas Police Homicide Report of Officer J. D. Tippit.

he reached the hood of car, suspect started shooting, striking deceased once in the right temple, once in right side of chest, and once in center of stomach. Suspect ran south on Patton from

100. Copy of Dallas Police Arrest Report of Lee Harvey Oswald.

location toward Jefferson. Suspect was later arrested in the balcony of the Texas Theatre at 231 W. Jefferson. Suspect's gun a 38 Special [which] was recovered and turned over to Homicide

101. Copy of Dallas Police Arrest Report of Jack Ruby.

Bureau. Deceased taken to Methodist Hospital by Dudley-Hughes ambulance and pronounced DOA at 1:30 pm by Dr. Liguori. Judge Joe B. Brown, Jr. ordered autopsy, transferred to Parkland Hospital.

Next of Kin has been notified. Personal effects placed in property room."

One error in the report is typically exploited in many assassination-related books. Oswald was seated in the main level of the theater as explained earlier, not in the balcony as stated in the narrative. The report is accurate in all other areas, and was written immediately after the shooting of Officer Tippit (within 4 hours). Captain Talbert evidently had not been informed at the time that Oswald was seated in the main, or lower, area of the theater.

THE ARREST REPORT COPIES IN RUSTY'S POSSESSION are interesting in their brevity alone. The details of the arrest of Lee Harvey Oswald state simply, "The subject shot and killed President John F. Kennedy and Police Officer J. D. Tippit and shot and wounded Governor John Connally" (Photo 100). The details of the arrest of Jack Ruby are even shorter, stating, "This subject shot and killed Lee Harvey Oswald" (Photo 101).

Rusty told me that there was a reason that few details were typically written on Arrest Reports. He said that these were normally released to the press, and so not much in the way of real information was given out with them. The Police Department made out their own internal reports which were not normally released to reporters.

PHOTO 102 IS A SCALED DRAWING OF THE SIXTH FLOOR OF THE Depository. It gives the approximate area of the rifle location and sniper's nest location found by officers. It indicates that the sixth-floor window is located 60.7 feet above the sidewalk below.

ONE PIECE OF EVIDENCE WHICH RUSTY HAS THAT WILL HELP SETTLE another controversial charge against investigators is a copy of a magazine ad found among Oswald's belongings. The 6.5 Mannlicher Carcano rifle and .38 special Smith & Wesson revolver were circled on the discovered magazine ad from Klein's Sporting Goods in the *American Rifleman* magazine (Photo 103). Rusty also

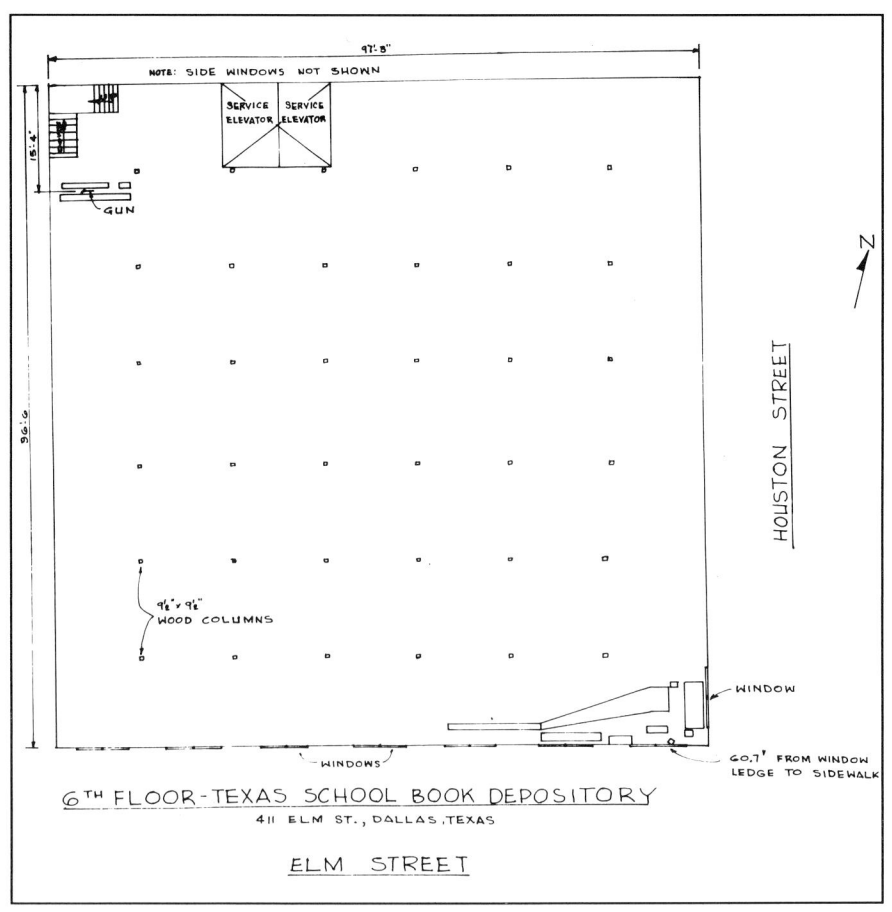

102. Dallas Police scaled drawing of the sixth floor of the Depository showing the location where the gun was found.

has a copy of the magazine page facing the one with the ad on it (Photo 104).

The importance of Rusty's copy lies in the fact that it was made from the original ad found by the Dallas police showing a rifle with a length of 40" overall. This was before the Warren Commission published a similar ad in the Commission exhibits showing a 36" rifle. The discrepancy was discovered by researchers, and another charge was leveled concerning manipulation of the evidence. The charge is understandable, but is here shown to be a moot point. The original ad, which Rusty

247

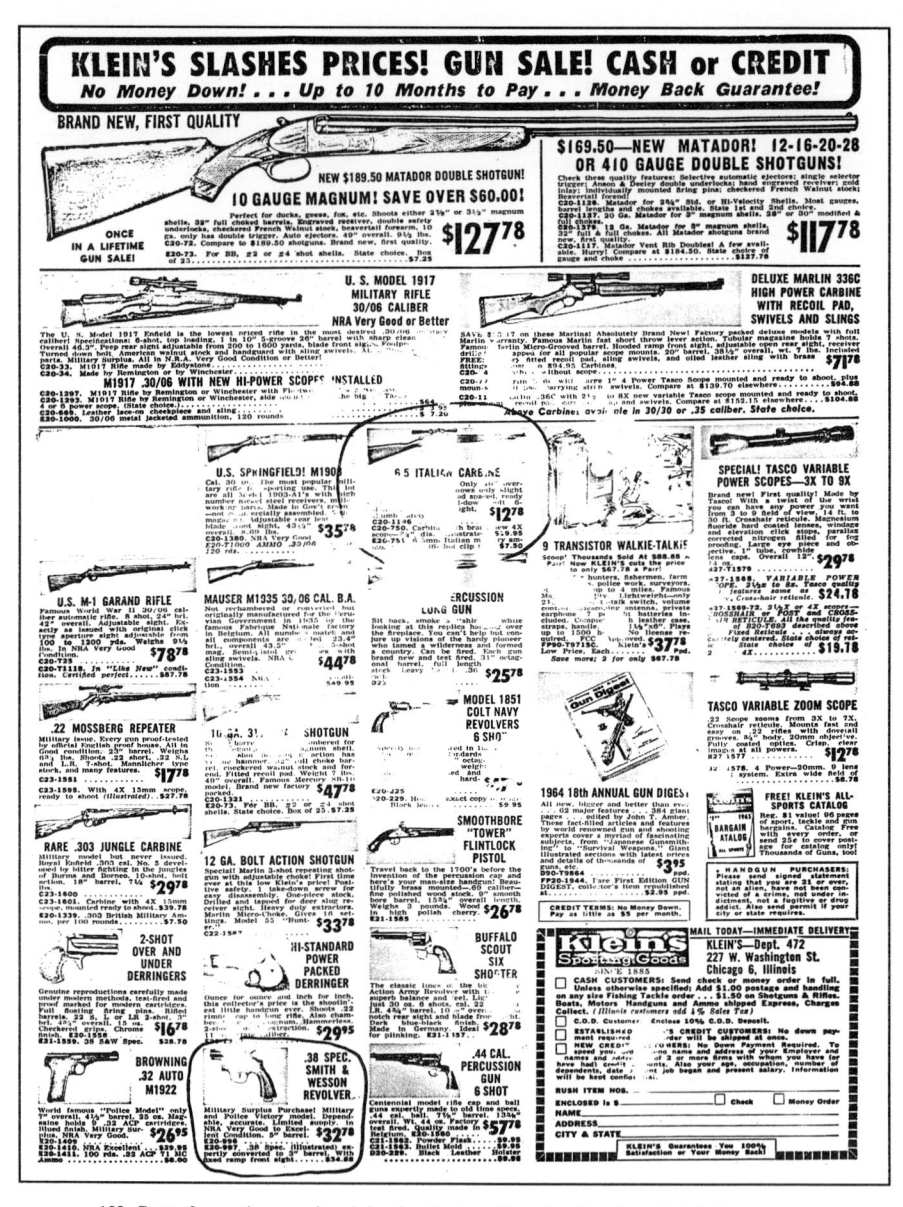

103. Copy of magazine page found showing the type rifle ordered by Oswald circled.

copied, shows the rifle to be 40" overall. Whatever happened to the ad later in its handling by others is meaningless since now an independent source can verify the validity of the original ad.

104. Copy of facing page of the previous magazine ad.

PHOTOS 105 THROUGH 111 ARE COPIES OF THE CASE REPORT of the investigation of the murder of President John F. Kennedy, listing Lee Harvey Oswald as the defendant. It includes a list of many of

249

JFK FIRST DAY EVIDENCE

```
                                 POLICE DEPARTMENT
              Disposition           CITY OF DALLAS                    Filed
                                  CASE REPORT        Date November 22, 1963
Court_____               With Alexander
Docket_____               By   Capt. Fritz
Method_____               C. N. Dhority - C. W. Brown
                                                     Investigating Officers
Disposition_____               Lt. L. E. Cunningham
                                                     H. W. Mc Donald
                                                     Arresting Officers
                                                     Deceased
                                                     Location of Defendant
Defendant Lee Harvey OSWALD
Race White    Age 24    Sex Male    Residence 1026 North Beckley
Date of Arrest November 22, 1963 - 2:00 PM          Identification No. 54018
Place of Arrest 231 West Jefferson                  Arrest No. 63-98155
Date and Time of Offense November 22, 1963, approximately 12:30PM Offense No. F-85950
Complainant John F. Kennedy, w/m/47, Deceased
Where and How Committed On Elm West of Houston - Shot with rifle
Charge Murder
Property Taken and Value_____
Evidence and Seizures Attached
                                                    Voluntary Statement No
Accomplices
List Witnesses and What Each Can Testify to on Reverse Side
Summary of Case Deceased was riding in motorcade with his wife and Governor Connally and
his wife. Witnesses heard gun shot and saw deceased slump forward. More shots were
fired and deceased fell forward. Governor Connally was also shot. Officers determined
where shots came from and covered the building and went into the building. Capt. Fritz
had name of Defendant, but Defendant was not in the building. Capt. Fritz received
information that Defendant had killed Officer Tippit in Oak Cliff. Arresting officers
brought Defendant to City Hall.

                    Any additional information may be placed on reverse side.
```

105. Copy of Case Report of Lee Harvey Oswald, page 1.

the officer witnesses participating in the investigation, as well as a list of many civilian witnesses to the events which occurred. The testimony of each witness was recorded by affidavit which was

250

OFFICER WITNESSES:

M. L. Baker
Solo Motor Officer
Traffic Division
    Saw Oswald in building after shooting. Identified him in line up. See affidavit.

Deputy S. Boone
Sheriff's Office
    Found rifle used in offense, Northwest corner of sixth floor of Texas School Book Depository Building. Turned rifle over to Capt. Fritz.

Deputy Seymour Weitzman
2002 Oates Drive, DA 7-6624
Bus. Robie Love RI 1-1483
    Same as above.

Capt. J. W. Fritz #9
CID
    Made investigation of offense. Found empty and live shells used in offense.

Lt. J. C. Day
Crime Lab
    Made investigation at Texas School Book Depository. Took charge of rifle used. Lifted prints on building and from rifle and paper rifle was wrapped in.

Det. R. L. Studebaker
Crime Lab
    Made investigation where offense was committed.

Det. Johnny Hicks
Crime Lab
    Made paraffin case of Defendant's hands and face.

Det. Pete Barnes
Crime Lab
    Made paraffin cast of Defendant's hands and face.

Capt. G. M. Doughty
ID Bureau
    Had charge of evidence which he turned over to F. B. I.

G.L. Hill, Sgt. 1180
Radio Patrol, Sta. 511
    Arrested defendant.

M. N. McDonald 1178
City P. D., Sta. 511
    Arrested defendant.

C. T. Walker 1529
City P. D., Sta. 501
    Arrested defendant.

Ray Hawkins 887
City P. D., APB, Sta. 515
    Arrested defendant.

T. A. Hutson 1146
City P. D., Sta. 501
    Arrested Defendant.

P. K. Carroll 923
City P. D., Spl. Ser. Sta. 566
    Arrested defendant.

Deputy Sheriff Luke F. Mooney
Dallas Co. Sheriff's Office
    Found 3 empty 6.5 rifle shells on 6th floor Texas Book Depository Bldg. and notified Capt. Fritz.

106. Copy of Case Report of Lee Harvey Oswald, page 2.

filed by a number indicated in the report.

Witnesses continued--Defendant: Lee Harvey Oswald   Murder offense F 85950

O. P. Wright
Security Officer, Parkland Hosp.
2502 Also, WH6 2736
: Recovered 6.5 rifle slug, turned it over to Secret Service at Parkland.

Det. Marvin Johnson 879
City P. D., Sta. 551
: Made investigation at Texas Book Depository. Recovered long brown paper rifle was wrapped in and Dr. Pepper bottle at scene. Took affidavit from cab driver Whaley and officer Baker.

Dt. L. D. Montgomery 1047
City P. D., Sta. 551
: Same as Officer Johnson above.

Det. L. C. Graves 702
City P. D., Sta. 551
: Took affidavit from Helen L. Markham and Mrs. Mary L. Bledsoe.

Det. R. L. Senkel 714
: Was in motorcade about seven blocks ahead of President's car. Followed President's car to Parkland Hospital. Made investigation at Texas Book Depository. Made search of defendant's room at 1026 N. Beckley. Took affidavit from defendant's wife. Made search

Det. F. M. Turner 809
City P. D., Sta. 551
: Same as Senkel above. Made identification of defendant's picture from witness Ronald B. Fischer who saw defendant before shooting. Not positive on identification. Made search 1026 N. Beckley.

Det. W. E. Potts 576
City P. D., Sta. 551
: Made identification of defendant's picture from witness Ronald B. Fischer who saw defendant before shooting. Not positive on identification. Recovered map, 1026 N. Beckley.

Det. C. N. Dhority 476
City P. D., Sta. 551
: Was present at lineup on defendant for William W. Whaley, cab driver who picked up defendant. Mr. Whaley made identification as #3 man in 4-man lineup, 2:15 pm, 11-23-63, city hall. Took affidavit and held lineup from Cecil J. McWatters bus driver who picked up defendant. Also made identification of bus transfer defendant had in his pocket. 11-23-63, 6:30 pm identified defendant as #2 man in 4-man lineup. Took 3 spent 6.5 rifle shells to crime lab. Made copies of defendant's identification papers for Mr. Stewart of Secret Service. Prepared case report.

C. W. Brown 759
City P. D., Sta. 551
: Made investigation at Texas Book Depository Bldg. Took witnesses from Book Depository to room 317 City Hall, took affidavits from William H. Shelley and Seymour Weitzman. Was present at lineup when Mr. McWatters made identification of defendant and transfer, which defendant had in his possession at time of arrest.

107. Copy of Case Report of Lee Harvey Oswald, page 3.

(2) supplementary witnesses-continued-Defendant: Lee Harvey Oswald, Murder Offense F 85950

G. F. Rose 1025 City P. D., Sta. 551	Made search of 2515 W. 5th St., Irving, Texas. Recovered blanket rifle was wrapped in, personal papers and pictures of defendant. Brought witness Wesley Frazier to city hall for affidavit and polygraph. Brought defendant's wife and Mrs. Ruth Paine to City Hall.
R. S. Stovall 1031 City P. D., Sta. 551	Same as above.
H. M. Moore 672 City P. D., Sta. 551	Made search of 2515 W. 5th St., Irving, Texas. Found picture of defendant holding a rifle similar to the one defendant used at time of offense.
J. P. Adamcik 1548 City P. D., Sta. 551	Made search of 2515 W. 5th, Irving, Texas. Was present when defendant's wife made identification of defendant's rifle. Took affidavits from defendant's mother and brother and Michael Paine.
F. L. Anderton 1506 V. D. Monaghen 801 City P. D., Sta. 551	Was present at Texas Book Depository when investigation was made.
J. R. Leavelle 736 City P. D., Sta. 551	Held lineup when Helen Markham made identification of defendant as the man who killed officer Tippit. Took affidavits from Ted Calloway, Sam Guinyard, R. S. Truly, Mrs. R. A. Reid and W. A. Scoggins.
E. E. Beck 45 City P. D., Sta. 551	Assisted officers in moving defendant from jail to Room 317. Took affidavit from Mrs. Geneva L. Hine.
R. M. Sims 629 City P. D., Sta. 551	Made investigation at Texas Book Depository. Recovered evidence from this building, took defendant from jail to Room 317, recovered bus transfer slip from defendant's shirt pocket.
E. L. Boyd 840 City P. D., Sta. 551	Same as above, also found 5 live .38 shells in left front pocket of defendant when searched in the showup room.
M. G. Hall 540 City P. D., Sta. 551	Took defendant from room 317 to showup room. Took affidavit from Lee E. Bowers. Was present when defendant's mother and brother talked with defendant in city jail.

108. Copy of Case Report of Lee Harvey Oswald, page 4.

(3) witnesses continued--Defendant: Lee Harvey Oswald Murder Offense F 85950

Marina Oswald w/f/22
2515 W. 5th St., Irving, Tex.
Wife of defendant. See affidavit #1.

Seymour Weitzman w/m
2802 Oates Dr., DA7 6624
Bus: Robie Love, FI1 1483
Was at place of offense. See affidavit #2.

James Richard Worrell, Jr. w/m/20
13510 Winterhaven, CH7 2378
bus: Thomas Jefferson High
Was at place of offense. See affidavit #3.

William Wayne Whaley w/m
619 Pine St., Lewisville, Tex.
bus: 610 S. Akard, RI2 9191
Cab driver who picked up defendant. See affidavit # 4.

Mrs. Mary E. Pledger w/f
621 N. Marsalis, WH421985
Saw defendant get on city bus knows defendant. See affidavit #5.

Lee B. Bowers, Jr. w/m/38
10508 Maplegrove Lane, DA1 1909
bus: Union Terminal Co., RI8 4698
Was at place of offense. See affidavit #6.

Cecil J. McWatters w/m
2523 Blyth, DA1 2909
Bus: Dallas Transit Co., RI1 1151
Picked defendant up on his bus. See affidavit #7.

Helen Louise Markham w/f
328½ E. 9th
bus: Eat Well Cafe, RI8 2475
Saw Officer Tippit killed by defendant. See affidavit #8.

Jeanette Davis w/f/22
400 E. Tenth, WH3 8120
Saw officer Tippit killed-recovered evidence. See affidavit #9.

Virginia Davis w/f/16
400 E. 10th, WH3 8120
Saw Officer Tippit killed-recovered evidence. See affidavit #10

W. W. Scoggins w/m
3138 Alaska, FR4 2955
Bus: Oak Cliff Cab, WH2 6203
Saw officer killed. See affidavit #11.

Ted Callaway w/m/40
805 W. 8th St., WH6 8045
bus: 501 S. Jefferson
Heard shots, saw defendant run with pistol when officer was killed. See affidavit # 12.

George Jefferson Arplin, Jr. w/m/21
3423 Meisenberger, no pho. or bus.
Saw defendant come into picture show. See affidavit #13.

Ruth H de Paine w/f/31
2515 W. Fifth St., Irving, Tex.
Owns house where defendant and his wife lived, also lives there. See affidavit #14.

Michael Ralph Paine w/m/35
2515 W. Fifth St., Irving, Tex.
Owns house and lives where defendant and his wife lived. See affidavit #15.

Buel Wesley Frazier w/m/19
2439 W. 5th St., Irving, Texas
BL3 8965
Works Texas School Book Depository. See affidavit #16. (All listed below were there when offence happened)

109. Copy of Case Report of Lee Harvey Oswald, page 5.

(4) Supplementary witnesses continued for: Lee Harvey Oswald Murder Offense F 85950

Roy S. Truly w/m
4932 Jade Dr., FR6 9893
Works Texas School Book Depository.
See affidavit # 17.

William H. Shelley w/m/37
126 S. Tatum, FE7 1969
Works Texas School Book Depository.
See affidavit #18

Mrs. R. A. Reid w/f
1914 Elmwood, FE1 6617
Works Texas School Book Depository
See affidavit #19.

Bonnie Ray Williams c/m
1502 Avenue P., Apt. B
Works Texas School Book Depository
See affidavit #20.

Linnie Mae Randle w/f/30
2439 W. 5th, Irving, Tex. BL3 8965
Works Texas School Book Depository.
See affidavit #21.

Jack E. Dougherty w/m/40
1827 S. Marsalis, WH6 7170
Works Texas School Book Depository.
See affidavit #22.

James Earl Jarman, Jr. c/m/33
3942 Atlanta St., HA 8 1837
Works Texas School Book Depository
See affidavit #23.

William H. Shelley w/m/37
126 S. Tatum, FE7 1969
Works Texas School Book Depository.
See affidavit #24.

Danny Garcia Arce w/m/18
1502 Bennett, TA1 3289
Works Texas School Book Depository
See affidavit #25

Billy Nolan Lovelady w/m/26
7722 Hume Dr.
Works Texas School Book Depository.
See affidavit #26.

Charles Douglas Givens c/m/37
2511 Carpenter, RI2 4670
Works Texas School Book Depository.
See affidavit #27.

Howard Leslie Brennan w/m/44
6814 Woodard, EV1 2713
Saw shooting; was at place of offense of President Kennedy, See affidavit #28.

Amos Lee Euins c/m/15
411 Ave. F., WH3 9701
Was at place of offense, saw shooting.
See affidavit #29.

Ronald B. Fischer w/m/24
4007 Flamingo Dr., Mesquite, Texas
FE9 0950
Dallas County Auditor's Office
Was at place of offense; saw shooting.
See affidavit #30.

Robert E. Edwards w/m/22
821 S. Nursery, Irving, Texas
Bus: Dallas County Auditor's Office
Was at place of offense, saw shooting.
See affidavit #31

Arnold Lewis Rowland w/m/17
3026 Hammerly St., FE7 1861
Student, Adamson High
Was at place of offense; saw shooting.
See affidavit #32.

Jesse James Williams w/m/40
1108 Allen St., Apt. 114, Irving,
Texas, or phone PL3 7086
Longview, Texas
Was at place of offense.
See Affidavits #33 and #34.

110. Copy of Case Report of Lee Harvey Oswald, page 6.

JFK FIRST DAY EVIDENCE

(5) Supplementary witnesses continued.Def: Lee Harvey Oswald Murder Offense F 85950

Hugh William Betzner, Jr. Was at place of offense. See affidavits #35 & #36.
5922 Velasco, TA7 9761

Ernest Jay Owens w/m/36 Was at place of offense. See affidavit #37.
3005 Peachtree, Mesquite, Tex.

Jim Braden w/m/49 Was at place of offense. See affidavit #38.
621 S. Barington Dr.
Los Angeles, Calif. Pho. 4725301

Jean Newman w/f Was at place of offense.
3893 Clover Lane, FL2 4222 See affidavit. #39.

Julia Ann Mercer w/f/23 Was at place of offense.   See affidavit # 41 & 40.
5200 Belmont, Apt. 208
Bus: 1720 Canton

Philip Ben Hathaway w/m/28 Was at place of offense.   See affidavit #42.
11021 Quail Run, DI8 6532

John Stevens Butter Lawrence w/m/23 Was at place of offense.   See affidavit, #43.
709 Devonshire, Richardson, Tex.

Barbara Walker Rowland w/f/17 Was at place of offense.   See affidavit #44.
3026 Hammerly St., FE7 1861

Jean Hill w/f/32 Was at place of offense. See affidavit #45.
9402 Bluffcreek, EV1 7419

John Arthur Chism w/m/23 Was at place of offense.
4502 Underwood Dr., no phone See affidavit #46.

Marvin Faye Chism w/m/19 See affidavit #47.
4502 Underwood Dr.

Mary Ann Moorman w/f/31 Was at place of offense.
2832 Ripplewood, DA1 9390 See affidavit #48.

Austin Lawrence Miller w/m Was at place of offense. See affidavit #49.
1006 Powell Circle, Mesquite, Tex.
AT5 2998

S. M. Holland w/m/57 Was at place of offense. See affidavit #50
1119 Lucille, Irving, Tex
PL3 2185

Gayle Newman w/f/22 Was at place of offense. See affidavit #51.
718 W. Clarendon, WH8 6082

William Eugene Newman w/m/22 Was at place of offense.
718 W. Clarendon, WH8 6082 See affidavit #52.

Larry Florer w/m/23 Was at place of offense.
3609 Potomac See affidavit #53.

Royce Glenn Skelton w/m/23 Was at place of offense. See affidavit #54.
2509 Reagan, LA1 2745
Bus: 215 Union Terminal, RI1 1396

111. Copy of Case Report of Lee Harvey Oswald, page 7.

256

MORE DOCUMENTS

PHOTO 112 IS A COPY OF A BUS TRANSFER FOUND IN OSWALD'S pocket after his arrest. Oswald had boarded the bus after leaving the Depository, and obtained the transfer from the bus driver after it became stuck in traffic due to the motorcade. Oswald then walked about two blocks and hailed a taxi, which then took him back near his rooming house on North Beckley in Oak Cliff. Photo 112 shows the key to Oswald's post office box used to mail order the rifle which figured in the assassination.

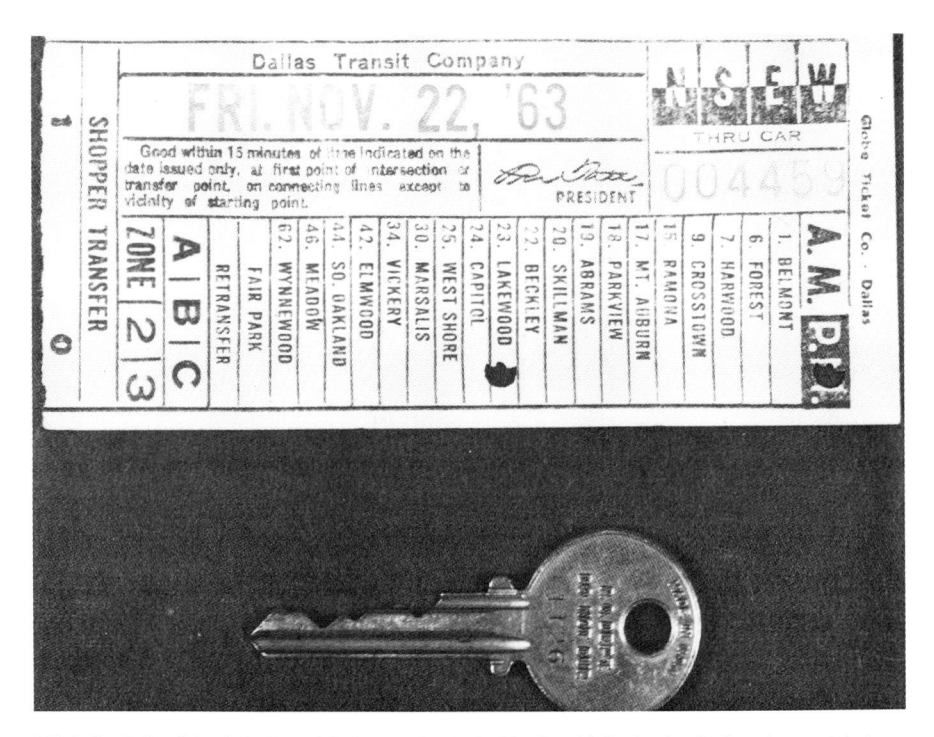

112. Dallas Police Crime Lab photo of the bus transfer obtained by Oswald after leaving the Depository and the key to a post office box used to order Oswald's rifle.

PHOTOS 113 THROUGH 124 ARE PERSONAL SNAPSHOTS OF MARINA and Lee Oswald with friends taken in the Soviet Union. Many of the photographs appeared in the Warren Commission exhibits.

257

JFK FIRST DAY EVIDENCE

113. Photo of Marina Oswald.

114. Photo of Lee Harvey Oswald.

115. Lee and Marina leaving Russia (WC Exh. 2629).

116. Marina on train leaving Russia.

MORE DOCUMENTS

117. Lee Oswald in Russia.

118. Lee and Anita Zieger in Minsk (WC Exh. 2616).

119. Lee and friend Alfred (WC Exh. 2612).

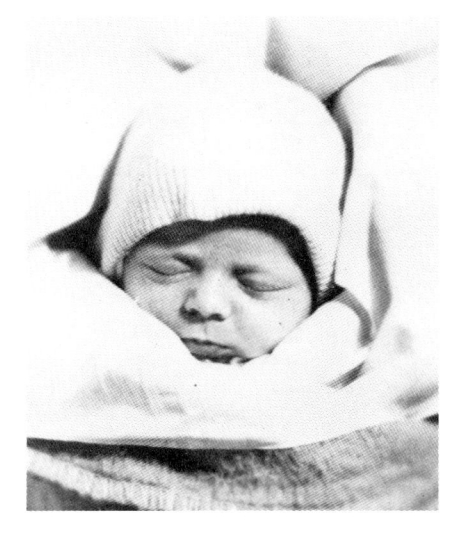

120. Child photo, presumably Oswald's.

259

JFK FIRST DAY EVIDENCE

121. Pavel Golovachev in Minsk (WC Exh. 2619).

122. Photo of Lee Oswald and friend.

123. Aunt Lubova, Marina and Lee (WC Exh.2610).

124. Lee and Marina at left in Minsk (WC Exh. 2628).

MORE DOCUMENTS

AFTER OSWALD'S ARREST, NUMEROUS FAKE IDENTIFICATION PIECES were found in his wallet by Gus Rose and other officers. Photos 125 through 128 include a fake Selective Service card with the name Alek James Hidell alongside Oswald's photograph. Other items found are shown in photos 129 through 139. Most, if not all, of the items were published in the *JFK Assassination File* by Jesse Curry. The accurateness of Curry's book is now independently verified once again through Rusty's evidence photographs.

125. Face-side of fake Notice of Classification ID found on Oswald with the name Alek James Hidell.

126. Face-side of fake Marine ID found on Oswald.

261

127. Forged card probably made by Oswald.

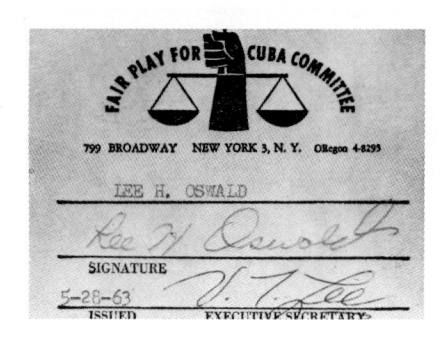

128. Fair Play For Cuba membership card.

129. Hand-written addresses found on Oswald.

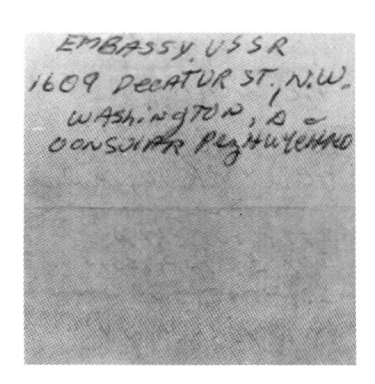

130. Hand-written address found on Oswald.

131. Social Security card found on Oswald.

Various pieces of Communist literature were sent to Oswald from *The Worker* address found hand-written in his wallet (Photo 129). A copy of *The Worker* magazine was held by Oswald while posing for the backyard photographs shown in Chapter 5.

MORE DOCUMENTS

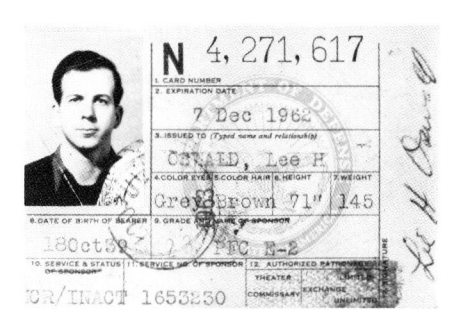

132. Military identification found on Oswald.

133. Face-side of Notice of Classification card of Oswald.

134. Military identification found on Oswald.

135. Reverse-side of fake Marine ID found on Oswald.

136. Face-side of Marine ID found on Oswald.

137. Reverse-side of fake Classification ID found on Oswald.

263

JFK FIRST DAY EVIDENCE

138. Military identification found on Oswald.	139. Front of library card found on Oswald.

THE COMPLEX NATURE OF OSWALD WILL CONTINUE TO FASCINATE the public as a curiosity. This man, with such an amazingly sordid background, altered the course of United States history. The name of Lee Harvey Oswald will be recalled with disdain by generations of Americans to come, just as the name of John Wilks Booth still is in the present.

264

CHAPTER

XI

The Acoustics Evidence Disproved

IN 1979, THE HOUSE SELECT COMMITTEE ON ASSASSINATIONS ISSUED a report stating that President Kennedy was probably killed as a result of a conspiracy. That conclusion was based primarily on what was referred to as the "acoustical evidence."

Recordings made by the Communications Department of the Dallas Police of radio transmissions at the time of the assassination were listened to by the Committee. They hypothesized that a five minute episode recorded near the time of the shooting contained four "impulse patterns" or sound impressions which were concluded to be shots from two different rifles emanating from two separate locations in Dealey Plaza.

They determined that one of the motorcycle officers riding in the motorcade was the individual who had an "open" microphone, caused by his radio transmitter button being stuck in the "send" position. The officer was hypothesized to be in Dealey Plaza at the time, providing a continuous sound transmission of rifle fire from the assassination.

The information presented here will prove beyond any reasonable doubt that the Dallas recording *does not contain any sound of gunshots.* The motorcycle officer that had the open microphone, in fact, *was not even in Dealey Plaza* at the time of the assassination. The "acoustical evidence," the mainstay of the HSCA, is totally incorrect. Their evidence is no evidence.

In 1991, Rusty and I were in Dallas to interview J. Carl Day. At the time, we had not located R. L. Studebaker, and were anxious to speak to him about his work in the assassination. Lieutenant Day mentioned to us that another of Rusty's police buddies, Jim Bowles, might know where to find Studebaker, so we headed over to see Jim.

JAMES C. BOWLES IS TODAY THE SHERIFF OF DALLAS COUNTY. AT THE time of the assassination, he was a supervisor of the Communications Department of the Dallas police. It is the information contained in a rebuttal authored by Jim directed towards the HSCA findings which led to the inclusion of this chapter as further Dallas police first day evidence. Jim has graciously allowed Rusty and me to include for the first time his previously unpublished work in its entirety as an appendix to this book. This chapter is intended as a summary of Jim's rebuttal, which goes into minute detail concerning the inner-workings of the communications systems of the Dallas police in 1963.

As we arrived at the Dallas County Sheriff's Office, Rusty and I were met by the upbeat former Dallas Communications Officer. After a warm greeting between the old friends, we sat facing Jim, who was seated behind his large wooden desk. A lower cabinet on the wall behind held a cassette player. We were soon to be treated to an unexpected remembrance of November 22nd, 1963.

Rusty explained to Jim that we were working on a book about the Kennedy assassination. After he finished rolling his eyes back in his head, Jim grinned at his Public Information Officer, Jim Ewell (the former *Dallas News* reporter), and said, looking at me, "Aw, here's another one. Shall we give him the treatment boys?"

They laughed and then seriously told Rusty and me about some researcher who had come and presented what Jim thought was another wild theory on the Kennedy assassination. Jim said he called a group of former Dallas officers into his office and bombarded the poor man with the recollections of a multitude of men that had worked the case. The outnumbered researcher eventually left Jim's office shaking his head. It seemed now that Jim was gearing up quickly for me to receive the same "treatment."

Jim began to tell us that in 1963 he was in possession of the original Dallas police dictabelt recordings made at the time of the assassination. They contained the actual voices of the officers' conversations on the Dallas police radio during the time of the presidential motorcade. He then asked us if we wanted to listen to them. After being somewhat taken aback by the offer, I told him, "Sure." I was unaware of the significance of the recordings before he played them.

Jim turned around, opened the small cabinet, and (since he had transferred them onto cassette tapes) dropped a cassette into his tape player. The tapes were about a half hour or more in length, and we listened at the time to the portions dealing with the assassination. As we listened, I bent down to the speaker along with Jim. He told me, "It's like it just happened when I listen to the tape. I know everybody on it, and I know right where they are and what they're doing."

Later on I learned that Jim had sent the original dictabelt recordings to the FBI in Washington, D. C., back in 1963. After listening to them, the FBI approached Jim again back in Dallas and asked him to do a transcript for them since they were having a hard time understanding the local codes used by the officers. Jim did so by first making a reel-to-reel tape recording of the original Dictabelts. He retained a copy of the reel-to-reel recording for his own personal reference and delivered another to the FBI. He then provided the FBI with a written transcript of the tapes explaining their meaning. Jim told us that most police departments have their own unique way of communicating, as did the Dallas police. Therefore the need existed for someone familiar with the local lingo, ideally a communications officer such as himself, to do a transcript.

The original dictabelt recordings were later returned by the FBI to the Dallas police and were stored away along with other evidence. Years later, Officer Paul McCaghren carried the evidence of the Dallas police home for safe keeping. After the HSCA convened in the late seventies, McCaghren heard of the new investigation and decided to turn over the Dallas police property to the Committee.

The significance of the actual audio found on the old Dictabelts was determined not to be an important factor by the FBI who had first received and listened to the recordings fifteen years before, but the Dictabelt recordings were seen by the HSCA as new evidence. The written transcript prepared by Jim had been easier to follow than the recordings, and the old Dictabelts had been stored away and practically forgotten until their "rediscovery" by the HSCA. Of course, their existence was known by the Dallas police and the FBI since 1963.

TWO CHANNELS WERE RECORDED SIMULTANEOUSLY ON NOVEMBER 22nd, 1963, at the Dallas Communications Department by two different brands of recorders. The first recording, referred to as Channel One, carried routine police radio activity and was recorded on a Dictaphone A2TC, Model 5 belt or loop recorder. The second recording, referred to as Channel Two, was used on that day exclusively for communications between the motorcade officers and was recorded on a Gray "Audograph" flat disk recorder. Both units were sound activated and remained operating for approximately four seconds following the end of a transmission. The HSCA were incorrect in their assertion that Channel One was serviced by a continuous recording. The only part of the recording which was continuous was a five minute stuck-open microphone segment occurring at the time of the shooting at approximately 12:30 p. m.

On the day of the assassination, Channel One, which carried all other routine Dallas police calls, was the channel which contained the five minute open microphone episode. The officers in the motorcade were tuned to Channel Two, which remained clear in order to broadcast instructions for the motorcade and so the officers might note their progress along the route. It is highly unlikely that the open microphone stuck on Channel One was in the motorcade, since all of the officers had been instructed to be monitoring Channel Two.

Portions of Channel Two are overheard in the background bleeding over into Channel One during the five minute open-microphone period. A broadcast of Channel Two from another police vehicle speaker was picked up by the open microphone.

THE HSCA DETERMINED THAT OFFICER H. B. MCLAIN WAS THE motorcycle officer with the open microphone and set out to prove it. An interview was set up by the Committee in Washington for Officer McClain. However, before it was conducted, an investigator for the Committee was in Dallas. The investigator was informed that Jim and others knew which officer had the open microphone. The investigator told Jim, "I'll get back to you. We'll probably need your statement on the record." However, he never did return for a statement from Bowles.

Being aware of the other Dallas officers' knowledge of who had the open microphone led the Committee into a selective investigation. Having knowledge of a fact which disproves your case and not presenting that fact in a hearing leads to a manipulated conclusion. This is referred to as "exculpatory evidence." The Committee possessed such exculpatory evidence in the case of Jim Bowles and other officers but continued to develop the deception that the open microphone was in Dealey Plaza.

Following Jim's encounter with the Committee's investigator, Officer McLain was brought to Washington. The Committee interrogation of Officer McLain was broadcast and seen back in Dallas. The Committee had formulated questions for McLain in such a way as to elicit a response which would be supportive of their findings, even though they had information from Dallas that the actual officer with the open microphone was not McLain.

After hearing the answers given by McLain to the Committee, Jim Bowles wondered why he would say what he did since Jim already knew whose microphone was actually stuck open. Jim recognized that McLain was testifying to the Committee in a loose format and the questions were asked in order to achieve only a "yes" or "no" response. However, McLain did not respond with

271

"yes" or "no," but with "I could have."

WHEN OFFICER MCLAIN ARRIVED BACK IN DALLAS, JIM CALLED McLain's division chief. He asked the chief to send McLain over with a supervisor of his choice as a witness so that no one could later say that McLain was manipulated in any way. McLain arrived along with Lieutenant Doug Sword to see Jim. Jim then had McLain and Lieutenant Sword go into his office and sit down. McLain was allowed to listen to the entire recording of Channel One and then the entire recording of Channel Two privately with his witness, which lasted over an hour. The tapes covered the time from the President's arrival at Love Field up to and immediately after the assassination.

As the two officers were listening to the two tapes, Jerry Cohen, a writer for the *Los Angeles Times,* along with some other newsmen arrived. They, along with Jim, witnessed the response of Officer McLain as he emerged from the closed office after listening to the two tapes, and his statements are recollected here by Jim.

Jim was about twenty feet away from Officer McLain when he asked, "Well, Mac?"

McLain said in his amiable way, "Hell, J. C., there ain't no way that was my microphone stuck open."

Jim then asked him, "Well, is there a reason why you testified contrary to that in Washington?"

McLain responded, "They didn't let me hear the other tapes. They showed me little spots of tape to listen to. They said, 'Listen to this: could this be, could this be and could this be?' And I said to them, 'It could be' and 'It might have been.' Hell, they were federal lawyers, and I figured they knew what they were doing. I wouldn't figure that the government was going to lie to me or trick me, and I answered as honest as I could. They just asked me could that have been my microphone, and I said, 'Yeah, it could have been.' I didn't know whether it was or wasn't. But after I've heard these tapes, I know it wasn't mine. I remember all that conversation just like it was yesterday."

Jim asked him, "Like what?"

Officer McLain then responded by telling Jim about recalling instructions and comments on Channel Two and a total lack of recognition of anything on Channel One. It would have been impossible for an average officer not to realize that he was tuned to the wrong channel for one half hour. McLain stated that he was tuned to Channel Two as he should have been.

He also said that there was an absence of siren sounds on the recording when the motorcade had started to Parkland Hospital and that the siren sounds he heard appeared to pass an open microphone on a stationary unit. He felt that the motorcycle he heard with the open microphone was running too fast to be in the motorcade and that, when the trip to the hospital began, the motorcycle slowed down and then sat still at idle, which was opposite to what the HSCA claimed to have happened. He also wondered why there was no crowd noise on the tape. All of those present were convinced that Officer McLain had been purposely misled while being questioned in Washington, D. C., by the Committee. The Committee found out later what their key witness had stated to the press. Their predetermined conclusions were now threatened, and suddenly they credited McLain with a "rusty memory."

THE COMMITTEE HAD SET OUT TO PROVE THEIR HYPOTHESIS, NO longer allowing the facts to undermine a conclusion. They had gone about their work backwards, attempting to form a conclusion first and then manipulate the facts to support it.

Since some witnesses to the assassination were now claiming that there was a "grassy knoll" shooter, it seems as though the Committee chose to pursue the accusation rather than the facts previously established back in 1964. The grassy knoll was the only location where a microphone was set up for their tests to determine the location of a second shooter.

Test firings were performed at the Depository and recorded by the Committee experts. It was then decided where the open microphone would need to be in Dealey Plaza to fit the recording's impulse patterns. They found a motorcycle in the approximate position they needed, and Officer McLain was selected.

The Committee determined the location of "inaudible sound impressions" at the point on the tape which they felt was when the shooting had occurred. They did not hear actual shots, which would easily be detected if they had actually occurred. Jim told us that tests had been made to demonstrate that shots would have been recorded by the Dictabelt equipment if they had occurred.

The Committee stated that neither the tapes nor the Dictabelts contained discernible sounds of gunfire, and referred to the areas where they needed shots to appear as supersonic "inaudible sound impressions." Jim wondered how the Committee was able to find supersonic waves on a low frequency recording system.

The Report contradicts itself later by stating, "The sound of a rifle is so pronounced, however, that it would be picked up even if it originated considerably further away from the microphone than other less intense noise sources, such as a crowd." (According to Jim, the previous statement is utterly ridiculous!) Then they said, "This corroboration was considered significant by the Committee, since it tended to prove that the tape did indeed record the sounds of shots during the assassination."

Jim responded to this contradiction in his rebuttal by stating, "What is the truth? Are there sounds of shots or aren't there? What do 'impulse patterns' sound like? Are they audible or inaudible?"

The original Dictabelt tape of Channel One was a low fidelity recording made by a blunt needle impressing a thin plastic surface. The quality of the recording was lowered considerably as a result of multiple playbacks before the reel-to-reel tape was made. A repetition of the lowering of the needle onto the belt created minute dimples which were later picked up by the sensitive equipment used by the HSCA. Such "impulse patterns" were present throughout the recording but were determined to be gunshots by the Committee only at the selected area. The other areas throughout the entire belt containing the same type of "impulse patterns" were not defined. They were not even examined!

THE SIGNAL FROM THE MOTORCYCLE HAD BEEN PICKED UP BY RELAY transmitters located at various areas throughout Dallas. It was then sent over standard telephone lines to a police transmitter at Fair Park where it was retransmitted as a radio signal to all mobile units throughout Dallas. Another telephone line was then used to send the signal back to the Dispatcher's Office, where it was monitored and recorded. The audio appearing on the dictabelt recording had therefore traveled over typical telephone lines. The quality of the signal was limited to the low frequencies carried over the wire.

Jim states in his report, "It would be amazing and a credit to the Dictaphone equipment used had it served so profoundly as to record inaudible impression patterns picked up by a low quality microphone, passed through a low frequency transmitter, then through a voice-grade telephone line to a second transmitter, then a second telephone line, then to the recorder without even losing the N-waves which preceded the inaudible impression patterns calculated to be the assassin's gunshots. Fantastic!"

THE HSCA USED THE VARIOUS TIMES BROADCAST ON THE TAPES AS an actual and precise tool in determining their split second analysis of when the "shots" occurred. This was another incorrect assumption on their part due to the various procedures used in the Dispatcher's Office for recording the time over the air.

The Communications Department was serviced by a dispatcher for each of the two channels. As routine calls were received by the telephone operators, a call sheet was made stating the nature of the service requested. It was then stamped by the operator with a "Simplex" time clock. The call sheet was next given to the dispatcher to broadcast to the appropriate officer. Finally, it was stamped once again by the dispatcher on another time clock to show the time the call was broadcast.

A large wall clock hung on the wall in the Dispatcher's Office. The times stamped by the time clocks often varied one to two minutes ahead or behind the wall clock. Since no clock was linked to another, and none were linked to the wall clock, the times were, therefore, not synchronized. However, the HSCA attempted to establish a split second time base to demonstrate when shots appeared on the tape, although such a time base did not and could not exist using the recording as a reference.

Although somewhat of a real time could be established during the five minute open-microphone episode, a precise-to-the-tenth-of-a-second analysis is absurd. The exact playback speeds of the various recorders used could not be determined, and indeed subsequent playback of the recording by different players had diluted a real time even more. It was, therefore, impossible to attempt to calibrate or coordinate the tape speed of the dictabelt recording to the 18 frames per second of the Zapruder film.

ANOTHER AREA DEALT WITH BY JIM CONCERNED THE MOTORCYCLE engine noise recorded during the five minute open-microphone episode. Remember that the motorcycle speeds in the motorcade along Main Street would have averaged less than 5 miles per hour during the first two minutes of the five minute open-microphone recording. However, the recorded motorcycle revolutions actually demonstrate a speed of approximately 30 miles per hour during that period. This is six times the speed of the motorcade at the time the "impulse patterns" found by the Committee appear on the recording.

One ridiculous statement made in the Committee's conclusions was that they had to filter out the repetitive noise, such as the repeated firing of the pistons of the motorcycle engine! Was it not considered that the repetitive noises represented by the motorcycle could be calculated in revolutions per minute and then into miles per hour, namely 30 miles per hour? It is impossible that the motorcycle was in the motorcade for this reason alone since, again, the motorcade's average speed was less than 5 miles per hour. Also, the frequent stops and starts of a motorcycle in the motorcade are not heard on the first two minutes of the stuck microphone episode, nor is any crowd noise heard at the time. The motorcycle is heard to run at an even speed.

The question might be posed as to whether or not the motorcycle engine might be "reved up" to a high RPM in a lower gear to achieve the continuous sound heard on the tape. This was not the case, however, since the motors were already overheating and backfiring. Reving up the motorcycle engine in such a manner in a low gear would quickly burn up the engine.

Experts for the HSCA determined that the motorcycle was moving at a rate of 11 miles per hour at the time of the "impulse patterns," which is the rate at which the President's limousine appears to be moving in the Zapruder film. They stated that this would move the microphone about five feet in three-tenths of a second, which would match their areas of "impulse patterns." The problem with this additional incorrect assumption is that the officer they chose with the open microphone had to be moving during the shooting. Officer McLain was actually stationary during the entire shooting! This multiplies the Committee's problems with the choice of McLain even more.

AN ANALYSIS OF BOTH THE ZAPRUDER AND BRONSON FILM (ANOTHER citizen film of the event), as well as various still photographs taken at the time, confirm the recollection of Officer McLain as to his location at the time of the shots. At the moment of the shooting, McLain was stopped about 100 feet south of Elm Street on Houston Street. As the first shot rang out from the Depository, he looked up to see pigeons fly from the roof of the Depository. He remained on Houston Street during the entire sequence of shots, and through an opening in an ornamental wall on Houston Street saw Clint Hill jump onto the rear of the presidential limousine. Neither the full frames of the Zapruder film nor the Altgen's photograph show Officer McLain on Elm Street at the time of the assassination.

THE HSCA ALSO STATED THAT THE MICROPHONES ON THE motorcycles were directional. This too is incorrect. The microphones were non-directional, and would react to sound from approximately 300 feet around. The experts placed themselves in the position of needing to have a directional open microphone in a precise position in order to support the "impulse patterns" they had deemed were shots one and two.

They claimed that McLain was 120' behind and moving in immediate coordination with the presidential limousine and said that certain distortions of the impulse patterns were produced by the windshield of the motorcycle blocking the direct sound of the gunfire. Shot number three they felt came from the grassy knoll, since it appeared to be of a different pattern than the first two "impulse patterns." A fourth impulse pattern was detected on the recording which they felt represented the fourth, fatal head shot of the President.

Immediately after the shooting stopped, Officer McLain used his siren and went with the motorcade onto Stemmons Freeway and on to Parkland Hospital. However, the siren heard on the tape fades in and then gradually fades out. A completely ridiculous scenario was put forth to explain this next anomaly by the Committee. They postulated that Officer McLain had lingered in Dealey Plaza for a while, then accelerated his motorcycle without his siren on, and later passed the motorcade. Or, they theorized, he may have reached the motorcade, then fell back before arriving at Parkland. This is entirely absurd and is not what happened!

THE ACTUAL OFFICER THAT HAD THE OPEN MICROPHONE WAS NOT IN Dealey Plaza. He had realized after the five minute period that his microphone had been stuck open and later, after the assassination, told other officers at Parkland Hospital what had happened. He was worried about it at the time because he regretted making a particular statement during the five minute episode heard on the recording.

The officer with the open microphone was tuned to Channel

One. He had just finished a traffic assignment at about 12:23 p.m. and was en route to his next assignment, the motor pool at the Trade Mart. He was to report there at 12:30 p.m. As he left to make the six and a half minute trip, traveling at approximately 30 miles per hour, his microphone began intermittently to stick open. Finally, at approximately 12:29 p.m., the microphone stuck open for a full five minutes.

For the first two minutes of the five minute period, the officer was completing his trip to the Trade Mart at about 30 miles per hour. The engine is eventually heard to slow to an irregular speed for less than a minute. The officer arrived at the front of the Trade Mart and stopped, where he remained at idle as he listened to a fellow officer's radio tuned to Channel Two. No crowds are heard over the stuck microphone as the officer waited. A replica of the Liberty Bell mounted onto a trailer had been backed nearby in front of the Trade Mart and perhaps produced a bell-tone picked up by the recording. Someone may have passed by and given the bell a thump which was picked up by the officer's open microphone.

As the motorcade exited Stemmons Freeway and then passed the officer's stationary position, the sirens are heard to produce the Doppler effect (See Appendix, p. 357) as many of the vehicles passed his location. The officer then started to follow the motorcade to the hospital. At that moment he realized that his microphone had been stuck open when his button released.

THE MOTORCYCLE HEARD ON THE TAPE IS ACTUALLY A three-wheel type, not a two-wheel model as was the type ridden by Officer McLain. Many officers subsequently listened to the recording and were positive that the motorcycle was a three-wheeler. This was determined by the difference in sound of the smaller three-wheel "flat-head" engine and the larger two-wheel Harley Davidson high performance "over-head-74" engine ridden by Officer McLain. Each engine had its own distinct sound.

THE TESTIMONY OF MOST OF THE OTHER MOTORCYCLE OFFICERS IN the motorcade was neglected and ignored. They consistently stated that three shots occurred, and no more. They basically ruled out a shot from the grassy knoll, since they were directly in front of the area and observed no one firing a weapon. Some of the officers stated that the first shot had missed the President, the second had hit the President in the back, and the third had been the fatal head shot. Another officer reported that he brought up the rear of the motorcade in the quick trip to Parkland Hospital and that no one passed him on the way, including Officer McLain. (So much for McLain's remaining in Dealey Plaza for a while and then catching up to the motorcade. And, so much for the Committee's acoustical evidence of "impulse patterns" which--according to Jim Bowles-- actually happened one minute before the shots were fired in Dealey Plaza!)

JIM BOWLES' FIRSTHAND PERSPECTIVE PROVIDES A UNIQUE rebuttal to the entire findings of the HSCA. It would be of real benefit to all who actually seek the truth to take the time to read his entire document contained in the appendix.

CHAPTER

XII

"Lone Nut" or "Lone Patsy?"

RECENTLY, RUSTY AND I TRAVELED TO A CONFERENCE ON THE assassination of President Kennedy in Dallas, Texas. It was well attended by many noted researchers, authors, book dealers and others simply interested in who shot JFK. We decided to take advantage of the opportunity and began telling those attending about *JFK First Day Evidence* and handed out a one page summary of the upcoming book.

Over two hundred of our fliers were given out, and over one hundred people were spoken to directly by Rusty and me concerning Rusty's actions on the night of November 22nd, 1963 in the Dallas Police Crime Lab. It quickly became apparent that almost all of those attending the symposium had read many of the researcher's books (as Rusty and I have) and believed the conclusions drawn in them without much questioning. I discovered consistently also, to my dismay, that practically none of the attendees had read the actual Warren Commission testimony of the Dallas officers who had investigated the sixth-floor crime scene, trusting others to do the detailed reading for them.

When I initially began to write concerning Rusty's evidence and eye-witness testimony of what really went on in the Crime Lab, I assumed that others around the country would be much more informed than myself since I was a newcomer to the investigation. But after speaking personally to many of the Kennedy assassination researchers, and having read for myself the testimony of the Dallas officers, I learned that many of the authors have made assumptions based on an incomplete knowledge of all of the facts in the case.

Having the advantage of someone inside the Dallas Crime

Lab Office on the night of the assassination has given me a unique perspective in weighing the impassioned pleas of researchers who feel they've been lied to, with the testimony of a trained observer who actually lived the history inside his office 30 years ago. I feel as though I've been given the opportunity to help shed light on a situation and let the reader decide if what he or she is being told is correct.

THE WARREN COMMISSION CONCLUDED THAT OSWALD WAS A "LONE nut" assassin who did all of the shooting by himself. According to their final report, Oswald brought the rifle to work with him that morning and later fired at and killed the President, wounded Governor Connally, returned to his rooming house, picked up his revolver, and eventually went on to kill Dallas Patrolman J. D. Tippit, who had evidently stopped him for questioning.

On the other hand, some assassination researchers today have taken an extreme opposite view, which disputes much of the evidence presented in this book. Oswald was innocent of the assassination, they believe, and was set up to take the fall, becoming a "lone patsy," having fired no shots at all (even at Officer Tippit).

In a careful review of the evidence, however, done with an open mind, I would hope that readers will decide for themselves what the evidence proves beyond any doubt.

THE FIRST SCENARIO CONSIDERED HERE IS THAT OSWALD WAS A "lone nut" assassin as determined in the Report issued by the Warren Commission in 1964. The government body of seven men and their staffs reached the conclusion that Oswald did all of the shooting and that one of the bullets had done damage to both Kennedy and Connally at one time. This was eventually challenged by researchers as not possible, and the government returned the criticism by labeling researchers as "buffs." The public was told that the Warren Commission Report would stand for all time as the definitive answer to the Kennedy assassination.

Over the years, however, the conclusions of the Report of the Warren Commission (not the testimony of the witnesses) have continued to attract microscopic criticism. Many facts have since become known that were not included in the Report due to work of private citizens interested in the case. A large amount of documentation was withheld from the Commission by various government agencies, including the CIA and FBI. As shown in this book alone, the FBI withheld the knowledge that Oswald possessed a spy camera which had been turned over to them from the Dallas Police Department. (See Chapter VIII.)

The "single bullet theory" evolved from the work of the Warren Commission by a study of the evidence provided by other government agencies. Chief Justice Earl Warren, the man who headed up the Commission, was told by LBJ that if he did not take on the task of investigating the President's death, the United States might be led into another world war.[1]

Later, with the establishment of the House Select Committee in the 1970's, the conclusion was drawn that President Kennedy was probably killed as the result of a conspiracy. The "lone nut" assassin conclusion was at that time discounted, largely as a result of the new acoustics evidence (shown in this book to be untrue). However, since that time, the public has been left basically on its own to rediscover if the "lone nut" assassin conclusion was, in fact, valid.

ON THE OTHER END OF THE SPECTRUM ARE NOW MANY PRIVATE assassination researchers. Some, having been shunned by official agencies for years, have decided not to trust ANY evidence which has been siphoned through governmental channels. The blacking out of large blocks of assassination-related documents released through Freedom of Information Act requests has proved extremely frustrating for them. The researchers' attitude is understandable, having worked on their own for so many years, attempting to separate the latest new rumor from the documented truth.

Some researchers studying the President's tragic death,

140. Dallas Police Crime Lab photo taken by Lt. Day showing the view seen by Officer Baker from the second-floor stairs. Baker saw movement through the glass in the door and ran to confront Oswald in the lunchroom.

however, have taken a giant leap of logic into the startling conclusion that Lee Harvey was a "lone patsy." They feel he was totally set up to take the fall for the shooting, having done nothing illegal at all. The argument has been put forth by some that Oswald was seen in the second-floor Depository lunchroom some twenty minutes before the assassination.[2] Today, that time period has been suggested to be as little as five minutes before the shooting. Researchers assert that Oswald was seen with a Coke in his hand in the lunchroom by Officer Baker only ninety seconds following the shots. They maintain that he would not have had the time to climb the stairs in five minutes, fire three shots at the President, and descend the stairs to be confronted by Officer Baker in that short period. Besides that, they contend that the motorcade was behind schedule and Oswald could not have possibly been so precise in

141. Dallas Police Crime Lab photo taken by Lt. Day showing the stairs up to the third floor of the Depository. The entry to the stairs going down is seen in the far left of the photo.

his timing.

According to the scenario put forth today by some of the researchers, Oswald was in the second-floor lunchroom during the time the shots were being fired from the sixth floor above and never actually fired his rifle. They believe that the boxes in the sniper's nest window were probably stacked by others. They further theorize that Oswald's rifle was planted by conspirators on the sixth floor in order to totally frame Oswald with the crime which he may have been unaware was about to happen. They feel as though he probably fled the building after somehow realizing that he might have been set up to take the fall for the assassination, two minutes after the event.

Researchers also question the eye witnesses to the shooting of Officer Tippit, and have great doubts as to whether Oswald

142. Dallas Police Crime Lab photo taken by Lt. Day showing a wider view of the second-floor stairway area with the door closed. A perspective may be gained by noting the position of the large safe, seen also in Photo 141.

actually did any shooting that day at all. They maintain his capture at the Texas Theater was probably a staged event and the Dallas police, in coordination with the government, may have falsely planted the palm print on the rifle found on the sixth floor by placing Oswald's dead hand on the disassembled rifle barrel as Oswald lay in his coffin at the Miller Funeral Home. Any evidence put forth by the Warren Commission is viewed with contempt since the lone assassin scenario is impossible for them to accept.

IN VIEWING BOTH POSITIONS WITH A NEW EYE, AS SEEN THROUGH Rusty's evidence, I feel a more rational approach should be considered. Remember that the FBI came and began seizing the evidence gathered by the Dallas Police Crime Lab on the night of the assassination. (They did not receive all of it, however, as has

143. Dallas Police Crime Lab photo taken by Lt. Day on November 25th, 1963, showing the entry door to the second-floor lunchroom. Notice the door with the glass insert, now seen from the opposite side (WC Exhibit 741).

been shown.) The Secret Service took the President's body from Parkland Hospital from Dr. Earl Rose, who under state law had jurisdiction to perform the autopsy in Dallas. The result was a controversial autopsy done at Bethesda Naval Hospital.

And please remember this statement as the most important in this entire book: RUSTY'S EVIDENCE IS DIRECT FROM THE CRIME LAB OF THE DALLAS POLICE DEPARTMENT. It did not go through the FBI or the Warren Commission. It is not tainted with the eye of someone who might wish to censor the evidence gathered in the case. The fingerprints on the trigger housing have here been re-examined to show that possible partial fingerprints of Oswald were found on the rifle from the sixth floor of the Depository in addition to Oswald's positively identified palm print.

The Warren Commission's single bullet theory has been

144. Dallas Police Crime Lab photo taken by Lt. Day showing the view seen while entering the second-floor lunchroom.

discounted today by many assassination researchers. A viewing of the Zapruder film of the assassination shows what they believe to be a physical impossibility of a shot from the rear causing the wounds to Kennedy and Connally. Minor discrepancies have been brought out in the government's handling of the investigation, and a call has gone out for a new, independent investigation.

Persistent researchers have shown that portions of the Warren Commission Report are inaccurate. The facts, when proven with documentation, cannot be disputed. However, *if the documentation has been proven false, it may then be discounted.* Much of Rusty's photographic evidence reinforces the known evidence in the Kennedy investigation. First generation quality photographs in Rusty's possession prove that the Dallas Police Department's evidence is genuine. Inside information contained in this book explains the innerworkings of the efforts of the Dallas detectives in handling the evidence. Simply because some of the points contained in the Warren Commission Report have been proven wrong, does not mean that all of the evidence is false. Complicity of the entire Dallas Police Department in a conspiracy to murder the President is preposterous. The Dallas Police Department was manipulated by outside forces to give up their evidence even as it was being processed.

ONE POINT NOTED BY THOSE ALLEGING COVER-UP AND CONSPIRACY charges in the Dallas Police Department concerns an accusation that Dallas Police Homicide Captain Will Fritz lied in his testimony to the Warren Commission concerning Deputy Sheriff Roger Craig. Before detailing the charge aimed at Captain Fritz, recall that the *Mauser* story told by Roger Craig in an interview 13 years after the assassination was shown to be inaccuarate, and that he changed his original testimony as told under oath to the Warren Commission. (See Chapter VI.)

Roger Craig also stated in his Warren Commission testimony that he had gone to Captain Fritz's office and spoken to him concerning someone whom he believed was Oswald leaving the Depository in a station wagon following the assassination. He stated that a Dallas officer had asked him to come down to the Homicide Office and take a look at Oswald in order to identify him as the man he'd seen. Craig claimed that Fritz "took me in his office--I believe it was his office--it was a little office, and had the suspect setting in a chair behind a desk."

Captain Fritz, in testifying to the Warren Commission, stated he remembered Craig, and recalled "One deputy sheriff . . . started to talk to me, but he was telling me some things that I knew wouldn't help us and I didn't talk to him, but someone else took an affidavit from him. His story that he was telling didn't fit with what we knew to be true."

Captain Fritz was then asked, "Did that man ever come into your office and talk to you in the presence of Oswald?"

Captain Fritz replied, "No, sir; I am sure that he did not. I believe that man did come to my office in that little hallway, you know, *outside my office* [emphasis added], and I believe I stepped outside the door and talked to him for a minute and I let someone else take an affidavit from him."

Later, a photograph was widely published showing Roger Craig standing inside the third-floor office door labeled "Homicide and Robbery Bureau." There was now proof, it was hailed, that Roger Craig was telling the truth about being inside Captain Fritz's office, and Fritz had lied to the Warren Commission.

Rusty told me that what Captain Fritz told the Warren Commission was the absolute truth. The area seen in the photograph where Craig is standing is an outer office of the Homicide Bureau, not Captain Fritz's personal office. Note that Oswald is not seen in the photograph, only various officers along with Craig. Captain Fritz's small office was located off of the area seen in the photo. Roger Craig was not telling the whole truth.

MANY FEEL THAT OSWALD DID NOT ACT ALONE. NEW FACTS AND witnesses continue to be uncovered by researchers in an attempt to prove a conspiracy existed in the assassination. For instance, one witness named Ed Hoffman (who attended the 1991 Dallas conference) stated that he saw two men standing behind the stockade fence on the grassy knoll area. He said he saw one of the men facing the motorcade turn around holding a rifle in his hands. The man was wearing some type of uniform with a hat and, after passing the rifle to his accomplice standing beside him, turned and straightened his hat and casually walked away. According to Hoffman, the accomplice then ran with the rifle through the parking lot to a railroad switching post and knelt to break the rifle down. He then placed the disassembled rifle into a small tool box and walked off into the direction of the railroad yards.

Hoffman was advised, he said, to keep his story to himself by his uncle, who at that time served on the Dallas Police Department. His uncle's stated reason was that the assassin had been caught and the case was being handled by the federal authorities.[3]

THE SECOND SCENARIO PUT FORTH BY SOME RESEARCHERS OF Oswald as a "lone patsy" will now be examined. First, and most importantly, the fingerprints issue must be explored. Faking fingerprints on the multiple and key items of evidence would, of necessity, have to be assumed, should the lone patsy belief survive.

The facts are that Oswald's palm print and partial fingerprints were found on the rifle on the sixth floor. Rusty's photographs of the original trigger-housing fingerprints and the original fingerprint card rolled by Rusty have been independently studied today by Captain Jerry Powdrill of the West Monroe Police Department and shown to be a possible match. There were no other prints found on the gun of any other conspirators who some claim may have planted the gun by the stairway. Rusty's photographs and fingerprint card are not fake.

It cannot be denied that the boxes found stacked in the sniper's window had the fingerprints of Oswald on them. The prints found of Oswald were the freshest prints on the boxes. He was the last one to have handled the boxes. An argument can correctly be made that since Oswald worked on the sixth floor that his fingerprints would have been on the boxes. However, remember that the three boxes in the window were deliberately stacked by the shooter and Oswald's prints were the freshest prints found on them. Rusty examined the boxes for Oswald's prints firsthand and found that they were Oswald's prints. The prints on the boxes were not fake.

A palm print was found on a box by the window in the position where Oswald's right hand would have rested as he was sitting waiting for the motorcade to approach. The location of the palm print on the box does not conform to where a typical palm print would be placed from Oswald carrying the box of books, but appeared to be made as he sat waiting for the motorcade. The palm print on the box used by Oswald to sit on was examined by Lieutenant Day and Pete Barnes and found to match his known palm print. This palm print was not a fake.

Other facts developed through the evidence of the sixth-floor photographs clearly show that Oswald had a clear path to exit the sixth floor by running down the east wall of the Depository and then along the north wall of the building by the elevators. The short stacks of boxes that the gun was hidden behind indicate that Oswald leaned over them with the rifle in his right hand, placing it on the floor behind the stacks.

Oswald then turned around and ran down the small corner stairs to the second-floor lunchroom where he was seen by Dallas Officer Marion Baker. Baker stated that when he first observed Oswald he "caught a glimpse of this man . . . through this window in this door, . . . walking away from me, about 20 feet away from me in the lunchroom"[4] (on the second floor). Oswald was not seen by Officer Baker sitting down eating his lunch as put forth by the "lone patsy" scenario.

One other extremely condemning fact pointing towards the guilt of Oswald is that immediately after the encounter with Officer Baker he walked out the front door of the Depository and left work.[5] After a head count of Depository employees carried out following the Dallas police arrival, it was determined by the building superintendent, Roy Truly, that Oswald was not in the building. Truly then notified Police Homicide Captain Will Fritz, who was on the sixth floor, of the missing worker.[5] Why would Oswald have left so quickly? It certainly makes sense that anyone firing a rifle at a presidential motorcade would flee the scene.

In order for the "lone patsy" scenario to be credible, it is necessary to believe that Oswald did not fire any shots. The palm print (seen by Rusty on the night of the assassination) would thus not have existed until three days later (remember Lieutenant Day stated that the palm print he had lifted was old and dry) and the partial fingerprints on the trigger housing examined today by Captain Powdrill would have never existed.

Researchers assert that the fingerprints found on the boxes were there because Oswald worked on the sixth floor. They contend that the bag used by Oswald to bring the rifle into the building was not photographed and may have been planted by unknown conspirators (possibly the Dallas police). In trying to determine the truth, naturally the best course of action would be to ask those nearest a situation what they saw, felt, etc. Researchers have had at their disposal a list, printed in the Warren Commission, of all of the detectives working in the Dallas Crime Lab (WC Volume XIX, Batchelor Exhibit 5002). It has been twenty-nine years since the assassination, and Rusty has NEVER been approached by any researcher to tell his story. Why was I the first one to discover that those nearest the investigation might possess firsthand knowledge of the evidence gathered in the case?

In defense of the researchers, I would think most have incorrectly assumed that John C. Day was the only man to examine the palm print before its release to the FBI. To the author's knowledge, no other researcher has asked the other men working in the Crime Lab if they saw the palm print lifted from the rifle by Lieutenant Day. Admittedly, having an uncle who worked in the Crime Lab has opened many doors to old friends. But why do I get the feeling that no one before me has tried to open those doors? Most of the men who were there that Rusty and I have spoken to are still alive and well and speak freely of what they saw. The evidence must be accepted along with the eye-witness testimony of those who were there.

I FAIL TO UNDERSTAND ANY ATTEMPT TO LINK THE FEDERAL government with the Dallas police in a coordinated conspiracy to murder the President. The Dallas police were a local entity. They were not part of the federal government. Haphazardly linking the two together as plotters is irrational.

The Dallas police were manipulated, however, by outside forces. The Dallas Police Department was deprived after the assassination of the use of the FBI training facilities. Why did this occur? Could it have been retaliation in response to Chief Curry telling the media that the FBI knew of Oswald's presence in Dallas prior to the assassination, but did not inform Curry of Oswald's being a threat to the President? Curry had unknowingly bucked J. Edgar Hoover, and eventually lost his job because of what he had said. The Dallas Police Department and the FBI were not working together to convict Oswald in the assassination of JFK.

Why is it necessary to take the giant leap taking Oswald totally out of the sniper's nest and make him totally innocent? The evidence is overwhelming that he actively participated in the events of the day. There exists eye-witness testimony of Oswald slaying Officer Tippit, as well as Oswald resisting arrest in the Texas Theater. He even pulled his revolver on the arresting Dallas officer and pulled the trigger. The fortunate "click" of a misfire was heard by many of the witnesses to his arrest. In other words, a second Dallas policeman was almost killed by the man arrested for the killing of Officer Tippit. Why are researchers quick to accept eye-witness evidence of a gunman on the grassy knoll verbatim, but question eye-witness testimony here?

IS IT SO DIFFICULT TO BELIEVE THAT LEE HARVEY OSWALD DID PULL the trigger of his rifle from the sixth-floor window of the Texas School Book Depository Building?

I would hope that the public will now begin to take another look at the role that Oswald played on that day in conjunction with the roles played by countless others. They all interrelate somehow, and all of the leads should be explored.

We cannot, however, summarily discount the evidence that does not fit our particular scenario and then accept only the evidence which does. I, for one, do not feel that the innocent bystander witnesses forever affected by what they saw on November 22nd, 1963, lied (unless it is proven). Let's accept what they said as forthright and try to put ALL of the pieces together to arrive at the truth.

1. Jim Marrs, *Crossfire* (N.Y.: Carroll & Graf Publishers, Inc., 1989), 464.
2. Ibid., 49.
3. Ibid., 83.
4. Warren Commission, *Hearings Before the President's Commission on the Assassination of President Kennedy,* 26 vols. (Washington D.C.: U.S. Government Printing Office, 1964), III: 250.
5. Warren Commission, *Report of President's Commission on the Assassination of President John F. Kennedy* (Washington, D.C.: U. S. Government Printing Office, 1964), 154-155.

EPILOGUE

BY R. W. (RUSTY) LIVINGSTON

WHEN MY NEPHEW GARY SAVAGE FIRST APPROACHED ME ABOUT writing this book, I was somewhat skeptical. Gary and I had been going over the evidence photographs and materials that I had of the Kennedy assassination investigation, and he thought what I had was important.

We both began reading many different books on the subject, and came to realize that some of the points stated as fact in them simply were not so. The photographs and other related materials which I've had in my possession since the first day, as well as my knowledge as an eye-witness, proved that some of the claims we'd read were false.

I eventually came to the realization that the things I recalled were important, and the skepticism I had at first about Gary writing the book began to fade. I felt I did have something important that needed to be said.

EVER SINCE THE ASSASSINATION HAPPENED, NOW ALMOST 30 YEARS ago, the Dallas Police Department has been criticized and maligned by the news media and others, and I've always wished that I could do something about it. Being an old burnt-out detective with little energy or resources left, I didn't think there was anything that I could do. I now welcome the chance to speak out.

Having had a small part in the investigation, and having been associated with the other officers that were involved, I have personal knowledge of many things that went on during those first few hours after the shots were fired in Dealey Plaza. The Dallas

Police Department gathered up a tremendous amount of evidence in a very short time before the investigation was taken out of our hands. No matter what the critics may say, I personally know that we did a damn good job in those first few hours when we had control of the investigation.

I knew the principal officers who handled the investigation. Captain Will Fritz, the Commander of the Homicide Bureau, was in charge of the murder investigation of the assassination of President Kennedy. Note I said "murder" because that's what it was, a murder committed in the city limits of Dallas, Texas. The Dallas Police Department had jurisdiction over the case.

CAPTAIN FRITZ WAS ONE OF THE MOST COMPETENT INVESTIGATORS I've ever had the priviledge to know. He was smart and he was tough. He ran the Homicide Bureau on his own terms. He was practically autonomous because he was so good.

I personally feel that if he had been left alone to investigate the case and been able to interrogate Oswald alone, he would have probably been able to get the true facts from him. I also believe that if Captain Fritz had been left alone to handle the transfer of Oswald the way he wanted to, Oswald would not have been killed.

Lieutenant Carl Day was the supervisor of the Crime Scene Search Section, more commonly known as the Crime Lab. He was a very dedicated officer, and very knowledgeable in crime scene search techniques. He specialized in development of latent fingerprints, comparing and classifying fingerprints, photography, and gathering and preserving physical crime scene evidence.

LIEUTENANT DAY IS ONE OF THE MOST CONCIENTIOUS AND HONEST men I've ever known. He's a good Christian man. He doesn't smoke, drink, or use profanity. To insinuate that he would take part in any conspiracy or cover-up of the assassination investigation is beyond belief. It just didn't happen. Any testimony or reports that he gave in regard to his part in the investigation were the truth, to the best of his knowledge.

EPILOGUE

The work done by Lieutenant Day on that first day is to be commended. Lieutenant Day personally was involved in the following:

1) Searching for evidence, and documenting the evidence found on the sixth floor of the Depository Building.
2) Taking charge of the rifle found on the sixth floor and developing the latent fingerprints and the palm print found to be Oswald's before he had been murdered.
3) Developing fingerprints and a palm print on the boxes stacked in the sixth-floor sniper's nest window.

On the first day, the Dallas Police Department

1) Arrested Oswald in less than two hours after the shooting of President Kennedy and less than one hour after the shooting of Officer Tippit.
2) Recovered the revolver on Oswald, later shown to be the murder weapon of Officer Tippit.
3) Recovered Oswald's rifle and empty hulls dropped on the floor by the sniper's nest window.
4) Developed the information leading to the Paine residence and recovered personal effects of Oswald.
5) Developed the information leading to a search of Oswald's rented room in Oak Cliff.
6) Arraigned Oswald for the murder of Officer Tippit and later for the murder of President Kennedy.

IT HAS BEEN STATED IN SOME BOOKS THAT OSWALD WAS NEVER officially arraigned for the murder of President Kennedy. This is not true. I personally observed his arraignment in the Identification

Bureau on the night of the assassination. I was standing to the left and slightly behind Justice of the Peace David Johnston when he arraigned Oswald "for the murder of One, John Fitzgerald Kennedy, white male, forty-seven."

These were his exact words. I'll never forget them because it sounded so strange to me. I had always held the Office of the Presidency in such high regard and had expected Judge Johnston to say the President of the United States. This brought it down to me that legally this was a murder just like any other murder in any city, and would be handled like any other murder. These were the cold, hard facts. At that time, it was not a federal offense to kill a president, as it is now. The case was under the jurisdiction of the city of Dallas, and no one else.

POLICE CHIEF JESSE CURRY HAS ALSO BEEN THE TARGET OF criticism in books on the assassination. Having known him personally, I can tell you that he was a good chief. He was well-educated and an experienced police administrator. He was a fair man. Being in the position he was placed in, he could not always do things the way he wanted. His concerns were to protect his police department and the city of Dallas from further criticism. His desire was to assure the continued privilege of cooperation between his department and the FBI, the media, and other agencies.

Chief Curry, in trying to accommodate the press, allowed them to stay in the Police Department Building. This proved to be the action which allowed Jack Ruby an opportunity to slip in and shoot Oswald. In hindsight, he should have cleared the press out, keeping them informed of the information developed in the case. This would also have allowed a discreet transfer of Oswald to the County Jail, preventing his murder.

ANOTHER GREAT PIECE OF WORK WAS DONE BY A FORMER DALLAS officer, and has been ignored until now. The study by James C. Bowles in his "Rebuttal to the Acoustical Evidence Theory" was done in response to the findings of the HSCA. (See Appendix.)

Although his work was written in the late seventies, he used his own first day evidence (the dictabelt tapes) to demonstrate that the sounds on the tapes were not shots.

Even though an excellent job was done by the Dallas police in those first few hours after the assassination, the case began to deteriorate when the Secret Service, for whatever reasons, illegally removed the body of President Kennedy from Dallas before an autopsy was performed. Had the body been left at Parkland Hospital and Dr. Earl Rose been allowed to do the autopsy, it would have been known in the first few hours how many times the President had been shot, and from which direction.

If the Crime Lab technicians had been able to photograph and examine the presidential limousine, there would have been less doubt and speculation that later arose concerning bullet fragments and the number of shots. Describing what might have been is an effort in futility. It does indicate, however, the outside forces at work to manipulate and influence the Dallas police in the investigation of the President.

I have never seen or heard any concrete evidence that there was a conspiracy in the Dallas Police Department to cover-up evidence in the Kennedy case. If a conspiracy existed, and please note I said IF, it happened after the investigation was taken out of our hands. I would hope that publishing every bit of evidence that I have in the investigation will prove and support that fact.

I SPENT 23 YEARS OF MY LIFE AS A POLICE OFFICER OR "COP" AS MOST people called us. I used to hate that word, but now I find myself using it sometimes when people ask me what line of work I retired from. The reason I disliked the word was that most people used it in a derogatory manner. I felt that it showed disrespect for the police profession.

I was always proud, and still am, that I was a policeman. The job is one of the toughest, most demanding, gut-wrenching, emotion-filled professions that I've experienced. Policemen get little credit for a job well done and little respect from most civilians. It can have a devastating affect on your psyche. It is, however, one of the most fascinating jobs that any person could hold.

Being a policeman is tough. People view you as a figure of authority, and many resent authority. No one wants to be told what to do. They feel the law should be enforced, but not when it comes to them. Catch a thief, and you'll get a pat on the back today. But stop them for a traffic violation tomorrow, and you'll be called every name in the book while being lied to and told they did nothing wrong. People don't realize you're trying to save their lives.

Many times it's not the thief that can frustrate an officer. The police are used to being treated badly by the bad guys. That type of behavior is expected from them. What really gets an officer is uncaring people who they are simply trying to protect. The good citizen is quick to criticize when seeing an officer not do his job perfectly. Quick criticism from good citizens is extremely frustrating.

ONE OF THE MOST FRUSTRATING EXPERIENCES IN ALL OF MY YEARS of police work happened one evening years ago which illustrates the points I've just made. I came closer to quitting that night than at any other time, but I hung in there because I wanted to be a detective.

It began on a cold Christmas Eve around 5 p.m. I was a young patrolman on my first regular beat. I was working the 3:00 to 11:00 shift alone since my partner had to be pulled away to work the evening traffic rush of last minute shoppers. It was about 5:00 when I received a call of an accident out at the edge of my beat in Dallas.

A vehicle had run a stop sign at a narrow intersection and plowed into a car with a family of four inside. Both streets were narrow two-lane roads with no way to pass on the shoulder. The man in the car which had been hit had been killed instantly, and his wife had been seriously injured. The kids in the back seat had been banged up badly.

I immediately called for two ambulances and asked the dispatcher to send an accident squad. I was told that all squads were tied up working other accidents at the time. I then asked for a backup squad car to come and help me clear the traffic which had backed up badly. I was told all were busy, so I was on my own.

Many of the good citizens that happened to be driving by began getting out of their cars to come up to see the gore of the accident. I now saw that the traffic had become blocked all four ways and had backed up a full two blocks. People were double parked on both sides of the street looking at the accident, preventing the ambulances from getting through to the victims. I began giving first aid to the woman and begging the people to get back to their cars and move them so that the ambulances could get around to the accident. Most of them just stood there staring at me, and some began to make wise cracks.

I yelled out for some of the men to help me get the traffic moving so that the ambulances could get through. Some did, but some stood there asking me why wouldn't I call for more "cops" to come help. They told me that's what I was getting paid for. Finally, with the help of some of the people, we got the ambulances in there and away with the injured people. The mother died on the way to the hospital.

After the ambulances had left, I tried to get the traffic cleared out so the wrecker trucks could get the cars out of the street. It took about 20 minutes for them to get through. At that time, it was a violation to park and leave your car at the scene of an accident, so I began to inform the people standing around to once again get in their cars and move them. I began writing tickets and placing them on the cars since no one was taking me seriously. One man started going behind me and began taking the tickets off the cars and tearing them up. By this time, I was emotionally wrecked from having just witnessed the little boy lying by his dead father, crying and patting him on the face.

My patience was gone. I grabbed the man who had been tearing up the tickets and threw him on the ground. I put my handcuffs on him and flung him in my squad car. On the way to the car, I heard the crowd yelling, "Police brutality," and "Somebody ought to report him!" That little action helped me let off some steam. Then I turned back to the crowd and tipped by hat and told them, "Thanks for your cooperation," and left.

LATER THAT NIGHT, MY PARTNER REJOINED ME AFTER HIS TRAFFIC detail was over. We got a routine call on a family disturbance. A man had been out celebrating Christmas Eve with the boys, and his wife had jumped on him about it. He had slapped her around, and she had called the police.

When we arrived, the man was good and mad. He was drunk and wanted to fight us. My partner and I tried to choke him down and get the handcuffs on him. He was almost as big as my partner and I put together, but we both managed to get him down. About that time, the man's wife began feeling as though we were using a little too much force on her husband. She began beating me over the head with her high-heeled shoe while I was holding onto her husband. I got a few knots on my head from that.

Before that night was over, I came very close to quitting the police profession. I kept thinking about that little boy losing his father on Christmas Eve after having probably been so excited about Santa Claus coming that night. What a tragedy!

This one story is an example of hundreds that I've experienced which demonstrate how tough it can be to be a policeman. Usually very little appreciation is shown towards officers, and most people could care less what might happen to you while you're on duty. You do occasionally run across the exception: Some good citizen will show their appreciation to you by writing a letter of commendation to the Chief. That small act of kindness makes you feel as though you're not entirely wasting your time and you want to hang in there a little longer.

A LARGE MAJORITY OF POLICE ARE CARING MEN AND WOMEN WITH families who have a sincere desire to help people. Most wouldn't stay in the profession if they didn't care about people. Few will admit it, but most could probably make a better living doing something else, but won't leave because they care.

Around a bad murder scene, the officers crack jokes and act as though what has happened doesn't bother them. They're supposed to be tough, and they certainly don't want the other officers to think they're softies. Away from the scene is another story. Inside, the officer's guts are wrenching, and many are deeply affected by what they witness daily. It has to be suppressed somehow, and you're expected to go on with the next case that comes your way. The job can be devastating to your emotions.

A policeman has to have control over his emotions. A good example can involve the situation of a high speed chase. Having been on several myself, I know it is an extremely frightening experience. Having to drive through traffic at a high rate of speed, risking your life, and knowing at any moment you might be injured or killed in an accident is tough on your mentality. Thoughts of your family float through your mind at a time like that.

When you finally get a suspect's car stopped, you are emotionally strung out. It can take a concerted effort to keep your temper under control. Sometimes you can and sometimes you can't. You may have had a bad day, but you are expected to control your emotions. You must walk up calmly and inform the person of his rights and calmly place him under arrest. If the suspect resists, you are expected to restrain him, getting him under control without using excessive force.

Controlling your temper can be one of the most difficult obstacles to overcome in being a policeman. I lost my temper at times because it always bothered me to see people foul up their lives. It still does. Many thieves I've known were intelligent and likable, with good personalities. They could have worked on a legitimate job, but would rather steal to make a living. They would get caught, go to the pen for five years, get released, and do the same thing again.

I ONCE KNEW A MECHANIC IN DALLAS WHO ALSO DID THE BEST bodywork around. He had a good business that he owned. He had invented a small hydraulic jack that was small enough to fit in a briefcase. He had a couple of safe burglar customers who had talked him into joining them in committing a burglary. The friends believed that his invention would enable them to jack the pin out of the safe. His jack worked quietly and quickly. He went along with them, and they all got caught. He lost his family and his business, and continued to steal all his life. I still cannot understand the thinking of a man like that.

A deep toll can be inflicted on a policeman by witnessing the carnage inflicted by one human being on another. I've seen wasted lives ruined by greed, alcohol, drugs, and carelessness. I've seen pain inflicted on good people who've been beaten and robbed of their hard-earned possessions by an uncaring thief. I've seen women who've been raped and degraded by violence. I've witnessed many incidents as they've happened or shortly after they've happened. The adrenalin of a call can be quickly replaced by the sickening reality of violence and destruction.

I've had the thrill of catching burglars and armed robbers in the act. I've captured murderers and those committing assaults on individuals. I've gone into darkened buildings after burglars, not knowing if they were armed or not. I've been in dark alleys searching for suspects. Several times I've had shots go past me. Fortunately, I was never hit. I never had to shoot anyone, which I am extremely glad to admit. Other officers I've spoken to through the years who have, explain that it is a troubling thing to go through. Many nights were spent with no sleep following a shooting by a policeman.

I've drawn my revolver several times through the years but never had to fire it. During a situation such as this, a split second decision must be made as to whether or not to fire. Many things race through your mind at the time. You wonder whether or not you'll be killed and if you have the legal right to take someone's life to protect yourself. Was there enough of a threat to justify firing?

The decision must be made on the spot, and many times the results can be devastating to the officer, both emotionally and legally.

Hesitation may result in your death. In the event an officer fires his weapon, an investigation routinely follows. The officer faces the possibility both of being fired on during the incident and of losing his job. An officer can make a split-second decision which may take the courts years to sort out.

Over the years, I've been spit on, bitten, kicked, punched, and scratched. I've had my nose broken twice, two ribs broken, my fingers broken, and a shoulder thrown out of place once when chasing an escaped prisoner. I've been operated on for a hernia incurred on the job helping a man push his car out of a ditch after he'd been speeding down a wet highway. I had to pay for the operation. Being a policeman can be a tough job sometimes.

Sensationalism sells newspapers. It is a sad fact that the public enjoys hearing and reading only the spectacular stories. Rarely do the good things and the heroic deeds done by the police get told. The officers on patrol are there trying to keep the streets safe for the good people and their families. It does my heart good to read about the good deeds that an officer has done. Hearing them inspires me to be a better person.

Although I've described many of the negative aspects of police work, I did, however, enjoy being a policeman. There was nothing as thrilling as working a good case to its conclusion. As you work the clues and the leads begin coming your way, you don't want to stop working. A breaking case can take many continuous hours or days. One particular burglary case I worked on for 19 hours the first day, 16 hours the second day, and 14 hours the third day before the case broke open. I didn't want to stop at the end of each day, and only did when I was completely exhausted.

The fascination for solving difficult cases was the main reason I stayed with police work. I've always had an inquiring mind and always enjoyed solving mysteries. Even as a child, I enjoyed reading stories of lawmen in the old West. In my late teens, I developed a desire to become a detective. I never particularly wanted to be a uniformed patrolman, even though I enjoyed being one at the time.

WHEN I JOINED THE DALLAS POLICE DEPARTMENT, YOU HAD TO spend at least three years as a patrolman before you were eligible to take the examination for detective. The exam was given once a year, and only the top 15 were placed on a list to wait for an opening to come up in the Department. I took the exam along with about 200 others, and I had to do a lot of studying in order to place in the top 15.

Openings developed when a detective was promoted, retired, or quit. If no opening developed during the year, you had to re-take the exam and place once again in the top 15. I placed in the top 15 the first time I took the exam. Fortunately, an opening came up towards the end of my year of eligibility. I spent four and a half years as a patrolman before I made detective. I was thrilled I had reached the goal set when I was young. I persevered through the hard times as a patrolman and reached the goal I had set for myself.

I WOULD LIKE TO DEDICATE THIS BOOK TO THE MANY GOOD MEN AND women who are pursuing the law enforcement profession, a sometimes thankless job, which so many are doing with commendable dedication. May you overcome the adversities, and may God bless you, because usually, He's the only one who will!

> R. W. Livingston
> Old Burnt-Out Detective
> July, 1993

P. S. I would still like to work one more good case before the Lord calls me home. I could tell you more. . .

A P P E N D I X

THE KENNEDY ASSASSINATION TAPES

A Rebuttal to the Acoustical Evidence Theory

by

James C. Bowles

Copyright 1979
(Printed by permission of the author.)

CONTENTS

Preface

PART I

CHAPTER ONE
    Setting the Stage
    ---Introduction
    ---Reference to Time and Recordings
    ---Technical Reference to Radios and Recorders

CHAPTER TWO
    Critique of the Committee Report

CHAPTER THREE
    What Did Happen in Dealey Plaza
    ---The Motorcade
    ---Dealey Plaza and the Assassination

CHAPTER FOUR
    The Rebuttal
    ---Defense of the Rebuttal
    ---Conclusion and Summation

PART II

CHAPTER FIVE
Technical Considerations
---Time Discrepancy in 12:30 Time-Check on Channel II
---Fixing the Time the Shots Were Fired
---Comparison of Shooting Times
---Reconstruction and Progression of Motorcade Trip to Parkland Hospital
---Time and Position Confirmation Through Officer Working Beat 38
---The Sound of Sirens on Channel I
---The Motorcycle with the Stuck Microphone
---Comparison of Cross-Channel Messages

CHAPTER SIX
Reflections
---Officer A
---Officer B
---Officer C
---Officer D
---Officer E
---Officer F
---Officer G
---Officer H
---Officer I
---Officer J
---Officer K
---Civilian L
---Officer McLain

APPENDIX
Transcripts of Dallas Police Department Radio Communications
---Introduction
---Channel I
---End Notes Commentary - Channel I
---Channel II
---End Notes Commentary - Channel II

PREFACE

The Select Committee on Assassinations was created in September, 1976 and terminated its activity in December, 1978. Its principal accomplishment, its so-called acoustical evidence, is at least inaccurate.

Briefly stated, the Select Committee on Assassinations received certain recordings considered to be recordings of the Dallas Police Department radio transmissions on radio channels 1 and 2 for Friday, November 22, 1963, covering the assassination of President John F. Kennedy and the wounding of Governor John Connally. The committee staff, in listening to the recording of Channel 1, more especially a five-plus minute period during the assassination when a microphone switch stuck in the "on" position resulting in an open transmitter, formulated a hypothesis: What if the radio with the open mike was in Dealey Plaza and recorded the assassination shots?

There was no reason to believe the open mike was in or even near Dealey Plaza, and more than ample reason to know that it was not. Nevertheless, the Committee staff pursued their hypothesis beyond ordinary means, resulting in what they declared to be **acoustical evidence.**

Through the process of developing and enhancing any notion which enhanced their hypothesis, and discounting or ignoring all challenges, the Committee staff concluded that there was ". . .a high probability that two gunmen fired at President John F. Kennedy." (Committee Report, page 93.)

The keystone to that statement is their **Scientific Acoustical Evidence**. If the acoustical evidence is true and correct-if it exists, it leaves no doubt that, contrary to the *Warren Commission Report*, a fourth shot was fired at President Kennedy and that the shot came from a position referred to as "the grassy knoll," a shot fired by at least a second assassin. Further, that while two assassins do not establish a conspiracy, such an event is too coincidental to have occurred by mere chance.

However, should it be established that the open mike was **not** operating in a position from which it could have transmitted the sound of shots in Dealey Plaza, or should it be established that there are defects in the scientific deductions sufficient to nullify the authority of their scientific conclusions, that keystone would be removed and their acoustical evidence theory would collapse. With the loss of the acoustical evidence, Committee conclusions based on that evidence would suffer the same fate.

The absolute rebuttal of the "scientific acoustical evidence" is the objective of this Report.

More emphatically than the Committee concluded that their scientific acoustical evidence was valid, it is here and now unequivocally rebutted and rejected from its initial hypothesis to its final assumption.

An effort will be made to present rebuttal in terms which are easy to understand, but with sufficient detail to enable the reader to personally judge its validity.

The names of most officers have been deliberately omitted. Those officers who unfortunately had roles in the assassination scenario have been contacted at all hours and uncounted times by official investigators, private speculators and quacks. For those readers who choose to believe there was a conspiracy, the inclusion of names would not change their minds. Those who feel the matter is closed would not miss the names. And then there is that body of people in between who don't care one way or another.

PART I

CHAPTER ONE - SETTING THE STAGE
INTRODUCTION

November 22, 1963 started without any suggestion of its becoming a day of infamy. It was a cool and rainy morning, but as the day progressed, the weather improved. The clouds cleared, a warm sun shone brightly, and thousands of well-wishers turned out to welcome the President of the United States. The Dallas Police Department, in support of the Secret Service, began executing carefully planned arrangements for the President's visit. The dreary day became cheerful, and the President's motorcade was progressing exceedingly well. Years later it still seems paradoxical that such a fine day and a careful plan being executed so exactingly could have experienced such a tragic end. Actually, that day has never ended, nor is it likely that it ever will.

To refresh the reader's memory, Texas politics in that period could be described as "changing." The concept of Republican and Democrat was giving way to the ideology of Conservative and Liberal. Democrats in Texas were at odds with each other. The headlines of *The Dallas Morning News*, November 22, 1963, read, "Storm of Political Controversy Swirls Around Kennedy on Visit," and "Split State Party Continues Feuds." In the 1960 election the Kennedy-Johnson ticket lost in Dallas while carrying Texas by an alarmingly small margin. Dallas had been described as a developing seat of conservative philosophy and Republican politics. President Kennedy had embarked on a tour of Texas in an effort to raise campaign funds and to unite party members. The President, accompanied by Vice-President Lyndon B. Johnson, Texas Governor John Connally, and an entourage of dignitaries, wives, staff members, and the media was in Dallas for a luncheon and speech at the Trade Mart, Stemmons Freeway and Industrial Boulevard. Some of the President's advisors were opposed to his appearance in Dallas, but he would not be dissuaded. Success in Dallas should be profitable, and rally the Democratic Party in Texas in support of his candidacy in 1964.

Plans for such a visit are lengthy and complex. The Secret Service is charged with the primary duty to protect the President. In that capacity, their representatives and Dallas Police executives were busily involved in developing plans a full week preceding the President's arrival. The Dallas Police Department furnished nearly 500 of its 1100 officers in support of those plans. Additionally, the Dallas County Sheriff's Department, the Texas Department of Public Safety, and the Dallas Police Reserves furnished nearly 100 more men. These were in addition to the local Secret Service and FBI personnel who were involved in the maximum effort to ensure the safety of the President. It was necessary to provide security for the arrival and departure area at Love Field, security along the 9 1/2 mile parade route, for the large gathering at the Trade Mart, and for the four-mile route back to Love Field. Obviously, the best of plans cannot recognize every contingency and respond successfully. There were numerous overpasses, uncounted manholes, storm sewers, trees, roofs and windows, and uncounted thousands of spectators who jammed the motorcade route.

The motorcade started a few minutes late but managed to proceed close to its schedule. The crowds were exuberant, encroaching on every vantage point along the route. Protestors were conspicuous by their absence. At Lemmon and Lomo Alto streets, a small girl held up a sign which asked the President to please stop and say hello, which he graciously did.

Incidents such as that, the clearing weather, the bright warm sun, and the tremendous and loudly cheering crowds were exactly what the president needed. He ordered the protective plastic bubble removed from his limousine. The Kennedy magic was at its best. Then, more than halfway along the route through Dallas, and just as the motorcade broke through the heaviest street crowds, with thousands more leaning and cheering from windows, the bottom fell out. Shots echoed through Dealey Plaza. President Kennedy was mortally wounded, Governor Connally was seriously wounded. The public was thrown into stunned disbelief. The local criminal justice community was thrust into momentary chaos, and the general reputation of the community was crucified.

Immediately after the assassination, the law enforcement community set into motion its investigation of the criminal offense. One person had been murdered and another wounded. Who had fired from what location, with what weapon? What was the motive? What was the ultimate objective? In addition there were the urgencies of national security and the succession to the presidency. President Johnson had to be securely guarded. Was there a conspiracy? What would happen next, how, where, by whom, and to whom?

The follow-up investigation and results were prompt, suspicioned by some, and in some ways, inconclusive. However, based on the legitimate evidence, they were complete.Rumors and theories were plentiful, but facts were scarce. Essentially, the initial investigation led to the Texas School Book Depository, the last building along the motorcade route, providing an assassin a reasonably convenient access to the President. Inside the building an officer found the assassin's abandoned rifle. A name and description were developed, and a search was begun.

Exactly what transpired in the 400 block of East 10th Street in the Oak Cliff section of Dallas will never be known. According to witnesses, Officer J. D. Tippett stopped to talk to a subject later identified as Lee Harvey Oswald. Oswald spoke briefly with Tippett through the right front window of Officer Tippett's patrol car. Then, just after Tippett exited his car to approach Oswald, Oswald shot Tippett, killing him instantly. Fleeing on foot, Oswald was last seen running west along Jefferson Boulevard. Moments later officers following witness information were led to the Texas Theater. "Cry of Battle" and "War is Hell" were being screened. Officers entered the theater and observed Oswald sitting in the center section some three seats from the right-hand aisle and three or four rows from the rear of the auditorium. As Officer M. N. McDonald approached Oswald, Oswald stood, said "Well, it's all over now!", reached for a revolver he had concealed in his belt and attempted to shoot McDonald. Wedging the web-like skin between his thumb and index finger under the firing pin on Oswald's pistol, McDonald and other officers then subdued, disarmed and arrested Oswald. Witnesses to Tippett's murder identified Oswald as the assailant, and ballistics investigation, while not conclusive, strongly suggest that Oswald's revolver was the same weapon used to murder Officer Tippett. Unfortunately, Oswald would never stand trial for Tippett's murder. Eighty brief minutes in Dallas had set into motion unending episodes of concern, controversy, and intrigue.

One such episode prompted this undertaking. Congress gave life to the Congressional Select Committee on Assassinations, authorizing its probe into the assassinations of President John Fitzgerald Kennedy and Dr. Martin Luther King. Two years later and fifteen years after the assassination, the Committee concluded that there is a virtual certainty that President Kennedy was the victim of a conspiracy. They based the conclusion of their investigation on a recording of Dallas Police Department radio transmissions made during the motorcade which ended with the assassination. Their acoustics experts were satisfied that they had found not only the three generally acknowledged shots, but a fourth shot, recorded inaudibly where they had no reason to be found. Additionally, the acoustics experts concluded that the fourth shot was fired from a location generally referred to as "the grassy knoll," a mound some one hundred feet to the right front of President Kennedy's limousine. This would confirm the presence of at least a second assassin. The application of statistical theory would support the improbability that two such assassins, each acting without the knowledge of the other, would through coincidence alone select the exact same site and time for their acts. Accordingly, if there was a fourth shot and a second assassin, there would be reason to assume the existence of a conspiracy. However, no direct or corroborating evidence of a second shooter or a conspiracy was found.

The validity of the Committee findings depends entirely upon the validity of the acoustical studies and opinions. It is the intention of this author to prove that their conclusions are invalid. No criticism is directed toward the acoustics experts. Criticism would have to come from someone with greater scientific expertise, and would prove nothing.

I have neither **evidence nor opinion** with regard to how many assassins fired how many shots from what locations. As a trained and competent police officer, I remain open-minded in this area. Should competent evidence be uncovered, that investigation would be reopened. Until such evidence is uncovered, it would appear that the case should remain closed. What assassination investigators--the amateur and the accomplished, the well-intentioned and the meddlers--fail to consider is that the assassination of President Kennedy is a criminal act in the jurisdiction of the State of Texas, and in the venue of Dallas justice. For the Committee to declare that a second assassin fired from the grassy knoll is reckless and irresponsible. No competent attorney would go into a court with prosecution founded on such evidence. Why then would they offer such a concoction of wishful thinking as evidence?

Not having the time, the staff, and 5.8 million taxpayer dollars proved to be no handicap. The truth was before the investigators all the time. However, for reasons of their own, they chose to ignore the truth to pursue a fantastic hypothesis. The only problem is the necessity for some step-by-step preliminary explanations to facilitate an easier understanding of what really happened that tragic day in Dealey Plaza. The correct explanation is easy to make and to understand. After all, the truth always is its best defense.

REFERENCE TO TIME AND RECORDINGS

A considerable number of references to exact times, even to tenths of seconds, exist in the Committee's Report and in the following chapters. Therefore, two things must be established here and remembered throughout:

1. How time was reported and recorded by Dallas Police dispatchers, and
2. An absolutely accurate time base does not exist.

Since an absolute time base does not exist, and since careful time margins are important, there should be an acceptable explanation as to how times are derived so the reader might form an individual opinion as to the accuracy.

First, consideration should focus on how the dispatcher's office operated with regard to determining and recording time, especially since the Committee Report did not mention their method for making such determinations, and since they reported the recording methods inaccurately.

A master clock on the telephone room wall was connected to the City Hall system. This clock reported "official" time. Within the dispatcher's office there were numerous other time giving and time recording devices, both in the telephone room and in the radio room. Telephone operators and radio operators were furnished "Simplex" clocks. Because the hands often worked loose, they indicated the incorrect time. However, their purpose was to stamp the time, day and date on incoming calls. While they were reliable at this, they were not synchronized as stated in the Committee report. Therefore, it was not uncommon for the time stamped on calls to be a minute to two ahead or behind the "official" time shown on the master clock. Accordingly, at "exactly" 10:10, various clocks could be stamping from 10:08 to 10:12, for example. When clocks were as much as a minute or so out of synchronization it was normal procedure to make the needed adjustments. During busy periods this was not readily done.

In addition to the times stamped on calls by telephone operators, the radio operators stamped the "time" as calls were dispatched, and the "time" that officers completed an assignment and returned to service. Radio operators were also furnished with 12-hour digital clocks to facilitate their time references when they were not using call sheets containing stamped time. These digital clocks were not synchronized with any time standard. Therefore, the time "actual" and time "broadcast" could easily be a minute or so apart.

Now, multiply this by two since the police department was operating on two radio frequencies. For convenience they were referred to as Channel 1 and Channel 2. Calls for police service or information as well as interdepartmental messages were placed through the police communications office. Telephone clerks trained for the task handled the initial contacts. Telephone calls which required that an officer be sent to render a service were transcribed by hand on "call sheets" to inform the radio dispatcher as to the location and nature of the service request. The telephone clerk inserted the call sheet into the nearest time clock, causing the call sheet to be stamped with a "call received" time. The operator then sent the call sheet to the dispatcher by way of a conveyer belt which passed continuously between operators sitting opposite each other at the telephone stations. The conveyer belt terminated at the radio operator's console. The radio operator, upon receiving a call sheet, would select the officer appropriate to handle the call, dispatch the call to that officer, and stamp the call sheet with a "call dispatched" time. When the officer assigned a call had rendered the necessary service, he would inform the dispatcher that he was "clear." The dispatcher would then stamp the call sheet to obtain a "call cleared" time, and inform the officer of his clearing time. On November 22, 1963, the regular business of the department was conducted on Channel 1, and radio traffic associated with the President's visit was conducted on Channel 2. Next, consideration should be given to the methods of individual radio operators. A given operator at a given time might broadcast "time" a little early in one event then a little late the next. Accordingly, a call initiated at, say, 10:10 might be stamped at 10:13 by the dispatcher, only to have intervening radio traffic delay his broadcast. He might go ahead and announce the dispatch time as 10:13 and the digital clock then showed 10:14. Time intervals of less than one minute were never used. Likewise, the time stated in periodic station identification time checks was not always exact. During quiet intervals, station time checks were usually on time. However, radio operators did not interrupt radio traffic in progress just to give a station check. Accordingly, an operator might give, say, the 10:30 check as 10:30 when it was actually 10:29 or perhaps 10:31 or later. On another occasion, that same operator might state, "10:31 KKB 364," the correct time even though he was at least a minute late.

In a later chapter more definition will be given to estimating time as exactly as possible under the circumstances. The reader may then decide whether those methods and assumptions are acceptable. For now, however, a brief statement with regard to "time" during the assassination period is as follows:

> Channels 1 and 2 were in close synchronization, with Channel 2 announced time running approximately 15 seconds ahead of Channel 1. Accordingly, where a determination was necessary, a 15-second adjustment is used. Therefore, Channel 1 plus 15 seconds equals Channel 2 time: Channel 2 less 15 seconds equals Channel 1 time.

There is no way to connect "police time" with "real time." The Committee Report stated that the Dallas Police Communications system was recorded by continuously operating recorders. That statement is incorrect. Channel 1 was recorded on a Dictaphone A2TC, Model 5, belt or loop recorder. Channel 2 was recorded on a Gray "Audograph" flat disk recorder. Both were duplex units with one recording and one on standby for when the other unit contained a full recording. Both units were sound activated. It is important to note "sound" rather than "voice" because either sound or noise from any source, received through the transmission line, would activate the recorders. Once activated, the recorders remained "on" for the duration of the activating sound plus 4 seconds. The four second delay permitted brief pauses or answers to questions without the relay mechanism being overworked. On occasion, the recorders would operate almost continuously because rapid radio traffic kept them operating. On November 22, 1963, the Channel 1 recorders became, for practical purposes, continuous recorders for just over five minutes starting at approximately 12:29 pm (Channel 1 time) because the microphone on a police motorcycle stuck in the "on" position. The resulting continuous transmission kept the Channel 1 recorders operating for just over five minutes thus giving us a real-time recording for that period. The only problem was determining a basis for an accurate time reference during that period.

By noting the stated times and the duration of messages in the minutes preceding the incident of the open microphone, I have, for practical purposes, fixed the time for the start of the five-minute open mike episode at 12:29:10 p.m. (Channel 1 time). Time statements broadcast later confirm this as a rational assumption. (See PART II, CHAPTER FIVE for technical details demonstrating this confirmation.) Since it is important to have a zero-base from which one might project future time points, a decision was necessary. In using the start of the five-minute interval, and 12:29:10 (Channel 1) as the zero-base, with subsequent time factored thereon, "time" would at least be constant if not absolutely accurate. If not absolutely accurate, time statements cannot be more than a second or two off. The reader is encouraged to reach an independent decision based on the transcriptions of the radio transmissions contained in the Appendix.

It is, however, important to remember that

1. No exact record of "time" exists;
2. The several clocks were not synchronized;
3. The radio operators were not exact with regard to "time statements" on either radio;
4. The recordings were continuous only on Channel 1, and only while the mike was stuck open;
5. For an accurate, although derived, time reference point, 12:29:10 (Channel 1), the time the mike stuck open, will be developed and used in this text.

TECHNICAL REFERENCE TO RADIOS AND RECORDERS

The Committee Report (Section B, page 79) stated that Dallas Police motorcycles were equipped with directional microphones. That statement is incorrect. The department only recently experimented with directional microphones. The motorcycles in 1963 were not so equipped. Being "omni" or non-directional, they would react to sound sources from many direction almost equally.

To the contrary of the Report, in 1963, the department used two types of microphones, carbon and dynamic. The radios then (and now) were limited to specifications authorized by the Federal Communications Commission. Police radio networks then (and now) were limited to frequency responses between 300 and 3000 hertz. While radio hardware has improved with technology, they are still limited to the 300 to 3000 hertz range. Microphones will not pick up with any better quality, nor will the telephone lines transport any better now than they did in 1963. To say they will is nonsense.

The radio network, broadcasting, receiving, and recording, involved only voice-grade circuitry. Microphones, carbon or dynamic, had an ordinary response of 300 to 3000 cycles. Sounds generated in the presence of a microphone which fell below 300 cycles or exceeded 3000 cycles were converted to a sound the system was capable of handling, provided the sound was sufficiently dynamic to be heard. In such cases it might be difficult to identify the specific sound or its source, but some sound would be present. Another consideration would be the condition of the microphone itself. Some were better than others while some were very well worn. A response of 300 to 3000 cycles would only be ordinary, not exact.

Next, the sound complex picked up was passed through the motorcycle's transmitter, and a signal was generated. This signal was picked up by any one or a combination of remote relay transmitters situated at locations throughout the city. There is no record as to which relay transmitter or transmitters were being used during the assassination, so it can only be said that the signal was picked up by a remote transmitter. The signal was then converted to a telephonic signal and sent over a telephone company leased line to the police transmitter at Fair Park, southeast of the downtown area. Telephone lines normally operate between 200 and 2800 hertz with perhaps a 10% variation on a given line, these too being voice-grade circuits. At the Fair Park transmitter, the telephonic signal was transmitted as a radio signal from the main antenna to the mobile units throughout the city, and was sent by another leased telephone line through telephone company equipment to the police dispatcher's office downtown. In the dispatcher's office, the signal was split, one to the radio channel monitor or speaker; the other circuit was directed to the recorder. The sound level of radio signals activated a relay system and started the recorder to record the transmission. The recorder normally operated for the duration of a sound level in excess of that necessary to open the relay system, and for an additional four seconds thereafter.

The recorders were voice-grade units operating normally from 300 to 2500 hertz. Sound was not recorded by sharp needle cutting a sharp groove, but by a comparatively blunt needle which pressed a furrow in the thin plastic surface thereby creating a low fidelity recording. It should be noted that the Dictaphone equipment was designed only for that purpose, and it served that purpose well. It was never intended that it should make sophisticated recordings which could be replayed endlessly without loss in quality. It would be amazing and a credit to the Dictaphone equipment used had it served so profoundly as to record **inaudible impression patterns** picked up by a low quality microphone, passed through a low frequency transmitter, then through a voice-grade telephone line to a second transmitter, then a second telephone line, then to the recorder without even losing the N-waves which preceded the inaudible impression patterns calculated to be the assassin's gunshots. Fantastic!

Another characteristic of the recorders should be mentioned. On occasion, line noise would cause them to run but record no intelligible sound. On other occasions, parts of some messages might go unrecorded. For example, an officer might state that he was now in service, but the recorder would only record the dispatcher's acknowledgment. The Gray Audograph had another peculiarity. This was an old and much used unit. There was a sensitive worm-screw adjustment in the recording needle mechanism. When it didn't function exactly, it might omit some of one message only to repeat another message two, even three or more times. This occurred several times during the Channel 2 recordings of broadcasts during the assassination. Also, when the needle did not "groove" correctly a ghost signal might occur. Again, this was not the fault of the equipment. The unit was old and well worn.

A significant consideration for both recording units is that of recording and play-back speed. It was a common experience to observe noticeable changes in speeds between units. This becomes increasingly important when attempting to make critical time measurements. In fact, time measurements in the thousandths, even hundredths of a second are virtually impossible since the exact recording speeds are unknown and cannot be determined.

Further discussions of radios and recordings will accompany specific situations in later chapters. However, these explanations are important to the reader's future understanding.

CHAPTER TWO - CRITIQUE OF THE COMMITTEE REPORT

This chapter follows the order of Section B of the Committee Report. Selected passages from the Report will be cited followed by critical commentary.

The Report got off to a bad start before it deteriorated. Footnote 2, (Committee Report, page 66) states that Channel 1 was serviced by a **continuous** recording.

As noted in Chapter I, this is **incorrect**. An insignificant error, but a needless error. One which should not have been made and one which would not have been made had the Committee staff asked someone who knew the details of the Dallas Police Department Communications system. An open microphone on Channel 1 kept the Channel 1 recorder running for just over five minutes during the time of the assassination. This five-minute period is the only segment of tape recorded continually.

The Committee Report states that the original Dictabelt recordings made on Channel 1 as well as tape recordings of Channels 1 and 2 were made available to the Committee and were furnished to Bolt Beranek and Newman Inc. for analysis. The Report added that there was no evidence that any of the materials had been tampered with.

The questions here is, "original" on whose authority? Where did the tapes come from? Untampered with by whose authority?

Shortly after the assassination the author made reel-to-reel tapes of the recordings for the Warren Commission prior to his using the recordings in preparing a transcript. The tapes were made with and without a scratch filter, and were necessary if the contents of the recordings were to be preserved. The belts had already been subjected to uncounted replays prior to their being preserved on tapes. Past experience had shown that multiple replays lowered the recording's quality considerably. More over, the repeated lowering of replay needle against the Dictabelt added minute dimples in the belts. It is possible if not probably that these dimples, when read by the acoustics experts' sensitive equipment, generated "impulse patterns" present throughout the belts. Is it possible that these indentations were concluded to represent gunshots but only where it was essential for gunshots to appear?

The Committee Report does not address itself to this point, but shouldn't it have done so? According to information furnished by members of the media, critical analysis was made only of a small segment of the recordings. Although the mike was open for more than five minutes, only that segment judged to be somewhere between 12:30:30 and 12:31:00 (per their estimate of actual time) received scientific acoustical analysis.

How many "shots" could have been found had they looked on either side of that segment?

Next, the Report states that neither the tapes nor the Dictabelts contained discernible sounds of gunfire. While bearing in mind that the "gunfire" was inaudible "impulse patterns" it is difficult to understand certain later statements in the Report.

On page 79, the Committee Report states, "The sound of a rifle shot is so pronounced, however, that it would be picked up even if it originated considerably further away from the microphone than other less intense noise sources, such as a crowd." On the same page, the Report states, "This corroboration was considered significant by the Committee, since it tended to prove that the tape did indeed record the **sounds** of shots during the assassinations." (Emphasis added.)

What is the truth? Are there sounds of shots or aren't there? What do "impulse patterns" sound like? Are they **audible or inaudible**?

On page 67, the Committee Report states that Bolt Beranke and Newman were asked to make certain determinations, one being "Whether the recordings were, in fact, recorded from a motorcycle with a microphone stuck in the 'on' position."

The Report does not clearly state BBN's answer to that question. However, one might infer that they did determine that the recordings were from the open mike on a motorcycle by the reference to their having filtered out "repetitive noise" such as the repeated firing of the pistons of the motorcycle engine. On the other hand, one might wonder if this is a correct assumption, for on page 73 the Report refers to ". . .during which time the motorcycle or other vehicle would have, at 11 miles per hour, traveled about five feet." Perhaps the Committee were not convinced the open mike was on a motorcycle.

At any rate, having isolated the beats of the engine, it would have been a simple matter to have counted the beats, translated those beats into revolutions per minute, then into miles per hour. However, to have done so would have been fatal to the project, for they would have found that the motorcycle was operating at 25 to 35 MPH, averaging approximately 30 MPH. This would in no way correlate to the speed of a motorcycle in the motorcade which, at the same time, was moving through the downtown central business district at a speed of no greater than 6 to 8 MPH.

The open mike started its prolonged transmission at approximately 12:29:10, Channel 1 time. The motorcycle ran at approximately 30 MPH for almost 2 minutes, during which time it would have traveled nearly 2 miles. During this same time interval the motorcade was approaching the west end of Main Street, then making a slow turn onto Houston Street followed by a slow turn onto Elm Street. The crowd along the motorcade route was extremely heavy, pressing out into the street with individuals breaking out of the main body and rushing forward for a closer look at President Kennedy. At no time did the motorcade reach 11 MPH during this period. Frequently, they were at "walking speed" and barely able to average 3 to 3 1/2 MPH, with a top speed of about 5 MPH.

It is impossible for the open mike to have been in the motorcade for this reason alone.

Furthermore, none of the essential sound characteristics of an escort motorcycle are present on the tape. The sound characteristics do, however, clearly indicate that the motorcycle was not in the motorcade. In addition to the conflicting rates of speed, the escort motorcycles stopped frequently, waiting for proper vehicle intervals; they revved their engines in short bursts to attract the crowd's attention so they could move them back out of the street; and there were the stops for the turns from Main to Houston, and from Houston to Elm. None of these characteristic sounds are present.

Also conspicuous by its absence is the crowd noise, but this will be addressed later under another heading.

Why did the Committee refuse to conduct these tests?

Bolt Beranke and Newman were also asked to determine the time interval between the shots. According to the chart, Committee Report, page 80, the times were set as being between 12:30:47 and 12:30:55.3, an 8.3 second interval, the time stated being their determination of exact time.

The commonly accepted time standard for the interval of the shots is the Zapruder film.[1] How were the Committee able to be so exact when there is no way of determining the original run-speed of the recorders, and no way to insure that the unit they used for replay 15 years later ran anywhere near the same speed? Yet they were able to pinpoint the times to tenths of a second, matching the intervals they judged to be correct from the Zapruder film. The accuracy of such timing is very doubtful. A slight disparity in the record and replay speeds would make an exact match-up impossible. A very small error in their calculation of time would throw the "impulse sequence" match-ups completely out of place and would thus have been fatal to their project.

Having found six "sequences of impulse patterns," screening tests were designed to answer questions. Three of those questions deserve close attention:

1. Do the impulse patterns occur during the period of the assassination;
2. Does the time span of the impulse patterns approximate the duration of the

assassination as indicated by the Zapruder film; and

3. Does the shape of the impulse patterns resemble the shape, and are the amplitudes of these impulse patterns similar to those produced when the sound of gunfire is recorded through a system comparable to that of the Dallas Police radio network?

The first question cannot be answered with exact certainty because the exact time of the assassination is not known. It can only be approximated. According to the chart on page 80 of their Report, the Committee indicated that the assassination shots were fired between 12:30:47 and 12:30:56.3 p.m. (Channel 1). This determination is **incorrect**. The acoustical experts examined and the Committee considered **the wrong interval of the recording**.

With regard to the second question, the irregular recording and play-back speeds make it impossible to calibrate the tape speeds with **anything**, much less the interval of shots as recorded by Mr. Zapruder's film, and certainly not within fractions of seconds. To claim that they can is a serious deception.

With regard to the third question, the Committee focused attention on the shape and amplitudes of impulse patterns as they would be recorded through the existing equipment. However, **no** mention was made regarding how many other sound sources they could (should) have considered which would have generated patterns of **similar** shape and amplitude. Are gunfire patterns so unique that they can be isolated from **all** other patterns, with absolute certainty? Wouldn't amplitude patterns be affected by several modifiers such as the dynamics of origin and distance, as well as natural and physical interference? Also, sound is not a **single** thing. Sound is a **complex of frequencies**. When a filter is applied to a given sound to remove a given frequency level, **it modifies all sources** containing that frequency, **not** those desired sources. Simply stated, when they added filtering, they modified their "impulses" as well. On page 72, the Committee Report acknowledges that their matches did not ". . .prove conclusively that the impulses on the 1963 dispatch tape did, in fact, represent gunfire from the book depository or the grassy knoll." Also, that there was ". . . a chance that random or other noise could have produced the pattern. . . ." After conducting additional tests, the Report still stated (Committee Report, page 75) that finding no evidence of any other cause of noise, the Committee ". . .concluded that the cause was probably a gunshot fired at the motorcade." Doesn't that sound like **"a very definite maybe?"** Can these patterns be summarily declared to be gunshot patterns to the exclusion of all else?

On page 70, the Committee Report states that the grassy knoll was chosen as the likely site to test for another shooter because ". . .there was considerable witness testimony suggesting the shots were fired from there."

There are some problems with the words **considerable** and **witness**. "Considerable" means a large or great number, and "witness" requires certain positive sight or knowledge. More correctly, the Report should have acknowledged that "**some bystanders had guessed** that the shots were fired from there."

Curiously, of the Committee's "witnesses" who thought or even believed the **shots** (plural) came from the area of the grassy knoll, only **one**, S. M. Holland (Committee Report, page 89) referred to a **single shot**. Typically, those people who considered that the shots came from the area of the grassy knoll thought **all** shots came from there. A few thought the shots came **either** from the knoll **or** from the Texas School Book Depository. Doesn't this suggest that most of those people were doing their best to truthfully describe what they had heard, and in reality, they gave the locus of echoes of the shots, and not the location of the source? At least one witness was misquoted. (See Part II.)

In contrast to those well-intentioned beliefs, several people, **witnesses**, actually **saw** the rifle pointed from the window in the School Book Depository. Remember, too, that everyone was focusing their attention on the President who, by the time of the shots, had **passed** the assassin's lair. The assassin was above and behind the center of attention. However, witnesses heard the shots, looked around and found the shooter. At the same time, while everyone (including several officers) either was or had just finished looking at the railroad overpass and the area of the grassy knoll, **they saw nothing**.

Isn't it strange that an assassin firing from a concealed position up on the sixth floor and inside a building was observed by several people, but the supposed second assassin, comparatively out in the open and in front of the action in the line of sight of many bystanders and photographers, was not seen **before, during or after by a single living soul**?

The Committee Report, on page 90, speaks more clearly with regard to witness reliability in citing experiments conducted for BBN by Dr. David Green.

Two trained observers who knew that test shots would be fired, as well as approximately when and from where, could not be exact in stating their observations. According to the Report, "Their comments, in short, frequently reflected ambiguity as to the origin of the shots, indicating that the gunfire from the grassy knoll often did not sound very different from the shots fired from the book depository."

Doesn't that tend to confirm the previous suggestion that however well-meaning they were, the bystanders who thought they had heard the assassin's "shots" from the grassy knoll were actually hearing shots from the book depository, and **echoes** from the knoll?

Had the Committee noted on a map of Dealey Plaza the positions of those bystanders who referred to the grassy knoll, the Committee would have discovered that the bystanders were in positions exposing them to the amphitheater effect of the bow-shaped pavilion on the knoll. Their positions exposed them to an ideal echo situation. Apparently the Committee didn't consider those observers' positions as being relative to what they heard.

On page 73, the Committee Report refers to Weiss and Aschkenasy[2] "pinpointing" locations, and while early impulses in pattern three matched those on the tape quite well, later impulses in the pattern did not. Then, realizing that a microphone in the motorcade would not be stationary while receiving the echoes, they included in their calculations the assumption of an 11 MPH speed during a three-tenths of a second period. This would move the microphone about 5 feet and permitted a match of both early and late impulses. This is an interesting move, but it is absolutely incorrect for two reasons.

First, the Report makes several references to "11 MPH," which represents the approximate average speed of the President's limousine as calibrated by the Zapruder film; it is in no way representative of anything else. A motorcade is not linked together like coaches in a train. Chief Curry and motorcycles in front of the limousine were stopped or stopping. Behind the limousine, the follow up car had to work its way through the crowd that encroached on the President.

Next, the Vice President's limousine slowed to a stop or near stop at Elm Street. Still further behind, vehicles which had just made their way slowly off Main onto Houston were now slowing and stopping again. In other words, 11 MPH relates only to the President's limousine and to an average, not a constant speed. Other vehicles, especially those on Houston, were barely moving if not stopped. Therefore, three-tenths of a second would not give the five feet necessary for a match up unless the open mike was in the limousine.

Second, since the Committee determined for their purposes that the microphone was "open" on Officer H. B. McLain's motorcycle, let's consider McLain's motorcycle movements singularly. McLain and others estimated the motorcade speed on Houston as no more than 2 or 3 MPH, when they were moving. Actually, at the time McLain heard the first shot, he was stopped. He cannot say unequivocally that he heard the first shot as hearing only one; he can't say which one it was. His assumption is that he heard the first shot because he saw pigeons flushed from the roof of the book depository. He watched that phenomenon momentarily while remaining stopped. He waited, unaware that the President had been shot, moving out only after he heard Chief Curry's instruction to ". . .go to the hospital. . . ." (See Part II, Chapter Six for additional details regarding Officer McLain's observations.)

Whether one applies the first or the second set of circumstances, the five feet essential for a match-up just aren't there. Accordingly, neither is the match-up.

In considering what could cause such a noise if it were not a shot, Dr. Barger[3] "noted it had to be something capable of causing a very loud noise--greater than a single firecracker. . . (page 74).

Loudness refers to the dynamics of sound and is measured in decibels as opposed to the frequency or cycles per second as measured in hertz. Going back to page 67 of the Committee Report we understand that the sounds were inaudible, and now the discussion turns to a "very loud noise." Then, moving ahead to page 79 of the Report, while discussing the characteristics of motorcycle microphones, the Report states that "The sound of a rifle shot is so pronounced, however, that it would be picked up even if it originated considerably farther away from the microphone. . . ."

Since loudness and frequency are two separate measurements, exactly what was Dr. Barger considering, greater decibels, higher frequency or both? Were the loudness and frequency of the impulse patterns measured? What were their measurements?

In discussing N-waves and supersonic bullets, the Report states that ". . . most pistols--except for some, such as a .44 magnum--fire subsonic bullets."

In a limited sense, the above is correct. However, what is not said is more correct. While "most" pistols will fire a subsonic bullet, many (with no idea of what proportion of all pistols) will also fire supersonic bullets.

More correctly, one must consider muzzle velocity. Typically, muzzle velocities are measured at the muzzle, and at certain distances down range such as 50 yards, 100 yards, etc. Next, one must consider the powder-bullet combination which produces a subsonic velocity when fired. For example, a certain cartridge, say a typical .38 caliber, might have a powder-bullet combination which produces a subsonic velocity when fired. Another .38 cartridge might have a powder-bullet combination which produces a supersonic velocity when fired. Next, one must consider each pistol separately. A given pistol is designed to accommodate "up to" certain loads. In addition, each pistol has a safety factor built into it so that it will not explode and injure its user if too "hot" a load is inadvertently fired.

If the safety margin is not exceeded too often or by too great a load, that pistol can fire a bullet of greater muzzle velocity than that which is considered appropriate. While this is not a wise practice, it is possible to fire bullets with supersonic muzzle velocities from any number of hand guns. Since "sonic" refers to a speed of approximately 741 MPH at sea level, a muzzle velocity greater than 1086.799 feet per second is supersonic.

Also, the Committee Report (page 75) states that there is an ". . . 80 per cent chance that the N-wave was caused by a supersonic bullet."

Some natural questions are, What else could they represent? Only bullets? Was anything else tested or even considered? Were the investigators so anxious to reach a foregone conclusion that they used **selective** validation? Did they **construct** validity to support a **preconceived** idea?

Footnote 11, page 74 of the Committee Report, describes the motorcycle as being 120' behind the presidential limousine when the shots were fired, adding that this ". . .put shots one and two from the book depository, as well as shot three from the grassy knoll, **in front** of the motorcycle windshield." (Emphasis added.) This point was crucial to the acoustical examiner's theory in explaining certain distortions which they concluded through tests were caused by the shot sounds passing through the motorcycle's windshield before they were recorded. The Report states that ". . .their predictions confirmed by the tape, indicated further that the microphone was mounted on a motorcycle in Dealey Plaza and that it had transmitted the sounds of the shots fired during the assassination."

Testimony before the Committee and published accounts of media personnel interviews with acoustic examiners placed significance on the point that the acoustics experts had committed themselves to pinpointing exactly where the motorcycle with the open mike would be **before** they knew for sure they could produce corroborating evidence.

This was a most courageous and exceedingly inaccurate postulation.

For the sounds of shots one and two, from the book depository, to have passed through the windshield, McLain's motorcycle would have to be traveling north on Houston approaching Elm. As a matter of fact, he was there, on Houston Street approximately 100' south of Elm, with McLain noting the flurry of the pigeons on top of the seven-story building. According to the Committee's data, these shots occurred at 12:30:47, :48.6, and :55.3 p.m.

By shot three, the motorcycle would have to have made it 100' to the corner through a crowd of scrambling people and completed an acute turn in time to be headed west on Elm, facing the grassy knoll in only 6 seconds! Egad, what skillfully reckless driving! Especially since McLain, the suspected motorcycle officer, was stopped at the time. To the contrary, McLain did not depart his northbound position on Houston until all three shots had been fired. He watched Secret Service Agent Clinton J. Hill mount the rear of President Kennedy's limousine, after the last shot had been fired. He observed that through an opening in an ornamental wall on Houston. The full frames of the Zapruder film do not show McLain at the corner at the time of the first and second shots. Neither does James Altgen's Associated Press photograph show McLain at the intersection. This is because McLain was where he said he was, back on Houston Street until all of the shots had been fired.

Since the experts and counsel were willing to declare that the accurate pinpoint positioning of the motorcycle further indicated that the motorcycle with the open mike was in Dealey Plaza at the time of the assassination, will they now, since their calculations are obviously incorrect, acknowledge that it was **not**?

On page 76, the Committee Report states that investigators checked but found no record of McLain transmitting a message on Channel 2; that if he had, it could not have been his radio.

It's impossible to judge whether this is simply an effort at demonstrating some form of open-minded objectivity, or an attempt to cause the reader to assume a corollary that since he had not used his Channel 2, he must have been on Channel 1.

Either way it is as ridiculous a statement as it is inaccurate. Channel changes can be made with the proverbial flick of the wrist.

More important in considering whether McLain was monitoring Channel 1 or Channel 2 is logic and probability.

The motorcade assignment was a major exercise and one of tremendous importance. Extensive preparation with emphasis on execution preceded the assignment.

In addition to preparations, numerous radio instructions were given to motorcade officers, instructions to move out on leaving Love Field, as well as those given all along the route. Officers heard and complied with those instructions, McLain included.

Had McLain been on Channel 1, he would have listened to some 39 minutes of totally unrelated radio traffic prior to his microphone sticking. In addition, he would have heard absolutely nothing that he had been trained, prepared and expecting to hear--vital motorcade instructions from Chief Curry for the conduct of the motorcade. While it is possible that even the most expert motorcycle officer could make an initial mistake in channel selection, how long would one logically expect it to take even an ordinarily competent officer to realize that he wasn't tuned in correctly.

During McLain's appearance before the Committee, Committee counsel asked whether McLain could have heard Channel 2 orders and radio traffic over someone else's radio, and McLain agreed that it was possible. He did not mention that no radio was near enough to be overheard and that the crowd noise was so great that one could barely hear his own radio. Upon his return to Dallas, and in response to the questions, "Was the statement correct with regard to what happened? Do you believe that you were actually monitoring Channel 1 but listening to someone else's Channel 2?" McLain said that this is not what happened. When asked why he had testified as he had, he responded that counsel had only asked whether it was possible, and he had to admit that it was **possible**--that they had not asked him whether it was **probable**.

This opened another perspective. The Committee staff used one of the oldest tricks in the book on McLain, and he fell for it because as a trained officer he had been schooled in listening to the attorney, in listening to the question, and in not volunteering unsolicited statements. Beside this, he trusted them. They were professionals. They were representing the government in a serious undertaking. They were trustworthy. They would do him no mischief.

They carefully calculated their intended direction, then carefully worded their questions to elicit the desired answers. For example, "It is possible that . . .?" Unless it is wholly **impossible**, the only truthful answer would be "yes." He was not asked to relate to probabilities. McLain was carefully coached into giving answers which supported counsel's preconceived positions. By limiting the range of information available to him, they allowed McLain to consider only that material which they had selected. With this strategy, they duped him into their plot. Being a conscientious officer, he cooperated fully.

However, on his return to Dallas, he was permitted a private review of the tapes of both channels for the full period of the motorcade. After listening to the recordings he was asked one simple question, "Well, Mac, what do you think?"

His instant, uncoached and unrehearsed answer was, "Man, there's no way that could have been my mike stuck open!" He went on to qualify his response with supporting examples such as his recall of instructions and comments on Channel 2, his total lack of recognition of anything on Channel 1, the absence of siren sounds when the motorcade started to Parkland Hospital, and that when siren sounds did appear, they seemed to be passing the open mike on a unit standing still. He also noted that the motorcycle was running too fast for the motorcade, but that when they started the speedy trip to the hospital, the suspect motorcycle slowed down to a moderate speed and to an idle, and that there was a total absence of crowd on the tapes.

These spontaneous observations were McLain's free choice when given an opportunity for choice. When asked what effect his having heard the same tapes would have had on his testimony, had he been allowed to hear them before testifying, he said that he would have responded in an entirely different manner. More specifically, his response would have been a flat denial that it was in any way possible for it to have been his microphone that was "stuck open."

In the interest of objectivity and freedom of expression, the news media were informed that McLain was listening to the recordings, and press conferences began as soon as he finished listening. Needless to say, they were as concerned as we were not only with what he had to say but the freedom with which he was allowed to speak.

When Committee counsel learned through the media that they had lost a key witness, a situation which threatened their position, they turned on him, crediting him with a ". . .rusty memory. . . ."[4]

It should be noted that the official life of the Committee had by then ended. They could no longer hold sessions and present witnesses. But they did have a decision to reach and a report to write. The Committee staff made no known effort to resolve the challenges in forum with anyone who could give them firsthand information. Instead, they made feeble and foolish attempts to explain away the challenges with any counter argument that sounded right. Perhaps this will prove to be their undoing.

Next, let's consider some of the Committee staff's discussion and explanation of some points of controversy. First, they discussed on page 77 and 78 of their Report why the sound of the sirens did not appear on the tapes until almost two minutes after the assassination, and why they are heard only briefly.

The Report suggests that since the microphone was thought by others to be on a motorcycle "on Stemmons," it was noted that McLain was on Stemmons when going to Parkland Hospital. This is an obvious attempt to avoid the truth. McLain entered on to Stemmons Freeway after 12:31, Channel 1 time, at which time he was traveling between 60 and 80 MPH. He was on Stemmons for just about one minute. At the same time, the engine on the motorcycle with the open mike had slowed down to a moderate speed and idle. . . hardly the same as 60 to 80 MPH. It is beyond belief that competent investigators would fail to recognize that difference.

Next, the Report suggests the possibility that the reason the sirens begin to appear almost two minutes after the motorcade left Dealey Plaza en route to the hospital was because McLain either forgot or didn't feel a need to use his own siren, and that the sirens are heard only when McLain drew close enough to pick up the sirens of the other motorcade vehicles.

Then, as an alternate "explain away" they suggest that the sirens begin to appear and then fade away for yet another reason. They decided that McLain didn't exit from Dealey Plaza promptly after the motorcade, but that he lingered a while. Then, having left later, the appearance of the sirens indicate his having caught up with the others. To explain why the sirens then fade away, the Report suggests that McLain either passed them up or fell back, unable to keep up.

If those reasons aren't enough to inform, convince or confuse, the Committee offered another "explain away." Maybe McLain reached the motorcade and picked up their sirens just as they were turning their sirens down on arriving at the hospital.

These notions are so foolish it is embarrassing to dignify them with discussion. . . but they must be refuted as though any of them had an iota of merit.

You don't "forget" or decide not to use your siren. When exceeding the lawful speed, an officer is required to exercise reasonable precautions. The mere fact that one is an officer, on duty and on an emergency assignment does not relieve the officer of civil and criminal liability in the event of culpability in an accident. In an emergency situation an officer doesn't add up and subtract sirens in an effort to decide what to do. . . he does what he has been trained to do, and is required by operating rules to do. He uses his siren instinctively. McLain has always stated that he used his siren.

McLain left Dealey Plaza in relation to his position in the motorcade, and this was but a few seconds after the President's limousine departed. Had he lingered long enough to have allowed the lead elements a 15-20 second head start, it would have been physically impossible for him to have caught the others in approximately two minutes. The same applies to his passing them. As for his falling back, he didn't as he was among the first officers to arrive at Parkland Hospital, not by his say-so, but by his conduct at the hospital such as assisting Mrs. Kennedy while President Kennedy was removed from his limousine.

As for the last suggestion, either the staff knows absolutely nothing about sirens or they did not seek out qualified advice before making an absurd suggestion. You can't turn a

329

siren "down." It's either on or it's off! Besides, how could they expect a motorcade to travel some three and one third miles from Dealey Plaza to Parkland Hospital in just under two minutes? That would be a 100 MPH trip on motorcycles which could hardly travel more than 85 to 90 MPH under ideal conditions on a good straightaway!

In the Committee's *Appendix to Hearings,* Volume VIII, page 112, paragraph 6.2, in discussing the sound of the sirens on the tape, BBN reported that "The effect is not that of a microphone being carried on a vehicle with a wailing siren, but rather of many vehicles with sirens coming and going around the microphone." **This is correct!** Why the contradictions? Why did they impeach their own expert witness and conjure up dishonest foolishness?

At approximately 12:31:20 p.m., Channel 1 time, (12:30:02.3 p.m. by the Committee Report) the tape recorded the single tone of a carillon or large bell, tolled in the background.

The Committee would explain away the sound of the bell on the tape in less numerous but equally implausible terms. On page 78, the Report simply declares that, "The logical explanation is that the dispatch tape contains the transmission of two or more radios."

Is it logical simply because they declare that it is? For this to have been correct, the reader must visualize and accept the following. The police have an "open mike" which has almost crippled their Channel 1 communications. Next, they have an officer somewhere who for no reason keyed his mike, said absolutely nothing, but held the mike open during one tone of the bell. Then, just as mysteriously as he started, he closed his mike, saying nothing. Is it really "logical" to assume that an officer would key his mike under such conditions only to add to the confusion?

There is a better explanation, but one which has thus far escaped conclusive proof. There is recollection of but no identification of a group which brought a replica of the Liberty Bell, mounted on a trailer, to the Trade Mart. At the risk of being too free with assumptions, is it too much to suppose that some passerby yielded to temptation and gave that bell a testing thump?

With regard to the absence of crowd noises which should have been on the tape, the Report states (page 79) that motorcycle radios were equipped with directional microphones designed to transmit only very loud sounds. That statement is incorrect.

More accurately, in 1963 the department used both carbon mikes and dynamic mikes. These are similar in quality to regular telephone equipment and would pick up sounds with much the same quality as regular telephone equipment. They were definitely **not** directional; nor were they "noise cancelling" mikes.

Curiously, the Committee were suspicious of an independent radio station's recording because, ". . .appropriate background noise was not present." (Report, page 66.) It would seem that they, too, expected background noise before it became necessary to explain its absence.

As the motorcade eased its way through the downtown area, the sidewalks overflowed into the streets while added numbers leaned out of windows and climbed posts in an effort to see President Kennedy. At no time while navigating through the central business district was any member of the motorcycle escort more than five feet from these screaming masses.

The escort often proceeded at "walking speed" with engines running at idle and not at the speed of the engine on the recording. Occasionally, officers would rev-up their engines in an short burst and retard the spark. That technique makes the engine momentarily noisy in an effort to attract the crowd's attention so they can be motioned back. The open mike recorded no such maneuver, only the even sound of an engine running approximately 30 MPH.

The spectators were so close that motorcycle handlebars occasionally bumped them. Yet, the Committee Report simply states that there was **no** crowd noise because the (non-existent) directional microphones **couldn't pick up the noise.** To the contrary, the microphones then in use, being quite similar to a telephone hand-set would pick up and transmit on the exact same order that a telephone would under the same circumstances. The same equipment had recorded background noise before the shots were fired. Background noises are clearly present with Chief Curry's transmissions in the downtown area, and he was in an enclosed sedan, not an open motorcycle. Further, during the August, 1978 firing tests, similar radio equipment recorded every shot very distinctly.

The Committee's efforts at denial amount to professional dishonesty and utter nonsense. But the absence of the crowd noise had to be explained in some manner. Why wasn't the truth determined by a simple test and the results published?

On page 78, the Committee writer made a profound observation that ". . .to contend that the microphone was elsewhere carries with it the burden of explaining what appears on the tape." Further, that ". . .those who contend it was not in Dealey Plaza must explain the sounds that indicate it was." This is **absolute truth.** Why wasn't the contention pursued?

To make such explanation would have been a privilege, not a burden. From the first day the Committee counsel suggested the recording might have been in Dealey Plaza and might have recorded the assassin's shots, that opportunity was sought. And that opportunity is what counsel would not grant. Why? If the Committee truly believed that the burden of explanation existed, why did counsel refuse to permit that explanation? If they had so permitted, much misinformation could have been avoided. Much time, confusion and taxpayer money could have been saved.

This writing accomplishes both of those challenges: An explanation as to why the open microphone was not in Dealey Plaza; and why it was elsewhere, namely, at the Trade Mart, two miles away. Further, there is **nothing** on the recording to suggest the open microphone was in Dealey Plaza other than the imagination or wishful thinking of some Committee staff.

On page 84, the Report acknowledges that "scientifically, the evidence of the second gunman was established **only** by the acoustical study, but its basic validity was corroborated or independently substantiated by various other projects." Well, if they say so. . .but one must wonder, by **what** other projects? In succeeding pages the Committee considered photographic studies and "witness" testimony but acknowledge that the results were **inconclusive.** So where is the "corroboration" or "substantiation?"

To the contrary, the Report makes use of negative logic. For example, on page 87, the Report states, "None of the scientific evidence. . .was inconsistent with the acoustical evidence . . . ." This seems to say that if something is **not inconsistent**, it **must be consistent**. This form of reasoning does not even meet the criteria for freshman-level research methodology. One is not necessarily the corollary of the other. For instance, data might be inaccurate, inconclusive or irrelevant. Data which leads to a dead-end validates, corroborates or independently substantiates exactly nothing.

With further regard to witness testimony, the Report on page 84 states, "There was considerable witness testimony, as well as a large body of critical literature that indicated the grassy knoll as a source of gunshots." (Once again, the plural, gunshots.) Several questions arise for the serious reader's consideration. How many constitutes "considerable?" And "witnesses" who were witnesses to what? How many constitute "a large body?" And who is to differentiate between those who are knowledgeable and qualified writers as opposed to sensation-seekers and crack-pots? These questions are not posed as sarcastic humor. They are serious questions regarding terms which should not be used carelessly.

As mentioned previously, a witness must see or have factual knowledge. One who only thinks or supposes is not a witness. The only reason the grassy knoll received any attention as a shooter-site was because some bystanders were under the impression that the **shots** had come from that general direction, with Mr. S. M. Holland being the principal

JFK FIRST DAY EVIDENCE

exception. Mr. Holland was positive that he saw a puff of smoke come from under certain trees on the grassy knoll, that he heard four sounds he presumed to be shots, and that the sound from the grassy knoll was not as loud as the three shot-sounds from the other direction.

It seems noteworthy that the Report gives preferential treatment to only that part of Mr. Holland's statement which served the Committee's purpose. However, in the Supplemental References to Section B, page 606, Reference 155, in association with another topic, the Report casually mentions that Mr. Holland's **entire** statement had some inaccuracies which caused Congressman Edgar[5] to question Mr. Holland's credibility. Why did the Committee shunt to page 606 of the supplements their unfavorable comments regarding a key witness? Was this an effort to **halo** the vital part of otherwise shaky testimony?

With further attention to Reference 155, why did the Committee Report relegate all reference to the testimony of Mr. Emmett Joseph Hudson to back page status? Mr. Hudson had vital information but, unfortunately, it was not what the Committee wanted.

Let's deal with Mr. Holland's information first. After giving very concise information in careful detail, he then said that an agent in the President's limousine pointed a machine gun toward the grassy knoll.[6] Special Agent George W. Hickey Jr., in his report following the assassination stated that he, ". . .picked up the AR 15 rifle, cocked and loaded it, and **turned to the rear.**" (Emphasis added - Warren Commission Exhibit 1024.) Film documentation proved the accuracy of that part of Mr. Holland's statement. It was useful for the Committee's purpose to suggest through the reference "pointed the machine gun toward the grassy knoll" that the agent had a target on the knoll. This was not the case, and Mr. Holland denied that it was his intention to suggest that it was.

Also, Mr. Holland described a puff of smoke coming from under some trees on the knoll. As touched upon in the Committee's Report, there was question as to whether one shot containing smokeless powder would produce a "puff of smoke." In the concluding paragraph of Reference 155, page 606, the Report states that their firearms panel explained that, ". . . modern weapons do in fact emit smoke when fired." That statement is correct to a point but the explanation stopped short of complete accuracy. Several significant features should be considered. First, Mr. Holland's conclusion points toward a subsonic or a low velocity cartridge as being fired from the knoll. ("Not as loud.") The smaller the powder charge in a shell casing, the less likely there would be a "puff of smoke" of sufficient volume to be readily spotted. Second, weather and climatic conditions would effect the presence and behavior of any smoke produced by a shot. This apparently was not considered by the experts. Third, the number of shots fired would have a bearing on the presence of smoke. A single shot, regardless of its size, would produce a modicum of smoke, if any. If there was a noticeable wind, the smoke would be dissipated almost immediately. If calm, the smoke would tend to become stratified rather than become a "puff." The wind at the time of the assassination was strong and gusting. A police sergeant who observed some smoke in the vicinity of the overpass described it as originating **after** the shooting, and of far too much volume to have originated from a gunshot. Also, during the August, 1978 tests, numerous shots were fired for acoustical testing. No "puffs of smoke" were noted even though it was a calm, warm, dry day.

Next, consider Mr. Holland's immediate response. He was standing but a few feet from a Dallas Police Officer. If he believed he had just seen the President of the United States shot by someone firing from a position immediately to his left foreground some 200 feet distant, why didn't he say something to the officer? It would seem to be a most natural reaction to say something like, "Officer, did you see that?" or some such exclamation. It would have been a simple matter for the officer to have rushed to the location and to determine whether anything had happened there. As it was Mr. Holland did not apprise the officer of his observation, nor did the officer looking in the same direction, see the same thing that Mr.

Holland saw. They did go to the rear of the fence but observed nothing consistent with an assassin fleeing his act.

The reader must decide for himself just how much weight Mr. Holland's entire testimony deserves.

Next, let's deal with Mr. Hudson's information. Mr. Hudson was just a few feet in front of and below the alleged assassin's position on the knoll, the only person known to have been that close. Because Mr. Hudson's choice of words permitted an alternate assumption with regard to meaning, the Committee assumed he meant the alternate interpretation and that he was coached into saying that the **shots** came from the direction of the Book Depository.

The Committee paid notice to what Mr. Hudson said but not to his entire meaning. While looking down toward Elm Street and the motorcade, the book depository was to his left **rear**. As he related orally to the shots coming from behind, he indicated off to his left rear. If there was a shooter on the knoll, and only a few feet directly behind Mr. Hudson, how could he have failed to notice? The truth is, he didn't. He heard the shots. He heard three shots, and they came from the direction of the Book Depository just as he testified. Had **they** come from the knoll, why wouldn't everyone (something like 4 out of 178) who thought shots had been fired from the grassy knoll thought shots--not just one shot--had been fired?

Several officers were near to and in sight of the knoll. They are still positive that not one single shot originated on the knoll. To the contrary, they are unanimous in their observations that all 3 shots (3 not 4) came from the general direction of the Book Depository. And these are veteran officers, some of whom are veterans of military service as well, and not strangers to gunfire.

Most notable of these officers was the motorcade sergeant who was paused along the south curb of Elm Street within 60' of the presumed grassy knoll position. Immediately before the shots were fired he had completed a visual sweep of the overpass and the grassy knoll, carefully noting the people he saw. He saw nothing unusual, and no one who appeared in a position to or getting into a position to fire at President Kennedy. Finishing his sweep from left to right his eyes fell on the President at the same instant the first shot was fired. He then heard and observed the results of the second and third shots.

An officer immediately to the right rear of the President's limousine stopped his motorcycle just after he had made the same visual sweep of the overpass and the grassy knoll. The same instant he looked at the President he too heard and observed the results of the shots.

Just as the sergeant is positive that none of the shots came from behind him, the second officer is positive that all three shots came from behind his position. The Committee investigators knew this and ignored it. Why?

With reference to Mr. Abraham Zapruder's account of the effects the shots had on him (Committee Report, page 89), he said that he described one shot as more pronounced than the others. This reaction was previously considered by the Report in discussing "blur analysis" (Committee Report, page 80) and "jiggle analysis panning errors" (Committee Report, page 83). The Report concluded that Mr. Zapruder's differing reaction to the shots was "consistent" with shots from the building as opposed to the knoll. Since no physical law compels or denies this, perhaps it is as valid a conclusion as some of the others.

However, while we are making assumptions, there is another one which is at least equally if not more consistent. An unsuspecting observer usually has a more pronounced reaction to the first startling stimulus than he does to any subsequent stimulus, with the degree of reaction diminishing in relation to degree of surprise, the frequency, the suddenness and number of following stimuli as well as personal factors. Let's look at an example of this in simple language. Have you ever been in an audience when a loud noise such as a shout startled you from your concentration, then a second, and perhaps a third loud shout recurs? Remember how the first surprise shocked your senses, but the next and any immediately following had a much less shocking effect? Consider this theory as well as the Report's conclusion and decide for yourself. Was Mr. Zapruder's reaction a product of noise from two sources, or simply a diminished reaction because the second and third shots were less shocking to his surprised nervous system than was the first? Consider also the numbing effect of what Mr. Zapruder was observing through the view finder on his movie camera. A "ringside seat" in the destruction of a human being is an awesome and soul-shaking experience.

Let's return to the information developed by Dr. David M. Green, a consultant to Bolt Beranek and Newman Inc., as discussed on page 90 of the Committee Report. Dr. Green conducted tests wherein two trained observers knew shots would be fired, approximately when, and from where. However, their ability to identify the origin of the shots was only 82% in overall agreement. Their descriptions as to locus were phrased with equivocations indicating uncertainty.

Now, let's connect their ambiguity to those bystanders and witnesses who were positive the shots came from the Book Depository. If trained and waiting observers could not be sure, consider the probability of accurate recall by people who were not expecting shots, but who were concentrating on the President. Not one shred of evidence has ever been found which puts a shooter on the knoll. However, the rifle and shells as well as the wrapping paper which concealed the rifle's presence were found near where witnesses had seen the assassin's rifle pointing from the window and toward the president.

Considering the fallibility of witnesses, shouldn't the Committee have reflected on their own data and responded to it in a more appropriate manner? After all, those who thought the grassy knoll could have been the shooting site generally believed that **all** shots had originated from that same point. The Committee were willing to place weight on these observers, but only to a limited degree. They believed them for **one** shot and no more. That demonstrates a profound confidence in their witnesses. More so, it demonstrates a willingness to select validity. In their zeal to put a shooter on the grassy knoll, they selected from those elements which supported the notion and conveniently dismissed, if not actually ignored, anything which suggested differently. The search for anything that would place and support a shooter on the grassy knoll became somewhat a quest for the Holy Grail.

Why did the Committee choose to ignore Dr. Green's conclusions?

> *First, it is hard to believe a rifle was fired from the knoll. Such a shot would be extremely loud, even if silenced, and it would be hard to imagine anyone in the vicinity of the knoll missing such an event...*
> *Finally, if one accepts the hypothesis that a marksman fired from the knoll and that other shots were fired from some other location, then it seems most unlikely that only 4 of 178 witnesses would report a single location as the origin of the shots...a second shot from a different location should be distinctive and different enough to cause more than four witnesses to report multiple origins for the shots.*

(Excerpt from *Appendix to Hearings*, Volume VIII, pp 150, 151.)

In summarizing the evidence on page 93, the Report states, "The Committee considered all other evidence available to evaluate the scientific analysis."

You would have to know just what is meant by "considered" and "evidence" to estimate the merit of that statement. As indicated throughout this chapter, much more information was available to them. Unfortunately, they failed to give the information due andproper regard. The truth was available, but either they could or would not recognize it.

On the day the public was informed as to the possibility of the "open mike" being in Dealey Plaza, and that it might have recorded the shots, the Committee investigators then in Dallas were told that there was no possibility of that being correct, and why. The response was, "We'll get back to you." However, instead of doing so, the staff pursued a course which seemed to indicate that they didn't want to know why the open mike could not have been in Dealey Plaza. Instead, they set out on their unwavering course to prove that it was.

It remained for the public news media to sense that something was being ignored. The media then started to ask probing questions. It is anyone's guess as to what impact the Report would have had on the public had the media not assumed the initiative and done what the Committee should have done--resolve the issue rather than alibi it to death. The media investigators and reporters who would not buy their feeble excuses and explanations deserve the credit for neutralizing the public impact of the Committee Report.

END NOTES - CHAPTER TWO

1. Abraham Zapruder filmed the assassination with an 8mm movie camera from a position on the grassy knoll, north of the motorcade, and barely 35' east of, and almost in the line of fire of, the Committee's presumed second shooter's position.
2. Professors Mark Weiss and Ernest Aschkenasy, Queens College of the City of New York.
3. Dr. James E. Barger, Bolt Beranke and Newman Inc., Cambridge, Mass.
4. Goldman, Shannon, Camper and Donosky, "Rush to Judgment," *Newsweek,* (January 15, 1979), page 7.
5. Representative Robert W. Edgar, Democrat, Pennsylvania, Member, Select Committee on Assassinations.
6. *The Controversy,* a probe recording, produced by Lawrence Schiller, recorded by Capitol Records Inc.

CHAPTER THREE - WHAT DID HAPPEN IN DEALEY PLAZA
THE MOTORCADE

So much for what didn't happen and why it didn't. Let's consider what did happen and how.

Behavior is largely a product of knowledge, training and opportunity. Behavior, when it cannot be analyzed by facts, can be analyzed by empirical data and reconstruction. Exotic exercises such as the acoustical analysis are unnecessarily extreme, and in this event, produced results which are incorrect.

To enable the reader to pick up a feel for what happened, let's start at the beginning and work through the motorcade. Limiting one's determination on a mere guess about what might be found on a few inches of tape is unreasonably impractical and violates the concepts of research structuring.

At 11:37 a.m.. (Channel 2 time), Air Force One landed at Love Field and taxied to its assigned parking area. President Kennedy assembled with his entourage, greeted a few people personally, waved to the crowd gathered about, and took his place in the right rear seat of SS100X, his black 1961 Lincoln Continental limousine. The first lady was seated to his left while Governor Connally occupied the right front jump seat and his wife, Nellie, the left jumpseat. Special Agent William R. Greer drove while Assistant Special Agent in charge Roy

H. Kellerman occupied the right front seat. The President objected to agents on the side or rear boards. Neither did he want escort motorcycles to be between him and the crowd. Four motorcycles followed the President as did a '56 Cadillac with eight special agents.

A few minutes after its start the motorcade reached Lemmon Avenue and turned south toward the downtown area. The carefully developed, carefully rehearsed, checked and rechecked plans would take the President through the heart of the central business district during the noon hour before it circled back toward its destination, the Trade Mart in the Industrial District, two miles northwest of downtown Dallas. This would afford the President maximum public exposure in the brief time available.

Continuing south on Lemmon to Lomo Alto, President Kennedy ordered his driver to stop so that he could recognize a group of young school girls holding a sign requesting him to say hello. The motorcade then resumed its southerly route with nothing more eventful than Chief Curry giving a few instructions to the escorting motorcycle officers: move up, hold back, speed it up a bit. Nothing of a significant nature, just a vast crowd viewing a lengthy motorcade containing a star visitor and an impressive supporting cast. It was then just a little past 12:06 p.m., Channel 2 time.

The motorcade crossed Oak Lawn Avenue, reached Turtle Creek Boulevard, then turned right toward town. A few blocks further along, Turtle Creek Boulevard becomes Cedar Springs Road. At 12:16 p.m. (Channel 2), Chief Curry reported the motorcade location as Cedar Springs and Fairmount Street. In some 26 minutes the motorcade had traveled almost 5 miles, an average speed of just over 11 MPH.

At 12:20 p.m., the motorcade reached McKinney Avenue, traveling south on Harwood Street. Between McKinney and Ross Avenue the crowd swelled in numbers, and as orders were passed by radio, the loud cheering was clearly audible in the background. Continuing south on Harwood to Main Street the motorcade turned right to go west through the heart of the retail and office district. Again, with each radio communication, the din of the well-wishers was audible in the background.

DEALEY PLAZA AND THE ASSASSINATION

The motorcade reached Main and Field Streets by 12:26 p.m. It had taken some 10 minutes to cover the last one and two third miles. There were only 2600 feet, less than a half a mile, and some five minutes remaining. The press of the crowd was at its worst, and the cheers of the crowd were deafening. Anxious spectators broke out of line to rush the President's limousine in hopes of taking a photograph or at least getting a closer look.

By now the motorcycles were heating up and running roughly. So much slow driving inhibited cooling and permitted carbon to build up on the spark plugs. The strain of precision riding, of listening to the radio and watching, and the constant crowd noise made the approaching west end a welcome sight.

By 12:29 p.m. (Channel 2), the motorcade had passed Market Street on Main. The horizon ahead opened up, indicating their nearness to Dealey Plaza, an open, green area, and for practical purposes, the end of the motorcade. After Dealey Plaza the crowd thinned out. The motorcade would turn north onto Stemmons Freeway where, only two and one quarter miles away, they would reach the Trade Mart and have a rest while President Kennedy addressed a luncheon. With less than 900 feet remaining, it was almost 12:30 p.m. Just a right turn off Main onto Houston Street, then 220 feet to Elm Street. A hard left turn would put them westbound on Elm, and then they would be out of the downtown congestion and on the freeway.

The lead motorcycles and Chief Curry slowed to a near stop some two-thirds of the way down Elm, near the Triple Underpass, so named because Elm, Main, and Commerce Streets merge at this point to pass under a series of railroad tracks. The motorcycle sergeant, supervisor of the escort, who will be identified hereafter as "A," paused near Chief Curry and along the south curb of Elm Street. Seeing the President's limousine well back, having just turned onto Elm Street and almost stopped, he took advantage of the opportunity for a careful look at the handful of people standing on the railroad right-of-way over Elm. Panning his eyes from left to right, he noted the occupants of the grassy knoll, and then, the President. At that instant, the first shot sounded. The sergeant, a veteran officer as well as a military combat veteran, knew instantly that it was gunfire rather than backfiring motorcycles or a firecracker. Before he could believe and react to his observation, he heard a second shot fired and observed that the President was hit. He was still watching when the third and last shot struck. The sergeant had just turned his back to the grassy knoll the instant before the shooting started, and he was less than 100 feet from the proposed second assassin's site. There was never a doubt in his personal determination that there were three shots and only three, that all three were fired from somewhere to the right rear of the limousine, and that none was fired from the grassy knoll which was immediately to his left. The sergeant was interviewed by a Committee investigator, but his information was neither used nor impeached.

Another motorcycle officer who will be identified as "B" was stopped along the south curb of Elm, near Chief Curry, and he, too, took a look around and saw nothing which in any way might resemble an assassin poised to fire. This officer, just as the sergeant, is certain that only three shots were fired, that they came from the direction of Elm and Houston, and that no shot was fired from the area of the grassy knoll. This officer was interviewed, but his testimony was neither used nor impeached.

An officer, identified as "C," was riding to the right rear of the President's limousine and a second motorcycle away from the president. He was coming to a stop as the first shot was fired. He had just finished looking ahead in the direction of the grassy knoll and saw nothing that would command his attention. He had thought the sound was from overheated motorcycle backfiring near Elm and Houston as the sound definitely came from the rear of his position. He was looking directly at President Kennedy from a distance no greater than ten to twelve feet. The first shot seemed to have missed, and Governor Connally started to turn. He heard the second shot and saw that the President had been hit in the back near the base of his neck, and that the President grabbed his throat. He also saw Governor Connally jerk, apparently hit too. Then, his eyes frozen on this sight, the third shot struck with ghastly effect, that shot, too, coming from the right rear of the limousine. His mind clearly recorded that three shots were fired and that they were fired from the direction of Elm and Houston Streets. He wrote a journal[7] recording his observations that same day, suggesting the "Single Bullet Theory" before there was one. He, too, was interviewed, but his testimony was neither used nor impeached.

Another motorcycle officer, identified as "D" and one of the two assigned to the left rear of the limousine, was looking at the same scene. He, too, observed the same order and effect of each shot. His recollections corroborate the other; that three shots were fired from the direction of Elm and Houston, and that no shots were fired from the grassy knoll. His testimony was taken, but it was not used, nor was it impeached.

Another of the officers escorting President Kennedy, the officer immediately to his right, Jim Chaney, is deceased. However, in his lifetime he related a like experience with regard to shots and direction. It was this officer who, immediately after the shooting, sped away, west to Elm to inform Chief Curry what had happened. His statement is in the record, but it was not used.

Chief Curry, driving a sedan, and accompanied by Dallas County Sheriff Bill Decker,

Dallas Area Secret Service Chief Forrest V. Sorrels and Special Agent Winston Lawson, was having trouble trying to determine through his rearview mirror what was happening. He was aware that the motorcade lead had slowed or stopped on turning. Then he noted some form of confusion back at the limousine. Moments later, Officer Chaney pulled up next to Chief Curry and informed him that the President had been shot and appeared dead. Receiving this information from a trusted officer with an outstanding reputation, Chief Curry ordered the motorcade to Parkland Hospital. His broadcast was on Channel 2.

A motorcycle officer, here referred to as "E," was northbound on Houston Street near the driveway to the County Jail and approximately opposite Officer McLain. He heard the first of three shots and his attention was attracted by the sudden flurry of a large number of pigeons roused from their roost on the roof of the Book Depository by the first shot. While still focusing on this, and while slowly continuing north on Houston, he heard the second, then the third shot. From what he had seen and heard, he concluded that the shots had been fired from up in the Depository Building. He drove to the entrance, parked, spoke briefly with the building superintendent, then entered the building. He has no doubt that three shots were fired, that they were fired from the Texas School Book Depository, an observation confirmed by physical evidence. His testimony, too, is a matter of record. But it was neither used nor impeached.

At the time motorcycle officer "F" made his turn from Main to Houston on the same course, at a distance of 100 to 150 feet behind Officer McLain, he heard the first, the second and the third shot. He, too, has never doubted the clarity and accuracy of his observations. Likewise, his testimony is a matter of record. He was interviewed, but his information was neither used nor impeached.

Officer McLain was northbound on Houston approaching Elm when the motorcade started to back-up ahead of him due to the press of the crowd and the acute angle of the left turn from Houston to Elm. At or about the time he stopped, some 100 feet south of Elm Street, he heard one shot, and noticed the pigeons flushed from the roof of the Book Depository, the same as officer "E" had noticed on the first shot. Having heard only one shot, McLain could only believe it was the first shot because of the flight of the pigeons. He remained stopped until he heard on his radio Chief Curry's instructions to go to Parkland Hospital. Since "E" continued north to the Book Depository, and since "F" was stopped well behind him, and since the crowd was cheering and screaming, there is no likelihood that he could have heard those instructions over someone else's speaker; no other speaker was within 100 feet of his position.

A few minutes before the motorcade reached Main and Houston Streets, a three-wheel motorcycle officer, referred to here as "G," passed through Elm Street and started up the on-ramp leading to Stemmons Freeway, northbound, when he heard the motorcade sirens coming from Dealey Plaza. He pulled over on the shoulder of the on-ramp and stopped while the motorcade passed him en route to Stemmons Freeway, northbound. He waited momentarily until the last vehicle passed, and then he reversed his course, driving the wrong way against the one-way traffic flow of the on-ramp for a few hundred feet to Elm Street. Next, he turned left and drove eastbound on Elm Street the wrong way, against the one-way traffic flow for nearly 1000 feet to Elm and Houston. When questioned regarding vehicles which passed him westbound during his eastbound, wrong-way travel, he stated emphatically that none had passed him. Asked how he could be so positive, he admonished that you watch for this when you are going the wrong way. Driving slowly over the route, it took from one to two minutes to complete the trip.

As the motorcade passed through Elm Street lanes of the Triple Underpass, they were witnessed by another observer, the officer working district #38 who had checked out of service, en route to Municipal Court.[8] He had been traveling south on Stemmons Freeway near the Trade Mart where he observed pedestrians walking across Stemmons Freeway, and he radioed that information to the Channel 1 dispatcher, the message ending at a projected time of 12:29:10 p.m. Continuing south, he exited the freeway at the Triple Underpass, Commerce Street lanes eastbound just as the motorcade exited westbound at approximately 12:31:14 p.m.

As the motorcade left Elm Street toward Stemmons Freeway northbound, Sheriff Decker used Chief Curry's radio. He told the Channel 2 dispatcher to instruct the Sheriff's Department dispatcher to order all available officers out of the sheriff's jail and offices and into the area surrounding the Book Depository in an effort to stabilize the area until additional Dallas officers could arrive and control the situation.[9] The Channel 2 dispatcher passed these orders along to the sheriff's dispatcher, who in turn carried out his sheriff's orders. He had office personnel to pass instructions, and then he broadcast over the Sheriff's Department radio, "Attention All Units, Attention All Units...."

The motorcade, having reached Stemmons Freeway, picked up speed on its northbound journey, passing over Continental Avenue, some units at near 70 MPH. Considering the estimated speeds possible in exiting Dealey Plaza, and for navigating the narrow on-ramp, and allowing for the "blind" approach from the on-ramp onto Stemmons, the motorcade passed over Continental at approximately 12:31:43 (Channel 1), some 35 seconds after starting its rush to the hospital.

Officer "H," a three-wheel motorcycle operator, had finished his earlier traffic assignment and was en route to his next assignment, the motor pool at the Trade Mart. Having been on Channel 1, he heard the noise caused by the open microphone before switching to Channel 2. He travelled west on Ross Avenue to Lamar Street, then north on Lamar to the Continental Avenue underpass, just north of McKinney Avenue. As he reached Lamar and McKinney, he heard Chief Curry order officers to "go to the hospital." Since nothing had been said regarding a problem, the broadcast was a bit baffling. Continuing on his way he reached the Stemmons Freeway overpass over Continental Avenue in approximately 34 seconds, in time to hear a "mass of sirens." (See Chapter Five for corroboration.) Then he saw the motorcade on Stemmons over Continental. As the motorcade was passing Officer "H," he turned right and accelerated up the on-ramp to northbound Stemmons, travelling some 55 MPH. He followed behind the last vehicles in the motorcade at full throttle. Officers on Stemmons north of Elm had blocked northbound traffic there, so no traffic approached him from the rear. The motorcade traveling 20 to 30 MPH faster (his estimate) was pulling away at a rate of about 36 feet per second, so that while he could not keep up with them, he could keep them in sight. He followed them to Parkland Hospital. During the trip, no police or motorcade vehicle passed him. When questioned as to his certainty, he responded that when you are travelling in the middle of a freeway at top speed on a vehicle as small and unstable as a three-wheel motorcycle, you are a bit paranoid about other traffic overtaking without seeing you, and that he was constantly alert to that possibility, and that none approached nor passed him.

At about this same time, the Channel 2 dispatcher asked Chief Curry for ". . . any information whatsoever. . . ," to which the chief responded, "Looks like the President's been hit." This message was acknowledged at 12:32 (Channel 2). Only those officers who witnessed the incident knew that he had, in fact, been shot and at least seriously if not mortally wounded.

Moments later, as the motorcade approached the Oak Lawn Avenue overpass, some trucks which were on Stemmons prior to the emergency were in the traffic lane the motorcade would use to exit the freeway a short distance ahead. Chief Curry instructed the lead escorts to "Get those trucks out of the way."

The motorcade passed over Oak Lawn and moved closer to the right-hand lane. Approximately 1000 feet further along, they exited the freeway on an off-ramp to their right, and continued in a northerly direction on the service road parallel to the freeway. The service road carried the motorcade to the intersection of Stemmons and Industrial Boulevard, the location of the Trade Mart. The motorcade arrived at that intersection at 12:32:59 (Channel 1).

They turned right onto Industrial Boulevard, passed the side entrance to the Trade Mart, the initially intended stop for the President's luncheon address, and continued on toward Harry Hines Boulevard. Immediately parallel to Hines, a pair of railroad tracks cross Industrial at grade level. On crossing the railroad tracks, Industrial drops downhill, losing several feet in elevation. Also, the roadway bears a little to the right before it starts bearing left to merge with northbound Hines Boulevard. This represented the worst section of roadway on the entire trip. Some motorcade vehicles crossed too fast and nearly wrecked.

Completing the turn, the motorcade continued north on Hines almost 3000 feet to the emergency entrance to the Parkland Hospital compound. They then continued to the emergency dock, arriving at approximately 12:34 (Channel 1). They had covered the three and one-third miles in about three minutes, a desperate but futile effort.

As they entered the emergency area behind the main building, Chief Curry ordered, "Keep everything out of this emergency entrance." Officer "B," a lead motorcycle officer, stopped at the last turn behind the building and set up a control point, screening those vehicles allowed to enter after the motorcade. In addition to Officer "H," Officer "J," also a three-wheel motorcycle officer, had joined the motorcade. Another three-wheel officer, "I," was nearer than the motorcade was to Parkland on hearing the orders to go to the hospital. He arrived moments ahead of the motorcade. Officers "C" and "I" assisted the Secret Service Agents in the back seat of the President's limousine as Officer McLain stood near. At first, Mrs. Kennedy would not allow anyone access to the President. Someone then suggested removing Governor Connally first. He was assisted up and out of the limousine and onto a stretcher and was taken inside. His recollection was substantially correct; he was raised up but was in a trauma state and required assistance. The removal of the governor seemed to stir Mrs. Kennedy to reality and she released the President. Officer McLain then assisted Mrs. Kennedy from the limousine and kept her nearby. Having access to the President, officers and secret service agents covered his head with Agent Hill's coat, lifted him out, placed him on a stretcher and took him inside, accompanied by Mrs. Kennedy, McLain, Officers "C," "I" and "J," and several Secret Service Agents.

Inside, the President was taken into Trauma Room 1, across from the Governor in Trauma Room 2. An officer waited outside for a while with Mrs. Kennedy. Officer "J" was posted at an outer door by a Secret Service Agent who assumed the initiative. Vice President Johnson was taken to an inner room and placed under close guard.

Considering the consummate state of shock and a total feeling of unreality, it is understandable that some of the participants would have difficulty in remembering everything that followed, much less the exact order of events. Officer "J" remembers an altercation between a Secret Service Agent and an FBI Agent which very few people witnessed and not many were even aware of; it was that sort of an incident born of stress, confusion and despair; it was the kind of a day you want to forget as soon and completely as possible. Officer "H" remembers how press photographers tried to enter the emergency waiting room window; that as fast as he collared one and removed him another would take his place. Officer "C" remembers refusing a judge entry even though he was present to hold the inquest. That officer had not been told that the President was dead, but he had been told to keep everyone out. Officer "H" recalled that after he assisted in transporting the President's body out of the trauma room and into an a waiting ambulance, a Secret Service Agent availed himself of the ambulance and drove away, leaving the ambulance owner-operator standing in bewilderment on the emergency dock.

Conditions at Parkland began winding down to mild pandemonium. Chief Curry left with an escort to return President Johnson to Love Field. Some officers departed, a few reporting to Elm and Houston, and some responding to a call in the Oak Cliff section of Dallas where Officer J. D. Tippett had been shot and killed in an unexplained incident. A few officers remained behind at Parkland and engaged in miscellaneous conversation, perhaps in an effort to release tension and emotion. One officer mentioned that it had been a particularly bad day for him as his microphone had stuck open during the emergency and he hadn't realized it, and that he had made a statement which he really regretted. All of this information was available to the Committee had they accepted.

END NOTES - CHAPTER THREE

7. See Part II, Chapter Six, for details.
8. See Part II, Chapter Five, for details.
9. Chief Curry and Sheriff Decker ordered men into the railroad yards as a reactionary and precautionary measure. They had observed people (Mr. Holland and his crew) on the overpass, a place where they should not have been. The chief and his party, the railroad crew, and an officer assigned to the overpass had a clear view of the area. They observed nothing specifically wrong.

CHAPTER FOUR - THE REBUTTAL
DEFENSE OF THE REBUTTAL

An orderly narrative detailing the events of the presidential motorcade certainly cannot be offered as proof for or against any argument. However correct the narrative is, it is basically a story; it cannot substitute for evidence. Society must always be demanding in what it accepts as **evidence.** Where **legitimate** evidence is found, it must be recognized and supported. Where evidence cannot be established to a reasonable certainty, it is the individual's responsibility to reach independent conclusions without being beguiled into another's determinations, or the conclusions are best left unresolved.

Certain points should be clarified, and certain questions answered:

* Was the "Open Mike" on Channel 1 on a motorcycle?
* Was it a two-wheeled or a three-wheeled motorcycle?
* Was it near enough to Dealey Plaza to record shots?
* Would the existing communications network have recorded an audible sound of a shot, had such a shot been fired in close enough proximity to the open mike?
* Do the projected time estimates, in the absence of **factual** time, correctly represent time for the needs of this undertaking?
* **Can** events be accurately reconstructed?
* Does accurate reconstruction enhance any hypothesis or theory as to what did happen when no proof exists?

The Committee Report acknowledges that the theory of a fourth shot, thus a second assassin, and thus the likelihood of a conspiracy rests **entirely** on the accurate determination of the **assumptions** based on a small segment of a recording, thirteen years of age. Before considering what might be found on such a tape, it should be determined whether the motorcycle was even in or near Dealey Plaza. If the open microphone was not in a position from which it could record events in Dealey Plaza, **anything** found on the recording is academic and irrelevant.

Consider the preceding questions:

FIRST: Was the open mike on a motorcycle?

Yes, it was. The Committee Report seems to generally agree with this. However, reference was made to a "motorcycle or other vehicle." At least two-dozen motorcycle officers with extensive motorcycle service, two-wheel and three-wheel, have listened to the recordings some several times. These officers independently agree that the recording was made through the open mike on a motorcycle. In addition, several experienced radio operators agreed to the same.

SECOND: Was it a two-wheel or three-wheel motorcycle?

It was a three-wheel motorcycle. **NOTE: The Committee could have and should have used the equipment available to them to analyze the motor-sounds in the recording. They would have proved that the chart generated by a three-wheel "flat-head" engine rather than a Harley Davidson, high-performance, "over-head-74" matched the chart generated by the motorcycle in the recording. This would have conclusively eliminated McLain as the suspect operator.**

THIRD: Was the motorcycle in or near Dealey Plaza?

It was not. Since the Committee chose not to analyze the motorcycle sounds, and since three-wheel units were near Dealey Plaza, it is important to consider why the motorcycle was elsewhere. **FIRST: Consider that to have recorded the shots, AUDIBLY OR INAUDIBLY, the open mike would have had to be within 300 feet of the sound source. Just "in or near" Dealey Plaza will NOT suffice.** The receiver must be within 300 feet of the source. The Committee declared that it **was** but with **no proof**. There are several reasons why it was **not**, and they should be considered.

Why the motorcade WAS NOT in Dealey Plaza:

During the 12:24 (Channel 1) time frame, the microphone "opened" for about 4 1/2 seconds. Moments later, it stuck open twice for about one second each time. Then, during the 12:28 (Channel 1) time frame, it opened for 17 seconds. Each of these times, the sound of the engine speed indicates the motorcycle was underway, travelling about 30 MPH. During the 12:22 to 12:26 period, the motorcade travelled on Harwood from Live Oak to Main Street, then turned West on Main and travelled to Field Street. That required an average speed not more than 8 1/2 MPH. Also, at 12:24, the motorcade was on Main near Ervay Street. The crowd had increased and the cheering was tumultuous. At 12:28, the motorcade was on Main near Market Street, averaging just over 4 MPH through a very heavy and loudly cheering crowd, the spectators overflowing into the street. How, then could the open mike have been on **any** kind of motorcycle in the motorcade when the subject motorcycle was travelling 30 MPH? With this consideration, the absence of crowd noise isn't so important, considering the suspect motorcycle was travelling some **FIVE TIMES FASTER** than the motorcade. It would have run off and left the motorcade long before the shots were fired.

At 12:29, the microphone again stuck open and remained open for more than five minutes. At that time, the motorcade was nearing Main and Houston Streets. In the next period of some two minutes, the motorcade would almost stop while turning right onto Houston, ease its way north to Elm Street, then turn left onto Elm, westward toward the Triple Underpass.

During this segment the motorcade speed was reduced to less than 4 MPH, and one or two stops were required as well as a considerable amount of "walking-speed" travel. During this interval remember, the motorcycle with the open mike was still travelling 30 MPH.

A little past 12:30, the motorcycle in question transmitted a noticeable slowing down and an irregular running speed, continuing in that mode for almost one minute. **This would embrace the period when the shots were fired.** Just after 13:31, when the motorcade was departing Dealey Plaza en route to Parkland Hospital **at an accelerated speed,** and with **numerous sirens** in operation, the open microphone began transmitting the sound of its engine running at a **slow idle** for about half a minute. Then it revved-up slightly for about 15 seconds, then it slowed down again and seemed to sit and idle. It remained in this situation until about **12:34 p.m., the time the motorcade reached Parkland Hospital.**

It is **impossible** for the rational mind to equate this **idling** motorcycle engine with that of Officer McLain **or any other** escort motorcycle **racing** to the hospital. The differences in the engine sounds and speeds are **so conspicuous** it is easy to perceive the differences by ear. The question of speed, again, **could** have and **should** have been determined by electronic measuring techniques available to the Committee. That could have been done much quicker and at much less expense than the amazing search for the inaudible shots. Why try so hard to prove the impossible when the obvious is before you, and more readily and economically accessible?

Consideration as to the probability of McLain **or any other escort officer** having negligently, deliberately or accidently been **on or switching to** the "wrong channel" will not be enlarged upon except to recall two principal considerations:

> 1) the radio traffic on Channel 2 was heard, obeyed, and recalled by the motorcade officers, and
> 2) it was impossible that an officer could have heard a speaker from across the street in the ambient crowd, much less do so for more than half an hour, **without realizing he wasn't listening to his own radio,** or that he was effectively listening to two frequencies when he could scarcely hear **one.**

Counsel's suggestion that this was a likely solution to their dilemma constitutes wishful thinking. Getting McLain to acknowledge such a possibility is at least shrewd and deceptive manipulation of an unsuspecting and obliging witness.

<u>Why the motorcycle WAS at the Trade Mart:</u>

Several three-wheel officers had traffic intersection assignments along the motorcade route as it approached the central business district. After the motorcade passed through those intersections and the traffic flow returned to normal, the officers reported to their next assignments. Some of them were to report directly to a motor pool detail at the Trade Mart, to arrive by 12:30 p.m. The motorcade cleared these early intersections between 12:20 and 12:24 p.m. At some locations, companion-officers remained to clear the last of the congestion, permitting the three-wheel officers to leave promptly. These three-wheel officers left, driving in normal traffic at normal speeds, generally, 30 MPH. The suspect motorcycle was running at this approximate speed for 6 to 8 minutes before it slowed to an idle. This time and speed would be correct to permit the three-wheel officers to travel the same approximate distances from those early assignments to the Trade Mart with perhaps a stop for a signal light or two for good measure. Incidentally, signal lights, if any, would have been encountered in the first minutes of the trip as there are virtually none along the routes farther out toward the Trade Mart. During the time period 12:24 to 12:29, the mike "opened" briefly 4 times. In the intervening time the motorcycle could have stopped a time or two without transmitting sound of the stop over the radio. The same time that the subject motorcycle engine slowed down was **the same approximate time that the suspect motorcycle would have reached the Trade Mart.** And at that time, the open mike picked up the first of several "cross-communications," events that would occur only when the motorcycle was conveniently near an operating speaker (sound source). The first "cross-talk" was the message, "I'll check it" at 12:32:02 (Channel 1). On Channel 2 at this same time, the message, "That's alright. . .I'll check it" was broadcast by a Deputy Chief to a Traffic Captain. The voice picked up on Channel 1 was that of the Deputy Chief. This Channel 2 Message was picked up by the open mike on Channel 1 because the subject motorcycle was very near to the speaker of a radio monitoring Channel 2 traffic. This message became a transmission on Channel 1, and was recorded.

At approximately 12:33:01 (Channel 1) the motorcade sirens can be heard, faintly at first, increasing to full loudness. The siren source appears to pass, not as a single cluster, but as three separate groups. The siren episodes ended by fading out of hearing in the opposite manner of their arrival. The "siren episode" was some 33 seconds duration, and generated a distinct **"Doppler Effect,"** which indicates that **the sound source was passing the recording source** rather than the opposite. This is a scientific fact which the Committee could have confirmed but didn't. NOTE: At that time there were **no other** emergency vehicles running singularly, and most certainly, **no large groups,** anywhere in the city. Accordingly, the siren source could only have been the motorcade and nothing else. Next: Where was the motorcade some two minutes after it left Dealey Plaza? Following its route, the distances measured in feet, and breaking the route into segments, then calculating the speeds of the motorcade in "feet per second," it can be demonstrated that the motorcade reached the intersection of Stemmons and Industrial at approximately 12:32:59 (Channel 1). Since the motorcade was the source of the "siren episode," and since the sirens were recorded passing the receiver at 12:32:59, where would practical thinkers expect the open mike to be? There can be **no doubt.** The motorcycle with the open mike was at the Trade Mart. It could NOT have been on an escort motorcycle either overtaking and passing or falling back. This is established by the COMPLETE ABSENCE of the sound of a siren or the attendant engine and wind noise of an escort unit.

At approximately 12:33:38 (Channel 1) the following message was recorded on Channel 1: "Attention all units; attention all units . . . ." That was NOT a Dallas Police broadcast. It was the Dallas County Sheriff's dispatcher. Referring to the Appendix, Channel 2, during the 12:32 time frame, Sheriff Decker told the Channel 2 dispatcher to contact the Sheriff's dispatcher and have him send ". . .all available . . ." to report to the assassination site. The "Attention all units. . ." is directly coincidental to the response to the sheriff's instructions by his dispatcher. The message was picked up and recorded on Channel 1 because the open mike was near to the outside speaker on a deputy sheriff's vehicle. The ONLY place where police officers and sheriff's deputies were working together in that manner was **at the Trade Mart.** The Texas Department of Public Safety used the same broadcast style, and they, too, had a unit at the Trade Mart Command Post. However, due to the time reference, it is more likely that it was the sheriff's dispatcher. That could have been confirmed by the Committee with a simple "Voice Print" of the operator and the recording. Even so, the Trade Mart was the only place where city and state units were working together.

At approximately 12:33:52 (Channel 1) the following message was recorded on Channel 1: "You want me to still hold this traffic on Stemmons until we find out something, or . . . ." Referring to the Appendix, Channel 2, during the 12:34 time frame, Motorcycle Sergeant #190 asked, on Channel 2, the same question. At that time, he was still holding up northbound traffic on Stemmons, north of Elm Street. It was his actions which kept the freeway clear of private vehicles while Officer "H" was northbound from Continental on his three-wheel motorcycle. (See pages 44 and 86.) This message was picked up by the open mike being close to a Channel 2 speaker. Since this "cross-talk" was within seconds of the Sheriff's dispatcher's message, and considering that the subject motorcycle was not moving, it suggests that the motorcycle was sitting still at the Trade Mart command post or motor pool.

During the 12:34 (Channel 1) time frame the subject motorcycle seemed to move about briefly, and the movement apparently jarred the stuck transmitter switch causing it to release for about 6 seconds, and then it stuck open again until about 12:36 (Channel 1).

Just before 12:36 (Channel 1) the following message was recorded on Channel 1: ". . . came from the 5th floor. . . (Channel 1 dispatcher interrupts: '24. .') . . .of the Texas Depository Bookstore. . ." (sic). Referring to the Appendix, Channel 2, 12:36 time frame, Motorcycle Sergeant #260 made that broadcast. The broadcast was picked up by the open mike being close to a Channel 2 speaker.

By now, attention was being directed toward learning what had happened, why President Kennedy had not stopped when he passed the Trade Mart, why they went to the hospital. Also, the police dispatchers had broadcast that there was a three-wheel motorcycle in the area with its microphone stuck open. The officer using that motorcycle, in preparing to leave the Trade Mart en route to Parkland checked his mike as he started to leave and discovered that his was the offending microphone. The problem of the open mike was corrected at that time, and the officer arrived at Parkland a couple of minutes later. He is the same officer referred to in Chapter Three. Only the Committee could tell why they decided to say the motorcycle was in Dealey Plaza and would not consider why it was not.

The foregoing should provide adequate reasons for practical observers to understand that it was **IMPOSSIBLE** for the subject motorcycle to have been in the motorcade, much less a specific motorcycle, Officer McLain's, and to state its exact position in Dealey Plaza. Additionally, the foregoing should provide abundant reasons for practical observers to believe that the motorcycle was, in fact, **at the Trade Mart, two and one-quarter miles from Dealey Plaza.**

The deductions through which the Committee concluded that the subject motorcycle was McLain's in Dealey Plaza are based on impressive acoustical analyses, and we would suppose the Committee are sincere. The problem is, they are sincerely wrong.

FOURTH: Would the radio equipment have recorded audible sounds, had the open mike been in Dealey Plaza?

Yes, there would have been sounds of shots rather than "impressions," but ONLY IF the open mike was within 300 feet of the source, and IF ambient noise didn't cover the shots.

The Committee goes two ways on this point. They alternately refer to the "sound of shots," and they also state that the shot sounds are inaudible, that they are "impression patterns," but they did not define "impression patterns." And, **more important,** they did not say whether shots **alone** would have made the referenced impression patterns.

It is not necessary to argue acoustics as a science. To even attempt to do so, one would need professional qualifications at least equal if not superior to those who promulgated the acoustical evidence theory.

With reference to Chapter Four and an explanation of the technical properties of the police communications network, the system **would** have recorded the **sounds** of the shots (not inaudible impressions) had the shots been fired within 300 feet of the open microphone. The **sound** recorded would have been quite similar to that same sound if heard over regular telephone equipment.

In fact, during the series of test firings conducted by the select Committee in Dealey Plaza in August, 1978, similar radio equipment clearly received the sounds of all test shots and

JFK FIRST DAY EVIDENCE

recorded them audibly, and easily recognizable, as shots.

The same would have applied to crowd noise. Had the open mike been in the motorcade, it would have clearly captured the noise of the crowd. Main Street is generally 50 feet wide, with sidewalks of 12 to 15 feet on either side of the street. The buildings are generally from three or four floors to 15 and 20 floors in height. People were massed along both sidewalks and overflowing into the street. They were clinging to posts and leaning out of windows. The motorcade passed through a canyon of loudly-cheering spectators, the walls of the buildings containing and echoing the sounds back into the arena of the street. The escort motorcycles were in the middle of all this. It is impossible that **none** of these noises are on the taped recordings. . .**unless the open mike was elsewhere.**

The recording of shot-sounds is not a new phenomenon. Police officers have heard shots and crowd noises over their radios for years. What else would one expect to hear?

FIFTH: Do time projections correctly relate to events?

Yes, those in this text do; those from the Committee do not. The Committee set the time of the assassins' shots as being fired at 12:30:47 through 12:30:55.3 (Channel 1) with the last shot being followed 7 seconds later by a single tone of a clarion-like bell. This is the only basis they offered by which one might establish where on the tape to find the 8.3 second shooting interval: by timing backward from the sound of the bell which sounded 7 seconds after the last (fourth) shot. Unfortunately, **they picked the WRONG time.**

Had the last shot been fired at 12:30:55.3, and the bell-tone sounded 7 seconds later, the bell sound would have occurred at 12:31:03.3 (Channel 1). Actually, the bell-tone occurred more nearly at 12:31:20, or 16.7 seconds **later** then estimated by the Committee. While 16.7 seconds is but a brief period in the entire episode, it is more than ample time to constitute a fatal error to the Committee's work.

To afford the reader a basis for making an independent judgment, let's consider how the Committee apparently derived their time-basis. Since their Report does not specify their methodology clearly, it is necessary to extrapolate. The reader can then decide which time-basis is the more accurate.

With reference to the Channel 1 transcript, (See Appendix, Channel 1, 12:28), the officer working district #83 checked out of service to handle a traffic situation. The dispatcher acknowledged, "Eighty-three out, 12:28." A stopwatch started at the instant the dispatcher gave the time-statement as 12:28, and allowed to run until the sound of the bell-tone occurred would run for 3 minutes, 3.6 seconds, or until 12:31:03.6, or **within .3 second** of the Committee's statement as to the time the bell-tone occurred. Apparently, the Committee made the mistake of assuming that the first time the dispatcher stated the time as "12:28" was the **exact** instant that it became 12:28 p.m. This would build in an **incorrect** time reference. They failed to consider several points:

* There were 21 seconds of radio time used from the **last** "12:27" to the first "12:28" statement. How much of that 21 seconds should be credited to the end of the 27th minute, and how much to the start of the 28th minute?
* The message that #83 was out of service on a traffic check, and the dispatcher's acknowledgment took 3.5 seconds, and they appear to have been arbitrarily allocated to the 12:27 time frame. They could have been during the 12:28 time frame.
* The Committee erroneously determined that the Channel 1 recorder ran continuously. **It did NOT**. It recorded intermittently. No recognition was given to any time-break in the transmissions between the call to the officer

346

APPENDIX

working #56 (12:27) and the dispatcher's next message. Likewise, the Committee's position assumes that #38's message and the dispatcher's acknowledgment followed instantly after the episode when the mike opened for 17.5 seconds.

Since it is impossible to guarantee the exactness of anyone's time estimates, some basis must be stipulated. What must be considered in making such a stipulation?

There was quite a bit of radio use prior to the five-plus minutes that the mike remained open:

* From the first "12:27" to the first "12:28" there was 37 seconds of radio use.
*From the first "12:28" until the last "12:28," (12:29 was never stated) there was 55 seconds of radio use. Since the radio cannot be used more than 60 seconds per minute, and might be used "zero" seconds, it is necessary to use a little logic based on ordinary use patterns and the specific message patterns at the time. Allowing for 12:28 real-time to have occurred a few seconds **before** the first time the dispatcher stated the time, and allowing a couple of seconds between #83's and #56's messages, and a few seconds between the "open mike" episode and #38's message and the dispatcher's responses, 12:29 real-time occurred shortly before the five-minute "open mike" episode. Accordingly, this text considers that the major open mike episode started at 12:29:10 p.m., Channel 1 time.

Since there is no **factual** proof, what **empirical** proof would support the 12:29:10 estimate?

* While the motorcycle microphone was still open, #103 cleared from his previous assignment, and the dispatcher acknowledged him at 12:34. Projecting 12:29:10 through the open mike episode, that acknowledgment occurred at 12:33:59, or within **one second** of the adjusted time.
* Next, #76 cleared and was acknowledged at 12:34. This "time" coincides with 12:34:00 and 12:34:07, with the acknowledgment coming at 12:34:09.
*The open mike closed shortly after 12:34:18 and remained closed for about 51 seconds, breaking the "real-time" effect of the recorder, putting the recorder a little behind real-time. The next "time" reference occurred when the dispatcher dispatched a call to #35 at 12:35 p.m. This coincides with 12:34:46, which is as it should be, the dispatcher's time being a little ahead of the projected time.

Should one start the preceding times 16.7 seconds later, the subsequent times would not have occurred so accurately.

As stated previously, the two dispatchers were some 15 seconds out of synchronization in their announced "time" statements, with Channel 2 being ahead of Channel 1. The time estimates offered in this text agree with that position. To confirm the accuracy of this projection, consider the time the simultaneous broadcast, and those times when Channel 2 broadcasts were picked up by the open microphone being parked near a Channel 2 speaker. (See Appendix, Channels 1 and 2 at times indicated below.)

* Early in the 12:36 (Channel 2) time frame, (12:35:58 to 12:36:06) the Channel 2 dispatcher broadcast simultaneously on both channels. By continuing the stopwatch on the Channel 1 recording (as if a real-time recorder) the simultaneous broadcast occurred at least during or after 12:35:46 (Channel 1), or from 12:35:38 to 12:35:46, some 20 seconds difference.
* At approximately 12:31:04 (Channel 2), the message ". . .I'll check it" corresponds with 12:31:02 (Channel 1), a difference of some 2 seconds.
*At approximately 12:34:16 (Channel 2), the message "You want me to hold. . ." corresponds with 12:33:52 (Channel 1), a difference of some 24 seconds.
* At approximately 12:36:21 (Channel 2), the message ". . .came from the 5th floor. . ." corresponds with 12:35:57 (Channel 1, a difference of 24 seconds.

Based on these time constructions and comparisons, this text postulates that the principal open mike episode began at 12:29:10 and continued until 12:34:19 (Channel 1), and that Channel 2 announced times were a little ahead of Channel 1 times, which is close to the 15-second allowable. Further, that the time projections in this text relate more correctly to events than does the time reference established by the Committee.

SIXTH: Can events be established accurately?
Yes. Times and motions occurred within specific and identifiable limitations. Although the time references are dependent on accurate projections, those events can be reasonably synchronized. In so doing, it must be remembered that some activity could not occur at or within certain time points or periods. For example, it was **impossible** for Officer McLain to have left Dealey Plaza at a time different than that which he has stated. It would have been impossible for a motorcycle to have caught the motorcade almost **two minutes after** the motorcade left Dealey Plaza, if the second motorcycle was more than a few seconds late in leaving. Officers "G" and "H" related their experiences and recollections, totally unaware of how they would fit with and confirm other, and independent variables. The arrival times at Stemmons and Continental, at Stemmons and Industrial, and at Parkland Hospital fit time and distance references perfectly.
It simply is not sufficient to declare something to be factual because it is necessary to support an existing theory. Such things must be developed within the limits of **fact** where facts are available, and within the limits of reasoning where facts are absent.

SEVENTH: Does reconstruction enhance theory in the absence of proof?
This question calls for a judgment answer. There are two approaches to a "Reconstruction Theory," Actual and Conceptual.
Actual reconstruction has established the time and speed of the motorcade into and through the central business district, and its time of arrival in Dealey Plaza.
Actual reconstruction has demonstrated that the motorcade arrived at and passed the Trade Mart at the same time the sounds of sirens appeared on the Channel 1 recording. Additionally, a motorcycle leaving Dealey Plaza a couple of seconds after the motorcade's departure could not have overtaken the motorcade in the two-minute period before the sounds of sirens appeared on the tape.
Actual reconstruction independently determined that Officer "G" precluded Officer McLain leaving as late as the Committee suggested in an effort to explain the total absence of

crucial sounds which would have necessarily been recorded. Further, that Officer "H" arrived at Stemmons and Continental when he did confirms both the presence of the motorcade there at 12:31:43 (Channel 1), and that no other vehicles, McLain specifically, joined the motorcade beyond that point and the Trade Mart.

Conceptual reconstruction has fixed the element of time for both radio channels with the conclusion that Channel 2 was about 15 seconds ahead of Channel 1. Further, that, while the shots were fired in the late 12:30 (Channel 1) time frame, the area of the tape determined by the Committee to be the place where the **assassins'** shots were found is actually 16 seconds-plus **too early**. Had the shots been fired when the Committee concluded, President Kennedy would have still been on Houston Street, not yet turned onto Elm.

Conceptual reconstruction indicated that the nature and distribution of the crowd in the downtown street, and their proximity to the motorcycle officers, and the rate of speed of the motorcade confirm that, had the subject motorcycle been in the motorcade, the crowd noise would have been recorded.

Conceptual reconstruction indicates that it would have been unlikely that a motorcycle officer could have monitored both radio channels or the wrong one for almost thirty-minutes without realizing his error, and that it would have been impossible for him to have heard the orders to go to the hospital over another officer's radio from a distance of 100 feet or more in such noise.

Actual and conceptual reconstruction has demonstrated that experienced officers were in positions from which they could accurately observe, and that they do state without equivocation that only three shots were fired, and that they were fired from, or from the direction of the Texas Schoolbook Depository, and that **no shots** were fired from the area called the grassy knoll.

Actual reconstruction of events of the day revealed the identity of the three-wheel officer who experienced the problem of the open mike, and it **was not** Officer McLain. It was a motorcycle en route to, and at the Trade Mart.

CONCLUSION AND SUMMATION

Now the questions are passed on to the reasoning of the individual reader: Does the reconstruction of time and events indicate that the motorcycle with the open microphone was not in Dealey Plaza? Was the subject motorcycle at the Trade Mart?

Since the questions cannot be answered absolutely through a complete set of facts, the answers can only come through reasoning.

The Committee Report acknowledged that the acoustical evidence was wholly dependent upon

1. The open mike being on McLain's motorcycle, and
2. McLain's motorcycle being at one exact point at the time the shooting started, and
3. That it moved at an exact speed to an exact point at the time the last shot was fired.

Further, the Committee claimed that there was supporting and corroborating details which validate the acoustical evidence.

Is there any acoustical evidence? Had the Committee truly proved anything?

Answers and opinion should not be force-fed under the color of **scientific research.**

JFK FIRST DAY EVIDENCE

Too many research techniques were ignored. Too many research principals were violated. Too many questions received poor answers, incorrect answers, or worse, no answers at all even though they could have and should have.

Do the following questions relate to the issues surrounding the Channel 1 recordings? Should they have been answered? Have they been answered? Are the answers and/or conclusions valid or reasonable? Whose conclusions are most representative of the truth? What should history say?

* Could a motorcycle running near 30 MPH for more than 4 minutes be part of a motorcade travelling less than 10 MPH? This text says no.
* Could on ordinary officer listen to the wrong radio for half an hour and not know? This text **and the officer** say no.
* Could an officer hear and respond to a radio 100 feet away and not know it, and not be able to hear his partner yelling at him from a distance of 5 feet? This text and the officer say no.
* Could the open mike, which **must** have been in an **exact** position, **and in motion,** have recorded the "sound impressions" when actually, the motorcycle was stopped or stopping about **100 feet** from the **essential position**? This text says no.
* Would a professional-level investigation test to determine the correct kind of motorcycle (two or three-wheel) and its correct rate of speed when the exact answers to both are **crucial** to conclusions? This text says yes. . .and wonders why it didn't.
* Would a professional, open and objective investigation neglect or ignore the testimony of experienced officers with significant information? This text says no.
* Did the officers in the motorcade (except McLain) hear three shots, and **no more**?. . .This text and the officers say yes.
* Did those officers who were in a position to do so, effectively rule out a shot from the grassy knoll? This text and the officers say yes.
* With one known exception, those bystanders who thought **the shots** came from the grassy knoll thought **all three** did. However, the Committee concluded that, while these witnesses' testimony was reliable enough to launch the search to confirm **one** shot from the grassy knoll, they were **not sufficiently reliable** for the Committee to accept their word for three or even four shots. . .This text believes that those few bystanders **did hear three shot sounds,** but that these were **echoes of the three shots from the Schoolbook Depository.** This text also believes that to materially alter their testimony will compromise their entire testimony. The Committee **selectively** used that which complemented the Committee's position, and, without explanation, dismissed that which didn't.
* Did the motorcade leave Dealey Plaza in **one** loosely organized group en route to the hospital? This text says yes.
* Did Officers "G" and "H" effectively close the door on other vehicles joining the motorcade from its rear? This text says yes.
* Did the motorcade generate the 33 second interval of siren sounds on Channel 1, and was the motorcade passing the Trade Mart at that time? This text says yes.
* Did the motorcade reach the hospital at the time, and with the composition

as in the reconstruction? This text says yes.
* Does the reconstruction of three wheel officers en route to the Trade Mart from traffic assignments demonstrate the time and speed correctly, and does the sound of the engine at idle reasonably suggest the motorcycle to be at the Trade Mart rather than in the motorcade? This text says yes.
* Does the three-wheel officer at the Trade Mart, who had the problem with an open mike, shed light on whose mike was open, and where? This text says yes.
* Does the fact that the motorcade sirens are recorded in three separate groups, with the Doppler Effect present, indicate that the sirens were passing the vehicle with the open mike? This text says yes. The Committee vigorously denied this. However, their subsequent Report acknowledges that this is **true.** (*Appendix to Hearings*, Volume VIII, Chapter 6, paragraph 6.2, page 112.)
* Since the radio network had, in the past, transmitted and recorded the sounds of shots and of crowds, shouldn't they have been recorded on Channel 1 in this event? This text says yes.
* Does the Committee's inaccuracy in **simple** facts, such as whether Channel 1 was served by a continuous recorder, the frequency range of the equipment, and the kind of microphones used, suggest a complete, competent, unbiased, professional investigation? Or does it suggest a hasty means to justify a preconceived end? This text suggests the latter.
* Does the Committee effectively explain away the legitimate challenges? Such as other mikes which conveniently stuck open when necessary...That an officer elsewhere happened to open his mike, record the "bell-tone," then close his mike without saying a word...That McLain "forgot to turn on" his siren...That an engine running 30 MPH is the same as one in the motorcade travelling 5 to 10 MPH...That an idling engine is the same as one racing along the freeway in pursuit of the motorcade...That siren sounds disappeared because the motorcade reached the hospital, 3 1/3 miles distance in less than 2 minutes...That everyone who "witnessed" to the Committee's satisfaction was a valuable, bona fide witness with valid information, but those who were true witnesses, but who contradicted the Committee's theories, were unworthy, unreliable, and unmentioned.

How far should rebuttal go? How much rebuttal is necessary? How valid is the Committee Report? How valid is the rebuttal?
This text has attempted to reconstruct time, the events and recollections for that interval of November 22, 1963, through a Reconstruction-Progression Theory. In that manner the text identifies and utilizes facts neglected by Committee investigators, and connects loose ends, permitting rational reasoning to inform one, in the absence of fact. The reader is afforded alternatives, but is not led to believe anything.
In fact, is it important for the assassination to be revisited so frequently? So much has been theorized and so much has been written, that it is increasingly more difficult to separate fact from fantasy and fiction.
Whether the Warren Commission were impressive in the manner in which they reached their conclusions, they nevertheless, appear to have reached the right conclusions. Whether it was a thorough and brilliant delving into and sorting out of endless files of data, reaching an accurate resolution of facts, or whether it was pure luck, the commission

concluded that there were three shots and only three shots fired at President Kennedy, that all three shots were fired by Lee Harvey Oswald shooting from the Schoolbook Depository, that Jack Ruby killed Oswald, and that each acted alone for reasons known only to them.

No one knows whether this is the full and absolute truth. If there was a conspiracy, it certainly must rank as history's best-kept secret. Scores of serious and capable official as well as independent researchers have spent years going over assassination information, and have brought out previously unknown information, but still reach the same conclusion. Others have concocted theories ranging from intriguing to idiotic. If there was an unanswered question, it remains unanswered.

Consider the nature of a secret and the reliability of people for keeping them, and then consider how many people would have been involved in a conspiracy and for how many years. Anyone having even partial knowledge of a conspiracy could claim instant wealth and lasting world fame by divulging such information. Still, nothing has been revealed.

The sum total of the Select Committee's conclusion is an irresponsible estimate of the possibility of a conspiracy, based on an unprofessional and incompetent hoax.

An unfortunate by-product of the Committee's conclusion is an **alibi**. The Committee majority declared that, to an almost-certainty a shot was fired by a second assassin from a position on the grassy knoll. Should someone eventually be discovered through competent evidence to have been a second assassin, and that his shot was fired from almost **any position OTHER than the grassy knoll,** prosecution would be virtually impossible. That second assassin could use the Committee's Report to slam-shut the door on all shooters from all locations other than one from the grassy knoll. That assassin has a 5.8 million dollar defense furnished him by the Committee, at the expense of the American taxpayer. The Select Committee had far more opportunity, time and money than did The Warren Commission, and achieved nothing.

It is unthinkable that learned and trusted employees of the people, and members of our law enforcement and legal profession would lend dignity to such a preposterous deception as that of the expert acoustical evidence.

This writer has no special or privileged information with regard to whether Lee Harvey Oswald killed President Kennedy, or if he did, whether he acted alone, or whether there was a tangible connection between Oswald and Jack Leon Ruby or anyone else.

There is an important fact which should be remembered: The murder of President Kennedy and the assault on Governor Connally were offenses against the laws of the citizens of Texas. There is no statute of limitation on murder in Texas. It would be proper for people, however skilled and well-intentioned, to think and to speak carefully lest they contaminate evidence and obstruct justice in the event justice has not yet been done.

PART II

CHAPTER FIVE
TECHNICAL CONSIDERATIONS
TIME DISCREPANCY IN 12:30 TIME-CHECK ON CHANNEL II

As it would appear, since the Channel 2 dispatcher gave the 12:30 time and station check, "12:30 KKB364" a few seconds before Chief Curry's broadcast, "We're going to the hospital. . . ," the assassin's shots were fired either just before or immediately after 12:30 p.m. (Channel 2). However, that would be an inaccurate assumption.

There is a simple way to determine more accurately the approximate time the 12:30 station check was actually given.

RECONSTRUCTION-PROGRESSION METHOD

The Channel 2 dispatcher acknowledged the chief's location at Main and Lamar Streets, giving the time as 12:28 (Channel 2). About 30 seconds later, the chief stated he confirmed this message and again gave the time as 12:28 (Channel 2). Assuming that the first "12:28 was stated at exactly 12:28, the second would have been given at 12:28:31. At that time, the chief was westbound on Main Street, and the President's limousine was several seconds distance behind him.

The chief travelled the remaining distance to Houston Street and turned right, or north, and traveled approximately 220 feet to its intersection with Elm Street. At Elm, the motorcade turned left to the west toward the Triple Underpass. That last turn involved an acute angle (120 degrees) and it could not be negotiated rapidly, especially in the existing crowd. The chief drove west on Elm Street before announcing his location as the ". . .Triple Underpass. . . ."

Since the 12:28:31 (Channel 2) position check at Main and Market Streets, the lead-car in the motorcade had progressed some 900 feet, including two turns. The escort officers and supervisor estimated that the motorcade was travelling at "walking speed" or about 3 to 4 MPH. It would require 2 minutes and 22 seconds to cover the course. That would place the chief at the point where he announced "Triple Underpass" **no earlier** than 12:31:04 (Channel 2). At that time, Chief Curry was about midway between Houston Street and the underpass. With the President's limousine several seconds behind the chief, the President was approaching his final turn and about to come into the assassin's sights.

Approximately 12 seconds after the chief's message, the dispatcher gave the station check. Actually, the 12:30 station check was given more nearly at 12:31:16 (Channel 2).

FIXING THE TIME THE SHOTS WERE FIRED

Chief Curry announced his location as being at the Triple Underpass at approximately 12:31:04 (Channel 2) while travelling west on Elm, midway between Houston and the underpass. The President's limousine, slowly approaching the intersection to negotiate its turn, would soon be following the chief. Projecting that the limousine completed its turn a couple of seconds later and accelerated to approximately 11 MPH as suggested by the Zapruder film, the limousine would have been in the position where the first shot was fired by 12:31:10 (Channel 2) or 12:30:55 (Channel 1). Allowing 8.3 seconds for all shots (the interval developed by the Select Committee) the shooting ended by 12:31:18.3 (Channel 2) or by 12:31:03.3 (Channel 1).

There was a slight hesitation in the progress of the motorcade. Officer Chaney raced forward to tell Chief Curry that President Kennedy had been shot. The chief then ordered the escort officers to proceed to the hospital. His orders were given on Channel 2 a few seconds after the 12:30 time check, or just after 12:31:16-17. Therefore, determining that the shooting had concluded by 12:31:18-19 (Channel 2) and by 12:31:03-04 (Channel 1), and then adding some 4 or 5 seconds for the hesitation, the motorcade would have begun leaving Dealey Plaza at approximately 12:31:08 (Channel 1). This determination of "time" matches with Channel 1 time when the officer working beat #38 observed the motorcade leaving Dealey Plaza. (See that section, this chapter.)

COMPARISON OF SHOOTING TIMES

There is a conflict between the committee's determination of a time-fix and that determined in this text. The Committee's estimate of a time-fix is 16.7 seconds earlier than that in this text.

Example:	Bell tone - Text	12:31:20.0
	Bell tone - Committee*	12:31:03.3
	Difference	- 16.7 sec.

*Seven seconds after the last shot or 12:30:55.3 Committee time.

Next, adjust the shooting times projected by the Committee according to their impulse patterns with the time differences in this text:

Shooting Time - Committee	12:30:47.0 thru 12:30:55.3
Less Difference	-16.7 -16.7
Committee time Adjusted To Text Time	12:30:30.3 thru 12:30:38.6

Now, contrast the shooting times projected by the Committee, and adjusted for the 16.7 second difference, with the shooting times established through reconstruction:

Shots-This Text	12:30:55.0 thru 12:31:03.3 (Ch. 1)
Shots-Committee	12:30:30.3 thru 12:30:38.6 (Ch. 1)
Difference	24.7 24.7 seconds

SUMMARY:

Allowing for a time-fix error of 16.7 seconds and an adjustment in the shooting times of 24.7 seconds, the conclusions here a built-in error of some 51.4 seconds. The Select Committee found its acoustical evidence approximately **one minute BEFORE the shots were fired!**

At the time established by the Committee, the President was just ending his turn from Main Street to Houston Street. He would still have to travel Houston Street, turn onto Elm Street and travel some 100-plus feet.

RECONSTRUCTION AND PROGRESSION OF MOTORCADE TRIP TO PARKLAND HOSPITAL

Consider the route to the hospital in measured segments as follows:
(See Appendix, Illustrations V, VI, and VII.)
SEGMENTS
A - Assassination site to Elm and the on-ramp to Stemmons Freeway . . . . . .800'
B - On-ramp, Elm to northbound Stemmons . . . . .800'
C - Stemmons, north, on-ramp to Continental . . . . .1475'
D - Stemmons, Continental to Oak Lawn . . . . 6000'
E - Stemmons, Oak Lawn to Industrial via off-ramp . . . . .2925'
Recap: Dealey Plaza to Trade Mart (2.273 mi) . . . . 12000'
F - Industrial, Stemmons service road to Harry Hines . . . . .1600'
G - Hines, north to Amelia . . . . .2075'
H - Hines, north, Amelia to hospital drive . . . . .900'

APPENDIX

I - Hospital drive, Hines to emergency dock . . . . 1150'
Recap: Trade Mart to Parkland (1.084 mi) . . . . .5725'
Total - Dealey Plaza to Parkland . . . . .17725'

PROJECTED TRAVEL TIMES

Dealey Plaza to the Trade Mart

SEG.	DIST.	EST. SPEED	TIME IN SECONDS	TIME DEPARTED 12:31:08 (Ch. 1)
A	800'	50	10.91	12:31:18.91
B	800'	55	9.92	12:31:28.83
C	1475'	70	14.37	12:31:43.20
D	6000'	85	48.13	12:32:31.33
E	2925'	70	28.49	12:32:59.82 (Trade Mart)
	12000'	73.2	111.82	

Trade Mart to Parkland Hospital

F	1600'	65	16.78	12:33:16.60
G	2075'	70	20.21	12:33:36.81
H	900'	65	9.44	12:33:46.25
I	1150'	40	19.60	12:34:05.85 (Hospital)
	5725'	59.14	66.03	

Total 17725'   67.98   177.85   Dealey Plaza to Parkland

SUMMARY:

The motorcade's projected arrival time at Stemmons and Industrial, the Trade Mart, is 12:32:59.82 (Channel 1). The sound of sirens began to be audible at 12:33:01.02 (Chan.1). Accordingly, the motorcade reached the Trade Mart at the time the siren sounds began to appear. This, and the fact that there were no other emergency vehicles operating in the city, more especially, not as a group, tends to corroborate that the open mike received the siren sounds at that time and place **and no other**.

The motorcade's projected arrival time at Parkland Hospital emergency dock is 12:34:05.85 (Channel 1). Adding a 15 second adjustment converts this to 12:34:20.85 (Channel 2). Chief Curry's last radio messages were on Channel 2 in the 12:34 time frame, and before 12:35.

The confirmation of arrival time at the Trade Mart and at Parkland Hospital confirm both the speed estimates for the motorcade, and the projected time-fix for the Channel 1, open mike episode starting at 12:29:10 p.m.

Committee counsel suggested that Officer McLain left Dealey Plaza "**. . .later than he remembered.**" Thus the siren sounds were picked up by his radio as "**. . .he caught the motorcade.**" For that to have occurred, McLain would have covered the entire route at speeds **greater than possible.** If he covered segments "A" and "B" at 60 MPH, segments "C" and "E" at 75 MPH, it would require that he cover the 6000' segment "D" at an average speed of 93.9 MPH. To have **averaged** that speed, he would have exceeded 100 MPH peak speed. That is impossible for a motorcycle with a top speed of 85 to 90 MPH. Furthermore, having been operated at such a slow speed for so long a time, the motorcycles were running hot, and were carboning-up. That inhibits their performances momentarily. The above tends to disprove the Committee counsel's explanations that McLain caught and either passed or fell behind the main body of the motorcade, thus explaining why the siren sounds began to appear, then disappear.

TIME AND POSITION CONFIRMATION
THROUGH OFFICER WORKING BEAT #38

During the 12:28 (Channel 1) time frame, the officer working beat #38 was southbound on Stemmons from Industrial. He was en route to Municipal Court by way of Stemmons to the Triple Underpass, then east on Commerce Street to City Hall.

At 12:33 plus, he informed the dispatcher of pedestrian traffic crossing Stemmons Freeway near the Marriott Motel, and suggested that the dispatcher inform the command post at the Trade Mart. The dispatcher acknowledged #38 and asked whether he was still en route to court. The officer acknowledged that he was. It was at this point that this text fixed Channel 1 time as 12:29:10 p.m., and the motorcycle microphone opened and remained open for more than 5 minutes.

The officer working #38 concluded his message as he approached Oak Lawn on Stemmons. He continued south to the off-ramp for the Commerce Street lanes of the Triple Underpass, eastbound. On exiting the freeway service road and starting east on Commerce, his attention was attracted ahead and to his left by the motorcade coming through the Triple Underpass, traveling west in the Elm Street lanes with their red lights on and their sirens "screaming."

The distance traveled from where he ended his message, to where he observed the motorcade is approximately 10,000 feet. His speed was about 55 to 60 MPH on the freeway and about 20 MPH on the off-ramp. After stopping at Commerce Street, he started east traveling some 150 to 200' at a speed of 30 to 35 MPH. At that point he saw the motorcade as described. His average speed was near 55 MPH over the course. Accordingly, it would require some 2 minutes, 4 seconds to drive the 10,000 feet. Starting at 12:29:10 (Channel 1) he would have observed the motorcade at approximately 12:31:14 (Channel 1).

This compares quite accurately with this text's estimate that the shots were fired, between 12:30:55 and 12:31:03, and when the motorcade departed for Parkland Hospital, 12:31:08 p.m. (Channel 1). This allows the front of the motorcade some 6 seconds to reach and pass through the underpass to be observed by the officer working #38. By confirming the departure time, we tend to confirm the times the motorcade reached Continental to be observed by Officer "H," and the times it would reach the Trade Mart and Parkland. Likewise, it tends to confirm 12:29:10 as the time Channel 1 experienced the open mike episode.

SOUNDS OF SIRENS ON CHANNEL I

Starting at approximately 12:31:01 and lasting until 12:33:34 the Channel 1 radio recorded 33 seconds of the sound of several sirens.

During #91's request for a lunch mark-out (a signal 5) the sirens became audible, starting faintly at first, and increasing in loudness until about the 7th second when it reached its first peak. A second series of sirens reached its peak at about 15 seconds, and a third group at 21 seconds, and a last not quite so loud as the first, at 28 seconds. By the 33rd second, the siren sounds had faded to inaudible. It appears that there are three distinct groups with a last vehicle as fourth. Several officers stated that a lone Secret Service car was the last vehicle in line, a little behind the others as the motorcade passed the side of the Trade Mart, eastbound on Industrial Boulevard.

In addition to distinct peaks of loudness, the peaks are accompanied by an instant of sound-blank (silence) as the peaks appear to be passing the open microphone. This is referred to by scientists as the "Doppler Effect," which deals with changes in frequency as a sound source and a receiving source pass one another. The presence of the "Doppler Effect" scientifically indicates that the sound sources (the motorcade vehicles) were passing a receiving source (the open microphone) as opposed to an open microphone passing the several sound sources. The open mike could not have been passing the sound sources as the engine on the motorcycle containing the open mike could be heard running at idle-speed. It was sitting still, stopped on the Industrial Boulevard side of the Trade Mart, north of the command post, near the motor pool. As the motorcade turned east on Industrial toward Hines, they passed the subject motorcycle.

The motorcycle was approximately 80 to 100 feet east of the east curb of Stemmons Service Road. After completing their turns onto Industrial, the motorcade vehicles had 100 to 150 feet in which they would accelerate to between 50 to 60 MPH. At an average speed of 55 MPH, a motorcycle travels 80.666 feet per second. Accordingly, a few seconds after turning, the motorcade vehicles would come into the maximum pickup range of the open mike. Since each group seems to be about seven seconds in passing, they would cover approximately 565 feet in two equal segments of 282 feet each, an approaching-half and a departing-half. (See Appendix, Illustration IV.)

It is unlikely that sounds originating at distances greater than 300 feet would register with the open mike due to equipment limitations. Also, it would depend to some degree on the loudness of the sound, surrounding conditions, and the condition of the equipment. But 300 feet is the approximate maximum operating range.

With the sound approaching from the left, entering the first 282 foot segment, and the subject receiving microphone some 80 to 100 feet to the south, the sound sources would be approximately 300 feet from the receiver. As the sound sources reached the mid-point of the two segments, we find the "Doppler" exactly where it must be. Then, as the sound sources pass through the second segment in departing, the sounds fade away exactly as they must, passing out of the 300 foot range.

SUMMARY:

The motorcycle with the open microphone was at or near the motor pool, on the north side of the Trade Mart, at position "A" in Illustration IV. The motorcade passed the receiver from the receiver's left to right at an average speed of 55 MPH, and travelled 565 feet in passing the receiver. This condition caused the sound sources to pass at the optimum distances at which they were recorded, including exactly where the "Doppler" would be, and at the exact time that it should have, 12:33:01 to 12:33:34 p.m., Channel 1 time. This could have been confirmed by the Select Committee's investigation but they declined.

THE MOTORCYCLE WITH THE STUCK MICROPHONE

Several three-wheel officers, assisted by relief officers, were assigned to work major intersections on the motorcade route along Cedar Springs Road and on Harwood Street to Main Street. One of these, Officer "K," completed his assignment about 12:23 (Channel 1) and left on his 2 1/4 mile trip to the Trade Mart where he was due to report to the motor pool by 12:30 p.m.

Shortly after he left his intersection en route to the Trade Mart, his transmitter stuck open for brief intervals during which the sound of the engine suggests a traveling speed of 25 to 30 MPH. During the 12:28 (Channel 1) time frame his mike opened again for 17 1/2 seconds. The engine speed still appears to be near 30 MPH.

Then, at the projected time of 12:29:10 (Channel 1) his mike stuck open once again and remained open for more than five minutes. During the first minute or two his speed held steadily near 30 MPH. Then, the engine sound slowed to an irregular speed for a little less than a minute.

Officer "K" left his corner with 6 1/2 minutes to travel two and one quarter miles to the Trade Mart. There was heavier traffic, a stop sign and three signal lights along the initial portion of his route. Estimating his overall trip at 25 MPH, he had no trouble arriving on time.

He went to the Trade Mart and passed time listening to a two-wheel motorcycle tuned to Channel 2. Not all three-wheel motorcycles had been furnished with two-channel radios. He, "K," doesn't remember moving his motorcycle after he arrived. At any rate, it isn't possible to determine absolutely whether the recorded sounds of engine changes represent activity of the subject motorcycle or of other motorcycles arriving and departing, as they were doing at the motor pool. At one point in the recording the sound does seem more like the engine of a two-wheel rather than a three-wheel motorcycle.

"K" was using a relief or spare motorcycle that day, one which was not equipped with a Channel 2 radio, and one which had experienced frequent radio trouble.

Shortly after the motorcade passed the Trade Mart, Officer "K" can be heard to speak but his message cannot be understood. Moments later he started off on his motorcycle, en route to Parkland. Apparently, in checking his radio, listening to find the opportunity to transmit, he found that his radio was stuck in the transmit mode.

At Parkland, after the immediate urgency had subsided and almost everyone had departed, Officer "K" commiserated with other officers over a couple of his personal misfortunes during the day. One of these problems was that his radio had stuck open during the emergency.

COMPARISON OF CROSS-CHANNEL MESSAGES

Since there was no time standard for radio communications in the Dallas Police system, and since each radio dispatcher's position operated independently, and each operator performed individually, and since "time" indications could and did come from several different sources, it is impossible to fix a time reference with absolute certainty. However, to reconstruct events of the day and to show progression through and the relationship of certain events, it is necessary to establish some "time fix" to serve as a standard reference base. In this text, "time" turns on a fix at 12:29:10 (Channel 1).

Since the Channels were **not** synchronized it was necessary to show as precise as possible a relationship. First, Channel 2's announced time was approximately 15 seconds ahead of Channel 1. To correct the difference and show the approximate "true time," 15 seconds should be added to Channel 1 times, or subtracted from Channel 2 times. These two time references when considered together, represent true or real-time as accurately as possible.

The best and easiest method for showing their relationship is through those incidents where Channel 2 messages are present on Channel 1 recordings. These events are also referred to as "cross talk." However, the reference can be misleading as it might suggest that one person was **knowingly** talking to another on a different channel. Such cross-talk is virtually impossible. That is, it could be done through awkward preparation, but there is absolutely no reason for doing so.

There are three occasions where the open microphone picked up portions of Channel 2 messages from outside speakers on radios which were tuned to Channel 2, and on one occasion, the Channel 2 dispatcher used his "simultaneous broadcast" capability to broadcast at once on both channels.

The relationship between Channels 1 and 2 in cross-channel recordings is as follows:

1. At approximately 12:31 (Channel 2), Deputy Chief #4 discussed a traffic problem with Captain #125. The last sentence in that message, "I'll check it." was picked up over the open mike and was transmitted and recorded at approximately 12:31:02 (Channel 1).

2. At approximately 12:34:16 (Channel 2), Motorcycle Sergeant #190 asked, "You want me to hold. . . ?" Part of his message was recorded by the open mike at approximately 12:33:52 (Channel 1).

3. At approximately 12:35:58 (Channel 2), the channel 2 dispatcher activated the simultaneous broadcast switch to announce at once over both channels, "Attention all emergency equipment . . . ." This was recorded at approximately 12:35:38 (Channel 1).

4. At approximately 12:36:21 (Channel 2), Sergeant #260 broadcast, ". . .came from the 5th floor . . . ." Most of this message was picked up and recorded at approximately 12:35:57 (Channel 1).

It must be remembered that these times are estimates based on several factors, However, it is useful to observe these events as they tend to confirm time estimates through their near relationships, and more so, that the subject motorcycle **was not** in the motorcade, but away from the downtown crowd and at a place where other police units were parked.

CHAPTER SIX
REFLECTIONS

Probably the most informed and the most ignored authorities on what happened and in what order in Dealey Plaza are the motorcade motor jockeys. They have been interviewed uncounted times by many people, ranging from official investigators to insufferable quacks. Again, they are referred to in this text by a "letter" name, hopeful that it will discourage further contacts, however well-intentioned.

While their recollections are presented in the first person, their comments should not be taken as unalterable quotes. Too many years have passed for them to remember with unimpeachable certainty what they might have said earlier and what they say now. Accordingly, what they say here should be considered for the **meaning** rather than exactness.

OFFICER "A"

The only thing different in this and all the other VIP escorts we had pulled was the length and the crowds. The crowd was there almost the whole length of the motorcade. In motorcades like this, we are constantly watching up, down, right, left, all around. If we see anything that looks in any way wrong, we radio back to the command car and they hold up the motorcade until it's checked out. That's nothing new.

I was about half way down the hill on Elm toward the Triple Underpass, going very slowly, so slowly it was actually a walking speed--you have to put your feet down to stay up-- and, periodically, you had to stop a moment. As I looked ahead I saw one officer on the overpass over Elm, and some civilians, and wondered who the civilians were because they weren't supposed to be up there. But since an officer was with them, and another officer was assigned up there too, I supposed it was all right. They all appeared to be calm and orderly.

Looking on around to my right, I noted that the hill to my right, the one referred to now as the grassy knoll, was clear up to the pavilion. Then, there were a few people standing in the open area from the steps on to the area in front of the pavilion. The number of people increased toward Houston Street, and there was a number of people across the street on the south side of Elm, mostly back to the east.

I had looked toward Chief Curry to get the signal to open interval and move out since he had the Secret Service man with him. Then I looked back toward the President. They had made it around the corner off Houston and were now headed west on Elm in my direction. They had passed the worst of the crowding, and were then coming more into the open, but they were moving real slowly.

That's when the first shot was fired. I was looking directly at the President, and I saw the concrete burst into a cloud of dust when that bullet hit the curb. I noticed, too, that with the shot, some people started running in every direction, while several people hit the ground. It seemed to me like they had been hit by shrapnel. Then, while looking back at the President, I heard the second shot. The President became rigid and grabbed his neck. It also seemed like the limousine stopped or almost stopped, and agents from the following car started running toward the President's limousine. The third shot hit the President in the head.

I was still moving west at a slow speed toward Chief Curry when Jim Chaney pulled up from his former position to the right rear of the President's limousine. Chaney said the President had been shot in the head and that it appeared to be a fatal hit. We then informed Chief Curry through his open car window. That's when the chief ordered everybody to go to the hospital.

During the shooting, my back or more accurately, my left side was turned to the grassy knoll, but I was never more than about 100 feet from the spot where someone is supposed to have fired. Just an instant before, nobody was standing there, and I didn't see anyone approaching. If a shot had come from that close to me, I would have known it. There was no shot fired from the grassy knoll. There were three shots fired, and all three came from back up toward the School Book Depository.

Just before the shooting started, I passed my niece, her husband and their children. They were standing on the grassy knoll, just north of Elm Street and near where the President was when the second shot was fired. They gave their statements to the Warren Commission, and I suggested to the Committee investigators that they should be interviewed. I told the investigators what had happened. I told them that there had only been three shots, and that no shot or shots had been fired from the grassy knoll. For some reason they seem to have ignored everything I told them, and I don't think they ever contacted the family.

There's a lot of people who have talked about all this who don't know what they're talking about. It seemed to me like those people from Washington didn't want to know what happened. It seemed like they had already made up their minds how they wanted it to be and were only looking for someone to agree with them. They didn't want to know the truth.

OFFICER "B"

I was assigned to the lead group of jockeys. We got through the crowd at Elm and Houston well ahead of the President. We were at least halfway down the hill from Houston, headed toward the Triple Underpass. Recognizing some friends standing on the south curb of Elm Street, I stopped to spend a moment while waiting for the motorcade to catch up.

As the President started down Elm, one of the group took a picture with a Polaroid camera. I still have that picture somewhere around the house--I hope I didn't lose it while moving. Anyhow, that was the same time the shooting started. At first I thought it was a motorcycle backfiring, as they were heating up. The first shot apparently missed the limousine as it hit the curb, not too far from where they were standing. The second and third shots hit the President from the rear. At the time, I was facing east on Elm with the grassy knoll to my immediate left, and the corner of the stockade fence was less than 100 feet away. I saw nothing on that hill that looked in any way suspicious. I'm absolutely positive that there were only three shots, that they all came from back up Elm Street from the right rear of the President's limousine, and that no shot was fired from the grassy knoll.

It seemed like all that took an awful long time to happen, maybe a minute or more. I then pulled out to the head of the motorcade with Grey (deceased) and that's when Chief Curry ordered us to Parkland. That was one wild ride. I almost lost it on Industrial when I crossed the railroad track west of Hines. I hit it way too fast and went airborne, landing almost at Hines. Chief Curry radioed to keep all traffic out of the emergency entrance so I stopped at the turn on the corner southwest of the rear of Parkland. I don't remember in just what order other officers arrived, but McLain must have come in with the main body as he didn't come in late by himself.

OFFICER "C"

Officer "C" did something unique. Late that night, after he returned home, he felt the weight of the day in a most personal way. Not wishing to permit time and circumstances to cloud his memory, he sat down with his child's school notebook, and in a fatigued but reflective mood, wrote a diary for the day. He intended to correct it later and have it typed. However, considering its contents, he decided to leave it unedited. It is well that he did, for in its original state it more clearly reflects the mood of the day. He graciously consented to publishing his unedited account herein for the first time.

I SAW THE PRESIDENT ASSASSINATED

The morning of November 22, 1963 started out to be cold and raining, a dark day. I made detail at 6:45 a.m. along with many other officers. I had escorted President Kennedy in 1961 when he came to Dallas to visit with Mr. Sam Rayburn who was in Baylor Hospital in serious condition. That day, when we got back to Love Field Mr. Kennedy shook my hand and thanked me for the escort. This time I was hoping that I could escort the President again, but I thought I would probably have to work a corner instead. In Detail I was assigned to ride on the right side and slightly to the rear of the presidential Limousine. The original plan was to have two officers ride on the left of the car and two on the right of the car. These officers were to ride one behind the other to keep anyone from getting too near the President but he did not want this so we were changed so as to ride side by side at the rear bumper of the car which was only slightly behind the President.

We rode our motorcycles out of the garage that morning in the rain. We were required to be on our assignments at Ten that morning. The planes were due to land at about Eleven Thirty. I got to Love Field at a little after Nine and it had about quit raining. By Ten it was beginning to clear off.

The planes landed at about Eleven Thirty Five. There were three of them; the first two carried the Staff, White House Press and other dignitaries. The third plane was Air Force One which carried the President.

We lined up our motorcycle escort preparing for the departure. The motorcade was led by Chief _____ who was to be about six blocks ahead followed by Sergeant _____ with two motor jockeys who were to be about three blocks ahead, then Sergeant _____ with four jockeys one block ahead, then Chief Curry only a few feet ahead of the President's car. I was riding beside Jim Chaney on the right side of the President's Limousine. Sergeant _____ and four jockeys were bringing up the rear behind the Secret Service car.

There was hundreds of people standing on the curbs as we came out of Love Field; it was to be this way all the way to the Market Hall. These people would walk out into the street as the first motorcycles went by so Chief Curry told them over the radio to fall back to about 50 feet ahead of his car. On Lemmon Avenue 4900 block near Loma Alto some people on the right hand curb were holding a long sign said "JFK and LBJ stop and shake our hands." Mr. Kennedy had his driver stop and he told these people to come on and they walked up to his car and did shake his hand. I saw people start to run toward the stopped car from as far as a block ahead of us. Jim Chaney called by radio to Chief Curry and he started backing up toward the presidential car. Sergeant _____ and the four Jockeys turned around and started toward us the Secret Service men dismounted and ran to the car and started moving people away and then we started moving again. Chief _____ called Chief Curry and told him the crowd was extra heavy at Turtle Creek and Lemmon and he replied "that's all right we'll take care of it we have a good motorcycle escort." Sergeant _____ and his four got the crowd pushed back and we proceeded with out to much interference. The closer we got to downtown the heavier the crowd got and the more they would walk out toward the President. If one of them got pretty close a secret service man would leave his car and get on back of the presidential car so he could be close enough to Mr. Kennedy to protect him.

We traveled west on Cedar Springs to Harwood then south on Harwood to Main Street without much trouble with the crowd but as we traveled west on Main the crowd was heaviest of all and they wouldn't back up. Several times my right handle bar and right hand hit people in the stomach because they weren't watching me they were only looking at the president. Along about Akard Street the crowd was so heavy and they would not back up so rather than bump them I slacked back and was riding directly behind Jim Chaney. A young man ran out of the crowd from behind me and ran past me on my left which put him between me and the presidential Limousine as he ran past me I saw he was carrying a small camera already placed to his eye but he didn't get to take the close up picture of the President because one of the Secret Service men caught him just in front of my motor and bodily threw him between me and Chaney into the crowd. The last glance I got of the crowd there were people still falling. About this time I saw ahead of me standing in the street a lady holding an umbrella, the type that had a long metal piece on the tip I rode up beside Jim Chaney forcing people to back up but this lady didn't right then. An Agent left his car and got on the rear of the presidential car. I rode closer to her forcing her back into the crowd. After we passed her the agent went back to his car.

We traveled west on Main the turned north on Houston Street without too much trouble with the crowd then we turned west onto Elm Street. Drove only a short way traveling very slowly. About that time I heard what I thought was a car back fire and I looked around and then to the President's car in time for the next explosion and saw Mr. Connally jerk back to his right and it seemed that he look right at me I could see a shocked expression on his face and I thought "Someone is shooting at them" I began stopping my motor and looking straight ahead first at the Railroad overpass and saw only one Policeman standing on the track directly over the street. . I looked back toward Mr. Kennedy and saw him hit in the head he appeared to have been hit just above the right ear. The top of his head flew off away from me. Mrs. Kennedy pulled him toward her. Mrs. Connally pulled Mr. Connally down and she slid down into the seat. I knew that the shooting was coming from my right rear and I looked back that way but I never did look up. Looking back to the front again I saw the Secret Service Agent lying down across the car over Mr. and Mrs. Kennedy the presidential limousine was beginning to pick up speed and the Secret Service men were running past the presidential car drawing their guns as they ran. I said to Jim Chaney "Let's go with them" and we sped away, he pulled past the President's car and up toward Chief Curry's car. Chief Curry came on the radio and notified the Dispatcher that a shooting had occurred that we were in route to Parkland Code three and to notify them to stand by. As we were traveling north on Stemmons Freeway Agent Hill raised up looked toward me and shook his head from side to side and held up his hand thumb down. He knew at that time as I did that the President of the United States was dead or dying.

We were driving at a high rate of speed the people along the shoulder of the freeway not knowing what had taken place were trying to get a closer look at the President and would run into the street in front of us. A very dangerous thing to do. After we passed Market Hall we had no trouble with pedestrian traffic but the automobile traffic was heavy. It seemed like an eternity but we finally got to Parkland Hospital.

I got off my motor stepped over to the presidential Limousine. An Agent opened the car door and started to get Mrs. Kennedy out but Mrs. Kennedy said no. It's no need she said and raised up from over Mr. Kennedy. I could see the top of his head was gone, his left eye was bulged out of socket. The agent said "Oh no!" and started crying pulled his coat off and placed it over Mr. Kennedy's head. I saw someone rolling a stretcher up and I said "Let's get Mr. Johnson out then;" thinking that Mr. Connally was Mr. Johnson; reached in the car and got a hold of him under his arms some other officers got a hold of Mr. Connally and we laid him on the stretcher and he was taken inside. I looked back to Mr. Kennedy as Mrs. Kennedy said all right but I'm going with him." I reached in and got a hold of him at his shoulders and helped lay him on a stretcher. I stepped back and some agents started pushing Mr. Kennedy into the hospital Mrs. Kennedy walked beside the stretcher. As we got to the door the emergency room an agent told me to take up a post here and not to let anybody but doctors and nurses in.

Some woman and a small boy walked up and asked "Is it true that the President was shot" and I said yes. "How bad is he hurt" she said and I said "I don't know Mam and if I did I could not tell you."

Mr. Pokey Wright a retired Deputy Chief of Police walked up and told me to clear the Hallway and I along with some Secret Service agents asked everybody to leave the hallway and did get it cleared out.

This was the first chance I had to relax a little bit and I lit a cigarette I noticed I had blood on my hands looked and I had blood on my left sleeve, down the left side of my riding breeches and on the outside of my left boot. I suppose I got this on me as I helped get Mr. Kennedy out of the car.

A man walked up and wanted to go into the Emergency Room. I asked him who he was and he said he was Justice of the Peace _____. I told him he could not go in because there was probably nothing he could do. He said Ok then he went on. Later the Hospital

Administrator came out looking for his J. P., I told him I turned him back and he said "Turned him back man he owns the body" and I replied "What body" and he said "I guess you are right," If you see him again we need him to authorize removal of the Body." This was the first official word I had that the President was dead. Officer L. C. Gray walked up and asked me if I had heard about Officer Tippett I said no and he told me that Officer Tippett had stopped a suspect and was killed and that they were looking for this suspect in Oak Cliff.

Mrs. Cabell walked up and asked if Mr. Cabell was in the Emergency Room and asked me to ask him if he wanted her to come in. I went inside to ask him and before I could say anything he said "Does your radio work" I said yes and he said come on and we went to my motorcycle as we passed his wife in the hallway he told her he would be right back. We got to my motor he told me to call the dispatcher and have them to get a Justice of the Peace to the hospital in a hurry. I did and we went back inside he went back to the Emergency Room and an Agent got me by the arm and told me he had information that the airplane had been moved wanted me to find out where it was and arrange for an escort back to Love Field. I liked to never found a phone in that hospital that wasn't busy. One line had already been hooked up direct to Washington. I finally got a line and called the dispatcher's office. I told them who I was and that I understood the airplanes had been moved instructed him to contact the Love Field officer and instruct him to pick up the escort at the entrance to Love Field and lead it to the President's plane. He asked if I was going to escort the president's body back to Love Field and I told him that I did not know. I then looked for the agent to tell him that everything was set and was unable to locate him so I went back to the door to the Emergency Room.

Shortly some officer walked up and told me they are taking the President out the other door come on he said. I walked outside just as they were putting the casket into the Hearse. Someone said "Jackson a secret service agent is looking for you" Sergeant ____ asked me if I was going to escort the body to Love Field I said I don't know about that time the agent walked up and asked if I had arranged for the escort and I said "yes I'm ready to go when you are." Officer ____ asked me if I wanted him to go with me and I said yes and turned to Sergeant ____ and told him that ____ and I were going to make the escort to Love Field with that we left. A chief's car pulled out in front of us until we got onto Hines Blvd. then he motioned for us to take the lead. We did and made a usual funeral escort, using only red lights and whistle to clear traffic to Love Field. Where the president was placed back on Air Force One.

OFFICER "D"
I was assigned to ride at the left rear of the president's limousine. At first, we had been told to ride beside the limousine, but President Kennedy didn't want that. He wanted us back some so he could greet people directly. So we moved back, two officers side by side on the right and two more on the left, staying about 5 or 6 feet behind him.

Nobody expected what happened. It's hard to believe it. I was looking at the president when the first shot was fired. It missed. The second shot hit the president in the back, and the third hit him in the head. I was still in my position some 10 to 15 feet from President Kennedy. I didn't change my position because I had been told to stay right there no matter what--don't leave the President's side. So I stayed there all the way to the hospital.

Somewhere during this, Chaney pulled up to Chief Curry and then the chief told us to go to Parkland. While we were on the freeway running 80 MPH or so, people who were standing along the median strip were moving around trying to see the President. They didn't know what had happened. I was afraid someone was going to step out and get hit. One of the

Secret Service Agents motioned me to pull up beside the limousine, but I didn't because that would have put me a couple of feet closer to the bystanders, and that would be too dangerous. When I got to the hospital, I worked an assignment to keep people out until it was all over and we were relieved.

OFFICER "E"

It had been a long escort. We had a lot of people all the way. There were no problems, just a heavy crowd and a lot of yelling and cheering, and the motors were getting hot. When you follow the lead, you do a lot of starting and stopping, trying to hold an interval. I was glad it was almost over.

The crowd was real heavy down on the end of the downtown area, but just past Dealey Plaza it would open up and we would be on the freeway and just a few minutes from the Trade Mart. The front of the motorcade started blocking up in the crowd in those last turns coming off Main and turning onto Elm. Back on Houston, where we were, we were just about stopped and moving real slow when we could move.

A little past half way down Houston (between Main and Elm), I heard the first shot. I could tell it came from somewhere in front of me, and high. As I looked up I noticed all the pigeons flushed off the top of the building on the corner ahead of me. And in the same period I heard the second shot, and then the third one. I couldn't see just where the shots came from but I knew they were from a high-powered rifle. I hunt a lot, and had just got back from hunting. There was no mistaking that; there were three shots, that's for sure. Though I didn't see exactly where the shots came from, I knew in my own mind they probably came from the corner building as the sound was right and because of the pigeons. So I headed there, got off my motor and entered the building (the Texas Schoolbook Depository). It took a while because of the crowd; they had started moving in every direction.

The man who said he was the building superintendent was outside and met me at the door and went in with me. Shortly after I entered the building I confronted Oswald. The man who identified himself as the superintendent said that Oswald was all right, that he was employed there. We left Oswald there, and the supervisor showed me the way upstairs. We couldn't get anyone to send the freight elevator down. In giving the place a quick check, I found nothing that seemed out of the ordinary, so I started back to see what had happened. Not knowing for sure what had happened, I was limited in what I could legally do.

The investigator from Washington contacted me for my recollection of what happened, but I guess they weren't interested in what I said.

OFFICER "F"

I had just turned off Main onto Houston and stopped. I was headed north along the west curb and just a little north of Main Street. Inspector Putnam was standing near the curb not 10 feet from me. While waiting there for the press bus to complete its turn, I heard the shots. They definitely came from ahead of me, all three of them.

The motorcade was backed up almost to a stand-still. Then, people started running and falling. I looked toward where I would expect to see the President's limousine but I couldn't see it. I looked at Inspector Putnam but could tell from his expression he didn't know anything more than I did, so I took off for the front of the motorcade to see what had happened.

I passed people while I was doing this. I remember passing some of the motorcade vehicles, but I don't remember specifically who I passed. As I went down Elm Street, I noticed a motorcycle down at the curb, and an officer crawling on his hands and knees. The lead vehicles of the motorcade had already cleared the Triple Underpass, headed for the Elm Street off-ramp to Stemmons. They slowed down on the access road and I caught the lead units on the access road just about where the railroad goes over it, but I couldn't pass them because the roadway was too narrow.

On the freeway I pulled up behind the president's limousine. Apparently I startled one of the agents in the limousine who didn't hear me come up because he spun around and pointed a 90 mm machine gun at me. . .at least it looked that large when it was pointed at my head.

Somehow, we made it to Parkland and got them out of the limousine. A young boy came up from somewhere with a small, cheap-looking box camera. The limousine door was open and the kid stepped up and snapped a picture of that mess on the floor. An agent reached over and took the camera, peeled it and told him that, "That's all the pictures for today." I spent the next little while doing security duty at the hospital.

I told the investigator that there were only three shots and that they had all come from the Book Depository, but it seemed to me he didn't believe me, or he didn't like what he heard. To ease his doubt I suggested he put me on the polygraph or use truth serum. He said the polygraph really wouldn't prove anything and that they couldn't use truth serum because if I woke up with a headache I could sue them. I offered to sign a release of liability, but he wasn't interested. In fact, since I didn't say anything he wanted to hear, I got the distinct impression he wasn't interested in anything I said. I couldn't tell whether he had been sent here to discover something or just to see whether anybody agreed with whatever they had already made up their minds about.

OFFICER "G"

I had worked traffic at Cedar Springs and Olive while the motorcade came through. The President came through by 12:20, and the traffic flow returned to normal in a couple of minutes. I was due to report to the motorpool at the Trade Mart for my next assignment. To get there, I passed through the downtown area by heading west on Elm Street, getting ahead of the motorcade which was westbound on Main Street. I reached Elm and Houston a couple of minutes ahead of the motorcade and continued west through the Triple Underpass as the motorcade reached the west end of town.

Just after I turned off Elm and was on the service ramp leading to north on Stemmons, I heard sirens starting. I didn't hear anything that sounded like shots. I assumed the motorcade was speeding up to get to the Trade Mart because it had been scheduled to be there at 12:30, but they were late. I pulled over on the shoulder to get out of the way and let them pass. Some motorcycles passed, but I can't say who they were.

I could tell that something had happened because of what you could see in the back seat of the limousine, but I didn't know what. I waited a moment and looked back to be sure that all the vehicles headed my way had passed. Then I started back toward Elm, driving the wrong way down the entrance ramp, and then I continued east on Elm against the one-way traffic sign, headed back toward Dealey Plaza to see what had happened and what I might be needed to do. While I was driving the wrong way on the ramp and on Elm, no vehicular traffic passed me. I'm certain of this because I was going the wrong way and had to be careful.

I rode back to Elm and Houston and joined the officers surrounding the Book Depository. Later, I was assigned to the front door to take the name and address of everyone allowed to leave the building.

OFFICER "H"

I worked the motorcade through Harwood and Pacific. The President got through and the traffic cleared enough for me to leave by 12:25 p.m. I was due at the Trade Mart for reassignment by 12:30, so to avoid downtown traffic, I went back to Ross Avenue and turned west toward Lamar. Then I went north on Lamar. When I was headed west on Ross, I became aware of an open transmitter on Channel 1 and switched over to Channel 2 because that was the channel we would be on anyway.

While I was northbound on Lamar and almost at McKinney Avenue, I heard Chief Curry come on the air saying something about, ". . .go to Parkland Hospital." Nothing was said about what was wrong, but I couldn't help but wonder. I made the turn where Lamar becomes Continental and goes under some railroad tracks, and continued west on Continental. The roadway through there is set between walls on either side for a few hundred feet before you come out into the open in the old Trinity Riverbed area.

As I came out into the open area at Stemmons Freeway and Continental, I could hear sirens off to my left. I made my right turn from Continental to northbound on Stemmons Freeway service road. As I did, I realized that the sirens were from the motorcade, and that they were northbound on Stemmons passing over Continental and were passing immediately to my left.

I realized that something was wrong. I was accelerating in second gear, so I stayed in second to about 50 MPH, which was about as fast as I could do, and then shifted into high gear, and entered onto the freeway, behind the rear of the motorcade. I could do a little better than 50 MPH in high gear, but couldn't catch the motorcade. Deciding to join them as best I could, I pulled into the center of the freeway and stayed wide open. The motorcade was pulling away from me, but not so fast that I lost sight. As they went over rises in the freeway, I couldn't see all of them all the time, but essentially, I kept them in sight until they turned off Stemmons service road onto Industrial Boulevard, by the Trade Mart. I continued to follow all the way to Parkland Hospital.

When I pulled onto Stemmons behind the motorcade several hundred feet north of Continental, I became the last vehicle running north. While in that position, no vehicle passed me. I'm positive of this because I was concerned with being overtaken by someone who might not see me. By the time the front of the motorcade turned onto Industrial, I was perhaps a quarter of a mile behind them. At Parkland, I joined with other officers providing security at the hospital. I was sent to the old emergency waiting room because some enterprising reporters were climbing through the windows in an effort to penetrate security. A couple of photographers even handed me their cameras to hold for them while they worked their way in. I obliged, and then, after they gained entry, returned their cameras and walked them around the corner and back outside.

OFFICER "I"

I was assigned to traffic at Cedar Springs and Maple. After the President passed and the regular traffic flow was restored, I left for the Trade Mart. I had more than enough time so I was working my way in that direction. I don't recall just where I was when I heard the chief order officers to go to Parkland, but I was fairly close and felt I should go.

I arrived at the emergency dock shortly before the motorcade. I wasn't ready for what I saw when they arrived, and I still haven't got over it. I couldn't believe it even though I assisted in removing the victims from the limousine. I think all of us were moving mechanically because we were in a state of shock. It just wasn't real.

OFFICER "J"

After roll-call, I left City Hall and went to Hines and Industrial to cut southbound traffic on Industrial when the motorcade was approaching the Trade Mart on Stemmons. This was to keep the regular traffic from interfering with the motorcade while they turned into the Trade Mart parking lot off Industrial. I parked my motorcycle, turned up my radio and waited.

I heard sirens coming from around Stemmons and Industrial and looked up there and saw the front of the motorcade turning the corner. My watch was running slow so I thought there was still a couple of minutes before they would even be due there. Then I thought maybe I had missed my radio call telling me to cut traffic, and for a moment, that worried me. I started to cut traffic when I realized that they were passing the Trade Mart and coming on down Industrial in my direction. It suddenly occurred to me that the President had attended a breakfast in Ft. Worth before his short flight to Dallas, and that it had been a long motorcade, and that perhaps he had become ill. As the limousine passed me, an agent motioned for me to join them, so I turned around and joined them.

After President Kennedy and Governor Connally had been taken inside, a Secret Service Agent stationed me outside the door to the President's emergency room. He told me that no one would be allowed to enter except for medical personnel. Shortly after this, a man who said he was an FBI agent flashed his folder and started past me. Just as I called for him to wait a minute and he replied that it was all right, the Secret Service Agent came back in and told him he couldn't come in. The man repeated who he was and started toward the door. The Secret Service Agent said, "I don't give a ____ ____ who you are, you aren't coming in," and he grabbed the other guy, gave him a quick flip and laid the man flat on the floor. The Secret Service Agent then told me to escort the man out of here and out of the building and don't let him back in . . . to keep him out, whatever it took. I escorted him out without incident and never saw him again.

Some time later, I assisted in taking the President's body out to an awaiting ambulance. After placing the coffin in the ambulance, a Secret Service Agent helped himself to the ambulance and drove off, leaving poor old "Peg" standing on the dock saying, "They're stealing my ambulance!"

After things died down, several officers were standing out back trying to settle down and collect their wits. We were in a kind of bull-session about what kind of day it had been when ____ mentioned that it hadn't been his day, that his mike had stuck open during all this, and he had made a comment on the radio that he shouldn't have.

OFFICER "K"

I was assigned to work traffic and the crowd along Stemmons at Industrial. Officer ____ was with me. I heard and saw the motorcade coming toward the Trade Mart, but I could tell something wasn't right as they were traveling too fast, and they were strung out. When they passed us and continued north on Industrial, I knew something was wrong.

Shortly thereafter we were sent to Elm and Houston. We were copying vehicle license numbers for a while. Then officer Tippett got shot over in Oak Cliff.

The dispatcher was calling for some help there, and there were enough officers at Elm and Houston, so we were sent to Oak Cliff.

About the time we reached the area the dispatcher was broadcasting information regarding the suspect and his escape route. We pulled up on Jefferson and started checking some cars parked behind a service station to see if the suspect was hiding in or under one of the cars. That's when we found his jacket. We saw Captain ____ in his car on Jefferson so I turned the jacket over to him. It isn't easy to handle a motorcycle and hang on to a jacket.

About this time some officers who had been checking houses in the area reached a church and wanted help to search it. By then, I had gotten separated from Officer ____. While I was around there and some officers were checking, another squad spotted a subject fitting the general description of the suspect running into the branch library at Jefferson and Marsalis. However, he turned out to be an employee.

A while later the suspect was arrested in the Texas Theater. I have heard that someone suggested that "the real suspect" had escaped by hiding in that church while officers were drawn away to the library on a wild goose chase. That's ridiculous. The church was searched, and the subject did merit being checked. From a distance, he fitted the description, and he was running as if he were being chased. The officer who spotted him would have been grossly negligent had he ignored that subject.

Later that day, after things had settled down, I was with another three-wheel officer and some others when he commented about his earlier troubles which included his radio microphone sticking open during the assassination.

CIVILIAN "L"

My wife, our two children and I went to Love Field to see the President, but we didn't get a good view. I knew the motorcade route, so I drove downtown so we could get a better look. I had loaded my 8mm movie camera but forgot to bring it. We were standing right on the curb near a street light post in front of the pavilion which was on the hill behind us.

When the President's limousine came around the corner, I had a good view from about 150 feet. About that time I heard two loud sounds about three seconds apart. I didn't associate them with gunshots, so I didn't consider where they might have come from. They seemed more like firecrackers. However, I did notice a change in President Kennedy; his arm went up and he seemed to stiffen.

Just after the two sounds which I now know to have been gunshots, the limousine stopped for an instant, a large man in the right front seat picked up what looked like a telephone, and then the car shot forward again. Some of the agents on the following car got off. By this time the limousine was about to pass in front of us.

From a distance of 12 to 15 feet, just one lane of traffic away, we saw the bullet hit the President from the right rear and literally tear away the side of his scalp and right ear. Apparently Governor Connally had been shot too as his eyes were wide open, his arm was down, he was rigid and his shirt was bloody.

Hearing this shot, the one that hit the President in the head, I realized someone was shooting and we were too near. I told my wife, "That's it, get them down!" and we fell down over our children.

Having not considered the first two noises to have been shots, and having been so preoccupied with what I had just seen, and my concern for our immediate safety, I was not concerned with where the shots had come from. Thinking about it afterwards, I had the impression that they had been fired from behind us. I noticed Mr. Zapruder with his camera and thought it was a gun. My impression was only "behind us," not from the stockade fence. I am certain no shot was fired from there. Also, I'm certain that only three shots were fired. We are positive about that. Had the Committee investigators asked us, we would have told them this. Instead, they used part of what I said in a statement I made that day, and it makes it sound like I believe someone fired from the grassy knoll. That's not true.

The truth is: First, there were three shots, not four. Second, when I said "I. . .thought the shots had come from the garden directly behind me. . . ," I was referring specifically to the third shot and assumed all three had come from the same place; I really hadn't thought the first two were shots until I saw that they were. To say "behind me" would depend on just which way I was looking at the time I made my estimate. Watching the President pass from left to right, I was turning my head, so I saw the third bullet hit and was aware of the sound of the shot while I was concerned with what I was seeing. The shot sounded like it was from "behind me," but there's no way I can be more specific. Third, I am certain no shot was fired from behind the fence on the grassy knoll as that would have been to my immediate right and within 100 feet of my ear. I would have known it if a shot had been fired from there.

OFFICER MCLAIN

Just after I had turned north onto Houston from Main Street, I was moving very slow along the west side of the street. Officer "E" was across the street and a little ahead of me. The motorcade seemed to stop at Elm and Houston as the crowd pressed in on the President. As the President got around onto Elm Street, I was approaching the middle of the block between Main and Elm. It was along there that I heard a shot. I suppose it was the first shot because I looked up and saw the pigeons flushed from their roost on top of the building on the northwest corner of Elm and Houston. I was either stopped or stopping at the time. I looked around in an effort to determine what had happened. I don't recall ever hearing the other shots--just one which I guess was the first.

While looking about, I looked through an opening in the decorative wall behind the fountain and pond in Dealey Plaza running parallel to Houston Street. I saw the President's limousine going west on Elm Street fairly slow, and a man was running along behind it, holding on to the handrail, and jumping onto the rear of the car. I was sure by that, that something serious had happened. Then Chief Curry radioed for us to go to the hospital-- Parkland Hospital, and the lead jockeys started off code 3 (using sirens with their red lights). So I did the same. I pulled up to Houston and Elm and turned left to go west on Elm. As I turned I saw Bobby (a presidential escort officer) on his hands and knees, and his motorcycle was on its side. For an instant I thought he had been hurt, but then I noticed that he was crawling and attempting to stand up. By the time I reached him, he was on his feet and heading up the hill to my right, the one they now refer to as the grassy knoll.

I accelerated to catch up with the rest of the motorcade. Turning right and up onto Stemmons Freeway, northbound, I opened it up. I neared them as we reached where Stemmons goes over Continental, and about even with the Cabana Motel (about 600 to 800 feet north). I was part of the motorcade en route to the hospital.

At Parkland Hospital, I parked my motorcycle right near President Kennedy's limousine and left it there. I went over to see if there was anything I could do. They got Governor Connally up and out to a stretcher, but they were having trouble with President Kennedy since Mrs. Kennedy didn't seem to want them to do anything. They finally persuaded her to step out of the car, and I escorted her aside far enough to allow the others to get the President out and on a stretcher. Then we all went inside.

I'm not sure just how long I stayed in the emergency room but it was at least an hour or more because when I came out I found out that Officer Tippet had been killed in Oak Cliff. I also found that my motorcycle had been moved across to the other side of the parking area. I don't know who moved it or when, but several had been moved over to the same place. Officers had been standing by listening to the radio to follow what was happening both at Elm and Houston, and over in Oak Cliff.

Now, the Committee staff Report says that I was from 80 to 90 feet west of Houston, west bound on Elm Street when the President was hit with the last shot. That's completely wrong! I never left Houston Street until after the chief said for us to go to the hospital and for someone to check the overpass. The agent didn't get onto the back of the limousine until some seconds after the last shot. I saw that happen while I was still on Houston Street, so while I only heard one shot, I could not have been on Elm Street until after the shots had been fired. Had the Committee staff told me what they had in mind, it would have made a difference in my testimony. They were at least deceitful if not outright dishonest with me.

APPENDIX TO THE KENNEDY ASSASSINATION TAPES

TRANSCRIPTS
of
DALLAS POLICE DEPARTMENT
RADIO COMMUNICATIONS
November 22, 1963
ANNOTATED

INTRODUCTION

Radio communications are often so brief and cryptic, so full of local slang and inuendo that meaning might not be clear even to police officers in neighboring communities. Therefore, the meaning and significance of these transcripts would likely be lost to the lay person if they were required to decipher them without some explanation.

Ordinarily, Channel 1 would handle police communications for those police districts lying east of the Trinity River, and Channel 2 would handle those districts to the west, a community commonly referred to as Oak Cliff.

On November 22, 1963, Channel 1 was assigned to handle the ordinary business of the police department units NOT assigned to the visit of President Kennedy, and Channel 2 was used as a special event frequency during the President's visit.

Both transcripts start just before the motorcade got underway and end after the motorcade disbanded at Parkland Hospital.

Lengthy commentary in the body of the transcript would interfere with transcript continuity. Therefore, commentaries are included as numbered end notes.

TRANSCRIPT

CHANNEL I

DALLAS POLICE DEPARTMENT
Communications

11:42 am to 12:37 pm

November 22, 1963

TIME	SPEAKER	MESSAGE	NOTE
11:42	41	41 clear	1
	Disp	41 clear, 11:42	2
	(2)	9...	3
	Disp	9.	
	2	This is 2 calling 9	
	Disp	Stand by, 2	
	9	9 to 2...	
	2	Go ahead, 9	
	9	Crowds along Harwood are...quite light. I was just wondering...if we could pick up 2 or 3 of these officers along here that I think we could do without and take them down on Main Street.	
	2	Are they on intersections?	
	9	No, they are in the middle of the block.	
	2	Yeah. .If. .that. .if that's the situation, go ahead and pick them up and move them in there.	
	9	10-4.	
	69	69, a Signal 5?	
11:43	Disp	233, a 7, Wood and Houston, 11:43.	
	233	10-4, from Pacific and Harwood.	
	113	113, a Signal 5?	
	Disp	Yes, 113.	
	69	69, a Signal 5?	
	Disp	Yes, 69...111...	
	210	210...	
	Disp	210.	
	210	Put 210 and 213 out on a 5, please.	
	Disp	10-4, 210	
	Disp	111...	
	111	Go ahead.	
	Disp	Are you at 2100 Lemmon? Correction, Leonard?	
	111	Right.	
11:44	Disp	10-4...Upon completion, meet 233 on a 7 at Houston and Wood, 11:44.	
	111	111's en route.	

APPENDIX

	607	607's Code 6 at the station.	
11:44	Disp	10-4, 11:44.	
	38	38. . .	
	Disp	38.	
	38	Mark me out with 35. This is gonna be a Signal 6.	
	Disp	10-4, 38.	
	66	66 on the phone.	
11:44	Disp	10-4, 66, 11:44.	
	71	71. . .	
	Disp	71.	
	71	Disregard 63. . .I'm clear.	
11:44	Disp	71 clear, 66 code 4, 11:44.	
	(41)	41 on traffic, 5000 Live Oak, on a pick up.	
11:45	Disp	10-4, 41, 11:45.	
	620	620, Code 5.	
	Disp	10-4, 620, 11:45.	
	212	212 clear. (Unreadable message followed)	
	32	32 clear.	
	Disp	32 clear.	
	280	280. . .	
	Disp	280.	
	280	See if you can contact 9.	
	Disp	9. . .	
	111	111. . .	
	Disp	111.	
	111	Disregard me on that call and put 111 and 224 out with a DWI.	4
	280	280. . .Will you try him on Channel 1 and 2 both? We need him bad at Main and Ervay. (crowd noise in background)	
	Disp	9. . .	
	9	(Crowd noise and unreadable message)	
11:45	Disp	11:45.	
	232	232 clear.	
11:46	Disp	9. . .	
	?	___9___out at Main___. .	
	104	104. . .	
	Disp	104.	
	104	I'm clear. I'll handle that prisoner.	5
11:46	Disp	10-4. It'll be H. L. Green, Main and Ervay, 104. . 118 Code 4, 11:46	
	118	118 received.	
	223	223 clear.	
11:46	Disp	223 clear, 11:46.	
	56	56. . .	
	Disp	56.	
	56	56 and 243's clear and request a signal 5.	6
11:46	Disp	10-4, 11:46. . .9. . .	7
	41	41 clear.	

373

11:47	Disp	41 clear, 11:47.	
	61	61 clear.	
	Disp	61 clear, 11:47.	
	48	48 clear.	
	Disp	48 clear.	
	68	68...	
	Disp	68.	
	68	Clear and request a 5.	
11:47	Disp	Yes, 11:47.	
	280	280...	
	Disp	280.	
	280	Been able to contact him (9)?	
	Disp	No, he hasn't answered yet, 280.	
	280	Try him on Channel 2?	8
	Disp	We're trying him in both places.	
	628	628...	9
	Disp	628.	
	628	What street do they have blocked off down here...off Ervay here?	
	Disp	Repeat.	
	Ch. 2 Disp	Channel 2 to 280...	10
	628	What street is it they have blocked off off of Ervay down here?	
	620	620's code 6.	11
	47	47 clear.	
11:48	Disp	47 clear, 11:48.	
	620	620's code 6.	
	Disp	628...	
	628	628.	
	Disp	Main and Ervay's blocked.	
	628	10-4. (then feedback)	
	23	23...	
	Disp	23.	
	23	Clear and remains out on a 5.	
11:49	Disp	Yes, 11:49.	
	606	606 out.	12
11:49	Disp	10-4, 606, 11:49.	
	38	38...	
	38	38 clear and request a signal 5.	
11:49	Disp	10-4, 11:49.	
	43	43...	
	Disp	43.	
	43	This is an attempt "pigeon drop" out here ...I'm clear.	13
11:49	Disp	Clear, 11:49.	
	77	77 clear	
11:49	Disp	77 clear, 11:49.	
	(97)	97, signal 5, in the car?	14
11:49	Disp	Yes, 11:49.	

APPENDIX

	606	606 Code 5 to Parkland.	15
11:50	Disp	10-4, 606, 11:50.	
	Disp	233...	
	233	Go ahead.	
	Disp	Have you arrived yet?	
	233	About uh...2 blocks away now.	
	Disp	10-4. Advise if you need a squad.	
	233	10-4.	
	65	65...	
	Disp	65.	
	65	Signal 5?	
	Disp	10-4.	
	81	81 clear.	
11:50	Disp	81 clear, 11:50.	
	78	78 clear.	
	104	104...	
	Disp	104.	
	104	Is the President going to come down Ervay Street?	
	Disp	He'll come down Main and cross Ervay.	
	78	78 clear.	
11:51	Disp	78 clear, 11:51.	
	233	233...	
	Disp	233.	
	233	I won't need a squad.	
	Disp	10-4.	
	95	95 clear.	
11:51	Disp	95 clear, 11:51.	
11:52	Disp	79 a Signal 18, 2712 54th Street, 11:52.	16
	(79)	2712.	
11:52	Disp	26 a Signal 32, in the upstairs, 4144 Prescott, 11:52.	17
	(26)	Is that 4144?	
	Disp	Yes.	
	(26)	En route.	
	102	102 clear.	
	24	24...	
	Disp	24.	
	24	I'm going to be on traffic here, about the 2000 block of West Mockingbird.	18
	Disp	10-4.	
	102	102 clear.	
11:52	Disp	102 clear, 11:52.	
11:53	Disp	32 a Signal 9 at Grant's Store, Webbs Chapel and Forestalling, 11:53.	19
	32	10-4.	
	32	You said Webbs Chapel and Forest Lane, didn't you?	
	Disp	Yes, at Grant's Store.	
	32	Yeah, we got it...Thank you.	
	24	24 clear.	

375

11:54	Disp	24 clear, 11:54.	
	223	223 a 5?	
	Disp	Yes, 223.	
	?	A signal 5?	
	Disp	10-4.	
	Disp	16 call 633.	20
	103	103...	
	Disp	103.	
	103	Is 100 clear?	
	Disp	No.	
	16	16, 10-4.	
	(103)	I said 103 and 100 clear.	
11:54	Disp	103 and 100 clear, 11:54.	
	Disp	61 call 511.	21
	(61)	10-4.	
	601	601 Code 5, Market Hall.	
11:55	Disp	601, 11:55.	22
	232	232...	
	Disp	232.	
	232	Be at Baylor on. .checking a victim.	23
	Disp	10-4.	
	104	104...	
	Disp	104.	
	104	Did you call me?	
	Disp	No.	
	104	I'm tied up in this traffic up here, and I got a million people. I don't know whether. . .when I'm going to get that prisoner out of H. L. Green's. (crowd noise in background.)	
	Disp	10-4.	
	(41)	41 on traffic.	
	Disp	Who's on traffic?	
	41	41.	
11:55	Disp	10-4, 41, 11:55.	
	21	21, Signal 5?	
11:55	Disp	79 code 4, 11:55.	
	79	79, 10-4.	
	242	242 clear.	
11:56	Disp	242 clear, 11:56.	
	21	21 Signal 5?	
11:56	Disp	Yes, 21, 11:56.	
	87	87 clear.	
11:56	Disp	87 clear, 11:56.	
	111	111...	
	Disp	111.	
	111	Is there any route to the city jail other than the regular one?	
	22	22 clear.	
11:56	Disp	22 clear, 11:56.	
	93	93 clear.	

APPENDIX

	Disp	You can get in on Main Street for the time, 111.
	111	10-4.
	77	77...
	Disp	77.
	77	_____telephone, 300 East...?
	Disp	10-4.
11:57	Disp	24 check for a blocked loading zone at the liquor store, 3507 Oak Lawn, 11:57.
	(24)	3507
	93	93 clear
11:57	Disp	93 clear, 11:57.
	53	53...
	Disp	53.
	53	Is 51 in service?
	Disp	No.
	53	We need a squad back here in about the 6000 block of Gaston. .Come back over here in the 700 block of Lowell.
	(43)	43's at Gaston and Skillman.
	Disp	10-4, 700 Lowell.
	(43)	10-4.
	(53)	Be downtown with a prisoner.
	Disp	Both of you?
	(53)	10-4.
	Disp	10-4, 43 and 53 out.
	19	19 clear.
11:58	Disp	19 clear, 11:58.
	606	606 Code 6.
11:59	Disp	10-4, 606, 11:59.
	61	61...
	Disp	61.
	61	Put us on a markout with 511.
	Disp	10-4.
	620	620, Code 6, Parkland.
11:59	Disp	10-4, 620, 11:59.
	?	_____out at Parkland.
11:59	Disp	10-4, 11:59.
	76	76...
	Disp	76.
	76	Signal 5?
	Disp	Yes.
	43	43...
	Disp	43.
	43	The 700 block of what?
	Disp	Lowell, I believe he said.
	Disp	53...
	63	63.
	Disp	63...
	63	You call?

377

JFK FIRST DAY EVIDENCE

	Disp	No.	
	51	51's clear.12:00	
	Disp	51 clear, 12:00 noon, KKB364, Dallas.	26
	51	51...	
	51	43 got a call on Lowell?	
	Disp	He's to meet 53 over there for a prisoner.	
	51	I can handle it.	
	628	628 out at...out at Parkland.	
12:00	Disp	10-4, 528, 12 noon.	
	?	(unreadable signal regarding 2010 Farrington...then about a 1 minute break in radio traffic)	
	72	72 clear.	
12:02	Disp	72 clear, 12:02.	
	83	83 clear.	
12:02	Disp	83 clear, 12:02.	
	85	85 a "5"?	
	Disp	10-4.	
	57	57...	
	Disp	57.	
	57	Can I Signal 5? (sounds like a 51 in the background)	
	Disp	87 your location?	
	87	Kiest and Lancaster.	
12:03	Disp	85 and 87 a Signal 6 on the parking lot in the rear of the school, South Oak cliff, Overton and Marsalis, 12:03.	27
	(85)	I got it.	
	87	87, 10-4.	
	222	222 clear.	
12:03	Disp	222 clear, 12:03.	
	116	116...	
	Disp	116.	
	116	We're clear at the scene of this accident...Can I have a "5"?	
12:03	Disp	Yes, 12:03.	
	22	22...	
	Disp	22.	
	22	Traffic, NA3062 at, uh, Westmoreland and Ft. Worth.	28
12:03	Disp	10-4, 12:03	
	83	83 clear.	
12:03	Disp	83 clear, 12:03.	
	41	41 clear.	
	Disp	41 clear, 12:03.	
	118	118 out on the phone.	
12:03	Disp	10-4, 12:03.	
	Disp	221 call 501.	29
	79	79...	
	79	79...	
	Disp	79.	

APPENDIX

	79	I believe 85 checked out on a "5" just before you gave him and 87 this call...I'll be with 87 on it.	30
	Disp	Are you at the location now?	
	79	Yeah, I'm close to it.	
	Disp	85...	
	85	85's en route.	
	Disp	Disregard...continue with the Signal 5, 85.	
	85	Thank you.	
	233	233 clear.	
12:05	Disp	233 clear, 12:05.	
	(83)	83's out on the traffic, 300 West Illinois.	
12:05	Disp	10-4, 83, 12:05.	
	Disp	Any squad that's en route to the Central Station with a prisoner at this time...make a left turn on Main Street from the 2000 block into the basement. That's about the only way they're going to do it.	
	Disp	Yes.	
	232-2	232 car 2...	31
	Disp	Car 2.	
	232-2	Clear and en route to Parkland for a follow-up.	
12:06	Disp	10-4, 12:06.	
	Disp	102 a Signal 6, 2611 Cochran, 12:06.	
	(102)	2611.	
	104	104 remains out.	32
12:06	Disp	10-4, 104, 12:06...104, you'll have to come in ...make your left turn in...off Main, into the basement.	
	41	41...	
	Disp	41.	
	41	Lewis and Henderson, traffic.	
12:06	Disp	10-4, 12:06.	
	(51)	51 on the phone.	
	Disp	51 on the phone.	
	24	24...	
	Disp	24.	
	24	You might notify anything running emergency out here in North Dallas that Mockingbird, Lemmon, Cedar Springs and Denton Drive is all jammed.	33
	Disp	10-4.	
	45	45 clear.	
12:07	Disp	83 clear, 12:07.	
	19	19 out at Methodist.	
	Disp	Where, 19?	
	19	Methodist Hospital.	
	Disp	10-4.	
	77	77 clear.	
12:07	Disp	77 clear, 12:07.	
	(no traffic during 12:08)		

	41	41 clear.
12:09	Disp	41 clear, 12:09.
	22	22 clear.
12:10	Disp	22 clear, 12:10.
	242	242 to 68...
	268	268 clear.
	Disp	268?
	268	10-4.
12:10	Disp	Clear, 12:10.
	242	242 to 68...
	68	68.
	242	What wrecker made pickup, Buckner and Military?
	68	Wallis.
	242	Thank you.
12:11	Disp	57 meet complainant regarding the found children at 1155 Templemore Drive, 12:11.
	Disp	57...
	57	57.
12:11	Disp	57 meet complainant regarding a found child at 1155 Templemore Drive, 12:11.
	57	1155.
	26	26...
	Disp	26.
	26	Remain out with a burglary suspect.
	Disp	Coming downtown?
	26	Yes.
	Disp	10-4. You'll have to make a left turn off Main, into city hall.
	26	10-4.
	41	41...
	Disp	41.
	41	Did I clear?
	Disp	Repeat.
	41	Did I clear a while ago?
	Disp	Yes.
12:12	Disp	22 a signal 6, 3811 Mican, 12:12.
	(22)	3811 Viking.
	Disp	M-I-C-A-N.
	(22)	10-4.
	222	222...
	Disp	222.
	222	A "5" in the car?
	Disp	10-4.
	31	31 clear.
12:12	Disp	31 clear, 12:12.
	69	69 clear.
12:13	Disp	69 clear, 12:13.
	61	61 clear.
	Disp	61 clear.

	72	72...	
	Disp	72.	
	72	Check registration on "Nolan Robert 4841...	
		and also wanted.	36
	Disp	Stand by.	
	232	232 clear.	
12:13	Disp	232 clear, 12:13.	
	(232)	If you should happen to get a call on an injured person...a white male 2 1/2 at Baylor, you can disregard it. I made an injured person offense on it.	
12:13	Disp	10-4, 12:13.	
	35	35 clear.	
12:14	Disp	35 clear, 12:14.	
	Disp	57...	
	57	Go ahead.	
	Disp	They belong at 8547 Forest Hills Blvd.	
	57	10-4.	
	260	260...	
	Disp	260.	
	260	Is 6 on Channel 2?	
	Disp	He's at Main and Harwood...on the street.	37
	260	10-4.	
	49	49 clear.	
12:14	Disp	49 clear, 12:14.	
	103	103...	
	Disp	103.	
	103	Stolen or wanted on Alabama '63, 1-A (Austin) 11113...on a '56 DeSoto.	
	45	45...	
	Disp	45.	
	45	A "5" at Northeast Sub?	
	Disp	10-4.	
	621	621 clear from VA	38
12:15	Disp	621 clear, 12:15.	39
	105	105...	
	Disp	105.	
	105	Clear that last call sheet...signal 5, please?	
12:15	Disp	Yes, 12:15.	
	(Unreadable-dispatcher thinks "101")		
	Disp	101?	
	(101)	10-4..Notify Public Works they got a big ol' tree limb out in the 1700 bk. Industrial.	
	Disp	Out in the street?	
	(101)	Yes, southbound.	
	Disp	10-4.	
	Disp	305 and 309, call 551...309 and 305 call 551. 72...	40
	(72)	Go ahead.	
	Disp	No wanted on it..A 1950 Chevrolet 2 door. (number deleted) Vista Drive, Mesquite.	

381

	?	Ninety____?		
		(72)	Check 3. The first one'll be (deleted) Pride, colored male, 21...(deleted) Pride, he's a colored male, 23. .and (deleted) Pride, P-R-I-D-E, he'll be a colored male, 29.	
		Disp	Stand by. .It's not registered to any of those.	
		(72)	All right.	
	12:17	Disp	____? Meet the complainant regarding lost property at the 33-11 Club, 3311 Hines, 12:17.	
		?	3311 Hines.	
		212	21 clear.	
	12:17	Disp	21 clear, 12:17.	
		78	78...	
		Disp	78.	
		78	Be out of the car a minute, 4100 block of Bonnie...view.	
	12:17	Disp	12:17.	
		157	157 to 159...	
		628	628 clear from Parkland.	
	12:18	Disp	10-4, 628, 12:18.	
		41	41...	
		Disp	41.	
		41	Put me out at the radio station.	
				41
	12:18	Disp	10-4, 12:18.	
		(66)	Do you show 66 clear?	
		Disp	No, are you?	
		(66)	Yes, sir.	
	12:18	Disp	12:18.	
		289	289...	
		Disp	289.	
		289	Give us an ambulance, 100 block North Houston Street. .Epileptic seizure.	
		Disp	10-4.	
		(289)	Make it Code 3.	42
		Disp	10-4...That'll be a white?	
		113	113 clear.	
	12:19	Disp	113 clear, 12:19. 72, number 1 has one alias.	
		97	97 clear.	
	12:19	Disp	97 call 544...Clear, 12:19.	43
		118	118 clear.	
	12:19	Disp	118 clear, 12:19.	
		80	80...	
		102	103 clear.	
	12:19	Disp	102 clear, 12:19...72...	
		(72)	Go ahead.	
		Disp	One on James.	
		(72)	All right.	
		289	289...	
		Disp	289.	

APPENDIX

	289	Make that ambluance Code 3, and could you give me the direction he will be coming in?	
	Disp	606...	
	606	606. (Covered by:)	
	(72)	See if that's a parking ticket.	
	Disp	What's your location?	
	(606)	We're about. .uh. .Harwood and. .Cedar Springs now.	
12:20	Disp	10-4. .Code 3 on a Signal 28, 100 North Houston, 12:20.	44
	(606)	10-4.	
	95	95...	
	Disp	Harwood and Cedar Springs, 289.	
	95	95...	
	289	10-4.	
	Disp	95.	
	95	Would like a "5."	
	Disp	Yes.	
	72	72...	
	Disp	72.	
	72	Will you check and see if that's a parking ticket?	
	Disp	Stand by.	
	Disp	289...	
	289	289.	
	disp	Go ahead and start your set-up.	45
	289	10-4.	
	97	97 on the phone.	
	Disp	10-4, 97.	
	78	78 clear.	
12:20	Disp	78 clear, 12:20.	
	223	223 clear.	
12:21	Disp	223 clear, 12:21.	
	38	38...	
	Disp	38.	
	38	Clear my "5" and remain out to Corporation Court 1 at 1:00.	46
	Disp	Remains out, 12:21. 72...	
	(72)	Go ahead.	
	Disp	It's not a moving violation.	47
	(72)	All right.	
	312	312...	
	Disp	312.	
	(312)	Try 305 or 309.	
	305	305.	
	(312)	Say, he's suppose to be up there around. .uh, 2421 Ellis, if you're close. .We're leaving the city hall now.	
	(305)	We're about a block from there.	
	115	115 clear.	
12:21	Disp	115 clear, 12:21.	

383

	111	111...	
	Disp	111.	
	111	We're going to have to take this prisoner to Parkland. Is Harwood Street blocked off all the way?	48
	Disp	Yes, all the way, 111.	
	111	10-4.	
	91	91 clear.	
12:22	Disp	91 clear, 12:22.	
	101	101 clear.	
12:22	Disp	101 clear, 12:22.	
	Disp	603...	
	603	603.	
12:22	Disp	603 and 61, a Signal 16 at the restaurant, Parry and Exposition, 12:22.	49
	603	603, 10-4.	
	Disp	That'll be at Kinzer's Restaurant.	
	?	All right. (Probably 61.)	
	23	23 clear.	
	243	66 and 243 clear.	
	Disp	Who's clear?	
	23	23.	
	243	243.	
12:23	Disp	23 clear, 12:23. . 243, did you clear?	
	243	Yeah, 66 and 243.	
12:23	Disp	10-4, clear, 12:23. .243, your radio is about out.	50
	231	231 clear.	
12:23	Disp	231 clear, 12:23.	
	606	606 out. (Siren clearly audible.)	
12:24	Disp	10-4, 606, 12:24. (Microphone stuck open for 4 1/2 seconds, transmitting engine sound of a running motorcycle.)	51
	79	79 clear.	
12:24	Disp	79 clear, 12:24. (Microphone stuck open twice for about 1 second each time, transmitting engine sound of a running motorcycle.)	
	Disp	65...	
	65	65.	
	Disp	Call "633."	52
	65	Out to use the phone. .	
	Disp	10-4.	
	97	97 clear.	
12:25	Disp	97 clear, 12:25.	
	309	309 to 312	
	606	606...	
	Disp	606.	
	606	We're en route to (unreadable-someone said "607") Signal 16.	

APPENDIX

	Disp	En route where, 606?	
	606	Parkland. (Siren in background.)	
	Disp	10-4. .Need a squad to meet you there?	
	606	10-4.	53
	Disp	10-4.	
	252	252...	
	Disp	252.	
	252	Out here at the intersection of Fairmount and Cedar Springs, uh, there's a V-shaped piece of land out here. . no uh, improvements on it. Someone, during the parade, backed over a water faucet out here and it's shooting water in the air. I wonder if you can contact the water department and have 'em come out here and turn it off.	
12:25	Disp	10-4, 12:25.	
	6	6 ___ (Unknown message.)	
	(252)	I'm clear.	
12:25	Disp	10-4, 12:25.	
	(91)	91 on traffic, P-Pecos, P-Pecos, 4700.	54
	Disp	10-4.	
	309	309...	
	(213)	210 and 213 clear.	
	Disp	309.	
	309	Need to talk to 312 just a minute.	
12:26	Disp	210 and 213 clear, 12:26. .Go ahead 312.	
	309	309 to 312...	
	(312)	Go ahead.	
	(309)	We have this subject. You want to meet up somewhere?	
	312	Right behind you.	
	?	All right.	
	Disp	23...	
	23	23.	
12:26	Disp	Meet 606 at Parkland on a Signal 16, 12:26.	
	23	10-4.	
	258	258 clear.	
	258	258 clear.	
12:26	Disp	258 clear, 12:26...305...	
	305	Go ahead.	
	Disp	Stand by.	
	103	103...	
	Disp	103.	
	103	Pecos, Nolan 6365 on a Buick...Industrial, 2100 block.	55
12:27	Disp	10-4, 12:27.	
	Disp	_____, 305.	
	(305)	10-4.	
	24	24 is clear.	
12:27	Disp	24 clear, 12:27.	
	56	56...	
	56	56...	

385

JFK FIRST DAY EVIDENCE

	(83)	83, traffic, 3200 South Westmoreland.	
12:28	Disp	83 out, 12:28.	
	56	56...	
	Disp	56.	
	56	Traffic, uh, on a . .'56 Chevrolet, I can't see the license number...(followed immediately by:)	
	(75)	75 clear.	
12:28	Disp	75 clear, 12:28. (This accompanied by microphone stuck open for 17 1/2 seconds transmitting engine sound of running motorcycle.)	56
	38	38...	
	Disp	38.	
	38	Might tell some of those people involved in handling this deal out here at Market Hall that there's people walking across southbound Stemmons here in front of the Marriott Hotel and all the way down south.	57
		(Microphone remained open while the dispatcher asked:)	
*	Disp	10-4, 38. .Are you still en route to court?	
12:29:10	38	10-4. (Microphone continues to stick open for next 5 minutes.)	
12:29:20	?	...Market Office...	58
12:29:27	?	...All right...	
12:30:55		(this is the approximate time the **first shot** was fired. While NOT recorded on the tape nor heard on radio, it is noted here for reference.)	
12:31:00		(Motorcycle engine slowed down.)	59
12:31:03		(Approximate time the **third and final** shot was fired.)	
12:31:02	4(Ch 2)	I'll check it.	60
12:31:10		(Motorcycle engine slowed to idle speed.)	
12:31:11	100	100...	
12:31:12	91	...Check wanted on P-Pecos...and other	
	S1(Ch2)	"Tell my men..." Sheriff Decker, Ch 2, 12:31 period, by voice analysis	61
(12:31:13)		Last Shot, according to Select Committee	
12:31:20		(A single tone of a bell.)	62
12:31:24		(Motorcycle engine at a very slow idle.)	
12:31:32		(A "bonk" sound is recorded and the motorcycle engine revved-up.)	63
12:31:40		(Motorcycle sounds like it started moving.)	
12:31:48		(Motor slowed down. Perhaps, another approached.)	
12:31:52	?	...on the phone. (Motor slowed to an idle.)	64
12:31:56		(Someone whistling a tune in the background of open microphone.)	65
12:31:58		(A "bonk, bonk" sound again.)	
12:32:04	?	(Unreadable, sounds like. .87. .)	

*Time fixed at this point and projected for remainder of transcript. Announced time, when given, is in parenthesis.

APPENDIX

12:32:05		(Hetrodyne sound of Morse Code "V" and the motor seems to speed up.)	66
12:32:08	603	603 out, Baylor.	
12:32:22	36	(Motor slowed, then:) 36...	
12:32:35	36	36...(Motor slow and irregular.)	
12:32:38	91	91 clear, request a "5."	
12:32:39	Disp	531 testing, 1-2-3-4.	
12:32:42		(Someone whistling again; the tune is unidentifiable.)	67
12:32:46	?	Loud and clear.	68
12:32:48	48	48, loud and clear.	69
12:32:56	56	56...(Motor revved-up.)	
12:32:56	91	91...	
12:33:00	(91)	91, request a "5."	
12:33:01		(Blending with the end of 91's message, the sound of sirens can be heard, faintly, but increasing in loudness.)	70
12:33:03	Disp	10-4..Anybody know where 56 is? (The siren sounds continue.)	71
12:33:08	?	He checked out on traffic.	
12:33:18	75	75, Signal 5? (Sirens continue; motor sounds slow and irregular.)	
12:33:26	76	76 clear. (Sirens continue; motor sound revved-up.)	
12:33:34		(Sirens fade to inaudible.)	72
12:33:55		(Someone whistling again.)	73
12:33:38	DSO?	Attention all units, all units...	74
12:33:50	?	(Unreadable.)	75
12:33:52	190 (ch2)	You want me to still hold this traffic on Stemmons until we find out something, or...	76
12:33:57	(103)	103 clear. (Motor is idling.)	
12:33:59 (12:34)	Disp	Clear, 12:34. (Motorcycle engine revved-up.)	77
12:34:00	76	76 clear. (Motor revved-up.)	
	76	76 clear.	
12:34:09 (12:34)	Disp	76 clear, 12:34.(Motorcycle sounds like it is moving.)	
12:34:18	75	75, a "5." (Motorcycle seems to gain speed.)	
12:34:19		**(Microphone closed.)**	78
12:34:22	Disp	24...	
	24	24...(Unknown___3...)	
12:34:25	Disp	Report to Inwood and Stemmons and cut all traffic for the ambulance going to Parkland, Code 3.	79
12:34:30	?	(Unknown___seventy, probably 75.)	
12:34:32	(24)	Inwood and Stemmons?	
12:34:35	Disp	Inwood and Stemmons, where they come off Stemmons, going to Parkland.	
12:34:40	(24)	10-4.	
12:34:43	Disp	Make your assignment Code 3, 24.	

387

12:34:45	(24)	10-4.	
12:34:46	Disp	35, a Signal 9A at Lobello's, Ames and Northwest,	
(12:35)		12:35. **(Motorcycle transmitter stuck open again.)**	80
12:34:52	Disp	Location, 93?...Disregard...21...21.	
12:34:58	Disp	Code 3, Stemmons and Inwood, cut traffic.	
	21	10-4.	
12:35:01	348/75	348...75...	
12:35:03	Disp	75.	
12:35:04	75	Signal "5"?	
12:35:05	Disp	10-4.	
12:35:06	65	65 clear. (More Hetrodyne noise.)	
12:35:07	Disp	65 clear, (4 interrupts), 12:36. .4, did you call?	81
(12:36)		(Motor at slow idle)	
12:35:12	4	...Cedar Springs and Mockingbord...(Noisy signal, unreadable; motor slow and irregular.)	
12:35:22	Disp	4, we have a mike butt stuck. .bike. . button stuck open. We can't hear anything. (Still unreadable; motor slow and irregular.)	
12:35:36	Disp	93...	
12:35:38	Ch2Disp	Attention all emergency equipment. .Attention all emergency equipment. .Do not use Industrial Boulevard. . Do not use Industrial Boulevard, 12:36. (Motor slow and irregular.)	82
12:35:47	93	93. (Motor idled-down.)	
12:35:48	Disp	Location?	
12:35:49	93	Sylvian and Fort Worth. (Motor still slow.)	
12:35:54	(4)	El. .uh. .Eleven...(unreadable.)	83
12:35:57	260 ch2	...came from the 5th floor...	
	Disp	24...(interrupting)	
	(260)	of the Texas Depository...Bookstore.	84
12:36:04		**(Transmitter closed with this message.)**	
12:36:05	Disp	35, did you receive?	
12:36:07	(35)	I got it.	
12:36:08	Disp	10-4.	
12:36:10	61	61 clear.	
12:36:15	Disp	61 clear, 12:37.	
(12:37)			
12:36:21	4	4 to 11...1131	85
12:36:26	21	21...(His siren slowing down in the background.)	
12:336:28	Disp	21. .continue. .(Interrupted.)	
12:36:31	24	24...	
12:36:35	93	93...(Dispatcher continued with:)	
12:36:36	(Disp)	. .to Inwood and Stemmons and assist 24...21, go up there to Hines and cut that service road off there where that ambulance can go on to Parkland.	
12:36:43	91	91...	
12:36:44		10-4. (Probably 21.)	86

APPENDIX

END NOTES
COMMENTARY - CHANNEL I

1. "Clear" means that officer is returning to service from some previous assignment; he is now available for another assignment.

2. The dispatcher indicates his acknowledgment of the preceding message, and states the time within a one-minute time frame. The time statement might be made according to a 4-digit clock before the dispatcher, or from a time stamped by a mechanical time clock. These were NOT synchronized; therefore, time statements are NOT consistent with ANY "real-time" reference.

3. A message should start with the officer wishing to speak identifying himself by call-number. In this event, Assistant Chief Batchelor did not give his call-number first, but called for "9," Inspector Sawyer, the party to whom he wished to speak. The dispatcher therefore acknowledged "9" rather than the caller, "2." Also, a number in column two in parenthesis indicates the speaker did not precede his message with his call-number. When that number is not known, a question mark is used.

4. #111 had been given a call to pick up a prisoner, but he will be unable to complete the call. (That call preceded this transcription.)

5. #104 announces his availability for 118's call. (The call preceded this transcription.)

6. A "Signal 5" refers to an absence from duty for the purpose of eating or for coffee, etc. The officer requesting authorization must first obtain permission to go out of service. Therefore, the message is in the form of a request, and the request must be recognized by the dispatcher.

7. "10-4" actually means "Message received and understood." More often, Dallas officers include in the meaning, "Yes," or similar affirmative meanings. In this event, the dispatcher's "10-4" represents both acknowledgment and permission granted.

8. With reference to Channel 2 transcript, the 11:47 time frame, a concurrent effort was made to get 280, a three-wheel sergeant, into contact with 9, Inspector Sawyer.

9. Call numbers 600-629 were assigned to ambulances under contract to the police department.

10. The Channel 2 dispatcher used his Channel 1 switch to broadcast on Channel 1. This was part of the simultaneous broadcast capability available to either dispatcher. Each could broadcast on his assigned channel, the other, or both.

11. "Code 6" means, "I have arrived at the location of my present assignment."

12. "Out" in this event means that the ambulance #606 will be off the radio and available by telephone.

13. "Pigeon-drop" is a form of fraud.

14. He will be available by radio as he will be in his car.

15. "Code 5" means "I am en route to. . ." a given location.

16. "Signal 18" is a fire call.

17. "Signal 32" is a suspicious person call.

18. "On traffic" and similar references indicate the officer has observed a traffic violation or situation which requires attention. The dispatcher notes the matter and avoids giving that officer a call until he "clears."

19. "Signal 9" is a theft call.

20. The dispatcher instructs #16, the Northeast Lieutenant, to telephone the Northeast Station, telephone extension 633.

21. The dispatcher instructs #61 to telephone the Central Patrol office, telephone extension #511.

22. Apparently the dispatcher said "10-4" before he fully activated his transmit key. Therefore, only the ambulance call number and the message time frame were recorded.

23. Refers to Baylor Hospital.

24. This message did not record fully, but #77 "telephone" and "300 East____" indicates that #77 was out of service in the 300 block (of an undetermined street) to use the telephone. In later messages other officers might use the expression "on the phone" or similar references for the same purpose. They do not always indicate a location.

25. #61 telephoned extension 511 (note 21). Now he tells the dispatcher to put them on a "markout," a duty status not on a call, but not available for a call.

26. The time reference followed by "KKB364" is the station identification required by the FCC, KKB364 being the Dallas Police Department's call letters. Ordinarily, time and station checks should be given on the hour and each quarter-hour, as nearly as possible at the exact indicated time. However, this was not always done, especially during busy periods. Sometimes they were given early, sometimes, late, and sometimes, they were not given at all.

27. "Signal 6" is a disturbance call.

28. The "NA3062" refers to the license plate number on the vehicle stopped for a traffic violation.

29. The dispatcher instructs accident investigator #221 to telephone the traffic commander's office, extension #501.

30. #79 volunteers to replace #85 on the "Signal 6" so 85 can continue on the "Signal 5" he had been authorized at 12:03 p.m. In the following messages, the dispatcher replaces 85 with 79.

31. Reference to a "car 2" indicated that two vehicles are using the same primary call number.

APPENDIX

In this event, there is a #232 and a #232-2.

32. "Remains out" and "remain me out" and similar expressions, while grammatically improper, inform the dispatcher that the officer indicated, and who is already "out of service" for some previously acknowledged purpose, will continue to be "out of service." In this event, #104 picked up a prisoner in connection with his previous call. Here, he tells the dispatcher that he will continue to be out while transporting the prisoner to jail.

33. Reference to "running emergency" refers to anyone operating a vehicle under emergency driving conditions. The officer #24 informs others that the streets indicated are obstructed by heavy traffic; that should someone be confronted with an emergency driving situation, avoid these streets if possible.

34. Refers to #242 attempting to contact #68 by radio.

35. Indicates that 26 will be out of service for an additional period of time with a burglary suspect in connection with his "Signal 32" mentioned in note 17.

36. Refers to vehicle license NR4841, and asks the dispatcher to determine the identity of the registered owner, and whether it is listed as stolen, or wanted in connection with an offense.

37. Three-wheel sergeant #260 asks whether Deputy Chief of traffic, #6, is on Channel 2. The dispatcher stated that he was not in his car, with a radio.

38. Refers to the Veterans Administration Hospital.

39. Note that the 12:15 station check was not given. This is the first statement of "time" given in the 12:15 time frame. However, there is no way to determine whether it has just turned 12:15, or whether it became 12:15 immediately after 49 cleared at 12:14, and before 103 requested a check of the Alabama license plate. Compare this illustration with references elsewhere regarding the difficulties encountered when attempting to fix a time reference point with a degree of exactness.

40. The dispatcher instructs Homicide detectives #305 and 309 to call the Homicide office, telephone extension #551.

41. Refers to the police department's radio transmitter and service center located inside Fair Park, the state fair grounds, southeast of the downtown district.

42. "Code 3" refers to an emergency response; the use of red lights and siren by responding personnel.

43. Instructs #97 to call extension #544.

44. "Signal 28" is a sick person call. Here, 606 is dispatched to meet #289 at 100 North Houston Street.

45. "Start your set-up" refers to 289's traffic assignment at Elm and Houston Streets. He was to set-up temporary control measures for the passage of the motorcade.

JFK FIRST DAY EVIDENCE

46. The officer working #38 has finished lunch but is not "clear" as he "remains out" to answer a 1:00 p.m. court call in Corporation Court #1 (City Court.) NOTE: His route will soon take him southbound on Stemmons past the Trade Mart at which location he will report pedestrian traffic on the freeway. At the end of his message the three-wheel motorcycle microphone stuck open on Channel 1 for more than 5 minutes.

47. Earlier, 72 had asked whether his subject's alias (past due) ticket involved a parking violation. The dispatcher tells 72 it is NOT a moving violation, but did not tell him what kind of violation it was.

48. Earlier, 111 and 224 picked up a DWI (an intoxicated driver) whom 111 is now taking to Parkland Hospital.

49. "Signal 16" is an injured person call, the injury being non-vehicular.

50. The dispatcher informs 243 that his radio is not performing well as evidenced by the dispatcher's inability to understand who was clearing.

51. Here, during the 12:24 time frame, is the first time during the day's events that the problem of the open mike occurred. The open mike transmitted the sound of a motorcycle engine running about 25 MPH. At this point the mike stuck for about 4 1/2 seconds. Moments later it opened twice in succession for about one second each time.

52. The dispatcher instructs 65 to telephone the Northeast Substation, extension #633.

53. At 12:20, 606 was dispatched to meet 289. Here, 606 tells the dispatcher he is en route to Parkland Hospital, and that he needs an officer to meet him there.

54. Refers to vehicle license PP4700.

55. Refers to a traffic markout on license PN6365.

56. Here, in the 12:28 time frame the open mike transmits the sound of a motorcycle engine running about 30 MPH for some 17 1/2 seconds.

57. The officer working #38, en route to court reported the pedestrians crossing Stemmons (note 46). At the end of 38's message the mike stuck open again, and it remained open for the next 5 minutes, 9 seconds.

The dispatcher acknowledged 38's message and asked,". . .are you still en route to court?" Thirty-eight answered, "10-4." It is at this point that this text determined the most likely time as 12:29:10 p.m. (Channel 1.) For the remainder of this transcript. 12:29:10 is the time-fix from which subsequent times and events are factored.

58. The city of Dallas operates a public market where truck-farmers vend their crops. Officers frequently used the market office telephone. It is likely that some officer checked out at the "market office" and moments later the dispatcher acknowledged, "All right."

APPENDIX

59. At approximately 12:31:00 (Channel 1) the open mike transmitted the sound of the motorcycle's engine slowing.

60. The "I'll check it" is the last of #4's (Deputy Chief Fisher's, communication with #125, Captain Lawrence, on Channel 2, and picked up by the open mike on Channel 1. (See Channel 2 transcription, 12:31;04.) Also, see Illustration #III which demonstrates how Channel 2 messages were picked up by the open mike and recorded as Channel 1 messages.

61. This transmission is not clearly understood. It appears to be 91 checking the vehicle he stopped during the 12:25 time frame, "P-Pecos 4700."

62. This is the sound of the single tone of a bell. While its exact origin cannot be established, it obviously was NOT in Dealey Plaza, and NONE of those people there, police officers, motorcade participants, news reporters nor observers ever mentioned hearing such a sound.

The Select Committee suggested the bell-sound appeared on Channel 1 because an unidentified officer keyed his microphone near a bell, conveniently as it tolled one time, then he closed his mike without saying anything.
There is a more likely explanation. There was a replica of the Liberty Bell at the Trade Mart. Perhaps a passerby gave it a rap. It was recorded on Channel 1 by the open mike.
The location of the bell is significant to McLain in that if the sound was recorded over his mike as he left Dealey Plaza, why didn't anyone else hear it? If the bell was at the Trade Mart, it further confirms that the open mike was at the Trade Mart.
However, the Committee's Report gives the sound of the bell a new and even greater significance. Their Report states that the bell sounded,". . .about 7 seconds after the last impulse believed to have been a shot. . ." (Committee Report, page 78). The Report logged the bell sound at approximately 12:31:02.6 (Channel 1), (Committee time-fix). This is in contrast to the 12:31:20 projection in this report, a difference of 17 seconds. In conclusion, the Select Committee was about one minute off, and was looking in the WRONG PLACE on the tape in their hopes of finding the sound of gunfire.

63. While the source of the "bonk-bonk" could not be determined absolutely, it was likely the result of the motorcycle passing a wheel over the cast iron grate to a storm sewer near the motorpool. Recent tests produced similar sounds; however, there have been considerable changes in the physical layout of the parking lot. Accordingly, it cannot be said with certainty whether these grates produced the 1963 sounds.

64. This transmission cannot be clearly understood, but it sounds like someone checking out to use a telephone.

65. This whistling is distinctly different from the screeching identified as "hetrodyne" which can occur when two transmitters open on the same frequency. In this event, someone is casually whistling an unidentified tune while near the open mike. If is highly unlikely that anyone was casually whistling in Dealey Plaza at the time, and less likely that whistling would be picked up but NOT the shouting. The whistling episodes were not preceded by the sound of a microphone being "keyed," which indicates the whistling was transmitted by the open mike.

66. Unidentified officers, in checking their mike buttons, unwittingly generated the sound of the Morse Code "V" or ". . ._" and this was recorded. Some assassination buffs have construed

393

this to be an officer signaling success to his cohorts by transmitting the World War II victory signal. This is absurd because the ". . ." is at a higher pitch than the "_" just as it is in the musical form from Beethoven's Symphony #5. A single officer keying his mike cannot make it play music. In fact, he would have no way of knowing that his keying would even produce hetrodyne.

67. Still a casual tune whistled by a passerby. Again, there is no keying-sound. Nor was this caused by officers "testing their mikes" as this is done by noting the control or pilot lights, "red" for transmit, "green" for stand-by.

68. An unidentified officer's response to the dispatcher's 4-count test.

69. Officer 48's response to the test count.

70. In the same transmission with 91's request for a "Signal 5," the sound of sirens appeared for the first time, starting faintly and gradually increasing in loudness. It cannot be determined how many, but there appear to be several separate sirens.

71. As the sirens are still passing by, the dispatcher keyed his mike to acknowledge 91's request and to ask about #56. The siren sounds increased in loudness, and the motorcycle engine can still be heard running slowly. Some unreadable radio traffic occurred, briefly overriding the siren sounds.

72. The siren sounds faded out in the same manner as they first appeared, gradually. In passing the open mike, it appears that some 3 or 4 groups of siren-sounding vehicles pass as opposed to individual vehicles. The Doppler-effect is present. The siren sounds from the first faint sound to the last faint sound were present for 33 seconds.

73. The passerby whistling the tune again.

74. The "Attention all units. . ." message received and recorded over Channel 1 was NOT a Dallas Police Department broadcast. It is most likely the Dallas County Sheriff's Department dispatcher, Deputy Jack Watson, broadcasting on 37.180 kilocycles while the Dallas Police broadcast in the 45.00 range. This was NOT a frequency skip nor interference; this has never been experienced between the two departments. The message was picked up and recorded because the open mike was near the outside speaker on a deputy sheriff's vehicle. The only place where the Dallas Police had a motorcycle and county cars working together was at the Trade Mart.

Both the Dallas County Sheriff's dispatcher and the Texas Department of Public Safety (the State Police) use the reference to "units" and both departments had officers working in conjunction with Dallas Police, but only at the Trade Mart.

It is unlikely that a state officer made the broadcast, for they were unaware of the emergency for quite some time. It is probably the sheriff's dispatcher because he had been informed of the emergency by direct telephone connection with the police dispatcher, and instructed per Sheriff Bill Decker to send his deputies into the area of the shooting. (See Transcript, Channel 2, between 12:31 and 12:32.) This is in all likelihood a response to that broadcast. The message is NOT on Channel 2.

75. A voice can be heard near the open mike, but he cannot be understood. By voice recognition, it sounds like the officer who reported experiencing the open mike.

76. The "You want me. . ." is part of the message Motorcycle Sergeant #190 was broadcasting on Channel 2 at the time. "One-oh-three, clear" cut off the remainder of the message. This portion of 190's transmission on Channel 2 appears on Channel 1 because the open mike was near the speaker of a radio tuned to Channel 2, and the open mike picked up the message. (See Transcript, Channel 2, 12:34:16.)

77. As the dispatcher acknowledged 103 clear, it appears that the motorcycle revved-up. There are sounds which might be the shifting of gears.
NOTE: The time projected from 12:29:10 is now 12:33:59 while the dispatcher stated "12:34" for a difference of 1-second.

78. While 75 requested a "Signal 5," the motorcycle seems to gain speed. Then there are a couple of "clicks," and the transmitter is closed.
 Based on the fixed time of 12:29:10 when the mike opened, and 12:34:20, when it closed, it was open for a full 5 minutes and 9 seconds. The time projections, measured with a hand-held stopwatch, were within 1 second after 5+ minutes.
 While the mike was open, Channel 1 radio traffic was recorded full-time or in real-time. After it closed, Channel 1 traffic is recorded only during radio use. Therefore, it cannot be considered a real-time recording. However, due to the steady radio use which followed, the recording stayed "on" almost constantly, and was virtually a real-time recorder. For that reason, the time-estimates during the remainder of the transcription will continue as if it were a continuous recording, although it was not. This will cause an error of a few seconds in the last minute.

79. In the confusion following the assassination, the Channel 1 dispatcher incorrectly thought that whoever was injured was enroute to Parkland Hospital by ambulance, and that the ambulance would travel Stemmons to Inwood, thence to Hines, thence to Parkland. Accordingly, he attempted to dispatch officers ahead of the "ambulance" to cut traffic. Actually, the victims remained with the motorcade, and they had already reached Parkland before traffic assistance was dispatched.

80. "Signal 9A" is an auto theft. This call was dispatched at 12:35 as opposed to the time estimate of 12:34:46. This loss of a couple of seconds is likely because the recorder was not recording real-time. (See Note 78.)
 The mike stuck open briefly here, and the engine sound suggests the motorcycle is operating slowly.

81. The engine appears to be running at a slow idle. Also, note the slight time difference. (See Note 78.)

82. The Channel 2 dispatcher used his simultaneous broadcast switches to make this announcement on both channels at the same time. Notice that according to the projected time, the message started at 12:35:38 and ended at 12:35:46. The time on Channel 2 was undetermined, but in the 12:36 (Channel 2) time frame. Allowing for Channel 1 to have lost a few seconds due to the recorder not now recording real-time, and allowing for Channel 2 to be broadcasting about 15 seconds ahead of Channel 1 time, this very close comparison of time

references tends to confirm both assumptions: That 12:29:10 was a valid time for computing future time on Channel 1, and that Channel 2 was running about 15 seconds ahead of Channel 1 time.

The motorcycle engine continued to run slowly and irregularly during this period.

83. This is probably #4, who had been trying to call but who was experiencing transmitting difficulties. It appears that the message started with an unsuccessful effort to remember a number, that as he started to speak, he forgot the number. Note that some 27 seconds later, 4 does, in fact, initiate a hesitant call to station #1131, the usual reference to the Northwest Substation desk.

84. The ". . .came from the 5th floor. . ." is part of a transmission initiated by three-wheel sergeant #260, broadcasting on Channel 2. The message appears on Channel 1 because the open mike was near the speaker of a radio tuned to Channel 2. (See Notes 60, 74, and 76; also Transcript, Channel 2, 12:36.) The motorcycle engine ran for part of this message; then the transmitter closed again, having been open for about 1 minute and 18 seconds.

85. Refer to Note 83.

86. The Channel 1 transcript ends at this point. By now, the motorcade had disbanded at Parkland, and activity was increasing around the Texas Schoolbook Depository. Nothing occurred past this point which would appear to have a bearing on the validity of the Select Committee's acoustical analysis of these recordings.

APPENDIX

TRANSCRIPT

CHANNEL II

DALLAS POLICE DEPARTMENT
Communications

11:37 am to 12:40 pm

November 22, 1963

TIME	SPEAKER	MESSAGE	NOTE
	30	It's on the ground. (Air Force one.)	
11:37	Disp	10-4, 30, 11:37. 30. . .	
	30	30. . .	
	Disp	30, weather and crowd estimate.	
	30	The weather's good. . .(unreadable). . .39. . .	
	540	Will remain clear the rest of the day. Temperature probably'll stay about the same.	
	Disp	10-4, 540.	
	20	20. . .	
	Disp	20.	
	20	So far as the crowd. . There's quite a crowd along Mockingbird Lane and Lemmon Avenue, around the Coca-Cola Bottling Plant.	
	Disp	10-4.	
	?	20. . .	
	20	Go ahead.	
	?	Where do you want me to meet you?	
	20	Over here at the fire station on Mockingbird, with your partner.	
	?	10-4.	
	9	9. . .	
	Disp	9.	
	9	Is 2 on the air?	
	Disp	Stand by. . .15 car 2. . .	
	15-2	15 car 2, I'll get him.	
	Disp	10-4.	
	250	250. . .	
	Disp	250.	
	250	Ask 125 if he wanted a man at Herschel and Lemmon at the signal light there.	
	Disp	125. . .	
	125	125.	
	Disp	250 wants to know if you want an officer assigned at the signal light at Herschel and Lemmon.	
	125	Uh, yes. . .Tell him to take. . .uh. . .Have one of those men from Lomo Alto there go . uh. .Lomo	

397

		Alto and Lemmon, go up there.
	Disp	Did you receive, 250?
	250	No, I didn't.
	Disp	Take one from Lemmon and Lomo Alto and assign him to Lemmon and Herschel.
	250	10-4.
	280	280 to 9...
	289	289...
	Disp	289.
	289	Somebody call?
	Disp	No.
	280	This is 280 calling 9...
11:45	Disp	280, try him on Channel 1, (unreadable) KKB364.
	Disp	280...
	5	5 to 1...
	1	Go ahead.
	5	Just checking Communications...I'm at the front gate out here.
	1	Loud and clear. (unreadable, followed by:)
	9	9...
(11:47)	Disp	280 wants to contact you. Stand by a few minutes.
	Disp	(Using his Channel 1 key, Disp. switched to Channel 1 and contacted 280.)
	280	280...
	Disp	Go ahead to 9.
	280	280 to 9...Ervay Street is completely blocked with pedestrians now. It's completely out of control.
	(9)	I've got 2 reserves..I'm bringing them down now.
	(280)	Well, we've..we've got 3 or 4 three-wheelers here and we still can't get the people off of Ervay, so we're...Ervay's completely closed.
	(9)	10-4, I'm on my way.
	15-2	15 car 2...
	Disp	15 car 2.
	15-2	Progress report?
	5	5...
	Disp	"...a few minutes..." (followed by:)
	Disp	5...
	5	5.
	Disp	Are they moving yet?
	(5)	No.
	Disp	They have not started yet, 15 car 2.
	1	1 to 5...
	(5)	Go ahead.
	(1)	I'm moving out, very slow.
	(5)	10-4.
	Disp	15 car 2...

APPENDIX

	(15-2)	10-4.
11:50	Disp	11:50.
	5	5 to 1...
	(1)	Go ahead.
	(5)	There's a little traffic up there around Mockingbird...You might send a motorcycle up there and try to get them over to one side.
	1	5 to. .uh. .1. .Disregard the motorcycle. Send 2 men to Mockingbird and Cedar Springs to help clear the traffic.
	(5)	What's your location now?
	(1)	Just made the turn out of the field onto Cedar Springs.
	(5)	10-4.
	(1)	Traveling 15 MPH at this time.
	(5)	10-4.
	Disp	15 car 2...
	15-2	15 car 2.
	Disp	15 car 2...
	15-2	15 car 2.
	Disp	Are you reading all right?
	(15-2)	No.
	Disp	They're just leaving the field, on Cedar Springs at 15 MPH.
	(15-2)	10-4.
	5	5 to 1...
	(1)	Go ahead.
	(5)	You might need a motorcycle at. .uh. .Manor Way and Lemmon. (unreadable. .then:)
	5	5 to 1...
	(1)	Go ahead.
	(5)	Quite a few people on Lemmon on both sides of the median strip and on the curb.
	(1)	10-4.
	5	5 to 1...
	(1)	Go ahead.
	(5)	Location now?
	(1)	At Airdrome Drive and Mockingbird Lane.
	(5)	10-4.
11:58	Disp	11:58.
	9	9...
	Disp	9.
	(9)	Any late developments?
	Disp	Airdrome and Mockingbird, proceeding at approximately 15 MPH, 9.
	(9)	10-4.
12:00	Disp	12 noon, KKB364 Dallas. (Unreadable with a "3" in it.)
	Disp	3, are you calling?
	3	(Unreadable reply.)
	Disp	Unit calling 531...Unable to read you. 3
	15-2	15 car 2...

399

	Disp	15 car 2.
	(15-2)	That's 3 calling 531.
	Disp	Uh, 10-4. . Go ahead 3.
	1	1 to 531...
	Disp	1.
	(1)	Approaching Inwood Road on Lemmon, travelling about 12 to 15 MPH.
12:01	Disp	15 car 2. .Now on Lemmon approaching Inwood, 12 to 15 MPH. . .12:01
	(15-2)	10-4.
	Disp	3...
	15-2	15 car 2...
	Disp	Go ahead.
		(The recorder repeated the last three entries without recording a message prior to:) 4
	Disp	Uh, yes. .601 was standing by at Love Field, and soon as he completes that assignment he's going to your location. There'll also be a transfer ambulance at that location.
	(15-2)	10-4.
	1	1 to motorcycles leading, drop back closer. (Background conversation and crowd noise can be heard.). .Hold up so you'll be about 50' ahead of us. .About 50' ahead of us. .Stay at about...
	Disp	15 car 2. . .(Interrupted 1's message.)
	(1)	. . .(Continuing). . .Ok, go ahead.
	162	162 to 15 car 2...
	15-2	15 car 2.
	(162)	This uh. .greeting committee is turning south on Hines at Mockingbird now.
	(15-2)	10-4.
		(Unreadable. .sounds like "57". .then:)
	Disp	15-2...
	15-2	15 car 2.
	Disp	601 is en route to your location.
	(15-2)	10-4.
		(Recording repeated from ". .about 50' ahead of us. ." then:)
	5	5 to 1...
	(1)	Go ahead.
	(5)	What's your location now?
	(1)	I didn't get you.
	(5)	What is your location now?
	1	1 to 5...
	(5)	Wha. .what is your location now?
	(1)	We're approaching Cotton Belt underpass near Lomo Alto.
	Disp	Did you receive, 5?
	(5)	10-4.
12:05	Disp	15 car 2. .Now on Lemmon and. .nearing Lomo Alto, 12:05. 5

APPENDIX

(15-2)	10-4.	
151	151 to 1...	
Disp	1, 151 is calling you.	
(1)	Ok, escort. .3 or 4 miles faster.	
4	4...	
Disp	4.	
(4)	Let me talk to Ed Wofford, motorcycle officer. .4 to. .4 to Officer Ed Wofford...	
157	157, go ahead, 4.	6
(4)	Return to my location.	
(157)	10-4.	
	(Recording repeated "151 to 1" through "157, 10-4.")	
5	5 to 1...	
(1)	Go ahead.	
(5)	Got a pretty good crowd of people down here on Turtle Creek. .It's. . (unreadable). .two lanes of traffic.	
(1)	10-4. .We've got a good motorcycle escort. .Get traffic off of it.	
Disp	1, are you nearing Oak Lawn?	
(1)	About a block away. .We're at Knight Street.	
Disp	10-4. . .15 car 2. .On Lemmon now nearing _____.	
(15-2)	10-4.	
130	130 to 15...	
(1)	Drop down and cut traffic at Turtle Creek.	7
Disp	Go ahead, 130...	
	(Sounds like 130 called again.)	
Disp	130, did you call?	
1	1 to 531. . .Crossing Oak Lawn.	
Disp	10-4, 1.	
(1)	Ok, escort...	
260	260...	
Disp	Go ahead, 260.	
15-2	15 car 2...	
Disp	15 car 2.	
(15-2)	Advise 3 that the ambulances have arrived and are standing by.	
12:11 Disp	3, the ambulances have arrived and are standing by. . .3, the ambulances have arrived and are standing by, 12:11.	
260	260...	
Disp	Go ahead, 260.	
1	1 to 531...	
Disp	1.	
(1)	Just turning onto Turtle Creek.	
Disp	10-4. .Now turning onto Turtle Creek, off Lemmon, 15 car 2.	
(1)	12 miles an hour.	
Disp	260...	
260	260.	

401

	Disp	260...
	5	5 to 190...
	190	190. (Considerable feed-back.)
	(5)	What's your location?
	(190)	Just crossed Cedar Springs. (Considerable feed-back.)
	(5)	10-4.
	260	260...
	Disp	260.
	289	289...
	Disp	289.
	(289)	Apparently 260's receiver's out. He's goona get on Channel 1.
	Disp	Uh, 10-4...Yes, I've been answering them. (260 made contact on Channel 1 during the 12:14 time frame.) 1...1...
	Disp	1.
	1	MK&T ove.. underpass at Turtle Creek.
12:14	Disp	10-4...12-14...15 car 2...
	(15-2)	10-4.
	(1)	Escort, 3 or 4 miles an hour faster...Let's try it.
12:15	Disp	12:15, KKB364.
	9	9...
	Disp	9.
	(9)	What's the location?
	Disp	Now turning onto Cedar Springs road off of Turtle Creek.
	(9)	10-4.
	(1)	Cedar Springs and Fairmount.
12:16	Disp	10-4, 12:16.
	139	139...
	Disp	139.
	(139)	For your information, you have cars lined up on Stemmons, on the shoulder, on both sides, from Commerce Street, north to Oak Lawn, it looks like.
	Disp	10-4.
	?	131, turn on your red lights.
	5	5 to 1...
	(1)	Go ahead.
	(5)	_____ about Ross Avenue. _____ pedestrian crowd _____.
	(1)	I can't read you.
	(5)	Gonna be a pretty good crowd from about Ross Avenue on, on Harwood Street. (Crowd noise clearly heard in the background.)
	(1)	10-4.

8

	2	2 to 1.
	(1)	Go ahead.
	(2)	Everything's in good shape out here at Market Hall. . .Traffic's moving well. . .Crowd. .is. .is. .Not any crowd on the side of the street. . .A good crowd along the edges of the barricades 9
	Disp	1, for your information, Stemmons Freeway on both sides is pretty well crowded from Continental, on to the Trade Mart.
	(1)	We're at Harwood and McKinney.
	Disp	10-4. . .Harwood and McKinney, 15 car 2.
	(5)	1 to 5. .uh. .5. .Let's kind of keep the crowd over about Harwood and Ross. . .They're kinda getting out into the street here.
	(1)	We've got 'em.
	disp	1, are you approaching Ross?
	(1)	Just approaching at this time.
12:20	Dsip	10-4, 12:20.
	Disp	15 car 2, are you reading all right now?
	(15-2)	10-4.
	Disp	Received.
	212	212. . .
	Disp	212.
	(212)	A telephone company construction crew out here wants to know approximately what time the President will be back through here so they can clear out.
	Disp	Back through where, 212?
	(212)	Around Mockingbird at, uh, near Denton.
	Disp	It will probably be after 2:20.
	(212)	10-4. (Diesel train engine airhorn in the background.)
	5	5 to 1. . .
	(1)	Go ahead.
	(5)	Crowd on Main Street is in real good shape. They got'em back off. .on the curb.
	(1)	Good shape. We're just about to cross Live Oak.
	(5)	10-4.
		(Crowd noise on both 1 and 5 messages.)
12:22	Disp	12:22.
	(1)	Escort. . .Drop back. . .(Very loud cheering in the background.). . .Have to go at a real slow speed now.
	Disp	10-4, 1. . .15 car 2, are you reading?
	(15-2)	10-4.
	Disp	Received.
	(1)	Hold up, escort. .Ok. .Ok, move along. . .531, check and see if we've got everything intact. .Check with the rear car.

		(Loud cheering continues.)
	Disp	10-4, 1...Uh, 1, who's in that rear car?
	158	158...
	Disp	158.
	158	158..Everything's "OK."
	disp	158 advises, "OK," 1.
	158	____Ervay Street.
	(1)	10-4.
	(1)	Just at Field Street.
		(Loud cheering in the background.)
12:26	Disp	10-4, 12:26.
	4	4...
	Disp	4.
	(4)	Is 125 on the air?
	Disp	125...
	(1)	Crossing Lamar Street.
	Disp	Pretty good crowd there?
	(1)	Big crowd...Yes.
		(Crowd noise loud in the background.)
12:28	Disp	10-4, 12:28.
	5	5 to 531...
	Disp	5.
	5	5 to, uh..uh. Notify Captain Souter that..The location of the convoy now.
	Disp	15 car 2...
	15-2	15 car 2.
	Disp	Now on Main, probably just past Lamar.
	(15-2)	10-4.
	(1)	Just crossing Market Street.
12:28	Disp	Now at Market, car 2, 12:28.
	Disp	125...
	125	125.
	Disp	Go ahead, 4.
	4	125, this is 4. What traffic personnel do you have on Cedar Springs in the vicinity of the field here?
	(125)	Stand by..Uh, Cedar Springs and Mockingbird?
	(4)	Yes. The traffic seems to be moving out of this lot awfully slow. What uh.. What's your location?
	(125)	I'm at the Trade Mart now. I'll head back out that way.
Approx 12:31:04 (Chan 1)	(4)	Naw, that's all right. **I'll check it.** 10
	(125)	10-4.
12:31:04 (Chan 1)	(1)	At the Triple Underpass.
	Disp	10-4, 1...15 car 2.

APPENDIX

12:31:16 (**Chan 2**)		12:30 KKB364.	
	125	125 to 250...	
12:31:23 (**Chan 2**)	Disp	15 car 2...	
----------	(1)	Go to the hospital.. We're going to the hospital, officers. .(Someone in the background: "On our way!").. Parkland Hospital. Have them stand by.. Get men on top of that over.. underpass. See what happened up there. Go up to the overpass. (At least one transmitter was open for a while, now.)	11
12:31:08 (**Chan 1**)			
	?	(Unreadable; sounds like:) 91 Champion.	
	?	_____ to 1..	
	(1)	Have Parkland stand by.	
	Dallas 1	1...Dallas 1...	12
	Disp	Go ahead, Dallas 1.	
	Dallas 1	Tell my men to empty the jail, and up on the railroad, uh, right-of-way there... I'm sure it's going to take some time for you to get your men in.. Pull everyone of my men in there.	13
	Disp	Repeat, 1.. I didn't quite understand all of it.	
	Dallas 1	Have Station 5 to move all men available out of my department, back into the railroad yards there in an effort to try to determine.. just what and where it happened down there, and hold everything secure until the homicide and other investigators can get there.	14
	Disp	10-4, Dallas 1, Station 5 will be notified.	
	57	57...	
	Disp	1...Any information whatsoever?	
	(1)	Looks like the President's been hit. Have Parkland stand by.	
12:32	Disp	10-4. Parkland has been notified, 12:32.	
	4	4...	
	Disp	4.	
	(4)	We have those canine units in that vicinity, don't we?	
	Disp	Stand by. 1...	
	5	5 to 1...	
	(1)	(We're) headed for Parkland... (Sirens loud in the background.)	
	?	Is something the matter with Channel 1? (Likely #57.)	
	5	5 to 1...	
	(1)	Go ahead.	
	(5)	You want.. What disposition do you want to make on these men I have with me?	
	(1)	Just go on to Parkland with me. (Sirens loud in the background.)	
	Disp	___3...	
	?	Dispatcher on numb.. uh, on "1" seems	

405

	?	to be. . have his mike stuck. .(Loud sirens covered any remaining comment.) (Unreadable. Might be 20 or 220.)	
	(1)	Get these trucks out of the way... Hold everything...Get'em out of the way.	15
	Disp	15 car 2...	
	15-2	15 car 2.	
	Disp	There's a motorcycle officer up on Stemmons with his mike stuck open on Channel 1. Could you send someone up there to tell him to shut it off?	16
	(15-2)	10-4.	
12:34	Disp	12:34.	
	(190)	I'm up on Stemmons. I'll check all these motorcycle radios.	
	Disp	10-4.	
	190	190...	
	Disp	190.	
12:33:52 (Chan 1)	(190)	**You want me to hold this traffic on Stemmons until we find out something, or let it go?** (Hetrodyne.)	17
	(1)	Keep everything out of this emergency entrance.	18
	(190)	10-4. (Unknown to what message.)	
	136	136...	
	Disp	136.	
	136	A passerby says...the Texas Schoolbook Depository...Stated the shots came from that building.	19
	(1)	Get everything out of the way. (Referring to the vehicles clustering around the emergency dock at Parkland Hospital.)	
	Disp	10-4. Get all that information, 136.	
	(136)	10-4.	
12:35	Disp	12:35.	
	142	142...	
	Disp	142.	
	142	142. .I talked to a guy up here at the scene of this, where the shots were fired at. .And he said that he was sitting here close to it. . And the very best he could tell, they came from this Texas Schoolbook De. .pository Building here, with that Hertz Rental sign on top.	
12:35	Disp	10-4. Get his name, address and phone number, and all information you can, 12:35.	
	15-2	15 car 2...	
	Disp	15 car 2.	
	(15-2)	(The) Captain advises, have all	

APPENDIX

		emergency traffic use some route besides Industrial. .Have 283 cut the traffic at Hines and Industrial.	20
	Disp	10-4. 283, cut traffic, Hines and Industrial. .283, cut traffic Hines and Industrial. (Then, using simultaneous broadcast:)	
12:36	Disp	Attention all emergency equipment . . . Attention all emergency equipment. . . Do not use Industrial Boulevard, 12:36.	21
	260	260. . .	
	Disp	260.	
12:35:57 (Chan 2)	(260)	I have a witness that says they **came from the 5th floor of the Texas. .uh. .Depository Bookstore** (sic) at Houston and _____ Building.	22
12:36	Disp	10-4, 12:36.	
	220	220. . .	
	Disp	220.	
	(220)	Where do you want traffic cut going into that area?	
	Disp	Keep all traffic out of the emergency entrance to Parkland Hospital, and all emergency equipment off of Industrial Boulevard.	
	(220)	10-4.	
	Disp	1. . .	23
	(125)	We have the emergency entrance secure at Parkland.	
12:37	Disp	10-4, 125, 12:37.	
	22	22. . .	
	Disp	Go ahead.	
	(22)	Get some men up here to cover this building. . this Texas Schoolbook Depository. It's believed that these shots came from that. . As you're facing it on, uh, it'll be Elm Street, looking toward the building, it would be your upper. .right-hand corner. .at the second window from the end.	
	Disp	10-4. How many do you have there?	24
	(22)	I have one guy that was possibly hit by a ricochet, from a bullet off concrete, and another one that seen the President slump, and another one here that. .that. . (137 covered the rest of 22's message.)	
	137	137. . .	
12:38	Disp	10-4, 12:38. 137. . .	
	(137)	We have a man here that said he saw'em pull a weapon back through the window off the second floor on the south. .east corner of that Depository Building.	25
	(22)	No, I'm about three-quarters of a block away from it.	

407

Disp	10-4. .Report on down there.
(22)	10-4. . .I'll leave the witnesses here.
257	257. . .
Disp	257.
257	Do you want us to go back to Mockingbird and Cedar Springs?
Disp	4. . .
290	290. . .
Disp	290.
257	See if you can contact 125.
(125)	I'm at Parkland.
(257)	Do you want us to stay on Industrial, or where do you want us to go now?
(125)	Stay at your location, right now.
2	2. . .
Disp	2.
2	Can you give us any information as to what happened, for these people out here?
Disp	Two, evidently there has ____ the President involved. .I do not know the seriousness of it. ____Dallas 1. We have the ____ floor of the Book Depository Store on the corner of Elm and Field. Officers are now surrounding and searching the building, 12:40.
(2)	Where did this happen. . .at Field and Main?
Disp	At Stemmons and the Triple Underpass.
(2)	10-4.

26

APPENDIX

END NOTES
COMMENTARY - CHANNEL II

1. "Unreadable" probably was "11:45" as the station call letters, "KKB," are only given on certain occasions, such as the quarter-hour time and station checks. Also, with reference to Channel I, 280 attempted to contact 9 on Channel I during that channel's 11:45 and 11:46 time frames before returning to Channel II and making contact during 11:47.

2. The motorcade, having formed in the vicinity of Air Force One, got underway at 11:50 on its journey of some 7 miles to its unscheduled ending in Dealey Plaza at 12:31 p.m.

3. Reference to "531" was a short-form for "the dispatcher." Actually, the number 531 was one of the telephone extensions serving the dispatcher's office.

4. From the best reconstruction, 15-2 relayed for 3 who wanted to know about the ambulance service scheduled for the Trade Mart. Due to a defect in the recorder, it occasionally repeated all or part of a given transmission, while sometimes not recording any of an incoming message.

5. The motorcade stopped a moment at Lemmon and Lomo Alto while President Kennedy greeted some children.

6. Actually, Wofford's partner answered for him.

7. "Down" is a colloquial reference to "south," north is up, east is over, and west is out.

8. Actually, this is not a "turn." Two blocks west of Lemmon, Turtle Creek becomes Cedar Springs. A turn would have them traveling north instead of west on Cedar Springs.

9. It is a common error to refer to the Market Hall and the Trade Mart synonymously.

10. "I'll check it" was picked up on Channel I. (See note 60, and 12:31:02 on Channel I transcript.)

11. See "Time Discrepancy In Time-Check on Channel II" for explanation in time differences between Channels I and II.

12. "Dallas 1" is the radio call number for the Dallas County Sheriff, Bill Decker, who, with the local Secret Service Chief Agent, Forrest Sorrels, was a passenger in Chief Curry's car.

13. Sheriff Decker instructed the Channel II dispatcher to mobilize the county deputies for assignment to Dealey Plaza. To do this, the police dispatcher had a telephone clerk to inform the sheriff's dispatcher by direct line telephone. The sheriff's dispatcher then had a clerk to make the telephone notifications, and he broadcast, "Attention all units. . ." (See channel I, 12:33:38, and Note 74), to inform field units.

14. "Station 5" is a short-form reference to the Dallas County Sheriff's Department dispatcher's office. Thus far, no word had been given regarding what had happened. One could infer that something had happened, but with no idea of the nature. Here, Sheriff Decker has ordered mobilization of "all available men" into a large area to "secure" everything until "homicide and other investigators can get there." This could suggest anything from an attempted assault to

409

JFK FIRST DAY EVIDENCE

homicide, for the Homicide Division detectives handled both offenses.

15. As the motorcade neared Stemmons over Oak Lawn in the vicinity of Dal-Hi Stadium (later P. C. Cobb Stadium, now the Infomart), some trucks were in the right hand lane. The motorcade would exit at the first off-ramp past Oak Lawn. These trucks posed a problem to the motorcade in making its exit to the Stemmons Freeway service road, en route to Industrial Blvd., the next cross street.

16. With reference to Channel II, Note 7, the term "up" is a colloquial reference. Officers were "out" at Love Field, downtown, and "up" on Stemmons. The Channel II dispatcher had heard the motorcycle engine at different times during the period the microphone had been open, and concluded that it would, in all logical reasoning, be one of those at the Trade Mart "up on Stemmons" rather than up on the freeway.

17. Refer to Channel I, Note 76, and Channel I Transcript at 12:33:52.

18. As the motorcade approached the rear of Parkland Hospital, the emergency entrance, Chief Curry ordered security on the entrance. Officer "B," hearing the order, stopped and closed the driveway to unauthorized vehicles. This helps to fix the time of arrival at the 12:34 time frame.

19. This is the first open reference to "shots" thus far. Chief Curry had reported "hit," which could have referred to a thrown object. Also, the witness stated, ". . .the shots came from. . ." as opposed to those who "thought."

20. Officer 283 had been standing by his motorcycle waiting for this order. However, the motorcade passed him while en route to the hospital. Receiving a hand motion to do so, he fell in with the motorcade. He was at Parkland before this message was broadcast, and he never received it.

21. Refer to Channel I, Note 82, and Channel I transcript at 12:35:38. This message was not fully recorded by the Channel II recorder. The text here was borrowed from Channel I so that it could be presented in full.

22. Refer to Channel I, Note 84, and Channel I Transcript at 12:35:57.

23. No answer was received from Chief Curry or any officer at Parkland. This tends to confirm arrival time. By now the officers were busy assisting Governor Connally, President Kennedy and Vice President Johnson.

24. Referring to how many officers are there now as a basis for how many more would be needed.

25. Actually the second floor from the top rather than just the second floor.

26. The recorder defect caused this transmission to be partially lost. Reference to Elm and Field is an error in statement.

Works Cited

Central Independent Television, P.L.C. *The Men Who Killed Kennedy.* Videotape. 1988.

Curry, Jesse. *JFK Assassination File.* Limited Collectors Edition. Dallas, TX: American Poster and Printing Co., 1969.

Dallas Police Crime Lab sixth-floor photographs. (See Chapter VI.)

Groden, Robert and Harrison Edward Livingstone. *High Treason.* N.Y.: Berkley Books, 1989.

House Select Committee on Assassinations. *Investigation of the Assassination of President John F. Kennedy.* 12 volumes. Washington, D.C.: U.S. Government Printing Office, 1979.

"I Was Mandarin." *Texas Monthly.* December 1990: 133+.

Kantor, Seth. *The Ruby Cover-Up.* N.Y.: Zebra Books, 1978.

Knight, Janet M. *Three Assassinations.* N.Y.: Facts on File, Inc., 1971.

Lifton, David. *Best Evidence.* N.Y.: Carroll & Graf Publishers, Inc., 1988.

Manchester, William R. *The Death of a President.* N.Y.: Harper & Row, 1967.

Map drawn by Crime Lab Detective R. L. Studebaker. November 22, 1963. (See photo 47, p. 146.)

Marrs, Jim. *Crossfire: The Plot That Killed Kennedy.* N.Y.: Carroll & Graf Publishers, Inc., 1989.

Moore, Jim. *Conspiracy of One.* Fort Worth, TX: The Summit Group, 1990.

Taped personal interviews:
    W. E. Barnes, 4 April 1992.
    Bobby Brown, 25 April 1992.
    John Carl Day, 18 December 1991.
    Jim Ewell, 8 January 1992.
    Gus Rose, 16 February 1993.
    H. R. Williams, 25 April 1992.

Tapeworm Distributers. *Two Men in Dallas.* Videotape. 1987.

Warren Commission. *Hearings Before the President's Commission on the Assassination of President Kennedy.* 26 volumes. Washington, D.C.: U.S. Government Printing Office, 1964.

---. *Report of President's Commission on the Assassination of President John F. Kennedy.* Washington, D.C.: U.S. Government Printing Office, 1964.

Selected Bibliography

Associated Press. *The Torch Is Passed*. Keith Fuller, Supervising Editor. AP Production by Edward T. Fleming. Western Printing & Lithographing Co.

Belin, David W. *November 22, 1963: You Are the Jury*. N.Y.: The New York Times Book Co., 1973.

Bishop, Jim. *The Day Kennedy Was Shot*. N.Y.: Funk & Wagnalls, 1968.

Blyth, Myrna and Jane Farrell. "Marina Oswald Twenty-five Years Later." *The Ladies Home Journal*. November 1988: 184+.

Buchanan, Thomas G. *Who Killed Kennedy?*. N.Y.: G. P. Putnam's Sons, 1964.

Central Independent Television, P. L. C. *The Men Who Killed Kennedy*. Videotape. 1988.

Crenshaw, Charles A., M. D. with Jens Hansen and J. Gary Shaw. *JFK Conspiracy of Silence*. N.Y.: Penguin Group, 1992.

Curry, Jesse. *JFK Assassination File*. Limited Collectors Edition. Dallas, TX: American Poster and Printing Co., 1969.

Davis, John H. *Mafia Kingfish: Carlos Marcello and the Assassination of John F. Kennedy*. N.Y.: New American Library, 1989.

Garrison, Jim. *On the Trail of the Assassins*. N.Y.: Warner Books, 1988.

Gentry, Curt. *J. Edgar Hoover: The Man and the Secrets*. N.Y.: W. W. Norton & Co., Inc., 1991.

Golz, Earl. "Oswald Camera Disappeared During FBI Investigation." *The Dallas Morning News*. 15 June 1978.
---. "Oswald Pictures Released by FBI." *The Dallas Morning News*. 7 August 1978: 4D.

Groden, Robert and Harrison Edward Livingstone. *High Treason*. N.Y.: Berkley Books, 1989.

House Select Committee on Assassinations. *Investigation of the Assassination of President John F. Kennedy*. 12 volumes. Washington D. C.: U.S. Government Printing Office, 1979.

Kantor, Seth. *The Ruby Cover-Up.* N.Y.: Zebra Books, 1978.
---. *Who Was Jack Ruby?.* Everest House, 1978.

Knight, Janet M. *Three Assassinations.* N.Y.: Facts On File, Inc., 1971.

Lane, Mark. *Rush to Judgement.* N.Y.: Thunder's Mouth Press, 1992.

Lifton, David. *Best Evidence.* N.Y.: Carroll & Graf Publishers, inc., 1988.

Manchester, William. *The Death of a President.* N.Y.: Harper & Row, 1967.

Marrs, Jim. *Crossfire: The Plot That Killed Kennedy.* N.Y.: Carroll & Graf Publishers, Inc., 1989.
---. "Dallas Man Claims FBI Had Oswald Film." *Star Telegram.* 20 September 1978, evening ed.

McMillan, Priscilla Johnson. *Marina and Lee.* N.Y.: Harper & Row, 1977.

Meagher, Sylvia. *Accessories After the Fact.* N.Y.: Random House, Inc., 1976.

Moore, Jim. *Conspiracy of One.* Fort Worth, TX: The Summit Group, 1990.

Ridge Press. *There Was a President.* N.Y.: Random House, Inc., 1966.

Scheim, David E. *Contract on America.* N.Y.: Kensington Publishing Co., 1989.

Shaw, J. Gary with Larry Ray Harris. *Cover-Up.* Collector's Editions. Austin, TX: Thomas Publications, Inc., 1992.

Summers, Anthony. *Conspiracy.* N.Y.: McGraw-Hill, 1980.

Tapeworm Distributors. *Two Men in Dallas.* Videotape. 1987.

Thompson, Josiah. *Six Seconds in Dallas.* N.Y.: Avon Books, 1966.

Warren Commission. *Hearings Before the President's Commission on the Assassination of President Kennedy.* 26 volumes. Washington, D. C.: U. S. Government Printing Office, 1964.
---. *Report of President's Commission on the Assassination of President John F. Kennedy.* Washington, D.C.: U.S. Government Printing Office, 1964.

Weisberg, Harold. *Whitewash: The Report on the Warren Report.* Hyattstown, MD: Harold Weisberg, 1965.

White, Jack. *Fake.* Videotape. Third Coast Productions, 1990. 50 min.